PIMLICO

D0533372

374

1066
THE YEAR OF THE THREE BATTLES

Frank McLynn was educated at Wadham College, Oxford, and the University of London. He
was Alistair Horne Research Fellow at St
Antony's College, Oxford, in 1987–88, and is
currently Visiting Professor in the Department
of Literature at Strathclyde University. A full-
time writer, he is the author of biographies of
H.M. Stanley and Richard Burton, as well as
several books relating to the Jacobite movement,
including *Charles Edward Stuart*, which was
shortlisted for the 1989 McVitie's Prize for
Scottish Writer of the Year, and *The Jacobite Army
in England*, which won the 1985 Cheltenham
Prize for Literature. His most recent books are
*Hearts of Darkness: The European Exploration of
Africa*, *Robert Louis Stevenson* (both available in
Pimlico), *Fitzroy Maclean, Carl Gustav Jung*,
which was shortlisted for the 1997 NCR
Award, and *Napoleon* (also available in Pimlico).

1066

The Year of the Three Battles

FRANK McLYNN

PIMLICO

Published by Pimlico 1999

2 4 6 8 10 9 7 5 3 1

First published in Great Britain by
Jonathan Cape 1998
Pimlico edition 1999

Pimlico
Random House, 20 Vauxhall Bridge Road,
London SW1V 2SA

Random House Australia (Pty) Limited
20 Alfred Street, Milsons Point, Sydney,
New South Wales 2061, Australia

Random House New Zealand Limited
18 Poland Road, Glenfield,
Auckland 10, New Zealand

Random House South Africa (Pty) Limited
Endulini, 5A Jubilee Road, Parktown 2193, South Africa

Random House UK Limited Reg. No. 954009

A CIP catalogue record for this book
is available from the British Library

ISBN 0-7126-6672-9

Papers used by Random House UK Limited are natural,
recyclable products made from wood grown in sustainable forests.
The manufacturing processes conform to the environmental
regulations of the country of origin

Printed and bound in Great Britain by
Biddles Ltd, Guildford and King's Lynn

For Colette

Contents

Illustrations

1. Edward the Confessor, detail from the Bayeux Tapestry, *by special permission of the City of Bayeux*
2. Silver penny of Harold, minted at Chichester © *The British Museum, London*
3. Seal die of Godwin the thegn © *The British Museum, London*
4. Anglo-Saxon sword from the River Whitham, Lincs., 10th–11th century © *The British Museum, London*
5. Theophilus with his Varangian Guard outside the church of Blachernae, Scylitzes Chronicle, folio 43v., 11th century © *Biblioteca Nacional, Madrid/Werner Forman Archive*
6. Detail showing Yaroslav the Wise from the icon of St Boris and St Gleb, c.1590, *Stroganov School, Moscow*
7. Danish *Penning* of Svein Estrithson (1047–75) © *University of Oslo*
8. Altar frontal of St Olaf, c.1200 from Trondheim Cathedral © *University of Oslo*
9. Viking picture stone from Gotland, c.700–800 © *Antikvarisk-Topografiska Arkivet, Stockholm*
10. The Gokstad Ship, 9th Century © *Viking Ship Museum, Bygdoy/Werner Foreman Archive*
11. Viking Armour, c.850 © *University of Oslo*
12. Seal of William the Conqueror © *British Library, London*
13. The Temple Pyx, 12th century © *Glasgow Museums: The Burrell Collection*
14–21 details from the Bayeux Tapestry, *by special permission of the City of Bayeux*

Details from the borders of the Bayeux Tapestry decorate the first page of each chapter and are reproduced by special permission of the City of Bayeux. Photographs for chapters 1,3 & 9 © *AKG, London.*

Author's Note

The research for this book has been carried out over a number of years, during which time new editions of basic sources have continued to appear; the 1990s, indeed, have seen a veritable explosion of such new versions, mainly under the aegis of that admirable series, Oxford Medieval Texts. To avoid the Sisyphean task of standardizing references to research long since undertaken, I have, as the occasion demanded, quoted from a number of different editions of the same text, in every case making it clear which one I have used. For help with old French sources I acknowledge the help of my wife, Pauline, for German sources of my daughter Julie, and for Anglo-Saxon of my daughter Lucy. For assistance with Norwegian and Old Norse I acknowledge my grateful debt to Anders Jarydd. Christopher Harper-Bill and Ruth Harvey kindly made research materials available to me, and I thank them for this. The responsibility for statements and opinion in the text is mine and mine alone.

Introduction

For five hundred years, until the middle of the fifth century AD, the Roman empire guaranteed stability in the Western world through the *pax romana*. When the empire fell apart (the last Roman emperor who could trace continuity from Augustus was Romulus Augustus, deposed in 476), the centre of gravity shifted to Byzantium, the city on the site of modern Istanbul founded by the emperor Constantine in 332. Despite attempts to revive the western Roman empire, most notably under Charlemagne at the end of the eighth century, the centre of gravity in the West, the cultural hinge on which everything turned, was Byzantium; western Europe itself for the most part remained a collection of petty kingdoms and principalities.

Two great seismic events broke up this basic pattern. From the middle of the seventh century, the great new religion of Islam was on the march, and within one hundred years had reached the Pyrenees. One hundred and fifty years later the Vikings erupted from their Scandinavian fiords and cut a swathe through northern Europe: such was the fear and devastation they spread that the old English prayer-book contained the plea *A furore Normannorum libera nos, Domine* (Lord, deliver us from the wrath of the Norsemen). Between them, the Vikings, pressing on France and northern Europe from the north, and the Islamic nations, pressing up through Spain from the south, bade fair to squeeze western Europe out of existence.

Once again the key was Byzantium. It was the Byzantine empire that provided the main line of defence against the encroachment of Islam, and it was the Byzantines who co-opted the Vikings into trading partners, so that the Scandinavian settlers in Russia and the Ukraine (the *Rus*) provided a crucial transmission belt between the Mediterranean and the Baltic Sea, North Sea and the Atlantic. In concentrating on a story that involves mainly England, France and Norway, we should not forget that the dramatic events of 1066 took place in a much broader context. In Sicily Byzantines, Normans and Arabs confronted each other; in Spain ferocious wars went on between Christian kings and Moorish emirs (Rodrigo Diaz of Vivar, 'el Cid', was an almost exact contemporary of William the Conqueror); and in the Atlantic the Norsemen had settled Iceland and Greenland and reached the shores of North America.

The three main characters in my 'triple biography' were all 'great men', to use a term that has fallen out of fashion. William of Normandy was the most cunning of the three, Harold Godwinson the most courageous and Harald Hardrada the most flamboyant. But they were not Prometheans: they could not perform deeds that were precluded by the technologies and economies of the age; they made history but not in circumstances of their own choosing. If at times we must immerse our heroes in the socio-economic milieu that produced them, this is partly because true biography is not possible for personages so remote in time, for whose lives the sources are so suspect, and partly to underline the fact that, considering the constraints each of them worked under, their achievements finally emerge as even more remarkable than we thought before.

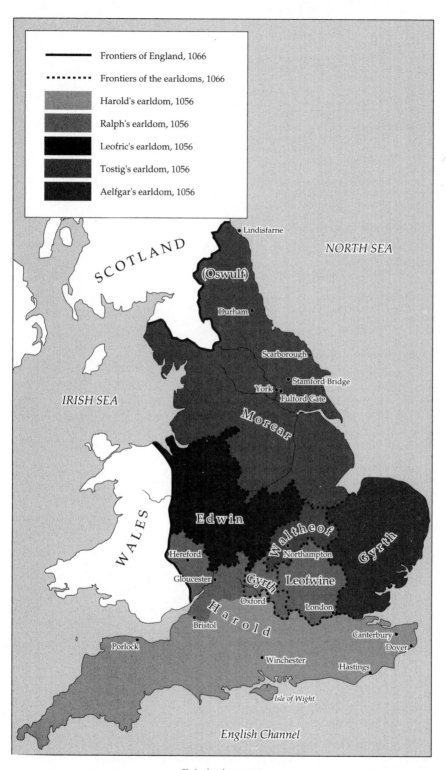

Legend:
- Frontiers of England, 1066
- Frontiers of the earldoms, 1066
- Harold's earldom, 1056
- Ralph's earldom, 1056
- Leofric's earldom, 1056
- Tostig's earldom, 1056
- Aelfgar's earldom, 1056

SCOTLAND

NORTH SEA

Lindisfarne

(Oswulf)

Durham

Scarborough

Stamford Bridge

IRISH SEA

York
Fulford Gate

Morcar

WALES

Edwin

Waltheof

Gyrth

Hereford

Northampton

Gloucester

Gyrth

Leofwine

Oxford

London

Harold

Bristol

Canterbury

Dover

Porlock

Winchester

Hastings

Isle of Wight

English Channel

Britain in 1066

1

Edward the Confessor

The England on which invaders began to cast covetous glances in the early 1060s had for twenty years enjoyed an unwonted period of relative calm and prosperity. But the fifty years 995–1045 had seen England in a turbulent condition, preoccupied with the 'Scandinavian question'. The key crossover point from the fairly tranquil tenth century to the violent early eleventh was the reign of Ethelred, known as the 'Unready', who was king from 978 until 1013.[1] Whereas the reign of Ethelred's father, Edgar, had been a peaceful 'golden age', his own was a miasma of warfare, conquest and uncertainty. Viking raids had been a factor in English life ever since the first terrible appearance of the Northmen at Lindisfarne in 795, but in Ethelred's reign Norse raids resumed, this time much more formidable both in degree and kind.

During the 'second Viking age' the Anglo-Saxon Chronicle recorded a series of raids of ever increasing ferocity by Norsemen seeking treasure and loot rather than a land on which to settle. In 980 there were attacks on Southampton, Thanet and Cheshire; in 981 Devon and Cornwall were the main focus of the Northmen's incursion; in 982 Dorset was ravaged and London itself put to the torch. In 991 one of Ethelred's ealdormen (the tenth-century equivalent of the eleventh-century earl) finally gave battle to the Norwegians under their famous king Olaf

Tryggvason but were utterly defeated in a battle at Maldon in Essex immortalized by one of the most famous exemplars of heroic poetry.[2]

After the defeat at Maldon Ethelred bowed to the seemingly inevitable and took the advice Olaf Tryggvason's herald had given ealdorman Byrhtnoth before the battle: 'Bold seamen have sent me to you and told me to say that you must send treasure quickly in return for peace, and it will be better for you all to buy off an attack with treasure, rather than face men as fierce as us in battle. We need not destroy each other, if you are rich enough. In return for gold we are ready to make truce with you.'[3] But buying off the Northmen turned out to be both expensive and hyperinflationary. In 991 the first of a series of *danegelds* was levied at £10,000, but three years later the Vikings returned to demand £16,000; the amount was said to have ascended to £24,000 in 1002, £36,000 in 1007 and £48,000 in 1012, though some scholars are suspicious of the neat arithmetical progressions.[4]

It is well known that the Anglo-Saxon Chronicle was unremittingly hostile to Ethelred, and its account of his spectacular incompetence may have been overdone. Certainly in recent years scholars have tended to rehabilitate him, stressing his efficient financial and administrative system and the burgeoning of vernacular literature in these years.[5] But history and legend had their final say with Ethelred by foisting on him the unforgettable nickname 'the Unready'. Even though this is a mistranslation of *un-raed* — literally lack of counsel or decision — a wicked pun derived from the proper name Ethelred (which means 'good counsel') and applied by the Anglo-Saxon chroniclers as an epithet to the king for his indecisiveness in the years 1011 and 1016, the mud has stuck.[6]

There are certainly good grounds for censuring Ethelred, who could never decide how to deal with the Vikings: whether to use force against them or simply to buy them off. Moreover, even as the Northmen landed on the east coast, Ethelred had embroiled himself in a conflict with the duchy of Normandy, so that he was liable to a war on two fronts.[7] At first he acted cravenly towards the Vikings, then he decided to back Olaf Tryggvason in Norway while identifying the Danes as a major target, trying at least to contain if not rule the Scandinavians by dividing them, and after all it was to the Danes that the major drain of treasure went.[8] Violent reversals of policies often denote the weak man attempting to make sense of events that threaten to overwhelm him, and so it proved with Ethelred. In 1002 he launched a murderous pogrom against all Danish settlers. But first he married Emma, daughter of Richard I of Normandy (and sister of Richard II), thus securing his southern flank by a dynastic alliance. Having already sired six sons and five daughters with his first wife, Aelfgifu, the prolific Ethelred produced three more children with Emma: Edward, Alfred and Godgifu.[9]

Denmark did not forget the massacre of its emigrant sons and daughters. In 1013 king Svein Haraldsson of Denmark invaded England with a mighty army, forcing Ethelred and Emma to flee to Normandy. But the following year Svein died, and in the interregnum Ethelred returned, having been handed a golden opportunity to expel Svein's Danes, since his son Cnut (Canute) had temporarily returned to Denmark to attend to the succession there. Despite strong backing from Normandy, by 1015 Ethelred's position was again desperate, since Cnut stormed back to England and quickly reconquered all the country except London. Worn out by battling against the odds, Ethelred died in April 1016, appointing his son Edmund Ironside as his successor. Cnut first defeated Edmund at Assandun in Essex, then agreed to temporary kingdom-sharing, but was handed the total sovereignty of England when Edmund conveniently died a month later.[10]

After a purge of all possible rivals and pretenders, Cnut set aside his English mistress Aelfgifu and contracted a marriage with Ethelred's widow, Emma; almost certainly his motive was to neutralize Edward and Alfred, her sons by Ethelred, and thus prevent them seeking military assistance from Normandy.[11] Since the Duke of Normandy still hoped that Edward would eventually succeed, or that Emma would have a son of Norman blood by Cnut, Richard II was happy to maintain friendly relations with Cnut. This cordial entente was ruptured under a later duke, Robert, for reasons that remain obscure. One apocryphal story was that Robert married Cnut's sister Estrith and then discarded her in favour of his mistress, Herlève, thus giving mortal offence to the king of England.[12] The story is implausible on many grounds, not least Cnut's unfailingly astute statesmanship, although it is clear Robert did at one time contemplate an invasion of England, before thinking better of the idea and departing on the pilgrimage to Jerusalem instead. Cnut, only twenty-one when he became king, was a master of international diplomacy. In 1018 he inherited the throne of Denmark from his brother and from Denmark directed operations which overthrew Olaf II Haraldsson (St Olaf) of Norway in 1030, after which Cnut installed his son Svein (by Aelfgifu) as the puppet ruler.[13]

When Cnut died in 1035 (the same year as his enemy Duke Robert of Normandy), the fissiparous tendencies in England which he had so skilfully integrated by his severe but popular government again manifested themselves. Svein, Cnut's eldest son by Aelfgifu, was still

trying to maintain himself in Norway and took no part in the struggle
for succession to the English throne, but the powerful earls in the
kingdom ranged themselves on opposite sides. Earl Leofric of Mercia,
who controlled all the thegns north of the Thames as well as the sailors
of the national fleet based in London, supported Harold Harefoot, the
younger son of Cnut and Aelfgifu and Svein's brother. Harold Harefoot
based his claim to the throne on the basis of one-one correspondence:
he argued that since Cnut possessed three sons and three kingdoms and
since, further, Viking law made no distinction between legitimate and
illegitimate sons, his brother Svein already held Norway and his half-
brother Harthacnut was king of Denmark, it followed that he himself
should be king of England. But Emma, who loathed Harold Harefoot
with a rare loathing, backed by the Archbishop of Canterbury and the
powerful Earl Godwin of Wessex, representing the nobility of the
south, vociferously asserted the absent Harthacnut's claim, in accordance
with Cnut's declared wishes that Harthacnut should succeed him in both
England and Denmark.[14]

In this tense situation two events occurred which at once clarified and
obscured matters. First, Svein died in Norway in 1036. In the same year
Emma's sons by Ethelred decided to make their own bid for the English
throne. In an ill-considered venture, they attempted a *coup d'état*,
supported with ships and mercenaries paid for by Normandy – for
Harold Harefoot was the only one of the pretenders who had no
Norman blood. The decision to stage this *coup* was dangerous folly, for
the implications had not been thought through; the most likely scenario
is that Emma summoned her two sons from Normandy out of sheer
rage at being unable to make inroads against Harold Harefoot. Certainly
Emma was sufficiently deranged to have spread a rumour that Harold
was not even Aelfgifu's child: allegedly Aelfgifu had substituted a
servant-woman for herself in the darkness with Cnut and he had
impregnated her instead.[15]

Emma's two sons disastrously botched their invasion attempts, mainly
through not having realized that Harold Harefoot already held the
military whip hand. Edward shaped his course from Normandy to
Southampton, where he landed, but, encountering stiff opposition, he
gave up, re-embarked and returned to Normandy.[16] Unfortunately this
prudent response, the reflex action of a survivor, was not copied by
his younger brother. Alfred, failing to co-ordinate his effort with
Edward's, used Flanders as his launching-off point and achieved initial
success by evading the English naval squadron that had been sent to
intercept him. But almost immediately after landing, he and his party

were ambushed by Earl Godwin's men, who took them as captives to Guildford and handed them over to troops under the direct command of Harold Harefoot. Alfred's companions were at once taken out and executed, but for Alfred a grimmer fate was in store: he was taken to Ely and there blinded so brutally that he died.[17]

Ever afterwards it was a staple of Norman propaganda that the murder of Alfred should be laid at the door of Earl Godwin.[18] His defenders pointed out that the murder was committed by Harold Harefoot's men who took Alfred out of the custody of the Wessex thegns, and that Godwin had neither control over nor responsibility for whatever happened when he no longer had power over him.[19] Later (in Harthacnut's reign) Godwin swore a solemn oath that he had handed Alfred over only after receiving express orders from Harold Harefoot.[20] It is interesting, too, that Emma never blamed Godwin for the death of her son, even though she was distraught with loss and anyway none too careful with wild accusations. Emma's version was that Harold had forged a letter in her name, luring her two sons to England, though it is clear that the main purpose of this story is to distance herself from responsibility for the fiasco which her own short-sightedness and overheated imagination had brought about.[21] The most likely explanation for this much-disputed episode is that Godwin was guilty of political machiavellianism rather than murder: seeing that Harold's triumph in the struggle for the throne was now inevitable, he decided to curry favour with the new ruler by handing over to him a dangerous pretender.[22]

With Harthacnut still preoccupied in Denmark, Svein dead in Norway, Alfred dead in England and Edward skulking, defeated, in Normandy, there was now no one to oppose Harold. At first he was merely regent for the legitimate heir to the throne, Harthacnut, but in 1037 he felt strong enough to expel Emma to Bruges and impose his own election as king on the ruling council of England or *witan*. Emma waited impatiently in Flanders for Harthacnut to make his bid, but her son showed good judgement by giving Scandinavian affairs his priority. By this time the followers of St Olaf had regained power in Norway in the shape of young King Magnus, who carried on a war of revenge against Harthacnut for the way Cnut had overthrown their beloved Olaf.[23] Harthacnut dared not leave a hostile and powerful Magnus on his flank while setting out on a risky venture in England, so that it was not until 1039 that he was able to move against England. In that year he made peace with Magnus, probably on the basis of a secret treaty pledging that, whichever of the rulers died childless, the other would succeed in both kingdoms.[24]

Next Harthacnut sailed for Bruges, to prepare for an invasion of England and concert matters with his mother. Civil war threatened, but suddenly, in March 1040, Harold Harefoot died. When Harthacnut crossed the Channel with sixty ships to Sandwich, expecting hard fighting, he met with no resistance. Once in London, almost his first act was to dig up Harold's body in Westminster Abbey and throw it into a bog.[25] Scarcely mollified by his pacific reception in England, he repaid the 'treachery' of the inhabitants during the years 1035–40 by levying a swingeing fleet-tax to pay the full costs of his journey from Denmark to England via Bruges. Universally detested by the common people, he died at the age of twenty-four in 1042, allegedly from convulsions after overindulging at a wedding feast.[26]

The year before he died, Harthacnut had made the apparently generous gesture of inviting Edward from Normandy to share the throne with him. This decision was undoubtedly dictated by circumstance rather than sentiment, for Harthacnut was aware that he was unpopular, had many enemies and needed to close ranks around him. The invitation to Edward, which was probably part of a grand design discussed with him and Emma in Bruges in 1039–40, made a lot of sense: on the one hand Harthacnut and the scarcely less unpopular Emma could palliate public hostility to them by using Edward as a smokescreen and thus camouflage their own position; on the other, Harthacnut, always essentially preoccupied by Scandinavia, wanted to renew the war with Magnus of Norway and needed Edward as his regent in England while he returned north. Harthacnut was prevailed on by Emma to recommend Edward as his successor in England, at which time he probably also designated his kinsman Svein Estrithson as his heir in Denmark.[27]

Edward was a shrewd reader of the runes, for on the face of it returning to England in 1041 was risky and he cannot ever have been unmindful of his brother's fate. Yet his judgement was rewarded, for, when Harthacnut died, he was on the spot while the two other most obvious claimants – Magnus of Norway and Svein Estrithson – were in Scandinavia. Edward was regarded with suspicion in some quarters, as the creature of the Normans, and there was a very strong pro-Scandinavian party in England that wanted the succession bestowed on a scion of the northlands.[28] The really salient fact, however, was that all the great earls of England supported Edward: Godwin of Wessex, Leofric of Mercia and Siward of Northumbria. The devious Edward accepted the endorsement of Godwin even though, in his secret heart, he hated him as the man responsible for the death of his brother Alfred and could never forgive him. None the less, for the present he kept his counsel and was rewarded by being crowned king of England at Winchester on Easter Day 1043.[29]

The central paradox of Edward's twenty-three-year reign was that he was a less powerful ruler than his counterpart William in Normandy, even though Edward was king of a nation much larger in extent and with almost twice the population. Before 1066 England was thought to be the maximum size for a polity under the direct control of a monarch, albeit one using nobles and the Church as intermediaries.[30] In this epoch Ireland was still completely independent and Scotland and Wales virtually so: kings on the Celtic fringes took a formal oath of fealty to the English king but were thereafter left undisturbed unless they intervened in England.[31] Nor is the answer to the paradox to be sought in the powers invested in the English monarchy.

Kingship was a prize worth having in eleventh-century England, for on paper the royal revenues were large and potentially vast. The king's income came from four main sources: from his own landed estates, known as the royal demesne; from profits from the boroughs and churches and from the administration of justice; from services owed the monarch by those under his direct lordship, plus gifts and offerings; and from the *geld* or land tax, payable from all parts of the kingdom, including the earldoms. The king had considerable reserve and residual powers: no one else could tax directly or issue coinage; a monarch could break an earl, declare him outlaw, and so come into possession of all his lands and thegns; and had sole command of national armies and fleets. Great nobles, royal thegns with estates in several shires and small freeholders, all held their lands provisionally from the king and in return owed him some service, rent or remuneration.[32]

Since England's economy was overwhelmingly pastoral and agricultural, the power to levy the land tax was a mighty weapon, especially as the *geld* was the first charge on property. Those who could not pay had their land sold to those who could, which meant that the *geld* was both deeply unpopular and deflationary in terms of local economies.[33] Moreover, the king exercised discretion in how the tax was levied: not paying tax on his own lands in the royal demesne, he could reduce or waive it elsewhere at whim. Unlike William of Normandy, notorious for his avarice, Edward was uninterested in money-making *per se* and sought wherever possible to lighten the fiscal load. Uniquely among

European nations, England levied an army tax or *heregeld*, used for hiring mercenaries – a burden introduced by Ethelred in 1012 – but Edward suspended it in 1051.[34]

The king stood at the apex of a social triangle where the hierarchy was reasonably clear-cut at the upper levels but became increasingly broad and confused at the base. Lordship was the key to the political structure just as producing goods to generate a surplus was the key to the economic; both the economic and political structures in turn rested ultimately on military might and, at the limit, the need to fight battles against powerful enemies.[35] Below the king in the pecking order was a handful of earls and below them in turn a heterogeneous group of noblemen known as thegns, which divided into king's and non-royal thegns, depending on the lord from whom they held their land. A thegn (or thane) by definition had to be a large enough landholder not to farm himself and was a member of the military élite and a local noble of influence.

Royal thegns were men who had been given lands for past services to the Crown and in expectation of future ones; such land was invariably still subject to the *geld* or land tax. The landed thegns owed the king service as a hereditary duty, and they 'owned' their land in a way alien to modern, capitalistic notions.[36] Property was always a provisional rather than absolute right, and every further land transaction by a landed thegn required the king's consent – which meant his actual, written approval, not just some tacit or assumed consent. When a thegn died, to ensure succession to his son the estate had to pay succession duty to the king, or else some part of the original land grant was taken back by the king as his 'fee' for ensuring the succession.[37]

Below the thegns were the non-noble classes, for whom the most common generic name was the *ceorls*, but here we encounter byzantine complexity of a kind that makes the famous Marxist division of Russian peasants into upper, middle and lower peasants pellucid by comparison. The Domesday Book of 1087 provides us with an invaluable key to social England in the eleventh century. Each manor is assessed by the acreage of ploughland, pasture, meadow and woodland and mills are included; the inhabitants are divided into a number of categories – for example, slaves, freedmen, villeins and cottagers – and the number of ploughs is stated.[38] The *ceorl*, properly speaking, was a prosperous peasant farmer who aspired to be a thegn; this ambition could be fulfilled in two main ways: by acquiring five 'hides' (600 acres) of land; or by deed of gift from an earl. Such promotions were by no means unheard of, since eleventh-century England shows some signs of accelerating social mobility.[39]

Descending from *ceorl* status, we encounter other types of peasants: the *gebur*, a kind of middle peasant burdened by rents and dues; the *sokeman*, a peasant owing light services or none at all; the villein or *villanus*, who held anything from fifteen acres to a full hide (120 acres) in return for labour, dues and services; the *bordar*, who held up to fifteen acres; and the cottar or cottager, limited to a cottage. Finally there was the *theow* or slave, who could be bought and sold by a lord. Slavery was a legal punishment imposed for an inability to pay fines and, since eleventh-century legal codes ordained heavy fines for many offences, the system produced many slaves by a process of spontaneous generation, to say nothing of those traded. The extent and role of slavery in eleventh-century England is still much debated, as is the question of whether it was in the interests of landlords to create it deliberately through fines.[40]

The same fundamental socio-economic system prevailed in both England and Normandy – yet another reason for rejecting the old model of violent disjuncture between 'pre-feudal' England until 1066 and feudal thereafter – though naturally custom and law produced different manifestations in the 'superstructure': what was a 'fief' in Normandy was 'bookland' in England, and so on.[41] As in Normandy also, towns were the centres for trade, and the walled towns or boroughs of England, with their streets set out in a grid system, were explicitly designed as safe refuges for merchants and rallying points against attackers. By 1086 about 10 per cent of the population lived in towns, which were increasingly linked with commerce and a burgeoning cash economy. Society in the towns was more complex, with specialized division of labour, represented by trades such as pottery, boneworking, leather manufacturing, long-distance trade, and – vital for a would-be military power – there were specialists in the storing and marketing of food.[42] The economic arrangements in the town tended to be more complex than in the countryside, for, although all profits from rents, tolls and lawcourts went to the king, he would often sublet to local landlords and, especially, churches and abbeys, in return for a fixed fee. By 1066, not only London, but Winchester, Canterbury, Nottingham, Stamford, Leicester, Northampton, York and Chester were all important towns.

Towns helped to increase royal power, and by 1066 all significant ones were controlled by the king. Another source of royal power was the coinage, which the monarch issued. There seems to have been a veritable explosion of coining in the eleventh century, initially to pay the *danegeld*, for which 36 million pennies were struck in Ethelred's reign.[43] This monetary inflation was part of a general picture of economic prosperity in Edward's reign, reflected in healthy demographic statistics. England's population was probably just under two million (though some estimates have put it as high as 2.5 million), with particular densities in East Anglia, eastern Kent and Lincolnshire and the lowest concentrations in Yorkshire, the Pennines, Cornwall and the north-west Midlands.[44] In this era of prosperity, short-term profit maximization was the watchword and, together with heavy rates of royal taxation, bore down hard on the peasantry. The get-rich mentality can also be seen in the trend away from demesne farming in Edward's reign. Instead of being actively involved in agricultural production, landlords increasingly rented out their estates for fixed rents.[45]

Despite all the sources of revenue, there is reason to believe that Edward, reluctant to mulct his people more than necessary, was not particularly affluent. One study has established that the value of the king's estates was about £5,000 (£30–40 million in modern money) and of the queen's £900.[46] One of Edward's problems was that his income did not far exceed outgoings and there was a shortage of silver with which to make cash payments: this meant that among the royal household all but a handful of mercenaries and retainers had to be paid in revenue-producing land, and the question was where this land was to come from. The consequence was obvious: either Edward had to risk antagonizing some of the powerful lords who had helped him to the throne by confiscating part of their lands; or he had to contract his own royal demesne to provide the land.[47]

Under Edward the great earls of England were more powerful *vis-à-vis* the king than under Cnut or later under the Normans. Hence the paradox of a relatively impoverished monarch in the midst of generally burgeoning economic prosperity. During Edward's mostly tranquil reign the mere fact of peace enabled the economy, diminished by the drain of money to Scandinavia under Ethelred and his successors, to recover. The necessary conditions for economic growth were already there, for the well-attested improvement in climate (the years 1000–1300 were among the warmest in all recorded time) produced in England the same consequences as in Normandy: population growth.[48] Pressure on resources; with a rising population outstripping the food supply, led both to dearth and increased profits for the few. The augmented demand for food resulted in cheap labour and an increase in the amount of land under the plough, though food prices continued steep. While the landless suffered, landlords prospered: the vast surpluses they extracted from the labouring peasantry were spent mainly on water mills, new churches and the purchase of luxury goods, which sucked in foreign imports. Unlike the situation in Normandy, none of the profits went into castle-building.[49]

It was the social sector occupied by the thegns that benefited most from economic growth, for studies have shown that on royal lands reeves and farmers hived off much of the profits. In addition, the royal lands under Edward were not nearly so extensive as those possessed by past and future monarchs. He had no estates in Middlesex, Essex, Hertfordshire, Rutland, Lincolnshire, Cheshire and Cornwall and merely tiny slivers of land in East Anglia and Yorkshire.[50] The greatest threat to the king's position was the vast earldom of Wessex which Cnut had created and given to Earl Godwin. It was not surprising that Edward's main problems throughout his reign centred on the Godwins and that he was obliged to 'solve' them initially by a curious marriage to Godwin's daughter.

The Godwin family would always overshadow Edward's reign. Godwin, probably a scion of a South Saxon family, was created Earl of Wessex by Cnut in 1018, and at around the same time he married Gytha, sister of Ulf of Denmark, himself brother-in-law of Cnut through having married Cnut's sister Estrith; Godwin was thus the uncle of Svein Estrithson of Denmark. He seems almost to have appeared from nowhere, for he first comes to the attention of history through having been left land in the will of atheling Athelstan.[51] His rise was rapid, not so much meteoric as comet-like, in that after him came a blazing tail, the issue of his union with Gytha. Adopting Homer's method in Book Eleven of the *Odyssey*, we might first deal with distinguished women and mention his three daughters: Edith, born some time in the 1020s, and later Gunnhild and another whose name has not come down to us. But it was on his six sons that the ambitious Godwin pinned his hopes of founding a dynasty that would make the Godwinsons the greatest power in England after the king. First born was Swein, around 1022; then came Harold, possibly with a date of birth in 1024 (but certainly not before 1022 or after 1026); Tostig, born between 1026–29; Gyrth, born around 1032; Leofwine, born around 1035 and finally the shadowy Wulfnoth, of whom little is known.[52]

Godwin, ambitious, cunning and dauntless, owed everything to Cnut. Plucking him from the obscurity of the South Saxon nobility, where his father, Wulfnoth, was just one among many thegns, Cnut took him with him to Denmark in 1017–18 and on his return in 1018 appointed him earl over the lands south of the Thames, intending the loyal Godwin to be his first line of defence in southern England against invasion or pirate foray.[53] It seems that in Denmark Cnut got to know Godwin well, and learned to appreciate the rare cluster of individual talents that encompassed courage, strength, wisdom, perseverance and eloquence. Wishing to bind him closer, he arranged the marriage with Gytha. Cnut was not disappointed. By 1023 the Earl of Wessex was clearly first among equals and always had pride of place when witnessing charters, ahead of the other earls. Godwin went with him to Denmark, where in 1025 he took part in the battle of the Holy River. This, one of dozens of major pitched battles that convulsed Scandinavia in the first sixty years of the eleventh century, ended in complete victory for the king of Sweden over Cnut's Anglo-Danish levies.[54]

If Godwin owed his elevation to Cnut, Edward no less owed his crown to Godwin. Since Edward on his accession found the English earldoms in the hands of powerful and virtually independent families, his obvious tactic would have been 'divide and rule'. But there were two problems with his ploy. First, throughout the 1040s there was an ever present threat of invasion from Scandinavia, especially from Magnus of Norway, and it would be folly to face this threat with a divided England. More seriously, Earl Siward of Northumbria and Earl Leofric of Mercia were preoccupied with their own bailiwicks; only Godwin had truly national ambitions. It was therefore difficult for the monarch to resist when Godwin, as the price for his support in the *witan* that had elected Edward king, all but insisted that Edward marry his daughter Edith.[55]

Edith is not an easy personage for the historian to pin down. Her date of birth is uncertain – she could have been anything from sixteen to twenty-four when she married Edward – and her historical personality has become encrusted with the barnacles of legend and the hagiography of would-be canonizers. Nevertheless, all the sources agree that she was an exceptionally intelligent woman, who had received a more academic education than was usual for one of her sex. At the nunnery of Wilton, a kind of finishing school for high-born ladies, she excelled in languages, mathematics, grammar and music.[56] An excellent linguist, with a fluent command of French, Danish and Irish, she was no blue-stocking, but a dignified and close-mouthed woman, in every way fit to be a queen, matching erudition with beauty, generosity and moral integrity.[57]

The marriage, which was celebrated in 1045, was childless and has always been considered something of an oddity. Some say that Edward never consummated the marriage, simply to show his hatred of Godwin, whom he sincerely believed to be the murderer of his brother Alfred;

there is also the curiosity that Edith later took an oath that she was a virgin and that her relationship with her husband was like that of father and daughter. Others say that Edward was himself a virgin, whether out of a fastidious disdain for carnality or simply because he was impotent.[58]

Others, again, consider that the evidence for Edward's lifelong chastity is not very strong − although it is likely that he never had another woman outside his marriage − and regard the legend of his celibacy as simply an 'expedient exaggeration' which was widely bruited about in order to enhance his claims to sainthood. These claims to a modern eye seem remarkably slender, especially if humbug has to be added to the indictment against Edward. If Edward knew himself to be infertile or impotent, or if he had no intention all along of having conjugal relations with his wife, then his promise to make Svein Estrithson of Denmark his heir in effect made Svein the indefeasible heir apparent − a fact about which a truly honest or saintly man would have come clean.[59] A careful review of the evidence suggests there are really only two plausible interpretations: either that Edward was homosexual or that he and Edith enjoyed normal marital relations, in which case either he was infertile or his wife was barren; given the fecundity of the other Godwin scions the former is more likely. It would have suited those who later promoted Edward for canonization to pretend that a normal marriage was in fact sexless and saintly − Edith indeed encouraged the rumours as part of her own self-hagiography − though how that squared with canon-law insistence that every marriage had to be consummated to be valid is less clear.[60]

The puzzle over his sexuality is only one of many enigmas surrounding Edward's personality. From the contemporary records it is hard to see how the legend of Edward the saint got started, for the personality described by eyewitnesses is that of a cross-grained neurasthenic, a neurotic with a tendency to paranoia and possessed of a fearsome temper that often made him impervious to reason.[61] It is tempting to say that he combined his father's indecisiveness with his mother's psychological instability and love of secret intrigue. His 'saintly' detachment can be read in quite another way, as the 'schizoid' alienation of the classic lone wolf, who has decided that since no one cares for him he in turn will care for nobody; interestingly, his most recent biographer writes: 'Edward always behaved like one who had been deprived of love.'[62]

Despite his Normano-Saxon blood, Edward had a characteristic that is more usually associated with the Celtic races: an elephantine memory for slights and an ability to bear grudges eternally. Edward was scarred by his early experiences in Normandy, where, later Norman propaganda notwithstanding, he had not been especially well treated, had been shown no particular marks of esteem nor given any lands of his own.[63] He blamed the Normans for slighting him, and for having sent Alfred to his death by not supporting him strongly enough with force of arms; most of all he blamed his mother for the long separation from her in his youth. Since his mother was Norman he made her a particular focus for all the rage he had had to suppress, and all the manifestations of resignation he had forced himself to display – something that his later champions absurdly read as saintly stoicism.

The final assessment we make of Edward is likely to depend on the interpretation we put on the enigmatic Emma. Was she the stoical, saintly, loving mother, oppressed by grief for her murdered son Alfred and, moreover, the classic female victim, dragooned into two dynastic marriages, first with Ethelred, then with Cnut? Or was she a venal, immoral woman, an inveterate intriguer as dangerous as she was indefatigable, who rode her luck too hard with Edward and was justifiably punished?[64] Certainly Edward, once raised to the throne, wasted no time in cutting her down to size. Attacked unexpectedly at Winchester in 1043 by the combined forces of her son and the Earls Godwin, Leofric and Siward, she was deprived of her great wealth in the form of gold and silver and kept under 'town arrest' in Winchester and allowed merely a subsistence allowance.[65]

Emma had played into Edward's hands by championing the claims to the succession of Magnus of Norway; her apologists, however, say she wished merely to do something about the growing power of the contumacious Earl Godwin. But it is typical of the fog of ambiguity that clouds eveything to do with Emma that the charge of conspiring with Magnus was only one count in a multifarious indictment. She was also suspect because of her friendship with the venal Bishop Stigand of Winchester, and there were even rumours that she was conducting a sexual liaison with him or another highly-placed bishop. Edward accused her of withholding from him treasure that was rightfully his and compounding her offence by promising Magnus that she would subsidize his invasion of England with her gold. But most of all, Edward hated her for having failed, as he saw it, to exert herself sufficiently on his behalf, for withholding her maternal affection from him, and even for having preferred his dead brother Alfred to him.[66]

It will already be clear that Edward was no saint; what was worse, he was the kind of weak, indecisive and ineffectual man who loathes all persons having talents superior to his. He evinced his 'lone wolf' status by wearing a long white beard, thus cocking a snook at both the Anglo-Saxon fashion for men to go about moustachioed and the Norman preference for clean-shavenness. His reputation for piety seems to rest mainly on the fact that, unlike most of his high-born peers, he refrained from carrying on conversations during Mass. His mania for hunting was a black mark against him, contrasting as it does so strikingly with the love for dumb beasts of his contemporary St Anselm. It is related that Edward once roundly cursed a peasant who trespassed on his hunting grounds; Edward Freeman is surely right when he remarks that Edward would have had no compunction about cursing St Anselm in a similar manner for the same offence. And another of Freeman's comments accurately sums up Edward: instead of a king, he should have been the head of a Norman monastery.[67]

The indecisiveness and confusion in Edward's mind can be seen clearly in his foreign policy during the 1040s. To assuage the anger of Svein Estrithson, who had confidently expected to succeed Harthacnut in England, Edward nominated him as his heir apparent and made his claim indefeasible by stating that the Dane would succeed him even if he sired children of his own.[68] But Svein was soon at war with Magnus of Norway, to whom Harthacnut had explicitly promised the succession. Magnus sent a forceful letter to Edward, reminding him of this fact and making it plain that in Danish eyes Edward was merely king *de facto*, a temporary viceroy on sufferance permitted to hold sway only until the day Magnus crossed from Norway to claim his own.[69]

To solve the Scandinavian problem called for superlative diplomatic skills; Edward, a great exponent of fudge and mudge, made no reply to Magnus and seemed simply to hope that something would turn up to rid him of these turbulent northern pretenders. Edward was lucky, for the something did turn up in the shape of a northern war. In 1045 as Magnus prepared a formidable armada for a descent on England, Svein, who had accepted a position as Magnus's satrap in Denmark, declared his independence; the result was a war between Denmark and Norway that went on sporadically for twenty years. Svein appealed to Edward for help in the form of fifty warships, and Godwin urged the king to send his fleet to aid his (Godwin's) nephew.[70]

Edward rejected this sensible advice – much more sensible than a policy of neutrality, as a *realpolitiker* like Godwin saw clearly, for Magnus was much the stronger of the two and when he defeated Svein was likely to revive his project for a descent on England. It seems that the counter-advice from a jealous Earl Leofric was the deciding factor with Edward; Leofric feared the consequences of the kinship ties binding the

Godwin family and Svein Estrithson, and suspected that Godwin was plotting to replace Edward with Svein as king of England, on condition that the Earl of Wessex and his sons would be the real power in the land.[71]

Events resulted exactly as Godwin predicted: Magnus was soon victorious over the Danes and immediately turned his attention to the invasion of England; only his sudden death on 25 October 1047 prevented the launch of his longships. Taking advantage of the confused situation in Norway, Svein Estrithson himself then resuscitated *his* plans for an invasion of England in pursuit of his claims. Edward stalled by reiterating his early succession contract by Svein, but this time the Dane seemed unconvinced by mere words from a man who had left him in the lurch when he was in mortal danger from Magnus. Once again by sheer good fortune Edward escaped the horns of the dilemma on which he had impaled himself, for Svein's plans in turn were laid aside as he faced a fresh outbreak of war with Norway under its new king, the redoubtable Harald Hardrada.[72]

Edward's foreign policy in continental Europe was also a muddle, even though he spent the first six years of his reign almost continually absorbed in it. His main aim was the containment of Baldwin of Flanders, who had allowed Flemish ports to become a launching pad for all manner of pirates and naval adventurers, such as the Scandinavians who raided the coast of south-east England in 1048.[73] To counteract Baldwin on the Continent, Edward made overtures to a number of putative allies but principally his brother-in-law Eustace II, Count of Boulogne (though his situation was complicated by being Baldwin's vassal), and his nephew Walter, then Count of Mantes, Chaumont and Pontoise and later pretender to the County of Maine – an ambition that led to his death by poisoning at the hands of Duke William.[74]

Failing to make much headway with these overtures, Edward was once again delivered from imbroglio by sheer good fortune, for after 1047 Baldwin became involved in his unsuccessful conflict with Emperor Henry III of Germany. The battle-lines on this occasion were drawn between two distinct camps: on the one side, Baldwin, Henry I of France and Duke William of Normandy; on the other, Emperor Henry III, Pope Leo IX and Geoffrey Martel of Anjou. Edward joined in on the imperial side (as did, confusingly, Svein Estrithson) and, as a result, in 1049 Henry III called on him to blockade Flanders so that the defeated Baldwin could not escape by sea. Based at Sandwich, Edward disposed his fleet so well that the result was achieved and Baldwin forced to make his obeisance to the emperor at Aachen.[75]

But the real confusion in Edward's foreign policy concerns his *rapprochement* with Normandy even as he allied himself with Duke William's enemies during 1047–50. To explain the zigzag pattern of Edward's policy it is necessary to trace the rise and rise of the Godwin sept during these years. Undoubtedly the black sheep of the family was the eldest son, Swein, who appears to have suffered from a kind of scapegrace hypomania that made him lurch from scandal to scandal.[76] Although by 1045 three of the Godwin kin possessed earldoms – Harold, created earl in 1044–5, held in East Anglia, while Bjorn (Estrith's son and Godwin's nephew) held a especially created earldom – and there were three other sons, Tostig, Gyrth and Leofwine, waiting in the wings, Swein was the first to receive glittering prizes. It was on him that the ageing lord of Wessex initially reposed his hopes, and accordingly he was the very first (in 1043) to join his father in a position of vast territorial power, commanding an earldom that encompassed the south-west Midlands, Somerset, Hereford, Gloucester, Oxford and Berkshire.[77]

With a reputation for preferring all things Scandinavian and Celtic and despising French and Norman influences, Swein capped an ill-advised raiding expedition in 1046 in South Wales with his freebooting ally Gruffydd ap Llywelyn, prince of the rival kingdom of North Wales, with an exploit that was an egregious scandal even for those case-hardened times. Making his way home through Herefordshire, he became captivated by the beauty of Eadgifu, Abbess of Leominster, and abducted her from her abbey. Whether this was rape or seduction is less clear – there are sources for either version – but Swein had already given grave offence at court by his wild allegation that Cnut, not Godwin, was his real father. Stung by this and the angry remonstrations of Gytha, whose fidelity was thus so openly impugned by her own son, Godwin raised no protest when Edward reacted adversely to the Leominster incident. Friendless anyway because his pro-Welsh leanings seemed unpatriotic and anti-English, Swein was obliged to seek sanctuary with Baldwin in Flanders.[78]

That Baldwin condoned a crime as serious as Swein's was surprising; that he welcomed the son of a man supposedly in league with Edward to abet the emperor's suppression of his (Baldwin's) rebellion seems even odder, once again illustrating the Byzantine intricacy of power politics in northern Europe. Godwin must have been secretly relieved, though he took care that Swein's earldom did not pass out of his family by putting the lands in the charge of his second son, Harold, and of Bjorn, the most senior Godwin kinsmen. Soon Swein was on his travels again, this time to Denmark, where he served briefly under Svein Estrithson until another scandal (this time of undivulged nature) drove him back to Flanders.[79]

By this time Edward's naval blockade of Flanders, requested by Emperor Henry III, was in full swing but the dauntless Swein managed to run the gauntlet and arrive back in Godwin lands with seven or eight ships. He made landfall at Bosham, then travelled overland to Sandwich to seek the king's pardon, hoping that his kinsmen would bring pressure to bear on Edward. But his brother Harold was not pleased to see the roistering Swein return, and still less was Bjorn Estrithson, who seems to have been managing most of the absentee earl's lands. To Swein's fury, he was unable to muster the support he needed with the king and then suffered insult added to injury when Edward ordered him and his ships out of the kingdom within four days.[80]

The sequence of events immediately afterwards is confused, for the malice domestic involving Swein was overtaken by a foreign levy coming from two different directions. First, the king of South Wales, Gruffydd ap Rhydderch, chose this precise moment to take revenge for Swein's raid a couple of years earlier. Approaching Wye and the Forest of Dean by way of the river Severn, Gruffydd raided across the Welsh marches and defeated a force under Bishop Ealdred of Worcester that went to intercept him. Edward immediately diverted the entire Wessex naval squadron, some forty-four ships, to deal with this menace, placing Godwin and Bjorn in charge.[81] But no sooner had they sailed than a new threat appeared. Osgod Clapa, one of the first of Edward's many expulsions, was reported to have cleared from Flanders with a fleet of twenty-nine ships, intending to raid southern England, presumably in collusion with Swein. Edward summoned the Mercian naval squadron to deal with this peril and achieved complete success. Twenty-three of Osgod's ships raided Essex but were caught in a storm on the way home; the few who survived the tempest were lured ashore by wreckers somewhere in continental Europe (possibly Ponthieu) and massacred to a man. Some instinct had made the circumspect Osgod remain in Flanders with just six ships to await the outcome; it is said that after this débâcle he gave up and sought refuge in Denmark.[82]

The Wessex fleet meanwhile was detained by contrary winds at Pevensey, and it was there that an apparently contrite Swein made his reappearance. Bjorn Estrithson, without the sagacious Harold to advise him, listened to the siren supplications of his kinsman and agreed to accompany him on another mission to seek Edward's pardon. The result was a double-cross only the gruesome Swein could have thought up.

Bjorn set out with just three bodyguards and allowed himself to be talked into diverting to Bosham, where Swein claimed to have gifts for the king. Once at Bosham, Swein ordered his men to seize and bind the luckless Bjorn; his fleet set sail and cruised west past the Isle of Wight and Portland Bill; and then at Dartmouth Swein put the unhappy Bjorn to the sword. Presumably Swein sought to terrorize Bjorn into accepting his terms and making an abject plea to Edward on his behalf, but, though frightened, Bjorn was not cowed and paid the predictable penalty for trying to call the bluff of a man as savage and murderous as his unruly cousin.[83]

News of the crime swept through England: to breach all laws of safe conduct and kill a kinsman into the bargain was morally reprehensible even in eleventh-century England, and made the previous scandal with Eadgifu of Leominster seem a bagatelle. Harold showed his disgust with his brother's conduct by recovering Bjorn's body and giving him solemn burial in Winchester's Old Minster, alongside his uncle Cnut. Edward, in the presence of his army, pronounced anathema on Swein: he was designated nithing, an outlaw. Swein's crime shocked even his atrocity-hardened sailors, most of whom deserted, so that it was with just two out of the original eight ships that he limped back to Flanders, where, amazingly, Baldwin again gave him sanctuary.[84]

It requires something of a suspension of disbelief to accept the sequel to these dark events, but the following year (1050) Edward pardoned the murderous Swein, despite the grave damage that had been done to England's relations with Denmark. The basic fact of political life was that the seemingly all-powerful Godwin dragooned the king into pardoning his son, but there were contributory factors. Since Bjorn had been the fleet commander, the leaders of the anti-Dane and anti-naval power faction in England, particularly those associated with Earl Leofric, moved in for the kill. Leofric argued that Bjorn's fortuitous demise afforded a suitable moment to take stock and wind up the expensive luxury of a fleet; it was obvious that neither the Danes nor the Norwegians would ever tear themselves away from their internecine conflict so as to be able to threaten England; and meanwhile the country was groaning under the burden of heregeld. Pardoning Swein could be a way of wiping the slate clean, of admitting that God worked in mysterious ways, and that he had given a sign of his displeasure with wasteful manifestations of naval power.[85]

Moreover, powerful voices in the Church called on Edward to exercise Christian forgiveness. Bishop Ealdred of Worcester, returning from Leo IX's Easter Council in Rome, is said to have met Swein in

Flanders, promised him his protection and brought him back to beg for mercy from the king. Ealdred, a friend and confidant of Godwin, persuaded Edward that England could never enjoy peace and prosperity if the Godwin clan was alienated, as they would eventually become if their leading representative of the next generation was not pardoned. Ealdred clinched his argument by offering to accompany Swein to Rome on a pilgrimage of atonement.[86] Swein was accordingly restored to his earldom, but met with considerable opposition from a disgruntled population. It is possible that Edward was being machiavellian, that he had already taken this likely result of the pardon into consideration, and thought that the return of Swein would tarnish the reputation of the Godwins irreparably. For his part, Harold Godwinson still thought his father was making a grave mistake in being so complaisant towards Swein. However, all his reservations were subsumed in a more general crisis, for Swein had not yet fully restored his fortunes when the Godwin family was confronted by its most serious challenge yet.

2

Duke William of Normandy

The man who would be known to history as William the Conqueror was born out of wedlock at Falaise in the autumn of 1027, the son of Robert, sixth Duke of Normandy, and Herlève, daughter of Fulbert. Exactitude is rarely possible when dealing with the ill-documented history of eleventh-century Europe, but the best estimate is that Robert was seventeen at the time of his dalliance and Herlève maybe a year younger.[1] Many legends have arisen about the first meeting of the lovers, and the circumstances in which Herlève became Robert's mistress. It is said that Robert was smitten by *coup de foudre* when he saw a lovely, innocent girl dancing in the street; in another version he was overcome by desire when he saw her shapely body bent over her laundry as she washed clothes in a stream. Needless to say, as in all such legends, the girl conceived after just one night of lovemaking, and even had a dream in which branches sprouted from her body to cover the whole of Normandy and England.[2] Sober history must leave the apocrypha to the troubadours and *chansons de geste* and be content with saying something about William's parents, where we are on firmer ground.

Despite the claims of certain historians, some of them eminent enough to know better,[3] and despite the legends, Herlève was *not* a

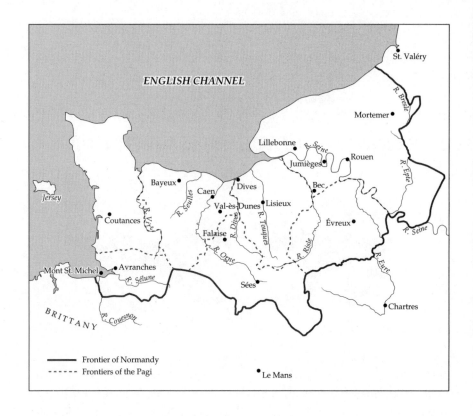

Normandy, showing the frontiers and the Pagi

tanner's daughter. Fulbert was a burgess, the household official at the Norman court whose title was *cubicularius* and, as such, a person of consequence, although all burgesses and household officials ranked below warriors in Normandy and would have been looked down on by those arrogant scions of a military élite. That Herlève was in no sense 'low class' is clearly shown by two items of evidence: her brothers appear in a charter as attestors for the infant William; and the Count of Flanders later accepted Herlève as a suitable guardian for his daughter.[4]

Why then did Robert not marry her? Immediately we discern the extreme cunning and ruthlessness of the duke – qualities which his son William would inherit in full measure. Only a year before the tryst with Herlève, Robert had seen his elder brother, aged eighteen, become fifth Duke of Normandy as Richard III. After a year of civil war, Richard died suddenly. His reign had been as difficult as it was brief, with younger brother Robert declaring his independence and building a castle at Falaise – the very fortress where Herlève consented to his embraces. Richard rode with his army into central Normandy, surrounded Robert's forces at Falaise and compelled him to sue for peace. Then came death, swift and black. Few dared speak aloud the suspicion that all entertained and would later harden into certainty: that Robert had poisoned his brother in accordance with the old Norman custom of using lethal toxins to dispose of enemies.[5]

Robert knew from bitter experience and long poring over the history of his land that when a Duke of Normandy had more than one son the upshot was always deadly rivalry, disputed thrones, murder, chaos and civil war. A dynastic marriage – the only one a Duke of Normandy could reasonably make – entailed obligations to kin and extended family which could be met only by the procreation of several children. The sole way to cut this Gordian knot was to take a mistress and beget a bastard, who would then be the one and only heir to the duke's fortunes. That is why, whatever his private feelings for Herlève, Robert cast her aside soon after William's birth. He married her off to Herluin, Vicomte de Contéville, to whom she bore two sons destined to play a large part in the story of William the Conqueror: Odo, later Bishop of Bayeux, and Robert, later Count of Mortain.[6] Herlève died around her fortieth year, in 1050, without doubt one of the most illustrious mothers of the Middle Ages.

Duke Robert ruled Normandy for nine years. It was not surprising that a reign that began with so signal an act of violence continued violent for some time. Normandy descended into chaos as powerful families enriched themselves by plunder and pillage and powerful magnates settled private disputes with the sword, even as Duke Robert waged an unnecessary war with his neighbour Alan III of Brittany – a conflict partly caused by increasing Breton influence in the Mont-Saint-Michel area.[7] No man's property – or, at least, no man not entrenched in a a mighty castle – was safe and the pillaging of Church property reached such a point that the influential Archbishop of Rouen, also called Robert, denounced his nephew the duke as a scourge of God. The irate duke at once exiled his ecclesiastical namesake, who responded with an anathema, laying Normandy under interdict.[8] Nothing daunted, Duke Robert proceeded to alienate his cousin Bishop Hugh at Ivry, to attack the powerful chieftain Niel in the Cotentin and to strike across Normandy's southern frontier to harry the powerful Counts of Blois-Chartres and Bellême.

By 1030 the reckless duke was losing his grip on the duchy. His supporters chafed at the increasingly violent, uncertain and strenuous way of life their lord imposed on them and at the warfare that threatened to bleed dry a Normandy potentially rich from the thriving trading towns of Rouen, Caen, Bayeux, Avranches and Coutances. Courtiers advised him that he should seek a reconciliation with the banished churchman, for only Archbishop Robert had the kinship connections, the ecclesiastical patronage and the personal *gravitas* that would enable young Robert to reasssert ducal authority. The duke recalled the archbishop and their compact was ratified by formal charters. The uncle's first task was to make peace between Duke Robert and his other nephew, Alan of Brittany; this was achieved on the basis of 'spheres of interest' leaving Alan to consolidate in Brittany while Robert achieved security on his western frontiers.[9]

In many ways Archbishop Robert thereafter became the real power in the land, encouraging and cajoling powerful magnates to link their power with that of the duke; such families prominent in the year 1030–35 were the Osberns and the Brionnes. But no sooner did Duke Robert's power seem firmly entrenched than he acted in a way that to modern sensibility seems like gross irresponsibility: he decided, and was inflexible in his resolve, to make a pilgrimage to the Holy Land. Pilgrimages of this kind by the royal and the mighty have to be seen in the context of an age that was, at least superficially, deeply religious: in the past thirty years many other French potentates, notably Fulk Nerra, Count of Anjou, and Geoffrey of Brittany, had made the journey to Jerusalem.[10] For all that, there is a mystery about Robert's true motives. Perhaps, worn out with the factionalism and internecine warfare in his duchy, he yearned for the more glamorous opportunities afforded by the tales of the Normans' success in southern Italy – tales which were already luring away the more wayward knights and barons of the north. Perhaps he simply wanted a quiet life and intended to abdicate if he could obtain a sinecure military office in Byzantium. One may speculate endlessly; the only certainty is that Robert lacked the stomach for the decades of conquest that were needed to bring all Normandy firmly under the ducal heel, and in this he showed himself a man far inferior to his son.

All the calm advice, pleas and even veiled threats as to the return of chaos to a recently pacified Normandy made and reiterated by Archbishop Robert, Gilbert of Brionne and Osbert the Steward swayed Duke Robert not in the slightest: his mind was made up and to Palestine he must go. But before departing he made the magnates who had assembled to remonstrate with him take an oath of fealty to the eight-year-old William as his heir. Early in 1035, taking leave of his son, who until then had lived with Herlève in Falaise, Robert left Normandy with an armed escort and a glittering retinue that won the plaudits of the nations he passed through on his way to the East. The details of the pilgrimage are not clear. He certainly reached Jerusalem and some good authorities add that he went on to Constantinople, where he paid his respects to the emperor Michael IV. On the homeward journey, in Bithynia, he died suddenly; once again poisoning was suspected.[11]

The eight-year-old was now Duke William of Normandy. What kind of land did he rule and how had it evolved? The Normans were originally Vikings (Latin *normannus* originally meant 'northman' or Viking) who had settled in northern France at the beginning of the tenth century. Throughout the ninth century Vikings had looted, raided, raped and enslaved across northern France, and even sacked Paris, swooping in from the sea and sailing up the Scheldt, Loire and Seine rivers. They preferred not to engage the Carolingians of France in battle but would do so if cornered; sometimes they would even enter into short-term alliances with the kings of France.[12] But in the year 911, the powerful Viking leader Rolf (or Rollo as he was more usually known in France) signed a treaty with Charles the Bald of France at Saint-Clair-sur-Epte which gave the Vikings a grant of land in the lower Seine around Rouen.

The Vikings' motive was presumably to establish a base in continental Europe for their widespread raids in northern Europe, avoiding the logistical problems of the long crossing of the stormy North Sea from Scandinavia. The French were actuated by the desire to tame the Norsemen by co-opting them into their own system of settled land and fixed alliances; they wanted to turn the poachers into gamekeepers and make the Vikings as vulnerable to armed incursions as they were. In the Romulus-and-Remus founders' myth later promulgated by Norman panegyrists, Charles the Bald gave his daughter Gisla to Rollo to seal the alliance. But this is unhistorical and it is anachronistic to speak of the 'founding of Normandy'. The French king simply gave a grant of land to Rollo to bind him and his men temporarily, and there was no intention that the enclave around Rouen should become a permanent colony.[13]

The colony survived, as all the other Viking land grants in northern France did not, through a mixture of good luck and cunning on the part of Rollo and his successors; it is interesting that this combination of characteristics would mark Norman history right through to the fateful year of 1066. Rollo's reign (911–930) saw the new territory in a state of flux, with no certainty of a permanent future. Although Rollo was portrayed by the first great Norman propagandist, Dudo of Saint-Quentin (who wrote the early history of Normandy in the 990s), as an Aeneas figure, he was so only in the sense that he had to fight constant warfare in his new land.[14] The sanguine French king Charles derived little benefit from his supposedly ingenious treaty. Defeated in a civil war by Raoul, Duke of Burgundy, and imprisoned at Château-Thierry on the Marne, Charles smuggled out a message appealing to his Norman 'vassals' to rescue him. To Rollo's credit, he heeded the appeal but his forces were too weak to secure Charles's release. Instead they reaped the whirlwind, for, having repulsed the Normans, Raoul invaded their enclave and devastated it; Normandy survived by the barest of margins.[15]

The Vikings were lucky in that their imperilled state was rescued in the 930s by a long series of civil wars that swept over France. Rollo's successor William Longsword proved a master politician, offering his services first to one side, then to another. His reign (930–42) was something of a turning point, for he ended the old Viking habit of raiding in return for a series of treaties guaranteeing the Norman enclave against raids. By these treaties and by marriages sealing the bargain, William Longsword built up a complex web of kinship relations which bound together the magnates of western France. Too late the French realized that they had, so to speak, created a Frankenstein's monster. They had called in the northmen to redress the balance in northern French politics, intending to use them as shock troops in harrying and besieging their enemies, but never intending that Normandy should be a fixture or that its rulers should be permanent players in the power politics of the area. So bitterly was Longsword's skill in playing one side off against another resented that an old enemy, Arnulf of Flanders, managed to lure him to a parley and murder him.[16]

But the momentum of the infant state could not be arrested, particularly as more and more settlers poured in from Scandinavia and intermarried with the indigenous inhabitants. Any hope that Normandy might disintegrate if ruled by sickly chieftains or feuding brothers was dashed by the fifty-year rule of Richard I, nicknamed 'the Fearless' and finally recognized as Count of Normandy. Under him the new nation finally took shape. Richard's reign was an era of stability and consolidation: links with Scandinavia were maintained, Viking armies were called in from the homeland to deal with French incursions, but increasing intermarriage meant that the official language, culture and institutions of Normandy steadily became French.[17] The early marriages of the Viking Norman nobility clearly show them trying to break into French society and live by French rules, and the Normans' patient diplomacy resulted in more and more land grants greatly extending the original enclave around Rouen. Most of all, Richard I took up and developed William Longsword's key idea – actually a very old notion in Scandinavia – that the way forward was to build up a system of interlocking kinship. By the last third of the tenth century the Normans were clearly committed to the idea that the true source of wealth was land, not loot, that agrarian wealth requires stability and that political alliances sealed by intermarriage were, in turn, the way to achieve this.[18]

The Normans of Richard I's reign were therefore a hybrid breed, half Viking, half French, but not wholly any one thing. Over the years they became more Frenchified but always had a strong sense that they were different from the Franks and were therefore never completely absorbed in the Carolingian ethos.[19] One of the conditions of the original land grant to Rollo was that he should be converted to Christianity, but in his reign and that of his immediate successor the official religion ran a poor second to traditional paganism. Only in Richard I's time did Christianity become the dominant faith, although links with infidel Scandinavia continued as strong as ever. The Normans allowed the Vikings of the north to use their ports as the launching points for raids or as secure havens afterwards, and as late as 1014 took part in the great Norse attack on Ireland defeated by Brian Boru at the battle of Clontarf.[20]

The Janus-faced Normans had a particularly ambivalent attitude to the so-called 'free Vikings' of the Cotentin peninsula, who owed no allegiance whatever to the Norman counts of Rouen: sometimes they made common cause with the Vikings against their traditional enemies the Bretons, but often they fought with the Counts of Brittany *against* their kith and kin.[21] As one historian has remarked about the twilight racial and cultural area the Normans of this era inhabited: 'Vikings who converted to Christianity and adopted Frankish ways in the . . . tenth century were like the Romanized Goths of the fifth century: caught between two worlds and accepted by neither . . . fear of not fitting in co-existed and conflicted with fear of fitting in too well.'[22]

Duke Richard's reign was notable for the twin-track approach to Normandy's mixed legacy. While retaining close ties with Scandinavia, he made great efforts to persuade his powerful neighbour, France, that Normandy was a permanent part of the political landscape. The first fruit of this approach was the pact of Gisors in 965 between Richard and the French ruler Lothair. Even more significant progress was made after 987, when the house of Capet replaced the Carolingians as France's reigning dynasty. In return for the title of Count of Normandy, Richard formally acknowledged Hugh Capet as his overlord. Under the Carolingian system a count had the right to administer justice and to charge what fees he saw fit for the privilege, and had fiscal rights over all lands that lay within his jurisdiction. But the importance of this should not be overdrawn; France was not giving the Norman ruler anything he did not already have, and the pact of Gisors was more a case of the recognition of necessity. In no sense was it formal recognition as count by the French that validated Richard's power, but his personal prestige, the growing numbers of warriors he could assemble under his banner, the extensive network of warlike kinsmen he had secured through alliance and intermarriage and, most of all, his control of the Seine trade.[23]

By the time of the pact of Gisors the Count of Normandy controlled the Seine but not yet the trade routes into and out of the land, nor even the whole of Upper Normandy itself; dominion over what became Lower Normandy was still a distant dream. Roughly speaking, one can distinguish between Upper Normandy – the eastern part of the province around the lower Seine – and lower Normandy to the west, including the Cotentin peninsula and the lands abutting on Brittany, and this division was to persist until the time of William the Conqueror.[24]

In the opinion of most historians, it was in the reign of Duke Richard II (996–1026) that Normandy first became a truly formidable military and political power. The circumstances of his election as count in 996, when his succession had to be ratified by the lesser territorial chieftains in the land, doubtless helped to give him a new sense of authority, for he was the first of the Norman counts to take the title 'duke'.[25] The expansion of Normandy through intermarriage and kinship is nowhere better illustrated than in the changes of nomenclature that can be observed during Richard II's reign. Having styled himself 'duke', Richard was quite content for the most powerful of his kinfolk in turn to adopt the title of count; below them in turn lesser magnates took the appellation 'viscount'. Of the complex semantics attaching to the word 'count' in the early eleventh century, one could perhaps point to the salient usage which denoted a man in possession of a castle or *castrum*. The first such count in Normandy was Rodulf of Ivry, who assumed his title some time before 1011, but by the time of Richard II's death there were half a dozen of them; there were also about twenty *vicomtes*.[26]

Believers in atavism would surely recognize the similarity between Richard II and his even more illustrious grandson William. Both were at once cruel and ruthless men and consummate politicians, both masters of *realpolitik* who shrouded their coldness and ambition behind a mask of piety and obeisance to Holy Mother Church. On Richard's cruelty, one story alone is eloquent. When the peasants of Normandy found themselves constrained by the consequences of the new ducal system, and its offshoots the counts – which entailed a much tighter control over land and income – they formed assemblies to demand the retention of their customary rights to fish in rivers and collect firewood in forests. Richard sent in his armed men, identified the ringleaders in the 'revolt', cut off their hands and terrorized the peasants back to the plough.[27] As for his political talents, nothing is more revealing than the cunning way Richard used religion to advance his purely worldly ambitions. Eight monasteries were founded in his reign, all owing military obligations to the duke and all useful in reconciling disaffected peasants to their lot. The rise of the monastic movement in early-eleventh-century Normandy shows how far the Normans of that time had come since their pagan Viking forebears first settled the land.[28]

Duke Richard II was also the first Norman ruler to look beyond the confines of France to the wider political scene in Europe and the first to entertain ambitions for a Norman role in England. It was a great *coup* when in 1002 he secured the marriage of his daughter Emma to King Ethelred II ('the Unready') of England. Richard thus had important links with both the English and French courts, but it was typical of the man to run with the hare and with the hounds.[29] Even as he linked himself dynastically to England, and became increasingly Gallicized by his adoption of a ducal style and title, he gave shelter in his ports to the Viking raiders who were harrying his English son-in-law's coasts and raiding into the Capetian realms.[30] Something of the multifaceted complexity of the man comes through in the very different nature of his three short-lived sons: the warlike Richard III; the reclusive William who became a monk at Fécamp; and the ambivalent Duke Robert who began his eight-year reign by poisoning his brother and ended it by a quixotic flight from Norman reality to Byzantine fantasy.

Such, in brief, was the legacy the eight-year-old William inherited in 1035. His father could scarcely have decamped at a worse time, and it was only through a series of fortunate circumstances – illustrating the phenomenal luck that would always attend the 'Conqueror' – that William survived at all. At least Duke Robert had surrounded the boy with the pick of his companions, instead of taking them with him on the pilgrimage. Chief among them, of course, was Archbishop Robert, one of four designated guardians, along with Count Alan of Brittany, Osbern Herfasston the steward, and Turold or Turchetil, magnate of Neuf-marché, but there were others: Ralph Tesson, Bishop Hugh of Avranches, Richard, son of Gulbert of Saint-Valéry-en-Caux, Roger, son of Humphrey Vetulus, and the Viscounts Niel, Gozelin and Thurstin; even Edward, future king of England, who spent his early years in Normandy, had a role. Moreover, before his departure, Duke Robert had secured the approval of the French king for William as his successor, and the boy probably visited the French court in 1036 to take formal vows of fealty to Henry I as liege-lord.[31]

William's principal tutor, Ralph Moine, a monk, brought the young duke up alongside two others of the same age, William Fitzosbern and Roger (the second) of Montgomery, and the slightly older cousin Roger of Beaumont. Although William's love for Herlève is well attested, he did not spend much time with her or her family and was probably brought up in Osbern's household with the other three boys, with whom he formed an unbreakable attachment.[32] The duke's education was scarcely liberal, being confined to Latin, the elements of castle-building and, above all, the pursuit of arms and training in combat: 'I was schooled in war since childhood' is one of the best-known sayings attributed to William the Conqueror.[33] At an early age he became a proficient horseman and it was clear to all that he possessed that indispensable attribute of medieval princes, a flair for warfare. While making due allowances for the rhetoric of a sycophant, we may concede some truth to the hagiographic portrait of the young William painted by his biographer William of Poitiers: 'It was both gratifying and awe-inspiring to see the prince grasp the reins, scythe the air with his sword while his lustrous shield defended him, and to behold him as a warrior, terrifying in his gleaming helmet and death-dealing lance.'[34]

But in the inevitable power vacuum left by the departure of Duke Robert and resulting regency in all but name, many local tyrants arose to bid for regional hegemony. It was with difficulty that the duchy survived at all, as Normandy descended into blood-feud, assassination and virtual civil war – a process which was accelerated after the death of Archbishop Robert in 1037. It was fortunate for the young William that the pretenders to his duchy were not yet ready to make a move, and that the violence was not directly aimed at him but at eliminating the inner circle of pro-Robert nobles, so that new groups could dominate and manipulate the boy born to be duke. Some historians, having claimed (rightly) that the violence in Normandy between 1035 and 1047 was never chaotic but always purposeful, spoil their case by minimizing the stress caused the young William.[35] Although we may doubt the more fanciful tales that Herlève's brother Walter used to sleep in the same room, ready to whisk the boy away to a peasant's cottage whenever danger threatened him, it is clear that, as with Louis XIV and the Fronde six hundred years later, a childhood memory of chaos helped to form an authoritarian personality and within that personality a determination to exert absolute and unquestioned control in his dominion.[36]

In the absence of effective lordship, a brutal struggle went on in the duchy for the reallocation of power and resources; in the maelstrom of murder and blood-feud, victory went to the most ruthless or those with the most influential extended families. The most notorious vendetta was that between the de Tosny and Grandmesnil families on one side and the Beaumonts on the other,[37] but the most signal acts of violence were directed at William's guardians. When Count Alan of Brittany died on 1 October 1040, his place was taken by Count Gilbert of Brionne, but Gilbert succumbed the following spring to the swords of assassins.[38] Some idea of the internecine vendettas, as also the kinship complexities, of Normandy can be gauged from a simple recital: Gilbert of Brionne was struck down in company with Fulk, third son of Giroie, but the assassination was planned by Rodulf of Gacé, second son of Archbishop Robert, and actually carried out by Odo the Fat and Robert, the fourth son of Giroie.

Turold, too, was murdered, but the most vicious act of blood-letting took place in the boy duke's very bedroom. One night William, son of Roger of Montgomery, stole into the ducal bedchamber at Vandreuil and cut the throat of Osbern the steward as he slept near William; according to some accounts the boy awoke and actually witnessed the murder. Roger of Montgomery was exiled to Paris for this crime, but nothing was done about his homicidal sons (William, Hugh, Robert, Roger and Gilbert) who remained to intrigue and plot further assassinations. But the blood-feud was carried on by Osbern's provost Barnon of Glos. One night Barnon collected a posse, broke into William of Montgomery's house and slew him and all his retinue.[39]

It was fortunate that none of the various pretenders to the duchy, actual or potential, made common cause with the murderers of the young duke's guardians. Nicholas, son of Richard III, had the best claim based purely on hereditary succession through the legitimate line, but he, having been placed early in life in the monastery of Saint-Ouen, showed no disposition to be other than an unworldly prelate and would indeed turn out to be a loyal supporter of William's. The real threat to the young duke would come from Mauger and William, sons of Richard II by his second wife, Papia, and from the so-called 'Guy of Burgundy', who through his mother Adeliza was Richard II's grandson. None of the three yet had a military or territorial base from which they could mount a challenge. To keep these dangerous claimants quiet, William's guardians gave them lucrative appointments, Mauger as Archbishop of Rouen, William as Count of Arques. The strategy of co-opting them was, however, fraught with danger, as it was precisely through their tenancy of these offices that they could advance to dominant positions in Normandy. William and his advisers tried to balance these perilous appointments by giving the late Gilbert of Brionne's castle to Guy of Burgundy, while to Gilbert's murderer went the palm as commander-in-chief of the Norman army.[40]

The years 1040–41, in which William's guardians were struck down, also saw the first armed rising against William himself, led by Roger of Tosny. A hero of the wars in Spain against the Moors, Roger was the first to make the young duke's bastardy an issue, and it was on these grounds that he and his two sons raised the standard of revolt, only to be defeated by Roger of Beaumont.[41] With 'malice domestic, foreign levy' threatening him, William found his situation eased by two develop-ments. The first was an attempt to introduce the so-called 'Truce of God' into Normandy, which, though ultimately unsuccessful, at least diverted the blood-feuders and intriguers for a while to rebuff this common threat to their depredations. The Truce of God was a scheme, originally initiated in southern and central France, to curb the Hobbesian state of warfare in the country by making violence, so to speak, a monopoly of the Church. The idea was that kings, dukes and counts, and their vassals, would bind themselves to conduct armed warfare only on certain days of the week or on certain months of the year.[42] Although Normandy's bishops were approached by the Abbots of Cluny and Verdun with a view to introducing the Truce, the Norman divines, linked by kinship and nexuses of power to the principal troublemakers, declined to call the necessary ecclesiastical council for authorizing such a move.

It was finally only the intervention of Henry I of France which saved William and his nation. Henry had several motives for being uneasy about the lawlessness of his western neighbour. In the first place he was concerned that the growing power of Normandy, based on the prosperous town of Rouen, controlled so many northern trade routes and cut off France from the Seine estuary. The route from Marseilles and Lyons to the English Channel, via Paris, ran along the Seine valley to emerge at the sea at Honfleur, while the produce of the Loire valley could reach the Channel ports only by the road from Tours to Le Mans and thence through Bayeux to the coast. A war of all against all in Normandy threatened French trade.[43]

Secondly, Henry had something of an obsession about his frontiers and especially the Norman fortress of Tillières-sur-Avre, whose castellan was the duplicitous Gilbert Crispin. In 1042 Henry demanded the fortress's surrender and was backed by a Norman faction who hated Gilbert; together they wrested the castle from Crispin's grasp.[44] On a later raid, in 1043, Henry stormed Argentan, again with support from one of the Norman factions. Thurstan Goz, Viscount of Exmes, supported Henry and established himself as lord of Falaise, from where he was ejected by Rodulph de Gacé, acting in Duke William's name. Gacé recaptured Falaise and consigned Thurstan Goz to exile. Henry did not engage with de Gacé and returned to Paris but not before reoccupying Tillières, which had changed hands once more, and leaving a garrison there.[45]

Thirdly, Henry's credibility was involved in the many attempts to dislodge the young Duke William or to turn him into a puppet of special interests. William, after all, was Henry's vassal and this status had been reiterated on many occasions, especially when Gilbert of Brionne replaced the deceased Alan of Brittany in 1040.[46] Henry was concerned to reinforce his rights as an overlord, and in this he was abetted by the faction in Normandy who supported William; these men reasoned that intervention by the French king might be the only way to end the chaos and factionalism in the duchy and to save their own positions and even their lives.[47]

Some scholars have objected that Henry was always more interested in *realpolitik* than credibility as a feudal overlord and that his real motive was to prevent his arch-enemy Baldwin V of Flanders from dabbling in the affairs of Normandy, which he showed every inclination to do.[48] But this is to make too strict a division between ideology and power politics. Henry must have had some confused idea that his credibility as lord was bound up with the survival of Duke William, and maybe he was opposed on grounds of principle to abetting rebellions against lords by vassals. For Henry's best interests were surely served by strict neutrality in the affairs of Normandy; with such a policy he could hope to see the duchy dismembered, after which he could establish a virtual suzerainty over the land. The net effect of his interventions was ultimately to confirm William as military strong man.

Whether Henry was principled but misguided or whether he read the runes incorrectly is uncertain, but it *is* certain that William owed his survival to the French king, when the long-threatened revolt finally took place in 1046. Centred on Lower Normandy, the rebellion was led by Guy of Burgundy, basing his claim to the duchy on his position as a legitimate male in the line of succession. Guy held the strongholds of Vernon on the Seine and Brionne on the river Risle, but his supporters came mainly from the west, and the most important of them were Nigel, *vicomte* of Cotentin, and Ranulf, *vicomte* of Bessin. They were joined by other powerful magnates in Lower Normandy, especially a group from the district of the Cinglais between Caen and Falaise, among whom were Ralph Tesson of Thury, Grimoald of Plessis and Haimo of Creully.[49]

The revolt began with an attempt to assassinate the nineteen-year-old duke at Valognes. William escaped the ambush but the incident has become encrusted with the barnacles of legend, for this was the occasion of William's legendary sixteen-hour ride through the night to Falaise after he had evaded his would-be murderers.[50] He then sped to Poissy to invoke the help of Henry I, whom he addressed as liegeman to lord. Henry, whose previous forays into Normandy had perhaps seemed ambivalent in their attitude to William, this time gave him full support and early in 1047 crossed the frontier into Normandy, heading for Caen. The army that sought out the rebels was overwhelmingly French, for William was able to bring in no more than an exiguous levy from Upper Normandy. Passing Argentan, the French army finally made contact with the rebels on the plain of Val-ès-Dunes just after they had crossed the river Orne. William was about to be blooded in his first real combat.

The rebel commanders had put all their trust in Ralph Tesson, for he was the only one of them who knew the country and his stronghold at

Thury-Harcourt controlled the only crossing of the Orne south of Caen.[51] The battle of Val-ès-Dunes showed neither commander to advantage and at first was merely cavalryman against cavalryman in isolated encounters, a clash scarcely warranting the historian Edward Freeman's description of it as a miniature battle of Granicus (where Alexander the Great defeated the Persians in 334 BC).[52] Norman hagiographers like to portray it as a miniature *Iliad* where a single hero (William, naturally) puts thousands to flight. There is some evidence that William might have killed Ranulf of Avranche's champion, Harder of Bayeux – an event said to have dismayed Ranulf unconscionably – but the real turning point in the battle came when Ralph Tesson switched sides and attacked his erstwhile allies in the rear.[53] Thereafter the fighting became more desperate: Haimo managed to unhorse King Henry but was then slain himself, while Nigel of Cotentin is said to have performed prodigies of valour. The rebel army panicked at the news that it was between two fires and tried to break off, but were driven into the river Orne, where hundreds were despatched by the sword or drowned while trying to swim the flooded waters; it was said that the nearby mill races of Borbillon were choked with bloated corpses.[54]

Val-ès-Dunes was a notable victory that changed the course of Normandy's history, and ultimately Europe's, but it was Henry's triumph, not William's, and might not have been secured at all but for the treachery of Ralph Tesson. William, who already had a cynical view of human nature, took a perverse delight in rewarding perfidy and rewarded the turncoat by marrying Ralph to Matilda, daughter of Herlève's brother. The badly wounded Guy of Burgundy escaped from the field and for some time carried on a form of guerrilla warfare but in the end was forced to surrender; to save his life he begged William for mercy, which was granted; thereafter Guy retired to exile in Burgundy.[55] William never killed a man if he thought he could still use him. The battle swung Normandy decisively over to the duke's side, to the point where the following year he was able to assemble an impressive warband and accompany King Henry to the siege of Mouliherne in Anjou.[56]

The triumph at Val-ès-Dunes gave William the confidence to aspire to great things, but first all Normandy would have to be brought firmly under his control. To achieve this William used three main methods. He began to assemble a personal bodyguard of knights as the nucleus of a Norman army.[57] He professed himself a pious champion of the Church, and to prove his credentials instituted the Truce of God in Normandy. In October 1047 an ecclesiastical council met near Caen, attended by

William and all the most important prelates of Normandy, where all present swore on holy relics to observe the conditions that had been so contemptuously rejected by the Norman warlords five years earlier: private war was prohibited from Wednesday evening until Monday morning and at all times during Advent, Lent, Easter and Pentecost. Anyone breaking these rules would be excommunicated, but, crucially, the Duke of Normandy and the king of France were excluded from all the restrictions of the Truce.[58] There could scarcely be a better example of William's political skill, for at a stroke he had managed to get the Church to give him the monopoly of violence in Normandy.

Even as he co-opted the Church, William eliminated a host of potential rivals by binding them to him by kinship ties. It was a favourite ploy of his to marry off defeated rivals to his relations, so that their interests became his. Even so, the core inner circle always consisted of his half-brothers Odo and Robert of Mortain and his trusted friends William Fitzosbern and Roger II of Montgomery. Since the Montgomerys were notorious predators, William's skill in attaching this particular family to his cause was notable, and even more so was his ability to prevent blood-feud between William Fitzosbern and Roger, whose father had killed Osbern the steward.[59] Perhaps because of their common education and upbringing under the same roof, perhaps because of a fortuitous affinity of temperaments, both William Fitzosbern and Roger of Montgomery saw the world through the same cynical, expansionist and power-worshipping eyes as the young duke. After 1048, therefore, one can see the first signs of centralization in the duchy, with William's power base emanating from central Normandy, making use not just of his four most trusted companions but also his stepfather Herluin and his new kinsman Ralph Tesson at Thury-Harcourt. In 1049 William brilliantly melded his two ploys of expansion through kinship and co-optation of the Church by replacing Bishop Hugh with his brother in the episcopate at Bayeux.[60]

The wider Church, represented by the papacy at Rome, still presented problems for William, as was dramatically illustrated in 1049, when the duke asked for the hand in marriage of Matilda, daughter of Baldwin V of Flanders. William had been urged to seek this match by his inner circle, who argued that it would be a glittering demonstration of his hegemony in Normandy and, by cementing the ties to the king of France (whose niece Matilda was), would demonstrate to any future pretenders in Normandy the military futility of their quest.[61] Baldwin, for his part, needed fresh allies approved by the king of France, for he had dabbled unwisely in wider European power politics. Baldwin accepted William's suit, but then all was thrown into turmoil by a papal interdict.

This is a story that cannot be followed without a keen appreciation of European political conflict at the time. In the years 1047–49, following his conquest of Hungary by the battle of Menfo in 1044, the German emperor Henry III was beset by the rebellion of the Lotharingians. Seeing an opportunity to dismember the Holy Roman Empire, Baldwin of Flanders and Henry I of France joined the conflict on the rebels' side; as Henry's vassal, William of Normandy had to give him nominal support and thus won the enmity of the emperor. War between Baldwin and Henry III was briefly interrupted by two peace treaties, in 1049 and 1050, but from 1051 the two potentates were continually at war.[62]

The Lotharingians had powerful allies, but the emperor had even more powerful ones, not just Geoffrey Martel, Count of Anjou, but the kings of Denmark and England, both angered by the sanctuary given pirates and sea-rovers by Baldwin of Flanders.[63] In some ways an even more important ally was about to appear. In December 1048 the German emperor Henry III secured the election to the papacy of Bruno, Bishop of Toul, the new pope taking the name Leo IX. Early in 1049 the emperor defeated Gottfried, count of Upper Lorraine, and Baldwin of Flanders, who were then summoned to make formal submission at Aachen. One of those who witnessed the ceremony of submission was the imperial protégé Pope Leo IX.[64]

It was time for Leo IX to repay the man who had elevated him to the throne of St Peter. Leo had already made a reputation as a reforming pontiff and had come to Aachen from Mainz, where he had held the second pontifical council of his first year in office (the first was in Rome). The purpose of these councils was to bring the entire area of sexuality within the domain of canon law; Leo was proposing celibacy for the clergy and the tidying up of all kinds of sexual irregularities, whether incest or marriage within the bounds of consanguinity or affinity.[65] From Aachen Leo proceeded to Rheims, the scene of his third council, where he intended to consecrate the church of St Remigius (famous Archbishop of Rheims) before pronouncing on morality within the French world.

The council lasted from 3 to 5 October 1049 and produced a series of shocks for Normandy. The first was the condemnation of Ivo of Bellême, Bishop of Sees, for having gutted his own church; Leo threw out Ivo's defence that he had burned the building as a last resort to scald out a gang of aristocratic roughnecks who had acted blasphemously by turning his church into a brothel.[66] But Pope Leo's next edict was much more serious. He expressly forbade the proposed marriage between Duke William and Matilda on the grounds that it was contrary to canon law. Ever since scholars have puzzled as to the true meaning of this delphic utterance. Did it mean that Matilda was already married? Or were the affianced couple within the prohibited degrees of affinity? Or was there some other reason for the Pope's action?[67]

There are four possibilities, outlined here in ascending order of probability. Was William's bastardy a problem? Some scholars say that from the early eleventh century illegitimacy was increasingly perceived to be shameful and hence a bar to dynastic advancement, but most students of William do not really think this was the issue.[68] The idea that Matilda was already married was popular for a time in the nineteenth century but can be emphatically ruled out. The story was that Matilda was married to one Gerbod, that Gerbod was still living, that he had already sired three children on her, and therefore that a divorce was necessary.[69]

If it is easy to discount this fantasy, the third possibility must be taken more seriously. The most plausible interpretation is that there are superficial but specious grounds for alleging that William and Matilda were within the prohibited degrees of affinity because Judith, William's aunt, had married Baldwin IV, or, more likely, that there had been a marriage agreement, never fulfilled, between Richard III of Normandy and Adela, later Baldwin V's wife and Matilda's mother; by sleight of hand this 'engagement' could be construed as an actual impediment to marriage between the ruling houses of Normandy and Flanders.[70] But overwhelmingly the most likely explanation is that Leo, either primed by the emperor or on his own initiative, was punishing the contumacious Baldwin for having supported the Lotharingians and that the marriage prohibition was a purely political action.[71]

What happened next is obscure, and the haste with which the Norman propagandists skate over William's marriage suggests that this is a murky episode which would not redound to the credit of the Duke of Normandy if properly investigated. It is clear that William, forever anxious to be seen as a devout son of Holy Mother Church, on this occasion defied the papacy, since William married Matilda, at the latest by 1053, and had two children by the time the interdict was lifted by Nicholas II in 1059.[72] That William's defiance caused severe misgivings among the Norman clergy is attested by the well-grounded story that Mauger, Richard II's son by Papia, was removed as Archbishop of Rouen for opposing the marriage, and that the great churchman

Lanfranc, later William's ecclesiastical bulwark, was deposed as Prior of Bec for remonstrating with the duke.[73]

How to make sense of all this? Theories proliferate. One is that William was not even given pause by the papal ban but married Matilda in 1050, as evinced by Matilda's name on charter documents from the year 1050. Other scholars object that this is not conclusive, since as seal-witnesses William and Matilda could have added their names to a letter some time after it was written.[74] Others say the wedding took place in 1053, following an informal lifting of the prohibition by Leo IX, by then a prisoner of the Normans in southern Italy.[75] Another plausible explanation is that William sent a delegation to Rome, that the pope was impressed by the argument that if the marriage did not take place Baldwin would be compelled to make war on Normandy to avenge the 'insult' and that all of northern Europe would be sucked into the conflict. According to this version of events, the pope granted a dispensation, waiving the objection arising from the alleged degrees of affinity, on condition that William and Matilda built two monasteries as a penance, which they duly did, at Caen.[76]

No breath of scandal ever touched the marriage of William and Matilda, who seem, subject to the constraints of the time and the attitudes taken to women, to have been a happy couple. William was famous for his marital fidelity, while Matilda, who would bear him four sons and six daughters, was a model of maternal love in the Dark Ages. Her most famous utterance is the following, relating to her eldest son: 'If my son Robert were dead and buried seven feet in the earth . . . and I could bring him back to life with my own blood, I would shed my own life blood for him.' William showed his high esteem for his wife by making her regent when he was absent from Normandy and by showering her with honours beyond what was considered normal for a duchess, associating her as a partner in his dominion. William was not an attractive human being, but his touching uxoriousness deserves to be recorded.[77]

3

Harald Hardrada

The Norway into which Harald Sigurdsson (later to be known as Hardrada) was born was similar in its economic and social organization to the rest of northern Europe, though very different in its laws and culture. Medieval Scandinavia, benefiting from the much milder climate of the early Middle Ages, seems to have been able to support a considerable population, though scholars dispute its nature and size. There is much evidence of demographic pressure on natural resources. Some say that overpopulation was a consequence of polygamy, others that it was *the* trigger for Viking expansionism from the late eighth century. But Norway seems to have been able to feed a population in excess of two million by the eleventh century. There was intensive farming of wheat, barley, oats and rye, a thriving dairy industry and large herds of cattle. A meat-eating diet was the norm in a land where vast herds of elk, reindeer and red deer could be hunted, and where million-strong flocks of ducks and geese were regular visitors. Then there was the abundant fishing off Norway's long North Sea coast, especially off the Lofoten Islands.[1]

Although commerce was probably more important in Scandinavia than elsewhere in northern Europe – the fame of the Vikings as warriors has obscured their great role as traders – the key to wealth and hence social organization was still land. The Norwegian aristocracy was originally composed of warrior chiefs with clan bands along the patrimonial model, but by the eleventh century, doubtless learning from their cousins in Normandy and from England, land ownership was the key to social success and intermarriage with powerful kinship groups the way to establish one's place in the pecking order of lords and vassals. But, as befitted the descendants of Vikings, the Norwegian oligarchs always had much more interest in commerce than their counterparts elsewhere in Europe: one great magnate had the monopoly of trade with Finland, another became wealthy through controlling the export of furs to England.[2]

One of the great features of Norwegian history in the hundred years before Harald's birth was the struggle by successive kings, beginning with Harald Fairhair, to establish their supremacy over the territorial magnates. Before Harald certain classes of nobility, the *odelsbondermen*, enjoyed full property rights in their land which were vested permanently in the family, who had the right to redeem the property if it was sold outside the immediate kinship group. Harald Fairhair's revolution was to make property-ownership provisional, as under feudalism; whether he forced the *bondermen* to pay a land tax or merely imposed a personal tax is uncertain, but it was widely felt that the *odel* had been abolished, and many magnates emigrated as a result.[3]

Harald Fairhair established a model of kingship which Olaf Haraldson (St Olaf) and Harald Hardrada himself would later follow. The king retained the right to levy a personal tax on his subjects, to tax special privileges and incomes, to receive tribute from vassal peoples and even to make trade a royal monopoly. To strengthen the monarchy, two new types of noble were created: the king's personal household of warriors and retainers known as the *hird* – roughly corresponding to the housecarls in England – and his local officials, sheriffs and administrators and tax collectors, known as *lendermen*. In return for making the royal writ run throughout the country, the *lendermen* held lifetime tacks of Crown lands; their fiefs were not hereditary, nor did their powers include the privileges and prerogatives over sub-vassals inherent in feudalism proper, but they drew income from their lands, in return for which they had to provide armed men whenever the monarch declared a levy. The more resistance there was to the king, the more lands were confiscated and added to the royal demesne, swelling the numbers of landowners bound to the Crown.[4]

The two key events in Norwegian history in the tenth century were Harald Fairhair's centralized monarchy and King Olaf Tryggvason's conversion to Christianity. Opposition to the new religion from devotees of Odin and the Aesir became confused with, and sometimes ran in tandem with, aristocratic opposition to the monarchy, and in the early years of Harald Sigurdsson's life these issues had not been fully resolved. In the year 1000 Olaf Tryggvason was defeated and killed by an alliance of recalcitrant aristocrats and the kings of Sweden and Denmark. Norwegian kingship received a crushing blow and for a time the aristocracy regained its power; Norway was divided between the kings of Sweden and Denmark and the jarls Eirik and Svein ruled the country as their vassals.[5]

For sixteen years Norway lay under the foreign yoke; the jarls, representative of aristocratic reaction, allowed the various districts of Norway to become semi-independent, with their own petty kings, as in the old days. One of these was Sigurd Syr, one of three kings of Oplandene (the Uplands) in south-east Norway, who ruled over the districts of Hadeland and Toten, with his capital at Ringerike. Another minor king was Harald Grenske, Harald Fairhair's great-grandson. Around 990 Harald Grenske married Aasta and in 993 a boy, Olaf, was born, but Grenske died before his son's birth. Aasta then married Sigurd Syr, who brought up the boy as his own. Legend says that Olaf was christened with that name when Olaf Tryggvason visited Ringerike in 996 and insisted that Sigurd Syr and Aasta should be baptised.[6]

At the age of fifteen Olaf Haraldsson joined a Viking expedition which took him first to Denmark, then Sweden and Finland and finally Holland. In 1009 Olaf arrived in England, where he lived for four years, then spent a further two years in Normandy. In 1015, at the age of twenty-two, well schooled in the arts of war and having seen a good deal of the world, he sailed for Norway, determined to regain the throne of his ancestors and fully Christianize Norway. Lacking Olaf Tryggvason's charisma and charm, he possessed great reserves of willpower, single-mindedness and even fanaticism. His first call was on Sigurd Syr, who backed him to the hilt and persuaded his fellow kings of Oplandene to proclaim Olaf king at the Uplands *thing*. More and more powerful chiefs joined him, until in 1016 Olaf felt strong enough to meet jarl Svein in a decisive battle. At Nesjar in 1016 Svein was defeated in a bloody battle, fled to Sweden and died the next year. Olaf was then proclaimed king of the whole realm at the *Orething* at Trondelagen.[7]

Olaf still had to fight hard against the intransigent king of Sweden until a peace was concluded in 1019, largely because King Olaf of Sweden, a treacherous and devious man, feared the rising power of Cnut. For nine years Olaf Haraldsson was free from foreign wars. He rewarded Sigurd Syr by abolishing all the petty kingdoms and began his campaign of imposing Christianity by force, even blinding or maiming those who would not accept the new dispensation. Crucial to the Christianizing campaign were the many bishops and missionaries Olaf had brought with him from England to Norway. The hasty, forcible conversion simply drove paganism underground, and a crude syncretism resulted whereby Jesus Christ was given the attributes of Thor and Freya was merged with the Virgin Mary. A great organizer, Olaf drew up an elaborate code of civil laws and an even more complex system of ecclesiastical law. He rebuilt the city of Nidaros, brought the Orkneys back to the Norwegian fold, and developed particularly close relations with Iceland.[8]

The rock on which he perished was his attempt to make royal power absolute and his insistence on equality before the law. Outraged by the loss of their privileges and their inability to hold sway in their districts because of the ubiquity of the *lendermen*, the old territorial magnates bided their time, thirsting for vengeance. Their chance came in 1028 when Olaf and the new king of Sweden, Anund Jacob, foolishly attacked Denmark at the very moment Cnut, after solving his problems in England, was again looking north. When Cnut assembled a mighty fleet to invade Norway in 1028, the disgruntled Norwegian oligarchs saw that their chance had come: they convened a *thing* at Trondelagen and proclaimed Cnut king. Overwhelmed by superior forces, Olaf fled to Sweden and thence to the court of Grand Duke Yaroslav at Kiev.[9]

The euphoria of the oligarchs was shortlived. Their leading lights Einar Tambarskjelver and Kalv Arnesson both hoped to succeed to the Norwegian throne when Hakon Eiriksson, the man Cnut appointed as his under-king in Norway, was unexpectedly drowned and died without issue. But to their great disgust, Cnut announced that he intended to appoint his own son king of Norway; Einar Tambarskjelver went into self-appointed exile and did not return for some years. The news of Hakon's death encouraged Olaf to attempt to return to Norway. He recruited a number of Varangian guards from Constantinople under Aasta, the Norse chieftain, and raised hundreds more in Sweden, where Anund Jacob, for fear of Cnut, dared not give him open support. In 1030 he crossed into Norway with an army of 2,500 men, many of them ill-trained levies.[10]

Among those who flocked to his standard was an immensely tall and strong fifteen-year-old youth named Harald Sigurdsson, his own half-brother. Harald was the son of Sigurd Syr and Aasta, and he must have been born right at the end of Aasta's reproductive life, for twenty-two years separated his birth from Olaf's. Of the first fifteen years of Harald's life we know nothing significant, but it is clear that it was the mother who was the vital influence. Sigurd Syr was a mild, peace-loving man of no great ability, who was said to have been helping his peasants bring in the harvest when Olaf Tryggvason visited him in 996. Aasta, though, was a determined and ambitious woman, who wanted her sons to gain power and renown and constantly dinned into the young Harald the message that these were the supreme values. She told Olaf: 'If I had the choice, I would rather you became king of all Norway, though you lived no longer than Olaf Tryggvason, than that you should remain at the level of Sigurd Syr and die of old age.'[11]

According to the sagas, Harald early showed his deep character. When Olaf came to visit Sigurd Syr around 1018, he amused himself by pulling demonic faces at Harald's two older brothers, who were so afraid that they burst into tears; Harald, however, stared back at him fearlessly. On another occasion Harald and his brothers were asked what they most wanted in the world; the brothers said, 'Corn and cattle,' but Harald answered: 'Warriors.' It is a fair inference, then, that Harald's early formation was in the harsh world of the warrior ethos. Perhaps the aesthetic side of his nature, which later manifested itself in a love of heroic poetry, was nurtured by childhood in Ringerike, a town then famous for its artwork and decorated rune-stones.[12]

When the fifteen-year-old Harald joined Olaf and his army he must have known what a desperate venture he was engaged in. The enemy had superior numbers and all the best generals, including Kalv Arnesson, Tore Hund and Haarek of Tjotta. Olaf marched across the Kjolen mountains towards Trondelagen and selected a field of battle at Stiklestad where he would command the higher ground. There he waited for the expected reinforcements under Dag Ringsson, but Dag reached the rendezvous only after the battle had been fought. On 29 July 1030, therefore, Olaf had to give battle to the forces of the pro-Cnut Norwegian aristocracy when he was outnumbered by two to one – the best estimates of the enemy army put it around 5,000 strong.[13]

Before fighting, Olaf slept and was said to have had a dream in which a ladder reached down from heaven to earth and Christ beckoned to him. The dream was certainly premonitory. At about one o'clock Olaf ordered the charge, hoping that the downhill impetus of his men would throw the enemy into confusion. The front line of the chieftains' army buckled but the ranks behind stood firm, and soon numbers told. Olaf's force was first outflanked, then surrounded, and finally annihilated. Olaf himself was wounded and then cut down by Kalv Arnesson and Tore

Hund, and almost all the great lords who had joined Olaf were also slain. Dag Ringsson arrived with the reinforcements in time to witness the final stage of the rout, but his brief counterattack could not reverse the verdict. In the confusion of the later stages of the battle the badly wounded Harald Sigurdsson managed to crawl away and hide in a ditch.[14]

One of those who fought that day with Harald was Rognvald Brusisson and it was he who rescued Harald, found a peasant family to nurse the young warrior and tend his wounds, and himself travelled east to Sweden to seek refuge with King Anund Jacob. Harald stayed with the peasant family until his wounds were healed; then, with the peasant's son as a guide, he made his way east to Jamtland and thence to Sweden, travelling at night or by little-frequented byways. While skulking in the hills on his way east, Harald was said to have begun his career as a versifier by composing the following: 'From copse to copse I crawl and creep now, worthless. Who knows how highly I'll be heralded one day.'[15]

Harald stayed in Sweden until 1031, then proceeded to Kiev, at that time the Mecca for exiled Scandinavians. The Prince of Kiev in the years 1019–54 was Yaroslav, formerly Grand Duke of Novgorod (1016–19), the son of Vladimir Monakh; a man who had come to power with the aid of Norse warriors after four years of civil war with his half-brothers. Vladimir had a bad reputation with Norwegian mercenaries because of his alleged meanness with money. There had been very close contacts between Yaroslav and Harald's half-brother King Olaf. Yaroslav's wife Ingigerd had, when a girl, nursed a romantic fantasy about Olaf (whom she had never met) and married Yaroslav only after her father, Olaf of Sweden, expressly forbade a match with his Norwegian namesake. But when Olaf came to Russia in 1029, Ingigerd found him as congenial in the flesh as in fantasy. She persuaded Yaroslav to offer Olaf the rule of the province of Bulghar on the Volga, baiting the offer with a suggestion that Olaf make a pilgrimage to the Holy Land first; Olaf hesitated, but in the end returned to Norway, Stiklestad and his death.[16]

As Olaf's half-brother Harald also received a warm welcome in Kiev, and for three years he fought with Yaroslav's armies, alongside his companion Eilif, son of Rognvald of Orkney. He served with distinction in campaigns against the Poles and East Wends, and on the strength of this made so bold as to ask for the hand of Elizabeth, Yaroslav's daughter, when she came of marriageable age. Yaroslav

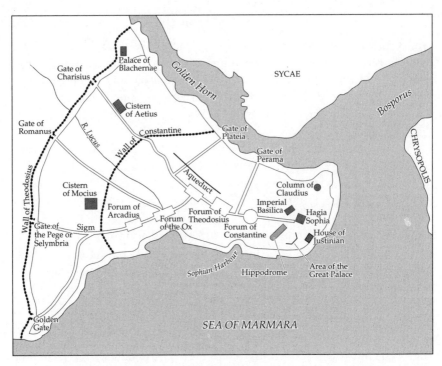

Byzantium

replied curtly that the young warrior would first have to achieve real fame and an individual reputation. The obvious place for Harald to achieve his ambitions was Byzantium, where the Varangian guard of Norse mercenaries had served the emperor for almost a century. Accordingly, in 1034 Harald took his leave of Yaroslav. We may discount all the fanciful skaldic stories that he first journeyed to Saxony and France and committed piracy in the Channel ports before decamping to Lombardy, Rome and Apulia and then proceeding to Constantinople; the obvious inference is that he sailed down one of the major Russian rivers to the Black Sea and then crossed over to Byzantium.[17]

Byzantium (or Constantinople, to use the name of its founder) was an empire seven hundred years old when Harald Sigurdsson arrived there and it was gnerally considered one of the wonders of the world. By the standards of the day a titanic megalopolis, with a population of one million, it had street lighting, sewerage and drainage, hospitals, orphanages, public baths, aqueducts, huge water cisterns, libraries and luxury shops like the 'House of the Lanterns', illuminated at night, where Byzantine silks were sold. The city was surrounded by twelve miles of high walls and gave on to a great harbour; there was a lighthouse or Pharos on a promontory within the palace enclosure. A chain of beacons linked the city to Asia Minor across the Bosporus, allowing messages to be sent rapidly to distant parts of the empire. Inside the huge fortress, doubly protected by walls and water, there was a cluster of great buildings, palaces and churches, stuffed with treasures from all over the world.[18]

There were seven palaces, including the imperial abode, where bronze gates were unlocked at dawn and then closed to the public from 9 a.m. to 3 p.m. – the hours when casual sightseers might be abroad. The Triconchus palace, built in 738, was roofed with gold; in the adjoining hall, Sigma, were fountains which flowed with wine and doors of silver and polished bronze. In the state throne-room, where foreigners were received, stood jewelled organs and the great throne of the emperor, guarded by two massive lions of gilded bronze. In front of the throne stood the phenomenon which most amazed observers then and since: a metal tree with mechanical birds in its branches. The imperial family rarely strayed outside the palace precinct except to go to the Hippodrome and the public rarely came in. There was little need to leave the precinct, for within the walls were the emperor's polo-ground, his private zoo and aviary and gardens and pleasure grounds with superb views over the sea of Marmora and the Golden Horn.[19]

Two things struck foreign observers of Byzantium: the power of its armies and the proliferation of its bureaucracy. In 1034 there seemed to be no serious military enemies in sight, as the Seljuk Turks were in abeyance and the threat from the Normans in Sicily had not yet materialized. The greatest danger to the Byzantine military came from within, from the jealous civilian and bureaucratic powers, who started to have the upper hand from 1025 onwards; here was paradox indeed – anti-military feeling in a society that was dependent on the military for survival. More than one commentator noted the rapid decline in the power of the emperor himself during the period 1025–1071, when there were no less than ten lacklustre emperors; Basil II, by contrast, who died in 1025, was an autocrat who reigned fifty years and brought the reputation of Byzantium and its armies to the highest pitch.[20]

After Basil's death, the dominant political figure was his niece Zoe, by common consent the one true descendant of the Macedonian line worthy of supreme power. Zoe was unintelligent, like her sister Theodora, but was a woman of undoubted sexual charms, where Theodora was a homely spinster. For three years Basil's brother, a notable weakling, ruled as Constantine VIII, but it was his daughter Zoe who captivated the Byzantines. Devoting herself to the life of a voluptuary, even though aged fifty in 1028, Zoe ran through three husbands in the space of fourteen years but never lost her hold on the affections of the public. The bureaucratic faction quickly saw that she was the key to their success and forced the feckless Constantine to nominate her first shadowy husband as his successor. The unlucky bridegroom was a sixty-year-old named Romanus Argyrus, who was already married. Forced by the bureaucratic élite to divorce and remarry on pain of blinding and mutilation if he did not comply, Argyrus married Zoe on 15 November 1028 and shortly afterwards succeeded as Romanus III.[21]

Romanus was a Walter Mitty character, who dreamed of reviving the glory of ancient Rome. A humiliating defeat by the Saracens outside Aleppo ended that fantasy and destroyed the myth of the Byzantine army's invincibility, so Romanus tried to retrieve his fortunes by toadying to the big landowners. Where Basil II had introduced progressive forms of taxation and been a champion of the smallholder, Romanus truckled to the *latifundistas*, abandoned Basil's reforms and reverted to the hated system of tax farming, which bore most heavily on the little man. But his parsimony with money, when extended to Zoe's household budget, proved his undoing. A low-born palace eunuch named John Orphanotrophus inveigled himself into the empress's good graces and introduced her to his attractive younger brother, Michael, who became Zoe's lover in 1033. Suddenly, on 11 April 1034, Romanus was found dead in his bath. So insouciant was Zoe about the inevitable suspicions concerning her husband's end that she married her lover the very next day. He assumed the purple as Michael IV and reigned seven years and eight months, though real power remained in the hands of John Orphanotrophus.[22]

Such was the Byzantium in which Harald arrived. The tall, broad-shouldered, blond warrior, with his certificate of service from Yaroslav, had little difficulty getting enrolled in the élite Varangian guard, for Russia had long been a source of supply of mercenaries to Constantinople. Kievan Russia was the transmission belt between Scandinavia and Byzantium, and the links between Russia and Constantinople were of the closest. There was a Russian colony in the city; the Russians acted as a kind of recruitment agency for the Varangians, architects, painters and merchants moved freely between Russia and Byzantium; there was a flourishing trade from Byzantium to Russia in jewellery, ceramics, glassware, olive oil, wine and fruit, and from Russia to Byzantium in slaves, furs, wax and honey. In normal circumstances Russian loyalty to Byzantium was guaranteed by the metropolitan Archbishop of Kiev, who represented the spiritual authority of the patriarchs of Constantinople.[23]

For all that, relations between Russia and Byzantium were often uneasy. The Viking states in Russia began life as forts – Norse trading posts that had to be secured against attack – but the ambivalent status of the Vikings, part traders, part marauders, is nowhere better illustrated than in the first (failed) attack by the Scandinavian *Rus* in 860, two years before the first permanent Norse settlements were established in the Ukraine. There was always mutual suspicion: as late as the mid-1020s it is related that 800 Kievan Vikings or *Rus* who sailed down to Byzantium in the hope of being enrolled as mercenaries were massacred out of hand by the Byzantine army.[24]

It was during the reign of Basil II that the Varangians really became established as a fixed point in Byzantine military life. His fifty-year rule from 976, which saw the empire at its apogee, depended greatly on his use of the élite Scandinavian bodyguard. They it was who were instrumental in securing for him the great victory at Abydos in 989, after which there were no more serious challenges to his rule. They, too, obeyed unhesitatingly when he ordered every single man, woman and child in twelve districts of the city put to death, even though it took them three months of butchery to achieve the objective. Most of all, the Varangians were the cutting edge of his military machine in a variety of foreign wars – for Basil was no bookish ruler like most of his fellow emperors but a brutal and bloody warrior. The Varangians heavily defeated the Georgians in one of Basil's last wars (in 1021) and earlier made their mark in Italy. A rising in Bari in 1011 by the local magnate Meles saw pro-Meles Norman mercenaries pitted against the Varangians in a campaign that dragged on for seven years before Byzantine victory in 1018.[25]

So fond of the Varangians was Basil that it has even been suggested that his second wife, Ingerina, was Scandinavian. Certainly by the end of his reign the Norsemen had acquired every conceivable military skill. They had mastered the art of warfare on horseback; they could fight on ground which other armies avoided, especially woodland; they were experts in night-time assaults; they knew how to improvize field fortifications quickly or to construct dykes fortified by stakes, palisades and advanced ditches; above all, they were masters of the surprise attack. A favourite strategem was to retreat into stone buildings, houses or churches, turn them into fortresses, and then sortie unexpectedly against an enemy who thought them cornered. The Varangians were also masters of guerrilla fighting and warfare of a socially subversive kind, freeing slaves or enslaving freemen, always trying to divide their enemies and turn them inwards against themselves.[26]

From the emperor's point of view these Norse mercenaries were invaluable. They were cost-effective in the sense that disciplined cavalrymen or axemen were worth twice their number in Arab or Bulgar infantry; as they came fully trained and armoured, the imperial treasury did not have to spend money bringing them up to fighting fitness; they were loyal to their paymasters as they had no local, territorial or family interests to defend; and their love of money was a stimulus towards economic growth and expansion, contributing to the well-attested prosperity of Byzantium in the eleventh century. So pleased with them was Basil II that he began to experiment with producing an élite within an élite, distinguishing the corps of 'guard Varangians' who remained inside the city from the 'mercenary Varangians' sent to fight foreign wars. It is interesting that Harald Hardrada's eight-year career marks a progress from the mercenary to the guard type.[27]

The Guard Varangians' main duty was to protect the person of the emperor, and to this end they accompanied him whenever he ventured outside the palace precinct, mainly for the purpose of coronations, triumphs, processions or visits to the racecourse at the Hippodrome. During Holy Week the Varangians' duties involved strewing the floor of Hagia Sophia with boughs of myrtle, laurel and olive, and stripping the Brazen House, on the route between the palace and Hagia Sophia, of all treasures. The end point for all processions, whether during a coronation or during the annual festivity on 11 May to celebrate the founding of the city, was always Hagia Sophia. After a victorious campaign the emperor would enter the city by the Golden Gate at the western end of the walls and proceed by the broad straight road (the Mese, or Middle Way, which bisected the city) to the mid-point of Byzantium at the Milion; thence he moved along the Mese to Hagia Sophia to lay the insignia captured from the enemy on the altar.[28]

But the most common Varangian escort duty was to the Hippo-drome, to attend horse races, chariot races, animal shows, boxing matches, athletic contests, circus acts or musical entertainments. Four-horse chariot races were the main attraction, and the fanatical racing factions, the Blues and the Greens, who functioned as primitive political parties, were still active, if not at the same strength that had triggered the notorious Niké riots in 531. The imperial box could be entered directly from the palace enclosure, and it was customary for the emperor to enter here, clad in state robes, carrying a lighted candle from his chapel.

He would bless the audience, then drop a white handkerchief for the races to begin. It was said that the Varangians used to assuage boredom on such occasions by noting the similarities of the frescos on the walls of the Hippodrome to their own gods and heroes, the Aesir and the Volsungs. Sometimes, however, the Norsemen had to preside over grimmer business. Although fights with wild beasts were by this time prohibited, the blood lust of the people was indulged in other ways. Offenders such as traitors and deserters were sometimes publicly despatched or the heads of executed rebels displayed. Anna Comnena relates that the leaders of the Bogomil heresy were burnt alive in the Hippodrome.[29]

The Guard Varangians were quartered in different places at different eras – at one time they were lodged in the palace of the Buceleon, and at another in Numera, a building near the Hippodrome on the upper floor above the prison. But in Harald's time both companies – the so-called great hetairia and the little hetairia – had their headquarters in the part of the great palace reserved for the Excubitores – a regiment exclusively formed from the Byzantine nobility – on the eastern side of the precinct. Reached through the Brazen House, the main route into the Palace of Daphne was through their quarters; to keep all entrances securely guarded the Varangians also had the use of their former lodgings in the old palaces. They were well paid by normal standards: guards in the great hetairia received forty-four gold coins a year, and those in the 'little' company forty. In addition to the salary, there were gifts at Easter and on the coronation of a new emperor, plus a share in the booty taken on campaigns and a percentage of revenues raised when the Varangians acted as tax collectors.[30]

The Varangians naturally attracted a good deal of jealousy from xenophobes and those irritated at the obstacle the foreign mercenaries posed to attempts at *coup d'état*. In élite circles it was whispered that it was unwise and self-destructive to have aliens occupying high offices of the state. The Varangians responded to their unpopularity by becoming increasingly ghettoized: they even had their own church – St Olaf's near Hagia Sophia, said to have been destroyed when the adventurers of the Fourth Crusade sacked the city in 1204 – where in later days the sword of the canonized Olaf of Stiklestad was said to have been kept as a relic.[31]

To deflect criticism of their status and power the Varangians maintained a very high level of *esprit de corps*, complete with savage military discipline meted out against any of their number who transgressed their code. Flogging, lopping off ears and noses, blinding and execution made up the ascending order of penalties for disobedience, cowardice or even being in the wrong place at the wrong time. Incompetent or unlucky generals could hope to escape this fate only at cost of being dressed up as a woman, mounted backwards on an ass and driven through the streets of Byzantium to the jeers, blows and missiles of angry crowds. The Varangians had the right to be judge and jury in cases involving their own members, subject only to the emperor's ultimate fiat, but there is no record of imperial intervention in any sentence. The draconian discipline of the Norse mercenaries was legendary: we hear of sentences of death for attempted rape and the attempted murder of the emperor Nicephorus III. In the very year Harald arrived in Byzantium, the Varangians met to try a case of a woman who had been raped in Lydia by a 'mercenary Varangian' and then killed her assailant with his own sword. The military court decided that the woman should inherit the dead man's possessions and that his corpse should be treated as that of a suicide and thrown out on a dunghill without proper burial.[32]

Harald made an immediate impression on the Varangians and was excited by the view of his messmates that an able man could get right to the top in Byzantium. Whether this was so is doubtful, for all the highest positions in the state were reserved for scions of Greek royal families, and the evidence for Varangians in élite positions is suspect. Harald's regal bearing led some to suspect that he was of royal birth and therefore ineligible for the Guard – since the Byzantines normally refused to employ foreign princes as mercenaries. Harald was lodged on the upper floor of the Excubitores section of the great palace together with the other great warriors he had brought with him from Russia, notably Ulf Ospaksson and Haldor Snorresson, an Icelander. It is stated in the saga sources that the Byzantines suspected Harald was a foreign prince and employed an Icelander named Mar to worm the truth out of Haldor in casual conversation, but the loyal Snorresson gave nothing away.[33]

As a newcomer Harald began his career in the 'mercenary Varangians' serving in foreign parts. His first job was to serve as a marine on the Byzantine galleys in the Aegean, clearing the sea lanes of pirates. The sources do not make it clear whether he fought against the pirates of Thrace and the Cyclades, who, though wounded by the recent loss of Crete, were by no means a spent force, or whether he was attached to the fleet Michael IV kept in Sicilian waters to deal with Arab privateers who preyed on shipping in the passage between Sicily and Africa. Yaroslav's credential may have sufficed to give Harald the command of a body of marines on an individual vessel, for this alone makes sense of later developments. Such commanders were supposed to pay the emperor one hundred marks for every pirate ship captured (they could keep the rest), but Harald very early realized there was no proper accounting system, so that it was easy to keep back more than his fair share. Harald, like William of Normandy, was a greedy man, and his avarice would soon land him in trouble.[34]

The details of Harald's maritime service are otherwise obscure. He may have been part of the fleet of Cibirriotes, who in these years won a great victory against the Thracian pirates, destroyed many ships and either enslaved or barbarously executed all prisoners. Or he may have opposed the great Arab fleet from Sicily and Africa that the annalist Zonaras mentions as active in the Aegean in the early years of Michael's reign; the Arabs raided most of the Greek islands, laid waste the Greek mainland, devastated Asia Minor and even captured the town of Myra. Since this raid coincided with the rebellion of King Adam of Sebaste, where the Varangians were definitely involved, the likelihood is that Harald was fighting the Arabs. The only thing certain is that he made his mark and that his deep character increasingly emerged: forceful, self-willed, determined, courageous, far-sighted, he had a talent for war, was attractive to women but was also a ferocious disciplinarian, wildly ambitious and coldly ruthless, greedy and avaricious, with a lust for loot that became legendary.[35]

Harald may next have been switched from naval warfare to campaign against the Pechenegs, since it was a characteristic of the Varangian fighting machine bequeathed by Basil II that crack troops could be switched from front to front at short notice. This extreme mobility means that the saga stories of Harald visiting the Holy Land in 1036 may not be so far-fetched. In that year Michael IV concluded a peace treaty with the Caliphate of Egypt, allowing the Christian places in Jerusalem to be rebuilt. Michael sent masons to begin a massive rebuilding programme in Jerusalem, and it is eminently plausible that Harald might have commanded a small detachment of Varangians on escort duty, to ward off attacks by marauding Bedouin, who were as much a menace to the Caliphate as to Christians. There is scholarly speculation that many high-ranking Byzantines took this unique opportunity to visit the Holy Land, including Zoe's two sisters, Eudoxia and Theodora. According to the saga tradition, Harald visited the sites of the Crucifixion and Resurrection, wore pilgrim's clothes, made money offerings at the sacred places and bathed in the river Jordan.[36]

For two years from late 1035 Harald served mainly in Syria and Armenia, under the command of Nicholas Pegonites. The Varangians captured the fort of Bekni in Armenia and in 1036 collaborated with regular forces under Constantine Katallakos to relieve Edessa, originally wrested from the Saracens by George Maniakes in 1032. It is in this period that we first hear of Harald as a fully-fledged composer of sagas drawn from his own exploits and those of other Varangians. A favourite story from just a few years before showed that the tradition of the blood-feud did not die when Norsemen went to Byzantium. It seems that in 1031, as a result of some obscure dispute, a Varangian named Grettir the Strong and his brother were slain by a man named Thorbiorn Angle. Now Grettir had another brother, named Thorstein Asmund Arson, who swore to avenge his siblings, followed Thorbiorn's trail all the way back from the Black Sea to Norway and killed him there. This was the kind of story that particularly enthralled the young Harald Sigurdsson.[37]

The most famous campaign in which Harald took part was the war in Sicily in 1038–41, which is particularly well documented from Greek, Latin, French and Arab sources. Sicily had always been a cockpit for Arab–Byzantine conflict and, after Basil II's death, two Arab chieftains battled for supremacy there. One of them, Akhal Aboulaphar, sought the emperor's help against his brother and opponent Abou Hafs, who in turn asked for military assistance from the Caliph of Tunis, Muizz-ibn-Badis. While Michael IV sent the catepan of Italy, Constantine Opos, to Sicily in 1037 to stiffen the military arm of Akhal, the Caliph of Tunis sent his son Abdallah-ibn-Muizz to reinforce Abou. This Arab alliance gradually prevailed against Akhal to the point where Constantine Opos was forced to retire from Sicily, though still in good order.[38]

Angry at the turn of events, Michael IV prepared a huge expedition for the reconquest of Sicily, which he put under the command of Georgios Maniakes, who had won fame by his victories in Asia Minor. Maniakes was given all the best troops in the empire, including the Varangians and three hundred Normans from Salerno commanded by the two sons of Tancred de Hauteville, levies from Lombardy, Apulia and Calabria, armies from Greece under Katakolon Cecaumenos, Armenian mercenaries and a fleet under the emperor's brother-in-law Stephen. Although the Byzantines were masters of amphibious operations, their imposing armada was vigorously opposed by the Arabs; the sagas claim that it was only through the exceptional bravery of Harald and his unit that the Byzantine forces secured a beachhead.[39]

This was Harald's first encounter with Maniakes, the greatest Byzantine commander of this era, the most notable captain in Constantinople between the reign of Basil II and that of Alexius

Comnenus. Maniakes was a Turkish-born former camp-waiter, distinguished by his giant stature and voice of thunder. At this stage Harald was not senior enough to challenge Maniakes's authority, but already he recognized a man cut from the same cloth as himself. As usual in such cases, where two over-similar individuals are vying for the same space, there was deep resentment, not least because Harald was used to being the only immensely tall individual in any gathering. They were at once both too alike and too unlike, for Maniakes was a self-made man, punctilious about military discipline and oversensitive to slights, real or imaginary. When campaigning Harald liked to take a relaxed attitude; he was a loner who liked to do things his way, even if this meant using unconventional methods. Maniakes was a by-the-book martinet who loathed any deviation from the normal chain of command. The campaign in Sicily saw continual friction between these two larger-than-life figures. In the sagas Harald is always given the last word or the crushing quip, but we should take this with a pinch of salt, as *l'esprit de l'escalier* imported into oral tradition.[40]

Despite the huge resources poured into the Sicilian war by Byzantium, the attempt to reconquer the island ended in spectacular failure. We know that by this time Harald commanded a regiment of 500 Varangians, but accurate details of the campaign and his role in it are hard to come by. The sagas are full of tall tales and absurd legends about his exploits. In one story, while the Varangians are besieging a castle, Harald pretends to be dead. The Norsemen then ask to be allowed to bury the body within the castle. Permission is granted, the Varangians carry the coffin to the gates, wedge them open with the heavy coffin, then their comrades rush in and slaughter the garrison. In another story the Varangians sap and mine under a castle, come up in the middle of a banqueting hall and then slaughter the feasters. In yet another Harald captured some birds, tied wood shavings to them, set fire to them and released the birds over the battlements, where they proceeded to set fire to the castle.[41]

Most of these episodes are commonplaces of the folk tales of many different cultures. The tunnelling and the mock funeral occur in stories of Russian kings and of the emir ibn-Khosran of Baghdad, while the incendiary birds feature in the history of the Mongols and in the saga of the capture of Cirencester by the Danish king Guthrum in the ninth century. The sagas featuring Harald seem to be a mixture of itinerant folk tales, military clichés and genuine oral tradition, usually signalled by distinctive circumstantial touches. One saga story about Harald in Sicily that may be true is how he outwitted the defenders of a town he was unable to take by siege. Mocked by the citizens for their inability to make inroads, the Varangians at Harald's command responded by holding an athletics tournament just out of missile range. This went on for three days, but on the fourth the Norsemen hid weapons under their cloaks as they approached the athletics ground. The defenders, who had become blasé, appeared on the walls unarmed to watch the spectacle, at which Harald ordered a general charge, which took the enemy by surprise and saw the Varangians shinning up the walls to open the gates.[42]

All we know for certain is that Harald spent two grim and largely fruitless years in Sicily. Bari, which fell to the enemy in 1038, was not retaken until 1040, when Argyros, son of the rebel Meles, made peace and recognized imperial overlordship. Harald and his Varangians were with the new catepan of Italy, Michael Dokeianos, when he arrived in Bari in 1040, but this was the year when the entire Byzantine position was destabilized by a revolt in Bulgaria and another rebellion in Italy. For the débâcle in Italy Maniakes must bear some of the blame. Having won a great victory over the Arabs at Traina in 1040, he ruined everything by his arrogance and niggardliness.

Three separate incidents underline Maniakes's folly. He had never got on with Admiral Stephen and now, in a fit of anger, he beat Stephen over the head with a whip, blaming him for Abdallah's escape to Tunis after the battle. Then he alienated the three hundred Normans, serving mainly as cavalry, who protested to Maniakes after the battle that they had not received their fair share of prize money and booty. Finally Maniakes had an important ally, Arduin the Lombard, flogged through the camp for contumacy after Arduin claimed as his prize a particularly desirable warhorse captured from the Arabs. Having already sampled Maniakes's arrogance, Harald and the Varangians openly sided with Stephen and the Normans.[43]

The sequel to the victory at Traina was utter disaster. Harald and his regiment of Varangians were recalled to help subdue the revolt in Bulgaria. Stephen complained to Constantinople about Maniakes, while Arduin raised Italy in revolt against his former allies, and was joined by the Normans. The result was a string of defeats for the Byzantines. At Mottola in 1040 Nicephorus Dokeianos was killed, Boianes, commanding another regiment of Varangians, was badly beaten by the Normans and later ransomed at huge cost, while his successor Synodianos was penned inside Otranto. In 1041 the Normans won two great victories, at Olivento, near Venusia, on 17 March and at Montemaggiore on 4 May. At Montemaggiore the Byzantine commander Michael Dokeianos had a clear numerical advantage but was outmanoeuvred by the Normans; in the ensuing fiasco large numbers of retreating Varangians were drowned in the river Ofanto, then in full spate. The net result was that by the end of 1041 the Byzantines were left with just Messina in their possession in the whole island of Sicily.[44]

Harald and his regiment, meanwhile, arrived in Bulgaria at the tail-end of the revolt there. In the summer of 1040 a runaway slave from Constantinople, named Peter Delianos, aspired to be a second Spartacus. Claiming to be a grandson of Bulgarian czar Samuel, he raised an army and was received with open arms by the people of Epirus and Macedonia, who were groaning under the yoke of Michael IV's regressive tax reforms. Greatly aided by Alousian, younger brother of Ladislas, last czar of the old Bulgarian empire, Delianos led his army into Greece and won initial victories which alarmed Michael IV's sufficiently to order the recall of troops from Sicily, including Harald's detachment of Varangians. On 26 October 1040, heartened by news that an imperial army was nearby, the besieged garrison of Thessalonica sortied and routed Alousian's army, which was completely destroyed, sustaining 15,000 casualties.[45]

Scholars debate about whether Harald and his men were present at the battle or whether he arrived just too late. In any case, either at Thessalonica or in mopping-up operations, Harald performed with such distinction that he was awarded the title of Manglavites with the rank of Spatharocandidatus; moreover, the emperor ordered a gold coin struck in his honour. It was almost Michael's last act, for the strain of the Bulgarian revolt turned him into a weary old man and he died on 10 December 1041 from some mysterious malady that made his limbs swell. Harald, promoted now from the mercenary Varangians to the imperial guard in Constantinople, seemed to face a purely ceremonial future. The duty of a Manglavites, who was entitled to wear a sword with a gold hilt, was to walk before the emperor in procession, carrying a jewelled whip on a belt, used to restrain the crowd. The Spatharocandidatus was something like an honorary colonel, though not a military title; it ranked sixth among the fourteen grades of Byzantine court official.[46]

Harald was now a person of some note and distinction in the Byzantine capital, but his elevation to the palace guard coincided with one of those sordid and bloody crises that so often disfigured Byzantine history. John Orphanotrophus, the power behind the throne for the last eight years and not a man to relinquish privilege and eminence gladly, persuaded Zoe to adopt his useless reprobate nephew as heir and ruler, but then pushed too far by having him crowned Michael V. Aristocratic sensibilities were offended by the idea of the son of a Paphlagonian dockworker as emperor, and the élite longed for an excuse to get rid of him. But for four months, while Michael appeared to live in harmony with Zoe, they had no pretext for action.

Having reached his apogee with Michael IV, Harald found himself at a nadir immediately on Michael V's accession. Part of the problem was Maniakes, whose fortunes oscillated in inverse relationship with Harald's. Following the altercation with Admiral Stephen after the battle of Traina, and even though Maniakes was completely justified in his reprimand, if not in his physical violence, Stephen predictably wrote to the emperor, accusing Maniakes of aiming at the purple. Maniakes was recalled and imprisoned, only to be released and given command of Byzantine forces in Italy when Orphanotrophus's nephew became emperor. Michael gave Maniakes a new fleet and army with which to retrieve the Byzantine situation in Sicily and southern Italy, where, by 1042, only Messina, Bari, Tranato, Brindisi and Otranto remained in Byzantine hands.[47]

One of Michael V's first acts, on the advice of Maniakes, was to disband the Varangians and replace them with a Scythian bodyguard. The Scandinavians, who were considered unreliable, were thrown on the scrap heap, but to the non-Scandinavian contingents in the Varangian guard fell the gruesome task of castrating all male members of the imperial family who expressed reservations about the new regime. Maniakes, angry that the insubordinate Harald had risen so high accused Harald of embezzlement, specifically of retaining for himself that portion of war prizes and booty he was duty bound to give up to the empire. To this (certainly justified) charge were added others: that he had insulted the empress Zoe by refusing to give her a lock of his hair when requested; that he had murdered a man while tax-collecting; and that he was a spy for the Russians, as evinced by his return to Kiev every winter during his first two years of service.[48]

It is interesting that most of these charges were entirely warranted. Harald had certainly already acquired a vast fortune, in part from retaining far more spoils of war than he was entitled to and in part from extortion during his tax-gathering missions (and the alleged murder could well relate to an incident when one of the mulcted was foolish enough to resist). It is also a moral certainty that he had given Yaroslav invaluable information about the Byzantine army, its state of morale and readiness, the city's fortifications and water supplies, to say nothing of political intelligence. The sagas prefer to pass over this solid ground in order to concentrate on arrant nonsense about the empress Zoe, who was said to have been madly in love with Harald; he, however, preferred her niece Maria. It need hardly be said that no such person as Maria ever existed, nor is there any evidence whatsoever of any romantic interest by Zoe in the young Viking.[49]

But the saga writers excel themselves when it comes to the details of Harald's imprisonment. Sober historical fact records that Harald was imprisoned alongside his faithful comrades Haldor Snorresson and Ulf Ospaksson in a tower located in the same street as the Varangian church, St Mary's near Hagia Sophia, and that he was released by the Varangians during the violent events of April 1042. According to the romancers, Harald was forced to do battle with a lion in the arena as a penalty for having seduced a noblewoman, but overcame the beast with his bare hands. In another version Harald, Haldor and Ulf had to do battle with a giant snake (a thinly disguised version of the earth-serpent in Norse mythology), which was overcome when Harald strangled it while Haldor and Ulf held it by the tail; in yet another version the monster is a dragon.[50]

Had he been imprisoned by any other emperor, Harald might well have languished in his tower for years, but events soon turned in his favour once again with the downfall of Michael V. Michael began by rounding on his old patron John Orphanotrophus and, in collusion with John's brother Constantine (who hated him), having him exiled to a distant island. Next he turned his attention to Zoe, whom he secretly loathed. After reigning for four months, Michael expelled Zoe's powerful spiritual mentor, the patriarch Alexius, then moved against Zoe herself, despite the warnings of the risk from his uncle Constantine. He had her arrested, divested of her imperial robes, and then removed to the Prinkipo islands in a nun's habit and with her hair shorn. Next he sent the non-Scandinavian rump of the Varangian guard to murder Alexius in his bolt-hole at the Stenson monastery. Alexius, knowing the venality of the Varangians, successfully bribed them to allow him to escape; he fled to sanctuary at Hagia Sophia and began organizing resistance to the new regime, summoning the high officials of state and army to him as Zoe's representative and thus the only legitimate authority extant.[51]

Meanwhile Michael V had learned to his cost of the immense popularity of the deposed Zoe. When he told the docile Senate that he had been obliged to exile Zoe as she had tried to poison him, the venal senators acquiesced in his version, doubtless remembering the real occasion when Zoe had tried to poison an emperor (Romanus III). But when Anastasius, the Serbocrator of Constantinople, tried to promulgate the credentials of the new regime in the Forum, he was nearly lynched; for the people of Byzantium the popularity of Zoe was inextinguishable and the dark tales of her behaviour seemed only to increase her lustre. In a spontaneous upsurge of grief and anger, a crowd formed on 19 April which swelled into a multitude; carried on a flood of pro-Zoe emotion, it began to attack the imperial residence, where, to its joy, it was joined by the Varangians, thirsting for revenge against the man who had humiliated them. To show their gratitude, the people's representatives issued a set of provisional decrees, ordering the release of all political prisoners, including Harald Sigurdsson.[52]

Elated by the turn of events, the Varangians released Harald and his comrades from their dungeon and, under his direction, pressed the assault on the palace. But 20 April 1042 turned out to be a black day for Byzantium when the emperor's Scythian guard resisted strenuously and bloody hand-to-hand fighting began. The palace was attacked from three sides – the Hippodrome, the Tzykanisterion and the Augusteum near the Excubita – and the net was being drawn tighter on the defenders, when the balance of power was suddenly upset by the arrival from Sicily of Katakalon Cecaumenos and a shipload of troops who joined in on Michael's side. Varangian now fought Varangian in some of the most vicious street-fighting Constantinople had ever witnessed. Finally, after 3,000 men lay dead in and around the palace grounds, the outnumbered defenders threw in the towel: some surrendered; others, including Katakalon Cecaumenos, fled under cover of darkness; the emperor and his uncle Constantine escaped by boat to seek sanctuary in the Studite monastery. The euphoric victors sacked the palace and destroyed the most detested symbol of imperial tyranny: the tax records.[53]

The newly appointed city prefect Campanares was inclined not to punish Michael and his uncle now that they were powerless, but a faction loyal to Zoe's sister Theodora was fearful that the weak-willed Zoe might forgive Michael and restore him. This faction accordingly drew up orders for the blinding of the ex-emperor and Constantine and gave them to Harald to implement. He set off for the Studite monastery on 21 April, only to find that the pro-Theodora mob had got there before him. Michael and Constantine clung piteously to the altar, claiming the right of sanctuary, but the enraged mob scorned the sin of sacrilege and tore them from their refuge. Apparently they intended to drive their victims through the city as figures of fun before deciding what to do with them, but they were intercepted just outside the monastery by a grim-faced Harald and his heavily armed Varangians. Harald showed his orders and at once set to work on the gruesome mutilation. First he gouged out Constantine'e eyes and then Michael's. Constantine endured the agonizing ordeal bravely, but Michael wept, pleaded and begged for mercy and had to be bound before the blinding could be carried out.[54]

Harald and the Varangians were restored to all their ranks and privileges, but these were anxious and uncertain times at Byzantium. For two months Zoe tried to co-reign with her sister Theodora but the experiment was not a success; in the end Zoe gave up and married for the third time (at sixty-five). Her new husband was Constantine Monomachus, who in June 1042 became Constantine IX and whose twelve-year reign was to epitomize imperial decline. During the interregnum Harald was appointed senior commander of the Varangians and in this capacity acted as judge, jury and executioner of those members of the Guard who had backed the wrong side during the uprising of 19–20 April. He was now at the height of his power, in possession of a vast treasure, and was rapidly building up a cult around his name. He liked to fight with a one-edged axe (the Varangians, like the Anglo-Saxon housecarls, usually fought with the double-headed axe) and he had made for him a mailed coat, which he called Emma, that protected him down to the calves.[55]

There were no further worlds for Harald to conquer at Byzantium, but he was faced with the problem of getting his vast hoard of gold and silver out of the city without running into objections from the imperial bureaucracy. Testing the waters, he applied for permission to return to Norway in late 1042, but Constantine IX refused him. Harald was now in a race against time. It is usually asserted that the fillip making him keen to leave Constantinople was news from Scandinavia that his eighteen-year-old half-nephew Magnus had been recalled and crowned king of both Norway and Denmark. But his reasons for wishing to leave were more pressing. On the one hand, he had word from Yaroslav that 1043 would bring a concerted Russian onslaught on the Byzantine empire; on the other, Georgios Maniakes had raised the standard of revolt in Italy and it was rumoured that Harald would be made commander-in-chief of the forces sent to subdue his old rival. Equally, Constantine's refusal to release him may have been because he too knew of Yaroslav's plans and did indeed intend to use the captain of the Varangians against Maniakes.

The great general Maniakes had performed miracles in Italy and partially restored the Byzantine position there after the terrible reverses sustained by Dokeianos and Boioannus. Then he fell victim to a serpentine intrigue directed by the powerful Sclerus family. Romanus, the leader of the clan, had a sister, Sclerena, who for eighteen months from late 1042 to 1044 was not just Constantine IX's mistress but officially recognized as such; she was given the title Augusta and attended official ceremonies openly, forming a threesome with the emperor and Zoe. With such powerful support at court, Romanus Sclerus, who nursed ancient grievances against Maniakes, moved in for the kill. In rapid succession he plundered the general's estates in Anatolia, seduced his wife and then denounced him to Constantine as a traitor. When Maniakes was deprived of his title of *magister* and ordered to relinquish his command in Italy to Pardus, he raised his army in revolt and defeated Pardus at Ostrovo in 1043 after being proclaimed emperor by his men. His death in the very moment of victory changed the course of Byzantine history, not least because the military élite, having lost its greatest leader, finally succumbed to the hegemony of the bureaucrats.[56]

The crisis with Maniakes gave Harald his chance to escape while Constantine IX's mind was elsewhere. Secretly purchasing galleys and the loyalty of a large body of men out of the vast treasure he had accumulated, Harald prepared to make his bid for freedom, taking his gold and silver with him. It may be that he was aided in his subterfuge by a mobilization order preparing the Varangians to move against Maniakes in Italy. One night he and his men stole down to the galleys and set sail, but their flight was a perilous one as they had to sacrifice a ship breaking through the boom across the Bosporus – a great chain or succession of chains set on rafts placed at appropriate distances apart, which were drawn into the shore during the day and refloated across the waterways at night. Sceptics have doubted that this incident took place on the grounds that the great chain spoken about was drawn across the Golden Horn rather than the Bosporus, but careful scholarship has established that a second boom was probably set up on the Bosporus to guard against the rumoured Russian attack.[57]

Harald and his men sailed north through the Black Sea to the estuary of the Dnieper, then set a course for Kiev. Almost as though by pre-established harmony, Yaroslav then launched the mighty attack on Russia he had planned with the aid of Harald's intelligence. A fleet of 400 ships under Yaroslav's son Vladimir, the Prince of Novgorod, set out with all the enthusiasm and appearance of an old-style Viking raid. Although Constantine IX had long expected this blow to fall, Byzantium was ill prepared, possibly because of the drain of resources to the Maniakes revolt in Italy. The Russian fleet appeared at the northern entrance to the Bosporus, where the Prince of Novgorod gave the emperor the chance to buy them off, but – at three pounds weight of gold for each Russian sailor – the terms were considered prohibitive. Constantine decided to equip the few triremes in the city, together with some old transports, with tubes for propelling the Byzantine secret weapon: Greek fire. But to prevent the emergence of a fifth column, he first ordered the arrest and deportation of every Russian merchant in Constantinople and the disarming of the Varangians, who were suspected of covert sympathies, if not outright collusion, with the enemy.[58]

Next morning the Byzantine triremes assembled in the harbour to confront the Russians, who were anchored on the opposite shore. The Russians then advanced to block the exit from the Bosporus, confident they had Constaninople in a stranglehold. It was only in the afternoon that the triremes emerged from the harbour, seemingly easy prey for the vastly numerically superior Russians. But as the Russians closed in, they were deluged with a devastating bombardment of Greek fire – an early version of napalm: liquid which burst into flames on contact. Since Greek fire was inextinguishable by the technology of the time and burned even on water, it caused the most appalling panic, with men abandoning ship in terror. To complete the discomfiture of the Russians a sudden storm blew up, wrecking ships and driving them into each other. Most of the Russian ships were either sunk, captured or driven ashore and the invaders had sustained astronomical casualties; it was said that 15,000 bloated corpses were later washed ashore. Among the damaged vessels was Vladimir's, and he was lucky to get away with his bodyguard to the Bulgarian coast to the north. Russian accounts speak of a running pursuit in which the valiant Vladimir managed to disable four triremes.[59]

This was disaster on a huge scale. All Russian prisoners had their right hands cut off and the severed limbs were exhibited publicly on the walls of Constantinople. The panic-stricken Slav army commander Vyshata tried to take his troops by the land route back to Kiev but was ambushed near Varna and cut to pieces. Some eight hundred survivors, including Vyshata, were taken back to Byzantium and all who were not ransomable were blinded – the traditional punishment for 'rebellion against the state'. A subsequent victory by the remains of the Russian fleet over a Byzantine squadron off the coast of Thrace changed nothing. Yaroslav was involved in protracted negotiations until 1046, when the surviving prisoners, including Vyshata, were released as part of a treaty stipulating that Constantine's daughter would marry Yaroslav's younger son.[60]

Meanwhile Harald had returned to Kiev in great triumph, his fame consolidated and his fortune made. Yaroslav's daughter Elizabeth was now of marriageable age and, with her father's eager approval, Harald asked her to be his wife. The suit did not go smoothly at first, it appears, for Harald composed a couplet in which he lamented:

> *Yet to the Russian queen I fear*
> *My gold-adorned, I am not dear.*

Seemingly, Elizabeth was regarded as a great beauty by the standards of the age, for she is portrayed, in company with three other princesses, in a wall painting in S. Sophia of Kiev dating from the early 1050s. Harald travelled north to Novgorod on some mission for Yaroslav and while there composed a series of verses which skaldic experts say are the best he composed. In the *Gamanvisur* series Harald boasts of his exploits in Sicily and laments that the Russian maid ('the goddess of the gold ring') gives him the cold shoulder. Nevertheless, by the end of 1043, whether through change of heart or under pressure from Yaroslav, Elizabeth finally consented to marry him. A glittering ceremony took place in Kiev, and Harald joined the list of notable marriages made by Yaroslav's daughters, which included unions of Anna with King Henry of France (1031–60) and Anastasia with King Andrew of Hungary. Still only twenty-eight, he was already the most famous warrior of the age.[61]

4

Earl Godwin

In 1051 Edward seems to have decided he was strong enough to seek
a decisive settling of accounts with the over-mighty Godwin family;
it is possible that the presence of increasing numbers of Norman
noblemen, Edward's kin, in England gave him a sense of security; or he
may simply have decided that it was 'now or never', that if he did not
take a stand against Godwin and his contumacious family he would be
reduced to the status of figurehead king or cipher. Edward still blamed
Godwin for Alfred's death and hated him for it, and, although he liked
Tostig and was ambivalent towards Harold, he cordially loathed Swein.
It is important to be clear that it was Edward who precipitated the crisis
of 1051 and that, in the words of his biographer, he 'provoked Godwin
beyond endurance'.[1]

The trigger for the confrontation between the king and his most
powerful earl was religious politics rather than international relations. In
October 1050 Eadsige, Archbishop of Canterbury, died, to be followed
in January 1051 by the other metropolitan archbishop, Aelfric Puttock
of York. These sees, with their extensive benefices, were highly
desirable political plums and intense lobbying at once began among the
various factions. Godwin, who was the political master of Kent, backed
the monks of Canterbury in their desire to see their brother in Christ
Aelric, a kinsman of Godwin's, raised to the archbishopric. Not only did

Edward spurn Godwin's representations on this score but he carried out a superficially very clever ecclesiastical *coup d'état* by taking the opportunity to pack the key dioceses with his own men. The Norman Bishop of London, Robert of Jumièges, was promoted to the archiepiscopate at Canterbury; Spearhavoc, Abbot of Abingdon, took Jumièges's place in London; while the king's kinsman Rothulf filled the vacancy at Abingdon and another royal favourite, Cynsige, was appointed at York.[2] It was a clean sweep, leaving Godwin's reputation as a powerful ecclesiastical patron in tatters; all three of his clerical protégés, Ealdred, Stigand and Aelric, had been passed over.

Edward could scarcely mount the defence that he had promoted the most saintly, the most able or the most popular; indeed the monks of Abingdon and Canterbury expressly and vociferously opposed the men placed above them. In a primitive version of later 'court' versus 'country' conflicts, he had tactlessly and brutally insisted on the letter of royal patronage, allowing himself the self-indulgent enjoyment of pure power and humiliating Godwin into the bargain. Moreover, Robert of Jumièges, a convinced enemy of Godwin, took the view that his elevation allowed him total freedom of speech and at once denounced Godwin as having usurped church lands in Canterbury. When Godwin tried to swallow the insult, possibly in return for a total royal pardon for Swein, Jumièges took his restraint as weakness and added the malicious slander that Godwin intended to do with Edward what he had already done to Alfred.[3]

Jumièges was pushing too hard, and even Edward grew alarmed at this point. But there was worse to come. The new Archbishop of Canterbury made a rapid trip to Rome in early 1051 and, on his return in June with his pallium, announced that he no longer recognized Spearhavoc as bishop, as Leo IX had decreed that he could not be consecrated in the see of London. Since the papacy never interfered with Church appointments in England, it was obvious to everyone that Jumièges had put the pope up to issuing this prohibition, possibly by peddling an unverifiable story about simony, known to be one of Leo's reforming preoccupations. It was also known that Jumièges had canvassed strongly for the Norman clerk William, his protégé, to have the bishopric in London and it was his obvious intention to install William there by fair means or foul. Edward showed his glacial disapproval of Jumièges's arrogant behaviour by confirming Spearhavoc in his see *de facto*, pending further investigation, and pointedly staying away from Robert's investiture at Canterbury.[4]

The conflict between Edward and Godwin was personal, not

ideological, and it is anachronistic to see it as a defender of Saxon modalities ranged against a king determined to make England Norman by granting High-Church rank to his mother's people, encouraging French-speaking settlers and provocatively planting Norman garrisons in Godwin demesnes. It must be emphasized that what rankled with Godwin was the loss of his ecclesiastical patronage, the blow to his prestige and credibility and the obvious attempts by the king to marginalize him.[5] Nevertheless, Godwin can hardly have been pleased by what seemed like a new pro-Norman bearing in Edward's foreign policy and by the favourites he had surrounded himself with, especially Earl Ralph, son of Edward's sister and her first husband Drew, count of Mantes and the Vexin, even though Ralph was more French than Norman.[6]

The presence of French speakers at Edward's court has to be seen in the context of his subtle and shifting foreign policy – so subtle indeed that it was hard to read his intentions. Edward had a cosmopolitan court, which included Bretons, Flemings, Germans, Lotharingians and non-Norman Frenchmen from all regions, and other Frenchmen were absorbed into Edward's England in the years before 1066, particularly as thegns in Hampshire, Wiltshire, Dorset, Somerset, Surrey and Kent; it is significant, however, that the only man he created an earl was not a Norman. The degree of normal Francophone assimilation was probably obscured by Swein's paranoid accusations about a Norman conspiracy in his earldom; and the king by foolishly promoting Norman bishops as a counterweight to the Godwins, merely fed that family's worst suspicions. Particular offence was given by two things: the promotion in 1047 of the king's nephew Earl Ralph as warden of the Welsh marches, where he established a kind of Norman colony extending through Herefordshire, Worcestershire and Gloucestershire that seemed a deliberate threat to Swein's earldom; and the guardianship of the harbour at Bosham, hard by Chichester, awarded to Osbern, brother of William Fitzosbern, the right-hand man of Duke William of Normandy.[7]

But we cannot go beyond the subjective feelings of the Godwin family to an objective reality: there is certainly not a scintilla of evidence that Edward had a conscious programme of promoting Normans in England in order to pave the way for an eventual succession by Duke William of Normandy. As in everything he did, Edward was singularly secretive, ambivalent and duplicitous. He was a man divided, who had pulls both towards the northlands and towards Normandy but who also hated and despised both regions: the Normans for their treatment of him in his early years and Scandinavia because of the threat it posed to his kingdom and the fact that its warriors had forced him from England as a young man. At the same time, Edward's attitude to the realms of the Viking was not simple – nothing ever was in his devious mind. He hero-worshipped the first Christian king of Norway, Olaf Tryggvason, and liked to have the sagas about Olaf recited to his courtiers on the first day of Easter, saying that Easter Day was superior to all other days just as Olaf Tryggvason was superior to all other kings.[8]

Whatever the reality of Edward's cynical playing off one side against the other, to Godwin in 1051 the king's actions looked like persecution. He was already smarting under the humiliation of the ecclesiastical rebuffs, with Swein whispering dark forebodings in his ear, when a head-on crisis between earl and monarch was triggered by the visit to England of Eustace of Boulogne in September 1051. Quite what Eustace was doing in the country has always divided historians. Some say that William of Normandy was now actively angling for a nomination as Edward's successor to the English throne and sent Eustace over as a plenipotentiary negotiator. Others say, more plausibly, that he was present on his own account or that of his family. There was a very strong faction at court which believed the best claim to the succession was not held by William of Normandy, or Svein Estrithson of Denmark, but by Earl Ralph, or Walter, Count of the Vexin, or even, assuming Eustace had a daughter and she was to be married, the putative grandson of Eustace and Godgifu.[9]

It seems that when Eustace landed at Dover with a considerable armed retinue, he gave offence to the citizens of Dover by his contumacious behaviour. After conferring with Edward at Gloucester, Eustace returned to his embarkation point at Dover, only to find he and his comrades were not welcome there. Some say the burghers resented the Frenchmen's depredations on the outward journey, others that Godwin, now in a white heat of fury that the king was making major foreign-policy decisions without so much as a pretence at consulting him, ordered the men of Dover, who were within his sphere of influence, not to offer the French any hospitality or accommodation. The exasperated and fire-eating Eustace ordered his men to don their chain mail, form battle stations and intimidate the burgesses of Dover into giving them what they wanted.[10]

It was a supremely unwise decision. When Eustace's troops began rampaging through the town, demanding food and lodging at sword-point and generally behaving in a high-handed manner, the put-upon citizens hit back. A soldier ran through one of the locals, who retaliated by killing one of them in turn. Eustace then ordered his knights to charge; they cut down men and women with their swords and trampled children and babies to death under their horses' hoofs. The enraged citizenry then rose up in a formidable armed posse, which expelled the intruders but only after a vicious running battle in which both sides took heavy casualties. When the Frenchmen were finally put to flight, at least twenty burghers of Dover lay dead and an unknown number of women and children; Eustace's men had lost nineteen dead and an unknown number of wounded.[11]

Eustace stormed back to Gloucester to report the grievous insult that had been offered to the king's 'guest' and doubtless talked up the role of Godwin in the affair. Without waiting to hear both sides of the story, Edward 'deemed' that Dover must have been to blame and ordered Godwin to punish the town. Godwin flatly refused, now more than ever convinced that Edward was seeking pretexts for a showdown. There is much justice in Edward Freeman's scathing judgement: 'The crime of Eustace was a dark one; but we may be inclined to pass a heavier judgement still on the the crime of the English king who, on the mere accusation of the stranger, condemned his own subjects without a hearing.'[12]

Godwin countered the king's demand by seeking a legal trial for the people of Dover, in which the full facts could be heard. Edward, goaded by Eustace and Osbern Pentecost, was enraged by this 'impertinence' and, egged on by hardliners like Robert of Jumièges (who continued his campaign of slander against Godwin), summoned his council or *witan* at Gloucester to consider charges of treason against the Earl of Wessex. For his part, Godwin was now disposed to listen to the most apocalyptical warnings from his hot-headed son Swein and to be convinced that Edward wanted war to the knife. He began to mobilize his forces and meanwhile demanded the surrender of Eustace and the expulsion of the French garrisons in Herefordshire. From the beginning of September 1051, when Edward summoned the *witan*, events escalated with the speed of a bushfire.[13]

Godwin, Swein and Harold summoned their armies to a rendezvous at Beverstone, fifteen miles south of Gloucester, on the Bristol–Oxford road, a handy position for menacing Edward's lines of communications. At Gloucester Ralph arrived with his levies to stiffen the king's military arm, and some of the French party advised an immediate attack on the 'rebels', but the ever-cautious monarch demurred, seemingly not totally convinced that the interests of the hardline war party were necessarily his. He played for time, meanwhile sending urgently to Earls Leofric and Siward to bring their power; he was well aware that it was on their attitude that the outcome of the crisis would turn.[14]

As long as the military power of the Godwins was formidable, and his own weak, Edward continued to stall, resisting the siren calls of the French party for a pitched battle. Before acting he needed to be sure of the attitude of the northern earls, especially as they seemed suspicious of the motives of Robert of Jumièges and the other 'hawks': Leofric was known to feel that an all-out military struggle with the Godwins would leave England unacceptably weak, whatever the outcome, and an easy prey for an invader. The obvious middle way (between battle or bowing to the Godwins) was to use legal machinery, especially as this was the course most favoured by the *witan*; it was accordingly decided that the Godwins be summoned to London to answer before a full council of the greatest in the realm, to take place on 21 September.[15]

Godwin now found himself in an unpalatable position. Failure to heed the summons to London would mean that he placed himself unquestionably in the wrong at the bar of élite opinion and would therefore have to undergo the perils of being dubbed rebel and traitor; Edward, on the other hand, seemed more uncompromising than ever, insisting that the 'rebels' must give sureties to him, while he was not obliged to give anything to them. There were protracted negotiations about hostages, but Godwin realized that, as the king was childless, the giving of hostages presented no such emotional wrench as it did to him or to Swein. And what charges would Godwin and his sons face? There was much loose talk about rebellion, but was it possible that the long-brooding Edward intended to raise the question of Godwin's complicity in Alfred's death?[16]

Edward's tactic of playing for time was triumphantly vindicated. Even as Godwin's army commenced the weary trek from Beverstone to London, a number of his thegns deserted, at the very moment news from London suggested Edward's forces were being daily augmented with troops sent by Leofric and Siward. A further blow came with the royal outlawry of Swein, on the grounds that he was doubly accursed, having forfeited a recent pardon for egregious crimes by his current treason. By the time both sides reached London, the king on the north bank of the Thames, Godwin in Southwark on the south bank, Edward held a clear numerical superiority in military force.[16]

Having the whip hand so clearly, Edward was in vengeful and vindictive mood. He curtly summoned Godwin to attend his trial, but the earl countered by asking for safe-conduct guaranteed by hostages. Edward made no direct reply to this but added the further demand that

Godwin surrender all his thegns. When Godwin complied with this, Edward brusquely informed him he should attend his trial with a retinue of no more than twelve men. Only a fool would have walked into such an obvious trap, so Godwin again made the rational request for a safe-conduct and an exchange of hostages. Edward refused bluntly: his position was that he neither would nor could give any assurances to men accused of heinous crimes. The result was a stand-off. Godwin was never going to cross the river, on the mere say-so of the king, to attend a trial where the counts in the indictment had not even been specified. It was clear that his rebuttal of the charges by an unsupported oath was not going to be enough; perhaps Edward intended to assassinate him as soon as he appeared before the council, or perhaps he favoured judicial murder by forcing Godwin, now a man of advanced years, to submit to one of the notorious medieval ordeals. At all events Godwin absolutely refused to cross the river on the king's terms.[17]

Seeking a way through the impasse, Godwin employed the good offices of his friend Bishop Stigand, a man from an Anglo-Norse family who was first appointed a royal priest in 1020. The problem was that Stigand was already out of favour with Edward through too close an association with Queen Emma, who had secured his appointment as Bishop of Elmham.[18] Predictably, Stigand got nowhere with the king, whose sudden sensation of being more powerful than Godwin seemed to have affected his judgement and even his reason. He told Stigand, when the bishop passed on Godwin's offer to submit to ordeal to prove that he had no part in the murder of Alfred, that he was not interested in Godwin's spurious attempts at purging; he would grant him the king's peace only when Godwin restored his brother Alfred to him, alive, together with all the men killed in 1036, and also all the land and possessions the Godwins had acquired since that time. Faced with this almost psychotic example of 'impossibilism', Stigand broke down in tears before conveying the uncompromising answer to Godwin.[19]

Godwin now knew there was no dealing with the king, who had become a purblind fanatic. His own weak position was both cause and effect of his inability or unwillingness to confront Edward either on the battlefield or before a council. After hearing what Stigand had to say, the earl saddled up and rode away, an outlaw in all but name (the formal sentence was pronounced by a jubilant Edward next morning), having failed to heed the third and final summons to his trial.

The Godwin family split into two groups: Godwin, his wife Gytha, Tostig and Swein made haste to Bosham, where they embarked at

Thorney Island for Flanders; Harold and Leofwine held on for Bristol, there to board a ship to take them to Ireland. Archbishop Robert led the pursuit after Godwin, riding hard to try to overhaul them; another divine, Bishop Ealdred, a Godwin sympathizer, played the laggard when on the trail of Harold and Leofwine. Some said that initially Edward granted the outlaws five days' grace to leave the kingdom, then, rather like Pharaoh with the Israelites, broke his word by despatching pursuit parties immediately.[20]

While Baldwin of Flanders was a known enemy and had sheltered Swein before, and thus his support for the Godwins occasioned Edward no surprise, the king was extremely angry that Harold and Leofwine had found sanctuary in Ireland, since he claimed the east coast of Ireland as part of his domain *de jure*. Some commentators have opined that Harold's flight to Ireland shows him typically mercurial and headstrong, forever looking for violent solutions to problems. But there was method in Harold's apparent madness, for his father already enjoyed close relations with the Irish monarch Diarmait Mac Mael-na-Mbo, king of Leinster (1042–72). Godwin had spotted Diarmait as a rising star in Erin, and he reciprocated the gesture with exceptional kindness to the two Godwinsson exiles. It was Harold who inspired Diarmait to his most signal exploit yet, the capture of the Viking town of Dublin.[21]

Meanwhile Edward revelled in the unwonted luxury of what seemed like perfect freedom. At the urgings of Robert of Jumièges, who knew well enough what to expect should the Godwin sept ever be restored, the king redistributed the vacant earldoms. All of Swein's lands except Somerset – that is to say, Herefordshire, Gloucestershire, Oxfordshire and Berkshire – went to Ralph of Mantes, while on Aelfgar, Leofric's son, was bestowed Harold's earldom of East Anglia. Godwin's Wessex earldom was subjected to the most complex subdivision: Odda of Deerhurst was given Cornwall, Devon, Dorset and Somerset, Jumièges got Kent to go with his see at Canterbury, while Edward himself retained Surrey, Sussex and Hampshire. Robert of Jumièges capped his triumph by getting Spearhavoc expelled from the bishopric of London and having him replaced by his protégé, William; in retaliation Spearhavoc first picked his diocese clean of all money and portable property and then vanished.[22]

Since the Godwin males were physically beyond his reach, Edward indulged his vindictive rage by meting out disgraceful punishment to his wife Edith. While announcing officially that his wife was merely going into retreat until the current disturbances were over, in fact he confined her in the very nunnery at Wilton where she had received her unusual education, stripping her of all land, movables and money, allowing her just one maid and no marks of royalty or even normal aristocratic distinction. Following his usual instinct to temporize, Edward kept the queen in seclusion until he could come to a final decision about her. There is no doubt that he was angry at the discovery that, when it came to the inevitable conflict of loyalties, Edith had unhesitatingly plumped for her family over her husband. Always prone to paranoia, the king would have been reinforced in a mentality described by his biographer as 'rootless, discontented, mean and irascible'. Misogyny may also have played a part, for the parallels between the disgrace of Queen Emma in 1043 and Queen Edith in 1051 are unmistakable; it cannot have helped the self-lacerating Edward to reflect that the two women supposedly closest to him had both, when it came to the push, preferred other claimants to supreme power rather than him.[23]

Edward was now supreme ruler of England in fact as well as name. How had he achieved what a year before all observers would have said was impossible? Did he set a trap for the Godwins or was the crisis of 1051 a happy (for him) accident? Was it essentially caused by Edward's pro-Norman policy, his entanglement in the general European system of alliances? Was it connected with his desire to solve the succession problem? Or was there some other factor at play?

We can, I think, discount the idea that the crisis was caused by Godwin's resentment at the increasing influence of the Norman faction in England. Godwin had noticed their encroachment and was irritated by it, but this alone would not have precipitated an inchoate civil war. It has sometimes been alleged that Edward made a serious offer of the succession to Duke William of Normandy in 1051, but this event, if it happened at all, clearly occurred *after* the flight of Godwin and his family.[24] Nor is it plausible that Edward would have precipitated a confrontation with the Godwin clan if he had merely wished to divorce Edith, his queen. It has been suggested that a childless Edward was becoming impatient with the lack of a clear successor,[25] but this would imply that Edward was both sexually active and convinced he could sire children – which in the nature of things would mean he had fathered offspring by other women. If this were the case, it is passing strange that we hear nothing of such women either from the Confessor's friends or his enemies. In any case, if the problem was Edith's barrenness, Edward would not have needed to become embroiled with Godwin because of the 'insult' to the family's honour connoted by a divorce petition; canon law allowed for papal dissolution of regal marriages in such cases. In short, Edward could have sheltered behind the pope, whose good opinion he was so anxious to foster.

The more one looks at the evidence, the more it seems as though the visit of Count Eustace of Boulogne really was the trigger for the crisis and not just a pretext used by a machiavellian Edward. The key precipitant towards the upheaval of 1051 was Edward's foreign policy, designed, as we have seen, to isolate and marginalize Baldwin of Flanders, the traditional provider of sanctuary for enemies of England; in this respect, his championing of the exiled Godwins shows a clear line of continuity. By 1050 Edward had made remarkable progress: he was on good terms with Henry III, the German emperor, Henry I King of France, Pope Leo IX and Eustace of Boulogne; his enemies at the time were Flanders and Normandy, who had just been bound closer together by the marriage (initially prohibited by papal interdict) of Duke William and Baldwin's daughter Matilda, and for this reason Edward also recruited into his network of alliances Hugh II of Ponthieu, and the Counts of Mantes, Charmont and Ponthieu.[26]

But the system of alliances in Europe contained many contradictions. Svein Estrithson of Denmark had also built up an entente with the pope and the emperor, yet he was at the time probably an even more dangerous enemy to Edward: Svein continued to feel that Edward had condoned or connived at the murder of his brother Bjorn by Swein Godwinsson. Cynics, who thought the Confessor one of the least saintly men in Europe, opined that he had not lifted a finger for Bjorn out of 'revenge' for the failure of the rest of Europe to protest vociferously about the murder of *his* brother Alfred. In any case, early in the 1050s Denmark fell out of step with Emperor Henry on ecclesiastical matters, and there were suspicions that Svein was trying to displace the German emperor as principal 'defender of the faith' in northern Europe. Possibly an even more glaring 'contradiction' was the way Duke William of Normandy, allied to Flanders, made overtures to Emperor Henry in 1050 to seek support against Geoffrey Martel of Anjou at the very time Baldwin was once again raising the banner of revolt against the Holy Roman Empire.[27]

The system of European alliances, then, was remarkably fluid and mutable and it was never beyond the bounds of possibility to reverse the pattern of allies altogether. Godwin was known never to have been happy with the main currents of Edward's foreign policy: he wanted friendship with Flanders and with Denmark, the two nations the Confessor regarded as his most deadly foes. It seems clear that what brought Eustace of Boulogne across the Channel in 1051 was not some chimerical errand undertaken on behalf of William of Normandy – a man who never trusted him and collaborated with him only after the exchange of the kind of hostages Eustace would not dare to forfeit by perfidy – but a desire to preserve his alliance with Edward which he thought to be in danger from the machinations of the Godwins. The one truly salient event that seemed to portend a new order in Europe was the marriage of Tostig Godwinsson to Judith, Baldwin's half-sister. With both William of Normandy and the Godwinssons apparently now allying themselves with Baldwin, Eustace felt singularly vulnerable and sought reassurances from Edward that he would not be abandoned to be eaten up by these powerful neighbours.[28]

It may be that Edward felt that he was on a winning streak, that he had already humiliated Godwin and his family over the promotions to archbishoprics and over Swein Godwinsson, and that he was steadily gaining the upper hand anyway; then came the fracas at Dover, the snapping of Godwin's already tested patience and the realization by the king that he suddenly had an unlooked-for opportunity for dealing a knockout blow. However, even if we discount the factor of the Normans in England as a major element in the crisis of 1051, it can scarcely be denied that Robert of Jumièges and the other senior French-speaking nobles were imbued with a sense of triumphalism and used their influence to nudge Edward towards *rapprochement* with Normandy. Yet here we confront the greatest mystery of all attaching to the year 1051: what were Edward's relations with Duke William at the time; did he make any promises to him; and if so, what exactly did he pledge himself to and how seriously?

The basic proposition all historians of the last days of Anglo-Saxon England have to contend with is this: did Edward promise the throne to William in 1051? Naturally, at the time, Norman propagandists asserted that he did, but their inadequate grasp of the precise historical context of 1051 makes their evidence not so much suspect as risible. Some later historians have swung to the other extreme and argued *a priori* that the whole idea of Edward's Norman alliance makes no sense: if the king was trying to forge an alliance with the emperor, and both he and the emperor regarded Baldwin of Flanders as a primary enemy, how could Edward have promised the throne to Duke William, an ally of their joint enemy?

The attempt to dismiss the persistent stories of an Edward–William entente in 1051 by this would-be syllogism is, however, specious. There can be many explanations of Edward's apparent volte-face. His attempt to conciliate the emperor may have been temporary and there may have been salient factors, on which the exiguous sources are silent, which induced him to change his mind by 1051. The years 1051–52, which saw the titanic struggle with the Godwin family and the negotiations with William, were notable for a number of virtually simultaneous events that may have played some part in Edward's thinking: Baldwin renewed his rebellion against the emperor; William defied the papal interdict and married Matilda; Edward's mother Emma died at Winchester; and Henry I of France and Geoffrey Martel were reconciled and began to make common cause against Normandy. A plausible interpretation for the new pro-Norman policy, given our knowledge of Edward, is that he was angered by the papal excommunication of Eustace for marrying Edward's sister Godgifu; since this marriage seems to have taken place in September 1051, Eustace's visit to England immediately afterwards, and the unintended consequences of the visit, would make perfect sense. Edward might also have been trying to detach Duke William from Baldwin or he might have felt exposed when the Godwins fled to Flanders and so tried to entice William away from Baldwin's web.[29]

His arguments would presumably have been twofold: William's alliance with Flanders was no longer important and certainly not unique now that the anti-Norman Godwins had built their own kinship link with Baldwin through Tostig's marriage to Judith; and since both of them lay under papal interdict (William for his marriage to Matilda and Edward for his sister's marriage to Eustace), their common interests were in an alliance with the papal/imperial axis. It is also possible that William himself wanted a closer relationship with the emperor and, as a first stage, tried to conciliate Henry's most reliable ally, Edward; it is certainly significant that one of the main reasons King Henry I of France turned against his Norman vassal was his anger that William had gone behind his back to make overtures to Emperor Henry.[30]

If the idea of serious negotiations between William and Edward in 1051 seems well grounded, we need to ask two further questions: did William come to England in person, as is often alleged; and did Edward offer him the English throne as his successor? The visit to England remains a possibility and certainly some of the arguments used by the sceptics, particularly the absence of all mention of this event in Norman sources, are not conclusive: it is a convincing rebuttal to point out that William of Jumièges and William of Poitiers, the duke's principal hagiographers, *never* show their hero as a suppliant – which he would have to be if he came to Edward's court – and for this reason could well have suppressed all reference to the visit. But against the visit is the powerful and, in the end, irrefutable objection that William was fighting for his very existence in Normandy then and would hardly have left the duchy on a foreign embassy at such a critical time.[31]

The most likely sequence of events is that ambassadors were exchanged between the two courts in late 1051, initially in connection with a problem of hostages, but William hoodwinked Edward into making him some kind of vague promise of the English throne. When the Godwins fled after Stigand's failure to mediate, they left behind the two family hostages who had originally been exchanged with Edward, namely Wulfnoth, Godwin's youngest son, and Hakon, natural son of Swein Godwinson from one of his many amatory conquests. It is known that Robert of Jumièges urged Edward to take precautions lest the unlikely happened and the Godwin sept managed to return from exile, and it is a moral certainty that Jumièges suggested Normandy as the one place from which Godwin would be unable to secure the return of his son and grandson. Nothing would be more natural for the supremely cunning William than to extract from Edward as a *quid pro quo* for his guardianship of the hostages the king's personal nomination as his heir.[32]

We need only compare this plausible reconstruction of the events of late 1051 with the absurdities in the accounts by the Norman apologists for William. According to William of Poitiers, Edward named William his heir for three clear and transcendent reasons: Edward was his kinsman, the king was grateful to Normandy for the help it gave him to win his throne, and from his early knowledge of the peerless William he realized that the duke was the most suitable person to help him in life and the best qualified to succeed him after his death. In a further layering of absurdity, we are told that Godwin, Leofric, Siward and Stigand all took an oath to accept William as king on the Confessor's demise.[33]

To take the most absurd part of the story first, it is evident that the Norman propagandists had no clear idea of the sequence of events in 1051–52, nor of the many nuances in Anglo-Saxon politics. Whatever transpired between Edward and William took place *after* Godwin and his family had been expelled; any request from Edward to Godwin to confirm a Norman succession before that time would certainly have precipitated the anti-Norman rising some historians have assumed the revolt of 1051 actually to have been. The circumstantial details are also hopeless nonsense: Siward was uninterested in affairs in southern England and scarcely cared who succeeded as long as he was not disturbed in the north; he would certainly not have travelled down to

Winchester to make common cause with his enemy Godwin on what he would have considered a fatuous errand. And why is there no mention of Harold? In 1051 he was a major earl, who would certainly have been privy to such a situation. The overwhelming likelihood is that later Norman propagandists, unaware of the true situation in England in 1051, simply plucked likely names out of a hat but in so doing exposed their own unreliability as sources. The story makes no sense anyway, for the banishment of the Godwin family later in the year and the humiliation of Stigand would have left William without his major guarantors.

Even more devastating to the Norman version of history is a study of the mentality of Edward the Confessor himself. We are asked to believe that the charisma of William, who was just thirteen when Edward last saw him, was such that the king stored the memory of the duke in his mind and then nominated him as his successor. The idea of such an 'attachment' is absurd even if we were not dealing with a person who notoriously made and discarded friends easily. Far from Edward's retaining fond memories of Normandy and its rulers and being suffused with gratitude for all the Normans had done for him, he was in reality livid with anger about the way the same people had, as he saw it, failed him at every point and treated him with contempt. Edward did not love William as a son and brother, as the Francophone hagiographers contend; he was not grateful to the Norman court for its generosity and assistance; he was quite manifestly no devoted son of a Norman mother and had no interest in his maternal kin. Besides, even if we grant for argument's sake that Edward was pro-William and pro-Norman, why did he wait nine years before repaying his 'debt of gratitude'? Why in the meantime did he take an English wife, who could have borne him children and blocked this 'favoured heir'? But the greatest implausibility is the idea of a one-sided exchange of oaths and hostages, purely from Edward to William; that was not how rulers operated in the eleventh century, even when they dealt with equals, and in this case there is the further difficulty that a duke is made to appear the senior partner in his dealings with a king.

The story of a visit by William to England in 1051 and of solemn oaths taken by the king, naming the duke as his successor, witnessed by the luminaries of Anglo-Saxon earldom, can safely be discarded. Let us assume, though, that Edward, having jettisoned the Godwins and his wife Edith, and, knowing that he was sterile, wished to nominate an heir to the throne. Let us assume, further, that he discounted the merits of those with claims to the throne superior to William's in point of blood kinship, most notably Eustace of Boulogne and Ralph of Mantes. Edward might have opted for William to detach him from Baldwin and bribe him into an alternative alliance, or because he felt isolated and vulnerable to the possible incursion of Svein Estrithson; either way, he was actuated by simple pragmatism and *ad hoc* opportunism. It is not wholly implausible, then, in the context of late 1051 that he might have made some informal, unbinding promise that William would be the 'inside candidate' for the throne if he died childless, provided he fell in with Edward's designs involving Baldwin of Flanders. This is a long way short of a formal oath. And to Edward such a promise would have meant nothing: he had already made a similar pledge to Svein Estrithson and would do so again to two further pretenders to the English throne. In any case, English kingship was not hereditary and Edward could not force the *witan* to do his will.

The entire elaborate edifice which Norman propaganda erected around the alleged 'oath' of 1051 is thus revealed as a house built on sand. The principal mistake of William's naïve apologists was to assume that Edward's promise, if there was one, was a unique, special and indefeasible pledge, instead of a conventional response to the many claimants who lobbied him about the succession. As Edward's biographer well says: 'I doubt whether anyone, at least on the English side, expected the promise to be honoured. Edward was still on the right side of fifty; William was in the hazardous early twenties, frequently on campaign. Much could happen before Edward died . . . .. If William had come over to see for himself what were his chances of succeeding to England, he must have returned discouraged.'[34]

While Edward plodded along his obscure, Byzantine and machiavellian diplomatic pathways in the winter of 1051–52, the Godwin family was regrouping. The two halves of the family, one in Ireland, the other in Flanders, kept in touch by means of couriers, and concerted plans for a return to their homeland. Godwin, an astute politician, thought that the threat of force alone might do the trick, if once he and his sons could effect a landing on English soil, for through his spies he had become aware of a change of attitude in England. A general consensus was forming that Edward was no saint, that the Godwins had been unjustly treated, and that Godwin was a kind of David ranged against Edward's Saul.[35]

Other factors seemed to make it unlikely that Edward would be able to reassemble the mighty host that had faced down Godwin and his family the year before. Leofric and Siward had already gone as far as they were going to go on Edward's behalf; whether the king realized it or not, they had no intention of risking their lives and those of their men in any future armed clash with the outlawed family. Moreover, public opinion had been alienated by the arrogant triumphalism of Robert of Jumièges and the Norman faction after their victory in 1051, and distaste was compounded by irritation and anger that the same forces which had obliged the Godwins to bow the head had not been able to prevent the Welsh king Gruffydd ap Llywelyn raiding deep into Herefordshire.[36]

It seems that many messages were passed along the sea lanes of the Channel and the Irish Sea before Godwin and Harold finally concerted their measures, which involved a rendezvous near Bosham, conjecturally established as meaning either in Spithead or the Solent. The year 1052 saw the elevation of Harold Godwinson as Godwin's right-hand man to take the vacancy left by Swein, who, in yet another amazing turn in his already astonishing career, suddenly announced that he would set out from Bruges to walk barefoot on a pilgrimage to Jerusalem. He reached the Holy Land but died on the return journey, either in Constantinople or somewhere near the city.[37]

The Godwin family, though deprived of its estates, still had wealth enough to finance a substantial expedition, much more imposing than Osgod Clapa's raid three years earlier. The military objective was neither mere tip-and-run raiding nor bringing Edward to a pitched battle, but a descent in force that would overawe the Norman faction under Jumièges and oblige Leofric, Siward and other half-hearted supporters of the king to consider where their best interests lay. Godwin's authority was still undiminished among his own supporters, as we can infer from his well-authenticated rebuke to the hotheads in his party who wanted to wage *guerre à outrance* in England. He had also lost none of his organizational and administrative talents, since he must have conveyed considerable sums of money across the Irish Sea to Harold, who was able to pay for the recruitment of Irish–Norse warriors and marines and the loyalty of nine ships' crews; meanwhile in Bruges Godwin fitted out at least twice that number.[38]

In the early summer of 1052 Godwin considered that he had weakened Edward's prestige sufficiently in England – constantly portraying the Godwin family as innocent victims – to be able to commence military operations. Harold and Leofwine crossed from Ireland with their nine ships and sailed up the Bristol Channel. Putting in at Porlock, near the Devon–Somerset border, to reprovision, they were surprised by one of Edward's armies and forced to fight for their lives. Harold won a victory of sorts, killing more than thirty thegns, before being compelled to re-embark. The two Godwinsons then sailed round Land's End and up the English Channel, making for the rendezvous with their father.[39]

Godwin had stiffer opposition to deal with, for Edward had assembled a formidable fleet of forty ships at Sandwich under Earls Ralph and Odda. The patriarch sailed from Nieuwpoort on 22 June, apparently without Tostig and Gyrth – it is thought he did not want to give (literal) hostages to fortune in case of a defeat – evaded the defending fleet at Sandwich and made landfall at Dungeness. Ralph and Odda responded by trying to catch him in a pincer movement, putting the levies of Kent on the march by land while they moved in with the fleet. Godwin re-embarked and stood away towards Pevensey; a sea battle seemed imminent. Then the elements took a hand in the form of a ferocious storm which dispersed the pursuing fleet and drove Godwin back in disarray to Flanders. Soon the outlawed earl was back in Bruges and Ralph and Odda in London, where they had to brave the wrath of Edward, who was bitter at their failure and wanted to replace them as commanders. In the ensuing confusion, the fleet, already impaired by losses in the storm and low morale, was allowed to disperse and so Edward lost the initiative.[40]

The dauntless Godwin refitted his ships and set sail again, this time directly to the Isle of Wight to rendezvous with Harold and Leofwine. It took time for the two flotillas to find each other, and in the meantime Godwin laid waste the island. At last, probably late in August, Godwin and Harold made contact; according to some sources the meeting was further west than originally planned, at Portland. Both father and son were full of aplomb and sanguine that events were moving their way. They slowly held their course up the Channel, landing to revictual at Sandwich, Pevensey, Hythe, Folkestone and Dover, being enthusiastically received by their old vassals in Kent and Sussex, collecting volunteers, and pressing ships and hostages from those clearly of the king's party. By the time they turned into the Thames estuary, they had assembled a host large enough to deal with any army Edward might throw at them. To keep up the morale of his recruits, Godwin loosened the strict discipline he had imposed since the Isle of Wight and allowed his men to ravage the Isle of Sheppey and sack the royal manor of Milton.[41]

Edward decided to make a stand at London, which was already showing dangerous signs of declaring for the Godwins. The response to the king's pleas for military help were slow and half-hearted, but Leofric and Siward dared not leave their own fate and that of the kingdom to chance by failing to heed the royal summons. Grudgingly they made their way to London with their picked troops so that, on the face of it, by mid-September, Edward again had a considerable force ranged against the Godwins, including a notional complement of fifty ships. As he lined the north bank of the Thames, waiting for Godwin to arrive at his old berth in Southwark, he must have been conscious of rerunning the events of the year before, except that this time his position was nothing like so favourable.[42]

Godwin reached Southwark on 14 September and was immediately encouraged when the citizens of London raised no difficulties about allowing him safe passage past London Bridge. Still on the south bank, the earl moved his forces within the city walls, so that soon the two armies stared at each other across the river. As in a similar position the year before, tough bargaining then commenced. Godwin began by demanding a full and unconditional pardon for himself and his family and the restitution of all their estates and worldly goods. When the stubborn Edward predictably refused, Godwin drew first blood by outwitting the monarch's naval commanders and encircling the royal fleet. In yet another instance of history repeating itself, Stigand crossed the river on Godwin's behalf as intermediary.[43]

Whereas in 1051 the northern earls and the Norman party had stood shoulder to shoulder, this time Leofric and Siward made it clear to Edward they would not fight kith and kin to protect Norman privileges. When he realized that the troops he had counted on to defeat Godwin were like so many toy soldiers, Edward flew into an apoplectic rage – his habitual reaction to being crossed. By his reluctance to be reconciled, Edward was playing a more dangerous game than he knew, for Godwin found it difficult to prevent his troops from attacking the king and deposing him. The Normans were much quicker to realize the parlous position in which they stood and, without waiting for the deliberations of the assembly, decamped at speed; Robert of Jumièges, together with his protégés Bishops Ulf of Worcester and William of London, fought his way out of the city and fled to Essex, there to take ship to the Continent. Godwin held all the cards and had it in his power to usurp the throne had he been so minded; but he merely asked that he be purged of all charges against him, especially the accusation that he had compassed the death of Alfred. With great reluctance Edward accepted that the game was up and he would have to make peace; as his chronicler put it: 'He gradually calmed the boiling tumult of his mind.'[44]

On 15 September Godwin and Harold, taking with them a large escort to guard against possible treachery, crossed to the north bank to attend a meeting of the *gemot*, where Godwin was allowed to declare his own and his family's innocence of all charges brought against them. The assembly voted for his restitution by spontaneous acclamation. Edward, doubtless fuming secretly, gave Godwin the kiss of peace, condoned all alleged offences and restored him and his sons both to the royal favour and to their estates. As a logical corollary to his acceptance that the charges against the Godwins were false, Edward announced the outlawing of all the Normans and French-speaking nobles who had perjured themselves and perverted the law. Most signally of all, he restored Edith to her royal dignities and place at court; if ever he had contemplated divorcing her, he no longer had the power to do so. But the rumours of marital strife between king and queen never went away, to the point where, many years later, Edith on her deathbed thought it necessary to clear herself of charges of adultery.[45]

Godwin's triumph was total but he showed himself remarkably free of vindictive spirit, once his Norman accusers had fled. He did not even seek to avenge himself on Ralph and Odda but contented himself with restoring his family fortunes. Edward made no attempt to undo the settlement into which he had been dragooned by events and may even have reflected later that he had been foolish to try to oust the Godwins. However, he persevered with his ill-starred policy of exiling those who displeased him. It is worth pointing out that, every time he banished a major personage during his reign, that person returned to plague him and often to humiliate him; so it was with Osgod Clapa in 1046, with Swein Godwinson in 1047, and with Godwin in 1051, and so it would be with Aelfgar in 1055 and 1058 and Tostig in 1065.[46]

One obvious consequence of the return of Godwin and the Godwinsons was that the Norman succession project, if it had ever existed, was dead in the water. This had been so totally predicated on the exile of the Godwins that only an unrealist, a cynic or his apologists could pretend it was still in being. Yet the myth of Edward's promise of the throne to Duke William dies hard, to such a point that it has even been suggested that the Godwins were allowed to return only after they had agreed to the Norman succession.[47] This is the most incredible of all the theories purporting to show a valid claim to the English throne by Duke William. To begin with, since the Godwin family so manifestly had the upper hand in September 1052 and forced their return on Edward virtually at sword point, what possible meaning can attach to the statement that they were 'permitted' to return solely on acceptance of the Norman succession? And how could the flight of Archbishop Robert and his Norman acolytes be explained on this basis: this would involve Normans fleeing in terror from a man who had sworn – nay, been forced – to accept their suzerainty.[48]

The flight of the Norman bishops cleared the way for Godwin's ecclesiastical protégés and especially for Stigand. This most worldly of clerics was now appointed to the archbishopric of Canterbury, in defiance of canon law on two counts: first, that the man who had received a valid papal commission, Robert of Jumièges, was still alive; and, secondly, that Stigand blatantly held on to the see at Winchester as well, out of sheer avarice. The tenure of plural dioceses was never likely to recommend Stigand to the papacy, but a brief opportunity presented itself in 1058, when the short-lived pontiff Benedict X granted him the pallium. This apparent seal of legitimacy suffered a boomerang effect the following year when Benedict was deposed for simony, thus leaving Stigand with a doubly tainted title to Canterbury. The venal divine comforted himself with the enjoyment of his vast wealth from Church lands and benefices: between his own private holdings and those of the see at Canterbury he was worth by the end of the 1050s about £3,000 – a staggering sum for those times and inferior only to that of the king and Harold Godwinson.[49]

Godwin did not enjoy his triumph long, for on 15 April 1053 he died suddenly while attending the king's Easter court at Winchester. He seems to have been seized by a stroke on the twelfth of the month and to have lingered for three days before expiring. Some later historians have seen his death as suspicious, but his own family, including Harold, Tostig and Gyrth who were with him and carried him from the banqueting hall to the royal chamber, do not seem to have shared these suspicions.[50] Poisoning does not appear likely, and still less can we credit the absurd anti-Godwin allegation later spread by Norman propagandists that he challenged God to strike him dead if he had had any part in Alfred's death, whereupon the Almighty duly obliged him. None the less, it was in many ways a highly convenient death, and it doubtless allowed Edward to reconcile himself more easily to the hegemony of Godwin's sons. That Godwin was a kind of *de facto* king seems underlined by the quasi-royal funeral obsequies: he was buried alongside Cnut and Emma in the Old Minster, and his widow, Gytha, made the kind of lavish endowments for the repose of his soul that were normally associated with departed monarchs. So passed away the last of Cnut's earls and yet another link to Scandinavia and the north. Increasingly, it seemed, the England of Edward would be a Wessex-based kingdom, with its interests in the south and its orientation towards continental Europe.[51]

5

The Conqueror

F rom 1050 onwards William pursued a policy of centralization and
expansion, at once bending the local Norman lords to his will and
rolling back the frontiers of Norman power and influence.
Following his successful strategy of state-building through intermarriage,
he had now formed around him a nucleus of powerful Norman nobles,
whose interests were also his interests: not just William Fitzosbern,
Roger of Montgomery and his half-brothers Odo of Bayeux and
Robert of Mortain, but also Roger of Beaumont, Hugh de Grandmesnil, and the other Williams, Vernon, Crispin and Warenne. William
dealt with these men in the same way Napoleon, eight centuries later,
would deal with his marshals: he made their wealth and success depend
on a never-ending series of foreign wars. Using these men as lieutenants,
William struck out at all cross-border interests that stood in his way: the
powerful Bellême sept, the clan of William de Moulins-la-Manche and
the Giroie family.[1]

Even if he had not been a belligerent expansionist, geopolitics would
have pushed him towards conflict with his neighbours, for, at the precise
time he elected to extend his sway beyond his southern boundaries, the
Count of Anjou was pushing north into the very same regions. Having
come to the limit of Anjou's southward push to the Loire, Geoffrey
Martel, Count of Anjou, a warlord second in military power among

Francophones only to the king of France himself, set his eyes on Touraine, Maine and even Normandy itself.[2] In 1049 William campaigned with the French king against Martel and took part in the expedition which captured the castle of Mouliherne near Angers later that year, leaving Roger of Montgomery a free hand to intervene in the country of the Bellêmes. William here once again showed his gambler's mentality, for he was striking out south in two different directions while Normandy itself was far from pacified.

In 1051 William was obliged to concentrate all his efforts in the Bellême border country, for Geoffrey Martel, having resisted the siege of his castle at Mouliherne, counterattacked by capturing Tours and seizing the town of Alençon in the country of the Bellêmes. William reasoned that the Bellêmes owed him fealty for Alençon; actually, in a complex skein typical of early medieval Europe their feudal obligations bound them three ways: to the king of France for the town of Bellême, to the Count of Maine for the castle of Domfront and to the Duke of Normandy for Alençon – which was why the Bellême family were past masters at playing off one overlord against another.[3] William consulted Roger of Montgomery, the specialist in the Bellêmes. He reported a clan riven with factionalism and private jealousies and also something more personal: Roger had fallen in love with Mabel, daughter of the Bellême patriarch, and wanted her for his wife.

With the explicit sanction of the French king, William took his army south to Maine. Geoffrey of Martel declined to meet him in open battle, but he and the Bellêmes heavily fortified the castle of Domfront and defied William to take it, hoping that a long siege would exhaust the Normans' supplies and *matériel*.[4] Displaying his customary military ingenuity, William settled down as if for a long investment of the fortress, then suddenly made a lightning dash to catch Alençon unprepared. He nearly managed to gallop his force straight through the gates of the town, but in the nick of time the burghers closed them against the invader. Confident that William could not besiege two places at once, the citizens of Alençon made the grave error of taunting William about his bastardy; it was said that they stood on the walls and cried: 'Hides! Hides for the tanner!'[5]

William, as always both lucky and ingenious, found a way to have the town betrayed to him. Brooding on the insult to him and his mother, in vengeful mood he paraded thirty-two of the leading citizens of Alençon to the bridge they had recently defended and, in full view of the rest of the citizens, cut off their hands and feet. Overcome by terror, the garrison that had retreated into the citadel at Alençon surrendered at once. Hearing of this atrocity, the men of Domfront, too, ran up the white flag, having first secured a solemn promise that they would not meet the same mutilated fate as their opposite numbers in Alençon. Between Domfront and Alençon there was just one other important castle, that of La Ferté-Mace; William made over the lord of this fastness by giving him in marriage a daughter of Herluin and Herlève.[6]

The 25-year-old duke's campaign had been a brilliant success at every level. Geoffrey Martel's prestige was severely dented, Roger of Montgomery won his bride, and the Maine frontier was made secure. The Bellême family passed within William's sphere of influence and became his vassals, partly through the loss of their strongholds and partly because of the alliance between the Montgomerys and the Bellêmes; Mabel of Bellême became both a staunch advocate of Norman expansionism and a personal favourite of William's.[7] Any fear that William Fitzosbern might still be harbouring thoughts of revenge against Roger of Montgomery for the murder of his father, Osbern the Steward, could be safely laid to rest, since William's two lieutenant-generals had co-operated brilliantly during the campaign.

The one cloud on the horizon was the alienation of the king of France. Too late Henry realized that he had probably backed the wrong horse and that Normandy was becoming an over-powerful military nation. With an abrupt switch of alliances he made common cause with Geoffrey Martel against the 'upstart' Duke of Normandy and sought an appropriate excuse to intervene in the duchy.[8] The pretext came in 1053 with the last, and most serious, internal revolt against William's authority. Suddenly the pretender William of Arques, who, with his brother Mauger, Archbishop of Rouen, was the most powerful man in Upper Normandy, renounced his vassalage and raised the standard of revolt. This brought to a head William's worst suspicions of disloyalty in Rouen; he had never liked the town and was trying to build up Caen as a counterweight. And he was well aware of the threat posed by William of Arques, who not only had a better claim to the duchy in terms of legitimate descent but was also aping William's ingenious system of building up a power base through intermarriage.[9] Now the duke had a fight for his life on his hands, and if Henry of France and Geoffrey Martel co-ordinated intelligently with the rebels he was surely done for.

At first things went badly for William. Sensing trouble ahead in Arques, he had already sent a detachment down to garrison the citadel, yet now the news came in that the troops had gone over to the pretender. But Henry of France wasted too much time building up a coalition that would be invincible. He enlisted the aid of William of

Arques's brother-in-law, Count Enguerrand II of Ponthieu and his brother Walerand, known firebrands; Enguerrand, indeed, had been excommunicated for incest by Leo IX at the council of Rheims in October 1049.[10] Henry's strategy was to invade Normandy with two armies, of which one, under Enguerrand, would advance into eastern Normandy through Neuchâtel-en-Bray while the other, commanded by the French king in person, would strike out for Rouen via Evrecin. With Geoffrey Martel coming in from the south and the Normans meanwhile preoccupied with the investment of the castle at Arques, the result, presumably, would be a military walkover.

And so it would have been if the ramshackle allies had co-ordinated their efforts successfully. But while Henry took an unconscionable time getting his ponderous military machine into full swing, William made another of his lightning strikes, hoping to force the fortress of Arques to capitulate before French forces crossed the frontier. On the way he met a despondent group of knights from Rouen, who advised their lord that the revolt was too widespread to contain. Talking them out of their despondency, the duke restored morale with a *coup de main* that nearly resulted in the capture of the fortress in a single afternoon. Baulked of his prey, William supervised the close blockade of Arques by his army, entrusting it to Walter of Giffard before hastening east for the next phase of the war.[11]

William had failed in his primary objective but by the autumn of 1053 he had a powerful force interposed between the stronghold and the invading armies. Next the allies committed the egregious error of invading separately. In October Enguerrand made his move but on 25 October was ambushed at St-Aubin-sur-Scie. The resulting battle has sometimes been described as a skirmish, but the invaders took heavy casualties, including (among the dead) Enguerrand himself. Among the many prisoners was Hugh Bardulf, lord of Nogent and Pithiviers.[12] Henry was forced to postpone his invasion and could only fume impotently as William compassed the fall of Arques. The defenders, enfeebled by hunger, agreed to surrender on the sole condition that the horrors of Alençon would not be repeated; when the gates opened, gaunt and starving knights on spavined and cadaverous nags limped forth, making a pitiful sight.

Once again a pretender had been defeated and once again a luckless claimant went into exile; this time it was Eustace of Boulogne who provided sanctuary.[13] Archbishop Mauger, already under a cloud for opposing William's marriage to Matilda, was deposed from the see of Rouen, replaced by the biddable Manilius, and exiled to Guernsey, where he drowned in a boating accident soon after.[14] Faced by the most dangerous threat to his hegemony so far, William had come through, aided by luck, the incompetence of his enemies and the soundness of his judgement: a key element in the contest for supremacy in Upper Normandy was that the local warlord Richard of Auffay thought his future looked brighter with the duke than with his namesake, the keeper of Arques.[15]

But Henry of France was determined to avenge the insult to his prestige from this contumacious Norman vassal. Now, too, jealousy and alarm were increasing among other Gallic princes, such as William of Aquitaine and Theobald of Blois. Finally, in February 1054, Henry and Geoffrey Martel, aided by Theobald and Guy of Ponthieu, finished concerting their joint venture and launched a two-pronged invasion of Normandy. To deal with this unprecedented threat, William called out the entire levy of Normandy, forming it into two armies that were to stand on the defensive until further notice. Meanwhile the two wings of the French army advanced slowly into the duchy, one progressing methodically along both banks of the Seine, the other aiming at Rouen and the original enclave granted to Rollo.[16]

The right wing of the allied army entered Normandy near Aumale, plundering, looting and ravishing as it went. The French soldiers reached the town of Mortemer and began what contemporary chroniclers called an orgy of rape and atrocity.[17] The Norman army which had been dogging this host made a forced march by night and came upon the carousing and raping French just as dawn was breaking. After blocking all exits from Mortemer, the Normans employed their favourite ruse of setting fire to houses to start a general inferno. As the French poured out of the town to escape the fumes and the flames, they found every exit blocked by the grim-faced Normans. Bloody hand-to-hand combat ensued and went on from daybreak until about 3 p.m. The slaughter was terrific, with most of the French being cut down in the blocked lanes leading from the town or, in the case of those who broke through the dragnet, in the nearby woods.[18]

When the Normans finally sheathed their swords after a frenzy of butchery the only Frenchmen left alive were those thought worth ransoming – who included Odo, King Henry's brother, and Guy, the new Count of Ponthieu who was taken prisoner and kept in a dungeon at Bayeux for two years. Enguerrand II's brother Walerand was among the fallen.[19] Evincing a flair for theatre, the victorious William sent a courier to the other side of the Seine, where King Henry was still toiling along with the main army. The herald arrived at the French camp at midnight and, in a histrionic manner, boomed out the news to the king. The French were at first demoralized, then the feeling turned to outright panic; Henry turned his army around and retreated pell-mell; William, well satisfied, did not bother to pursue them. The Norman duke proved beyond any doubt on this February day that he was a gifted captain. He had employed Fabian tactics, allowed the French to ravage his lands and to become overconfident, and contented himself with the thought that patience would bring him ultimate victory. Most of all, he proved that he knew how to win wars without fighting to the death. As the historian Edward Freeman, certainly no great admirer of the duke, wrote: 'One army was cut to pieces with hardly the loss of a Norman life. The other was hurried out of the land without so much as striking a blow.'[20]

Henry was forced to conclude a humiliating peace, simply to redeem the French nobles still rotting in Norman prisons. He agreed not to interfere in future Norman expansion at the expense of the Count of Anjou and to regularize any such conquests along feudal lines as the nominal overlord. Henry was prepared to agree to this, as he was piqued at the nonappearance in the field of Geoffrey of Anjou. To rub salt in the wound, William seized and fortified the disputed fortress of Ambrières, thinking this at least might goad Geoffrey of Martel into fighting, but still the Angevin was not tempted. For once the panegyrists who spoke of the 'terror of his name' had a point in their eulogies of William, for as soon as the duke departed Geoffrey Martel did appear, together with William of Aquitaine, to lay siege to the fortress, but as soon as William sped back they in turn decamped. To ram home his triumph, William imprisoned Geoffrey of Mayenne, hitherto an Angevin ally, and refused to release him until he had acknowledged the duke as his lord.[21]

From 1055 to 1057 there was peace in Normandy, with neither foreign wars nor domestic revolts. But Henry I had not forgotten Mortemer and plotted his revenge together with the equally humiliated Geoffrey Martel, who was still managing, just, to hold his own in Maine against Norman encroachment. The two rulers met early in 1057 to concert a new invasion, the first time at Tours on 19 January, the second at Angers on 1 March.[22] Once again the strategy was for a two-pronged incursion, with particular emphasis on the duchy west of the Seine. Alerted by his spies, William tried to ensure that the French would not benefit this time from the support of Norman quislings: to this end he exiled all unreliable grandees, including a namesake who married a daughter of the Count of Soissons and on the death of his father-in-law became count himself.[23]

In August 1057 Henry I's army crossed the frontier into Normandy, aiming to bisect it and reach the sea at Dives, laying waste the land as he went. Once again William employed Fabian tactics, allowing the French to penetrate his land unopposed, but planning to smite them on the return journey when they would be laden with spoils. However, the extent of French devastation forced him to make his move earlier than intended; Henry's army reached the river Dive, ravaged the Bessin area and sacked Caen; their next move would be to cross the Dive and carry fire and sword even deeper into the duchy. Once again displaying a mastery of timing, William marched from Falaise to intercept the enemy to the north-east of Caen and take them unawares.[24]

Henry had planned to get his entire army across the river at low tide, but the bridge collapsed halfway through the passage of the troops, leaving the van in an exposed position on the far side of a rising river, with the rearguard, baggage and booty vulnerable on the other bank.[25] When the Normans came swooping in on the rear, there was general panic and a massacre ensued: those who were not put to the sword or captured perished in the engorged river, being swept away and drowned in the swollen flood. From the far bank Henry surveyed the destruction helplessly, as impotent as Xerxes at Salamis; his shaken courtiers advised him that the only sensible course was to get out of Normandy as soon as possible.[26] A chastened French king shook off the dust of the duchy, determined never to cross the frontier again. As a final humiliation, William agreed to peace terms only on condition that the much-disputed border fortress of Tillières was restored to him. This was conceded, but no formal peace was concluded until Henry's death in 1060, as William claimed the fortress of Driment near Dreux on French territory; Henry found this unacceptable, and so desultory warfare continued.[27]

By 1058 Duke William of Normandy was the most redoubtable warlord in all France. Always fortune's darling, he achieved virtually complete hegemony in the French-speaking world after 1060 when all his most formidable rivals died. On 4 August Henry I expired at Dreux, leaving his eight-year-old son Philip, the fruit of his second marriage (to Anne, daughter of Yaroslav of Kiev), as king in name only pending his majority, until which time he was the ward of Baldwin V, Count of Flanders, both William's ally and his father-in-law.[28] On 14 November Geoffrey Martel died, immediately plunging Anjou into a civil war between the brothers and rival claimants Geoffrey le Barbu and Fulk le

Rechin – a fratricidal conflict which William could easily manipulate for his own ends. The only remote challenger to Normandy as chief military nation within the confines of modern France was Aquitaine, but William of Aquitaine would never have acted alone against his namesake in the north and was in any case preoccupied with the wars in Spain.[29]

It is probable that after 1060 William was already projecting ahead to a possible invasion of England, the most promising domain for his aggressive expansionism. But as a final touchstone to his hegemony in France he needed to conquer Maine on his southern flank. He therefore made careful preparations for a conclusive campaign, again displaying his political subtlety by recalling many leading Norman nobles from exile – notably Rodulf of Tosny, Hugh de Grandmesnil and Arnold, son of William Giroie – and allying himself with Thibaud, Count of Blois.[30] In 1063, after concerting measures with a pretender to the county of Maine, Herbert Bacco, he launched the invasion, quickly overrunning Maine, laying waste the countryside but avoiding a direct attack on Le Mans, possibly because he was already thinking ahead to an invasion of England and wished to avoid unnecessary casualties.[31]

Le Mans was formerly the very symbol of Geoffrey Martel's dominance in the province. William wore its defenders down by a policy of attrition and scorched earth, promising the burghers of the city that his reign would be mild and benign if they surrendered but harsh otherwise. Le Mans surrendered meekly, giving William success without hard fighting. Geoffrey of Mayenne, the ruler of Maine and frustrated defender of Le Mans, left the city before it was handed over and consistently refused to do homage to William.[32] This seemed to enrage William, so he proceeded to invest the castle and town of Mayenne, which had not been on his original list of objectives. Having taken the citadels of Alençon, Domfront and Arques, William was confident he could add Mayenne to his list of successful sieges, but soon discovered that this fortress was a tough nut, seemingly impregnable to catapults, battering rams and normal siege engines. The latent pyromania in William's soul took over: he ordered his men to set fire to Mayenne by shooting flaming arrows over the walls; when the defenders left the walls to put out the inferno that was consuming their wooden houses, the Normans swarmed over and began putting their victims to the sword. Once again Geoffrey of Mayenne evaded capture, having ensured that the citadel would hold out long enough for him to make good his escape.[33]

By the close of 1063 William was the dominant power in modern

France: all conceivable rivals, whether in Angevin France, Flanders, Maine or Anjou, had been defeated, humbled or neutralized. Less than fifteen years earlier, the continued existence of the duchy of Normandy itself had been in doubt. William's achievement was spectacular and deserves further analysis. There are many interconnected factors involved: William's ingenious use of kinship, castle-building and extension of ducal authority to produce a highly centralized nation; the manipulation of the Church both in Normandy and abroad for his own purposes; and, most of all, the establishment of a formidable army composed of his own household troops and those of cousins and close allies.

The four most powerful men in the duchy, after William, were his half-brothers Odo of Bayeux and Robert Mortain, together with Roger of Montgomery and William Fitzosbern, who by this time had married Aeliz, daughter of Roger de Tosny.[34] Beyond this inner circle were the overlapping groups formed by intermarriage, all bound to William's court by ties of blood and self-interest – a Mafia-like extended family in pursuit of maximum profit and loot. The same names in this kinship network recur in the sources with predictable regularity: Ralph Taison, Walter Giffard, Manilius of Rouen, Hugh of Lisieux, Geoffrey of Coutances, John of Avranches, Ivo of Sees, Robert, Count of Eu, Richard, Count of Evreux, Roger of Beaumont; as has been well said: 'Almost all could call one another cousin . . .. they were more than an aristocracy; first and foremost they were a family.'[35]

In return for their local rights and privileges, these men had ceded to William the prerogatives of ducal power held by Richard II but since lost during the chaos of the 1030s and 1040s. William had now regained ducal control over castle-building, the right to nominate to vicecomital and household offices, to deal with crime and dispense punishment (including the sentence of exile and the confiscation of lands), to seize the younger sons of the leading families and hold them as hostages to guarantee the good behaviour of their kinfolk, to issue charters and control the coinage. Put simply, William now enjoyed a monopoly of violence and command of the economy. This was a process which began immediately after Val-ès-Dunes in 1047 with the introduction of the Truce of God and the destruction of all 'illegal' castles.

The suppression of the two risings by pretenders, that of Guy of Burgundy in 1047 and William of Arques five years later, inculcated the lesson that the *vicomtes* were not independent agents but the servants of the duke, holding office at his pleasure and removable if they incurred his displeasure. All Norman counts and viscounts had to realize that they had an appointed place in the ducal hierarchy, and had only been given their positions because they were members of a favoured kinship group. The *vicomtes* were responsible for the collection of ducal revenues – receipts from broad demesnes, tolls, internal customs, feudal dues, profits from the administration of justice and direct taxation – and the discharge of ducal payments; the collection of taxes was farmed out to them, but a handful of picked administrators at William's court checked that a proper accounting of the monies was rendered. The efficient collection of taxes explains economic growth in Normandy under William, the development of a money economy, and ultimately the surplus with which to build abbeys and monasteries and hire mercenaries in 1066.[36] The most important duty of the *vicomtes* was to provide military service to the duke when called on and on this strict understanding they were allowed to build castles; William's trusted inner circle of magnates, in turn, oversaw the castellans to make sure none of them toyed with ideas of independent power.[37]

By 1060 a pro-William aristocracy occupied all the key positions, both secular and ecclesiastical, in Normandy. William made the four great ducal offices – steward, constable, chamberlain and butler – permanent and appointed his most trusted counts to these posts. Below them were the *vicomtes*, next came the fighting men, and then the artisans (tanners, blacksmiths, etc.) essential for oiling the wheels of the Norman military machine. At the bottom of the pyramid were the agricultural serfs, toiling to provide the surplus with which William's aggressive wars of expansion could be financed.[38] In the towns, of which Rouen and Bayeux were the only ones of importance, and in the spinning mills slavery was still employed, and the market at Rouen did a flourishing trade in slaves from Ireland.[39]

It is well known that the monastic movement made great strides during William's reign, that the Church in Normandy was considered a bastion of the faith, and that the duke's ecclesiastical appointments were shrewd.[40] Without falling into the trap of promoting incompetent cousins to high office, William made sure that all the Norman bishoprics went to favoured kin. If Manilius was his best episcopal appointment, he did even better when it came to selecting abbots, for here he managed to inveigle the two theological luminaries Anselm and Lanfranc.[41] Dismissed from Bec for opposing the controversial ducal marriage to Matilda, Lanfranc displayed remarkable moral courage, and even the physical variety, given that William was such a dangerous man to cross; on his way to exile he chanced upon the duke on the road, sought a reconciliation and talked his way back into favour. The new entente was most fruitful: in 1059 Lanfranc went to Rome with arguments that persuaded Pope Nicholas to rescind the earlier papal interdict; four years later Lanfranc became prior of the newly built St Stephen's Abbey in Caen.[42]

In supporting the monastic movement, William was carrying on and reinforcing the tradition of the earlier dukes: as with so many other facets of life, he was not different in kind from them but simply excelled them in all areas. There were sound financial, political, ideological and cultural reasons for the support of monasteries. The Normans, conscious of their Viking past, always liked to present themselves as devout Christians, thus consolidating cultural integration, for it was after all their Viking forebears who had destroyed the early monasteries in the first place. William, a master of political camouflage, liked to conflate the Norse culture of the past with the culture of the Frankish present to present an image of fearsome but god-fearing and pious warriors, crusaders *avant la lettre*. Additionally, the monastic movement could be manipulated for the purposes of the state, provided it was tightly controlled. A student of Norman monasticism has established that the Norman dukes, jealous of the potential independent power of monastic orders, endowed abbeys exclusively in Upper Normandy, which was firmly in their power; in Lower Normandy, where their influence was weakest, they liked to bind their military vassals to them with lands.[43]

William's genuine solicitude for the Church is partly explained by the fact that he was, unlike Harald Hardrada in Norway, a true believer in Jesus Christ and in Heaven and Hell, and partly because it was a quirk of William's psychology that he always needed to occupy the moral high ground: he believed in the use of main force but he liked it to be camouflaged and obfuscated by his putative role as the fighter for justice, the devout Christian, the wronged man, the bringer of peace, or whatever other ideological persona suited him at the time. Although he was a generous lay patron of the Church in Normandy, it was always on the basis that his supreme authority should be unquestioned.[44] He had a cynical attitude to the Church temporal and, as he showed later, would not hesitate to steal ecclesiastical property if it suited his book. And when Lanfranc crossed him he laid waste the consecrated grounds of the abbey at Bec just to show who was top dog. For all that, as his biographers have pointed out, he would have been shocked at Henry II's murder of Thomas Becket and incredulous at Henry VIII of England's wholesale expropriation of church property.[45]

William's attitude to the Church was never put to a serious test, since, in yet another of those wellnigh incredible slices of luck he always enjoyed, the previous enmity of papacy and empire to his duchy came to a sudden end. In 1053, while William was battling with Henry I of France and William of Arques in northern France, in southern Italy his Norman confrères under Robert Guiscard signally defeated a papal army at Civitate. This was a calamity for the policy of the German emperor in Italy, for the pope it had virtually imposed on the college of cardinals was now a prisoner of the Normans at Benevento. In 1054 Leo IX died, but not before uttering a solemn curse on all Normans from his deathbed.[46]

Two years later the emperor Henry III died, leaving the throne to a mere boy (the future Henry IV). After no less than three phantom popes had flitted across the scene in five years (including the deposed Benedict in 1058),[47] the conclave of cardinals decided to reverse their pro-imperial policy and elected the pro-Norman Nicholas II. At his very first synod in April 1059 Nicholas decreed that the emperor would no longer have the power to appoint popes and placed papal elections in the hands of the cardinal archbishops.[48] In August 1059 Nicholas II enfeoffed the great Norman captains Robert Guiscard and Richard of Capua in the lands they had seized in southern Italy, thus cementing an alliance between the papacy and the Normans against the German empire. This was the context in which Lanfranc approached the pope to lift the canonical ban on William's marriage to Matilda; it is hardly surprising that the petition was successful.[49]

William's great success in centralizing Normandy, and achieving in his duchy a personal power close to the absolutism of monarchs of a much later era, is all the more impressive since it ran against the main currents of the age. In general the eleventh century was an epoch of fragmenting, centrifugal power, both cause and consequence of the extreme violence of the era. Much of Europe at the time was characterized by what has been called 'feudal anarchy' – a situation where a new class of private lords based on castles became more powerful at the expense of those who previously acted as agents for the central government. Once private justice dispensed crime and punishment, the unbridled violence of the Hobbesian stateless 'natural man' took over, with its concomitant of the war of all against all. By contrast, in Normandy central authority not only constrained local aristrocrats but dragooned them more tightly even than under Carolingian France, hitherto regarded as the very model of centripetal political control.[50]

The extent and meaning of eleventh-century violence is much disputed by scholars, as is just about every facet of Norman society under Duke

William. Was Normandy by 1060 a completely Gallicized society or did a Norse residue still remain? Did William represent a completely new bearing in Norman policy or had it always been a rapacious and expansionist state, and was it just that William was the most able practitioner of primitive 'imperialism'? Was William's rise to supreme power simply a lucky accident or were there dynamic social forces that he energized, possibly a 'new class'? Most of all, was Normandy before 1066 a feudal society, with settled military and economic rights and duties?

There are two views on the Viking legacy in Normandy. One is that the warlike qualities of the Norsemen took the form of Norman expansionism throughout Europe and, consequently, that we should perceive Duke William's exploits as part of a common 'Norman achievement', manifesting itself not just in the wars of conquest in northern Europe but also in the spectacular gains in Sicily and southern Italy by Robert Guiscard and other notable captains, culminating in the 'imperialism' of the First Crusade.[51] The other view is that the Normans were not especially gifted in warfare from 911 onwards and that the so-called 'Norman achievement' is simply a reading back into history of the exploits of two distinct warriors, William of Normandy and Robert Guiscard, who both happened to be Normans. But it is true that William maintained contacts with his confrères in the Mediterranean, that he learned military skills and techniques from them, and that, learning from them the importance of Byzantium, he sent many young Normans there to acquire useful knowledge and technology; a notable envoy to Constantinople was Ivo of Bellême, Bishop of Sees.[52]

As to whether there was continuity or discontinuity between the post-1050 Normandy and the situation under the five earlier dukes, once again the experts are divided. The old view of Normandy before 1066, popular in the 1940s and 1950s, was that, as part of the Europe-wide phenomenon of extreme violence, disorder and militarization, a new military aristocracy arose in the eleventh century and cut a swathe through the old oligarchy; this new class of knights was allegedly the basis on which William built his power.[53] Much scholarly ink has been spilled over the meaning of the Latin word *miles*: does it mean a 'knight' in the sense familiar from the high Middle Ages or does it simply denote a mounted soldier? The most persuasive view is that there was no 'new class', even though some formerly obscure families did start to climb the greasy pole to positions of high influence: often mentioned are the Montforts, Beaumonts, Bernons and Tosnys. The notion of 'knight-hood' is an anachronistic displacement from the period after 1066, so there was no 'rise of the knights' but simply an aristocracy perceiving itself in a new, highly martial, way; the military culture and ethos may have changed but the class composition of the ruling élite remained the same.[54]

Similar considerations apply to the vexed question of feudalism. It is often said that Normandy was a feudal state and introduced the 'feudal system' to England in 1066. However, there was not, contrary to the myth, any fully articulated 'system' that the Normans took to England in 1066, and medieval feudalism is a much later development. The best scholarship envisages Normandy as much more inchoate than this; at best we can talk of 'pre-feudalism' or 'proto-feudalism'.[55] William drew service from his vassals not by a fixed system of military duties but through the fearsome charisma of his personality; in many ways he was more like a Latin American *caudillo* of the nineteenth century than a feudal lord properly so-called. Under feudalism the individual fief was held not absolutely but contingently, depending on a set of well-defined obligations. William's system of government was nothing like so clear-cut, being essentially a loose collection of duties based on a purely personal dependence. As a distinguished historian of the period has written: 'Norman society in 1066 . . . .. was one in which the holder of a dependent tenure was not a prestigious figure in a reasonably articulate hierarchy, but usually a simple soldier whose main responsibility was to fight . . . .. pre-1066 Norman feudalism was probably not much more than a loose association in fidelity.'[56]

In a sense, this makes William's creation of an efficient Norman military machine all the more impressive. When he called out the armed levies of his counts and barons, they responded to the call not out of a tightly feudal system of fixed military quotas and fixed periods of service but in response to kinship ties or a personal relationship with Duke William.[57] Naturally, those beneath him in the hierarchy feared that if they did not heed his appeal their lands would be taken from them, but this is still a long way from an ineluctable nexus binding liege-lords to vassals, even though historians of an earlier era were adamant that pre-1066 Normandy was feudal and therefore there 'must have been' fixed quotas.[58] It was only after 1066, when William faced problems of an entirely different dimension, that quotas of military contingents and terms of service became paramount. Before this date in Normandy there was only a tangle of inchoate feudal customs, some established from below and the result of custom rather than imposed from above and the result of law.[59]

What William lost in terms of predictability through not presiding over a feudal system he gained in flexibility. Whereas in Anglo-Saxon England the military levy called out in times of national emergency was required to serve for forty days and not a day longer, in Normandy William could keep his troops in the field as long as he needed them.[60] Naturally, this informal arrangement was always likely to break down if a warleader sustained serious military reverses, but by 1066 William was in the very rare position of never having lost a battle he had fought nor failed to take a citadel or castle he had besieged. Once again we see the personalist nature of William's hegemony in Normandy: his power was not a product of feudalism but depended on older, Norse, values and moral imperatives, where men followed a warchief as long as he could inspire or constrain them, as long as he won victories and distributed the spoils.

By 1060 the Normans had the reputation for being the finest cavalrymen in Europe. Each lord and sub-lord in Normandy had his own band of highly skilled horsemen who fought in groups or *conrois* which often combined and executed complex manoeuvres together. It is difficult to overestimate how hard the Norman warrior class worked to hone their martial skills, sustaining themselves through hours of backbreaking practice each day by the thought that they were Europe's élite warrior caste. Apart from their general prowess in arms, the Norman cavalry had the edge over their opponents in two main areas: their horses were bigger and stronger, and they had developed special battle lances that made their mounted charges almost irresistible.[61]

The Normans were noted for their selective breeding of warhorses. Here we see clearly the interaction of social and military factors, for the warrior élite had perforce to be also a socio-economic élite as selective breeding was expensive (to say nothing of the specialist training of cavalrymen) and as such required the generation of a considerable economic surplus. The famous *destrier* or battle-steed on which the Norman knights went into battle stood about fourteen hands high, as against the normal ten hands of the indigenous horse of north-western Europe. Although the great nobles of Normandy had their own stud farms, in the area of selective breeding they were eclipsed by the monasteries, who made this aspect of animal eugenics their speciality, demonstrating once again the value of William's encouragement of the monastic movement. Normandy needed to be rich in the supply of chargers, for each Norman knight rode to battle with three mounts beside his *destrier*: one to ride to the battlefield, so as to keep the *destrier* fresh for the actual combat, another for his squire and a third for his baggage and impedimenta, for it was the custom for knights to change into their armour only when they had reached the battleground.[62]

It is interesting to observe Viking Normandy and Scandinavian Britain heading in different military directions in the first half of the eleventh century. Before Duke Willliam's reign cavalry had been far more important in England than in Normandy, but under King Cnut resources were switched to the navy, with the construction of a powerful fleet and the neglect of warhorses; some speculate that English studs had been disrupted during the protracted wars of Ethelred's reign (978–1016). At all events, by the time of Val-ès-Dunes, Normandy had already overtaken England in the provision of a cavalry arm.

However, it should be made clear that the Anglo-Saxon élite in England *chose* to neglect cavalry as a matter of policy; there is no question of the Normans' opening up a technological and military gap over England, an idea which is refuted straight away by the virtual identity of the arms, armour and equipment in both societies; in particular, missile technology was at the same level and one should beware of the seductive legend that the Normans had a superiority in archery or the technology of the bow.[63] Both Normans and Saxons wore the hauberk or long coat of mail, with a coif of mail around the head, similar in appearance to the Balaclava helmet. Except for a handful of the most powerful counts, ordinary knights appear to have fought with their legs unprotected, mobility of the lower limbs being assured by criss-cross bindings. Mail as a form of armour gave some protection against most weapons, though not against a direct sword slash, a blow from a two-handed axe or a quarrel shot at close range from a crossbow.

The equipment of warriors was completed by helmets in the shape of conical domes, with a metal bar over the nose called a nasel and a neck-guard at the back; these helmets were made of curved plates, fitted inside a circular headband. The most spectacular item in the knight's equipage was the kite-shaped shield, which was standard issue for cavalrymen as, unlike the circular shield often preferred by infantrymen, it fitted neatly into the space between the rider and his mount without touching the animal. These shields were made of wood, covered in leather, with a reinforcing strip of metal around the rim, and with a central dome-shaped boss. Although it is commonly believed that the Normans used exclusively kite-shaped shields and the Saxons wielded circular ones, the truth is that both sides used both kinds.[64]

The one really interesting Norman military innovation was the couched lance, which was just coming into fashion around the time of William's later wars in France. Although the Normans continued to use spears for stabbing, thrusting and throwing, they had begun to experiment with the use of lances as a weapon of last resort, in case their initial attack with swords failed to make the required impact. Between 9 and 11 feet long, made from ash or applewood, such lances could be used either with an overarm thrust, as in the Ancient World, or underarm, in a couched position. Couching the lance concentrated the weight and velocity of horse and horseman at a target to achieve maximum momentum, and long stirrups and deep saddles gave the rider a firm seat and optimum purchase. Clearly there was a danger that it might be difficult or impossible to withdraw the lance from a transfixed foe, so they were fitted with cross-pieces to prevent too deep penetration into the flesh.[65]

The couched lance, familiar from medieval jousts, was normally used against enemy cavalry, and was one of the factors giving rise to the legend of the invincibility of the Norman knight. The use of heavily mounted cavalry in crushing charges with the couched lance astonished the Byzantines, against whom the Normans of southern Italy and Sicily increasingly warred in the late eleventh century, and the noted emperor's daughter and historian Anna Comnena asserted that such a charge could shatter the walls of Jericho.[66] Although cavalry were usually employed as shock troops against other cavalry, it did not escape the notice of William and other Norman captains that the charge with the couched lance could also be used against infantry defending high ground.[67]

By 1063, then, Duke William could bask in the achievement of a centralized political system, with every facet rigidly in his control, and a highly efficient war machine. Out of a likely population for Normandy of one million souls, William could in a grave emergency put about 30,000 soldiers in the field. The thirty-six-year-old duke was feared as peerless warrior, able strategist and supremely ruthless politician. All sources agree that he was a cold, grim and overweeningly ambitious man, who could be extremely harsh and cruel and brooked no opposition to his personal will; he was violent but scheming, deadly as a snake when he struck but prepared to be as patient as Job to achieve his eventual ends.

There are no reliable portraits of William, but the sources concur that he was a heavily-built, thickset man with a tendency to run to fat, and that this corpulence manifested itself increasingly from middle age. Impeccable scholarship has established that he was 5 feet 10 inches in height – very tall for those times – and had a harsh guttural voice. All eyewitnesses and contemporary chroniclers speak of his indomitable willpower, his physical strength and stamina, his ruthlessness and his dogged determination to see through to the end any project he put in hand.[68]

His frugality in eating and drinking has been much commented on, so that the incipient obesity must not have been due to overindulgence but have had a genetic cause. He was apparently very close to being teetotal and deplored drunkenness in the same obsessive way that, nine hundred years later, Hitler would deplore smoking. Overindulgence in wine was a very serious offence at William's court – a fact all the more remarkable when one considers the general propensity to imbibe in the eleventh century. Nor, unlike most of the autocrats of his time, was he a womanizer; he remained devoted to his wife Matilda and could even be considered uxorious.[69]

Matilda, apparently a woman tiny enough to be classified as a dwarf by modern standards, was a strong personality in her own right, who on at least one occasion publicly opposed her husband's will. Her small stature notwithstanding, she was remarkably fertile as a childbearer and presented William with four sons and six daughters. Little is known about the girls except their names – Cecily, Constance, Matilda, Adela, Adelaide and Agatha – but, of the four sons, three were destined to play a major role in history. The second son, Richard, was shortlived and died in his early twenties but the eldest son, Robert (born in 1051), took his rightful place as the seventh Duke of Normandy in 1087. The other two boys attained an even higher niche in history, for the third son, William (born about 1060 and later nicknamed Rufus), was king of England from 1087 to 1100, while the fourth, Henry, became the first English king of that name and reigned until 1135.[70]

Although is has been suggested that William had a grim line in gallows humour, most observers found him overbearing and terrifying; the only person known to have elicited a more gracious amd affable side to his personality was St Anselm, in the period after 1078, when he was Abbot of Bec.[71] And if he was free from the usual rulers' 'sins' of lechery and gluttony, he did possess one of the seven deadly sins in full measure: avarice. Even allowing for the fact that he often had to raise substantial revenues to pay mercenaries, William's tax-gathering methods were cruel and inhuman, and his personal rapacity notorious. His love of gold and silver became infamous in later years and in the last two years of his life is twice emphasized by the Anglo-Saxon Chronicle as an egregious shortcoming.[72]

Avarice aside, the one clear distinguishing mark of William was his cruelty. The atrocities at Alençon in 1051 would be matched by similar horrors at Mantes in 1087, while if the devastation of northern England in 1069–70, in the euphemistically named 'harrying of the North', was not a war crime, then that term has no meaning. William's troops often looted, raped and pillaged their way through towns with his consent; there was no question of 'licentious soldiery' being out of control, for every man in his army had a mortal terror of him and would never disobey an express order from him not to sack a town. The only thing that can be said in extenuation of William was that he was sparing of the death penalty for aristocrats guilty of rebellion or other high political crimes. But against this in turn can be set the duke's liking for mutilation and for confining people for a lifetime in the most noisome dungeons; many were the prisoners 'found dead' in their cells.[73]

There is also strong circumstantial evidence that William favoured the old Norman 'remedy' of poisoning dangerous rivals or those who, inconveniently, had a superior claim to some territory he coveted. The eleventh century was an era rich in suspicious deaths – in England during the duke's rise to power alone those of Harthacnut, Edward the Atheling and Lord Godwin can be so classified – but Normandy had more than its fair share.[74] Alan III, Count of Brittany, was poisoned in 1040 by agents directed by powerful figures at the Norman court, and his son Conan also died of poison, so very conveniently for William, in 1066. Walter, Count of the Vexin, a nephew of Edward the Confessor, together with his wife Biota, died of poison just after being William's guests at Falaise. Walter's 'crime' was to have been a pretender to the land of Maine when William lusted after it in 1063.[75]

The death of another claimant to the same land was even more mysterious and even more convenient. Herbert Bacco, deadly rival of Geoffrey of Mayenne, made a deal with William to support the duke in the conquest of Maine on condition he was then allowed to hold the county as a fief of Normandy; he also pledged that if he died childless, the sovereignty over the territory would pass entirely to William. Immediately after the conquest of Maine in 1063 Herbert died mysteriously, childless.[76] William's apologists have tried to defend him against the charge of poisoning, but the stories persist. Because of the lack of modern forensic evidence, each one can be dismantled in a way favourable to William, but there are just too many of them for this method to be ultimately convincing. The most sober conclusion is the one Kant came to about ghosts: that while one can be sceptical about each individual instance, the sum total presents a body of evidence difficult to ignore.

The harsh, cold cruelty of William can be explained, though not justified, by his troubled childhood. Even if some of the more far-fetched stories about the deadly peril in which the young duke stood can be discounted, there can be no doubt that the iron entered into his soul at this time, and that he became convinced that power was the be-all and end-all in this world; such a perception is the norm for all who have suffered disturbed childhoods, as thousands of case studies demonstrate. It may be that in some obscure, possibly unconscious sense William blamed his father for his predicament and that is why he always favoured his maternal over his paternal kin.[77] It was noteworthy that Herlève's family controlled the strongholds of Bayeux, Thury-Harcourt, La Ferté-Mace, Mortain and Avranches, while his paternal connections were driven into revolt as pretenders. Even though common sense suggests that William could never have favoured his father's family as he favoured his half-siblings, the sons of Herlève, since these had no claim through the legitimate dynasty of Normandy, nevertheless there is room to wonder whether there may not have been a psychological 'superplus' at work here, in that he unconsciously associated paternal kin with the principles of abandonment, betrayal and chaos.

The juvenile sensation of being an Ishmael, with every man's hand turned against him, may also account for a self-justifying, almost paranoid streak in William. It was not enough for him that he could prevail because he had the power; he had also to be seen to be always in the right. The obsession with himself as an injured party, which at another level he must have known was absurd, accounts for the Byzantine machiavellianism with Herbert Bacco before the invasion of Maine. It was important for William not just to defeat Geoffrey of Mayenne in battle but to be able to claim that his invasion of Maine was in pursuit of a rightful claim to the county, which he had inherited as a result of his deal with Herbert. The mixture of high talent as a warrior and serpentine deviousness as a politician was a hard one for any opponent to deal with, as other great European generals were about to learn to their cost.

6

Svein Estrithson

Harald remained in Kiev for two years, until 1045, for reasons that remain obscure. Was Harald advising Yaroslav on the protracted negotiations with Byzantium that followed the disastrous war of 1043? Or was Yaroslav, aware of the Norse custom of polygamy, reluctant to allow his daughter to depart for a life in the northern lands, where she might be set aside on a whim? Maybe Harald was hoping to use the prosperous state treasury of Kiev as a kind of bank in which he could deposit the vast treasure which, so Adam of Bremen reports, it took twelve of the strongest young men to lift? For a while at least Harald was prepared to let the pent-up waves of his fame wash over him in Russia, as more and more tales of his exploits percolated from Byzantium. It was even said that there was a great marble lion in Piraeus (where Harald had never been) covered with runic inscriptions describing his deeds of valour.[1]

But at last Harald was able to return to his homeland. Travelling from Kiev via Novgorod, he arrived in the spring of 1045 with a private army at Ladoga on Lake Ladoga, not far from present-day St Petersburg, and from there, in the summer, entered Sweden. Olaf, king of Sweden, was Elizabeth's grandfather and Astrid, the king's sister, was the mother of Svein Estrithson, then also fortuitously at the court of Sweden. At this

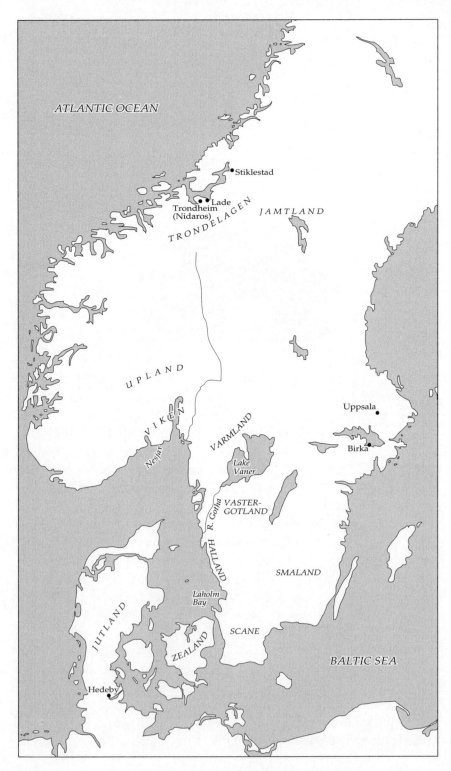

ATLANTIC OCEAN

•Stiklestad

Lade•
Trondheim
(Nidaros)

TRONDELAGEN

JAMTLAND

UPLAND

VIKEN

Nesjar

VARMLAND

Uppsala•

Lake
Vaner

Birka•

R. Gotha

*VASTER-
GOTLAND*

HALLAND

SMALAND

Laholm
Bay

JUTLAND

ZEALAND

SCANE

BALTIC SEA

Hedeby

The Viking homelands

stage Harald's relations with the man who was to be his lifelong enemy were cordial but it may be, as Svein later alleged, that Harald was merely using him and everyone he met for his own design of gaining the Norwegian throne. Svein began to interest him in an alliance, with the aim of securing kingdoms for them both: Svein in Denmark and Harald in Norway.

Harald did indeed have his eye on the Norwegian throne, but his ambition was unlikely to be realized in the short term, for the young king Magnus was a ruler of exceptional quality: wise and enlightened in policy as well as a doughty warrior in battle. The alliance of Cnut and the Norwegian aristocracy which overthrew Olaf Sigurdsson at Stiklestad did not prosper, especially in face of the lightning growth of the cult of the late king, who was now openly referred to as 'St Olaf'. Cnut's son Svein, who ruled Norway from Denmark from 1030 to 1034, made the further mistake of trying to turn the northern kingdom into an economic appanage of the Danes. A humiliating attempt to summon a *thing* in Nidaros in the winter of 1033–34, which no one attended, led Svein to fear the worst and withdraw to Denmark. In 1035 Magnus, son of Olaf Sigurdsson, was proclaimed king and restored effortlessly.[2]

Cnut died in 1036 and there ensued the struggle for mastery between Harold Harefoot and Harthacnut over the succession in England. In order to concentrate on this and to ensure he was not attacked in the rear by Norway, Harthacnut signed a treaty with Magnus at the mouth of the Gotha river in 1038. Harthacnut recognized the independence of Norway and, in a separate compact, it was agreed that when one of them died the other would inherit his kingdom. Having settled Norway's external relations, Magnus then faced the problem of the Norwegian aristocracy who (in his eyes) had murdered his father. He identified Kalv Arnesson as the chief culprit, invited him to tour the battlefield of Stiklestad with him, and there and then accused him of Olaf's murder. Kalv stowed all his portable property on board ship and left the kingdom the very same night, fleeing first to Thorfinn, Earl of the Orkneys, and later embarking on a career as a pirate in Ireland and the north of Scotland.[3]

Magnus then effectively declared war on the other great Norwegian oligarchs who had opposed Olaf at Stiklestad, confiscating their estates and refusing them due legal process. Einar Tambarskjelver, the greatest magnate of all, who had taken no part in the Stiklestad campaign against Olaf but who had been a deadly rival of Kalv, became a close friend and adviser of Magnus and admonished him not to risk civil war by such draconian actions. According to tradition, Magnus paid no heed and was determined to continue with his vendetta, until he was won over by a song entitled 'Bersoglisvisur', composed by the skald Sighvat Thordsson. Seeing the light, Magnus had a sudden change of heart, abandoned his autocratic ways and pledged himself to the rule of law.[4]

In 1042 Harthacnut died, to be succeeded in England by Edward the Confessor. In accordance with the Gotha river agreement, Magnus claimed Denmark as his own and set out to take it by force but was acclaimed king without having to fight; to Edward the Confessor he wrote that out of compassion for his harsh early life he would waive his claim to the English throne for Edward's lifetime but reserved his right to reclaim it then. Yet by 1045 he was writing to Edward in harsher terms and there is even evidence that he intended to invade England that year until war with Svein Estrithson supervened.[5]

The genius of the young Magnus as king showed itself in his ability to deal with three or four serious crises simultaneously. A running sore throughout his reign was the situation in the Orkneys, nominally a Norwegian possession but in reality virtually independent. At the time of Magnus's accession the Orkneys were ruled by Earl Thorfinn, Sigurd's son and uncle to Rognvald Brusisson. Wishing to assert sovereignty over the islands, Magnus sent Rognvald Brusisson to Kirkwall, capital of the Orkneys, to request that Thorfinn should give Rognvald his patrimony, viz. a third part of the islands. Thorfinn acceded but the contumacious Rognvald brooded away, convinced he should really have been given *two-thirds* of the Orkneys and Shetlands – the share his father Brusi had had in St Olaf's day. The result was a feud that endured for eight years (1038–46).[6]

To assuage Brusisson's feelings Thorfinn agreed to make over two-thirds of the Orkneys to Rognvald, provided he retained the Shetlands, but Brusisson's was an all-or-nothing mentality. Finally, in 1046, Thorfinn, having built up a powerful military following in the Shetlands and northern Scotland, invaded Rognvald's domain, overran his territories and forced him to flee for his life to Norway. There he lamented his fate to a sympathetic Magnus; preoccupied with other wars, Magnus could not give him much direct help but promised Kalv Arnesson a pardon if he would fight for Rognvald. Brusisson raised a new fleet, which clashed with Thorfinn's armada in the Pentland Firth in 1046, while Kalv Arnesson and his forces looked on, undecided which side to support. Finally, finding himself in danger of defeat, Thorfinn sent an urgent plea to Kalv, who at last committed himself and was instrumental in Rognvald's rout. Thorfinn then took possession of all the islands and Kalv Rognvald's old domain in the Shetlands.[7]

Brusisson was reduced to desperate measures. In the winter of 1046 he led a commando raid with a single ship's crew, hoping to assassinate Thorfinn in Pomona. The raiding party burnt down the earl's house, but Thorfinn and his wife escaped and rowed over to Caithness. Nothing daunted, Thorfinn tried to turn the tables on Rognvald, burning down his abode just before Christmas. Rognvald got clear of the blazing house but was found skulking on the shore by one of Thorfinn's men named Thorkel Fosterer. Concealing the news of their leader's death, Thorfinn then surprised Rognvald's followers in Kirkwall, massacred most of them, and executed thirty members of Magnus's personal bodyguard that he had sent over with Rognvald, sparing just one so that he could take the news back to Magnus. Incandescent with rage, Magnus was locked in warfare on several fronts and unable to take punitive action. In an evil hour Thorfinn took it into his head to journey to Norway, plead repentance and secure a lasting peace. The hard-pressed Magnus was minded to agree, but then the solitary bodyguard whom Thorfinn had spared claimed the right of blood-feud since Thorfinn had massacred his brother. Thorfinn was then forced to run for his life before judgement could be passed on him.[8]

Yet far more serious than Thorfinn's high-handed actions in the Orkneys was the disaffection of Svein Estrithson, son of Earl Ulf, whose mother was Astrid, Cnut's sister, and who claimed to have been named as heir by Edward the Confessor in England and to be the nearest blood descendant of Cnut's line. With consummate cunning, Svein did not at first reveal the scope of his ambitions, but pretended to be a man resigned to the buffets of Fate. Making the acquaintance of Magnus at the Gotha river in 1038, he became the king's chief adviser and confidant. Magnus was mightily taken with him, created him an earl and, when Denmark acclaimed him as its king in 1042, appointed him his viceroy in that country, following the example of Cnut, who had made Svein's father his plenipotentiary in Denmark while he ruled in England. The shrewd Einar Tambarskjelver, who was genuinely devoted to Magnus, warned the young king that this was a foolish act, as it placed temptation within reach of a supremely ambitious man. 'Too great an earl, too great an earl!' were Einar's resigned but prophetic words. Magnus rewarded Einar's fidelity by rounding on him, pointing out that he was forever running down the men he made earls: either they were useless or they were too strong.[9]

Despite the claims of his apologists, it is abundantly clear that Svein swore an oath of loyalty to Magnus and therefore that his subsequent actions were arrant treachery. At first Svein bided his time in Denmark, making himself a very popular ruler and finding reasons to keep out of the ferocious fighting Magnus found himself involved in during the year 1043. The Slavic Rus or Wends who had pushed west as far as the Elbe had an independent kingdom based on the fortified town of Jomsborg, which paid nominal allegiance to Magnus, but in 1043 they poured over the border in large-scale raids. Faced with a revolt against his authority by the Vendland people of Jomsborg, Magnus showed his harsh side: he sacked the fortress, razed the town to the ground and laid waste the countryside round about; Svein managed to be absent in Sweden during this campaign. Having forced the submission of the Wends, Magnus went north to Jutland to deal with a fleet of independent Vikings, whom he defeated in a sea battle off Rugen.[10]

Hearing that most of Magnus's land army had been demobilized, Svein Estrithson decided to strike. He invaded Denmark with an army lent him by the friendly Swedish king, declared himself the rightful successor of Cnut, and was well received by the peoples of Lund, Zealand and Funen. The Wends, seeing the authority of Magnus apparently in ruins, repudiated their treaty with him and went on the rampage. Calling up his land army again, albeit with reduced numbers, Magnus waited until the Wends reached Ribe. Marching to Hedeby, some twenty miles north-west of Kiel, together with his kinsman Otto, the Duke of Brunswick, he intercepted the Wends on 28 September at Haithabu on Lyrsog heath. After a long, hard-fought battle, he routed the Wends with great slaughter.[11]

Then he turned to deal with the treacherous Svein. On 18 December 1043 he defeated him in a great sea battle at Aarhus in Jutland, taking seven of Svein's ships as prizes. He dogged Svein relentlessly through Denmark, pursuing him through Funen, Zealand, Scania and Lund, until Svein finally sought refuge in Sweden. Denmark then submitted to Magnus, but he did not feel confident enough to return to Norway until the spring of 1044. As soon as he had retired, Svein again invaded from Sweden and was again rapturously received by the Danes. Once more Magnus headed south and this time he inflicted a severe defeat on Svein at Helganes, east of Aarhus in northern Jutland. Svein repeated the flight of the winter before, into Sweden, and it was there, in 1045, that he met Harald Sigurdsson on his return from Kiev. Magnus meanwhile, by visiting severe punishments on the disloyal Danes and trying to extirpate whole communities that had been particularly supportive of Svein, merely alienated Denmark even further.[12]

In 1045 Magnus was riding high. He seemed invincible in battle, had demonstrated his military superiority over Svein Estrithson and, angered by a reply from Edward the Confessor claiming that the English throne was rightly his, was contemplating an invasion of England. Edward was seriously alarmed and determined to placate Magnus by strict neutrality in the conflict between him and Svein; when Estrithson asked for help in his war against Norway, Edward turned him down on the grounds that Magnus's fleet was too large. At all points Magnus seemed poised for outright victory in Scandinavia. Suddenly Svein reappeared, having secured the alliance of Harald Hardrada.[13]

Harald's strategy was first to try to negotiate with Magnus, with the implied threat of a campaign in alliance with Svein if he did not get what he wanted. He proceeded to Denmark from Sweden in a beautiful Viking ship with a gilt dragon's head and dragon's tail and a sumptuous sail woven with the fabrics of Byzantium. He found Magnus's fleet anchored at Oresund on the coast of Skane, and the appearance of this imposing ship caused a sensation among the king's oarsmen. Magnus sent a herald to ask the stranger's business and Harald adopted his favourite trick of standing forth himself as his own envoy and answering in the third person as if on behalf of a superior. When the 'envoy' asked how Harald Sigurdsson, the king's uncle, would be received by Magnus, the reply was: 'With joy and open arms.' We can only speculate about the circumstances of the first meeting between these two great warriors. Magnus, about twenty-five at the time and thus five years Harald's junior, was said to be a man of medium height, long-faced, light-haired, clear-complexioned; admired by enemies as well as friends, he was brisk, decisive, eloquent, generous and, if the sagas may be believed, quick to anger.

Serious negotiations then began. Harald asked if Magnus, who was childless, would recognize him as his heir apparent and give him half the kingdom as an earnest of this. Magnus referred the request to his council, at which Einar Tambarskjelver first appeared as Harald's unregenerate enemy: Einar suggested that as a *quid pro quo* Harald should share half his treasure with Magnus – for by this time news of the fabulous hoard brought back from Byzantium had spread. The greedy, gold-loving Harald refused the suggestion indignantly, to the angry stupefaction of Einar, who considered it a generous offer and reproached Harald for his selfishness: he added, tauntingly, that Magnus had defeated all Norway's enemies while Harald was making money in

Constantinople and that, as long as he had any voice in the kingdom, Norway would never be divided on any other basis.[14]

Harald took this as a declaration of war and returned to Sweden to seal a formal alliance with Svein Estrithson. Their joint expedition set out and was soon harrying Funen and Zealand with fire and sword, Harald playing the role of the old Viking raider with gusto, Svein less enthusiastically, as he could only alienate the people by such depredations. It is abundantly clear that in this era Scandinavians took slaves from their own people, for the Icelandic bard Valgard wrote about Harald and Svein's raid on Zealand with a motley force of Swedes, Danes and Norwegians: 'The Danes, those who still lived, fled away but fair women were taken. Locked fetters held the women's bodies. Many women passed before you [Harald] to the ships; fetters bit greedily the bright-fleshed ones.'[15]

Magnus ordered a general levy of his kingdom to meet the renewed threat in the south, but baulked at fighting Harald and Svein together, so used diplomacy to try to detach Harald from his alliance of convenience. Secret messages were sent from Magnus to Harald, stressing the ties of kinship, pointing out the near-sacrilegious folly whereby the son of the saintly Olaf waged war on Olaf's half-brother, and renewing the offer to divide the kingdom on the exchange of half Harald's treasure. Svein soon got wind of these overtures, and one night there was a furious row when he made slighting remarks about the scant success achieved by Harald's beloved war-banner 'Land Ravager'. Harald replied coldly that there was no guarantee he would always be carrying Land Ravager into battle against Magnus in the future. Svein now stated openly the suspicion he had always harboured in his own mind – that Harald had only fought Magnus so far to wrest concessions from him. Harald replied that despite the sacred ties of kinship binding him to Magnus, he had always remained true to his word given to Svein – which was more than Svein could say about the word *he* had given to Magnus.

The two men parted angrily, and Harald told his lieutenants that he would not sleep that night in his ship, as he suspected treachery. To test Svein's intentions he left a block of wood wrapped up in his bunk and, sure enough, that very night an assassin climbed on board ship and severed the block of wood with an axe. There could be no denying a murder attempt on such visible evidence. Harald told his men to row all night and get clear of Svein's territory. His problem now was that he was out on a limb, having broken with Svein without having an accord with Magnus. Hearing that Magnus's fleet was on its way south to engage Svein's, Harald slipped into Norway by the back door, hoping to have himself proclaimed king in Magnus's absence. In his homeland of Oplandende he received a lukewarm reception – proving the truth of the old saw that a prophet is not without honour save in his own country – but he fared better in the district of Gudbandsal, where he was helped by his powerful kinsman Thor of Seig. Harald convened a *thing* where Thor proclaimed him king, and recruits began to trickle in. All seemed set for civil war, when Magnus suddenly asked for a fresh conference with his uncle.[16]

There are conflicting accounts of the basis on which peace was finally made between Harald and Magnus. Some say that Magnus stepped up to Harald at the council with two reeds in his hand, held one of them out to him and said: 'With this reed I give you half of Norway.' The trouble with this story is that Magnus did *not* give Harald half of Norway. The aristocratic advisers on either side were adamant that Norway should not be divided, as in Harald's initial proposal, but that Magnus and Harald should be joint kings, with joint sovereignty over an undivided realm, and that, if Magnus remained childless, Harald would succeed him. In some sources it is stated that Harald finally agreed to give Magnus half his treasure, but this is far less certain. For one thing, Einar Tambarskjelver always refused to recognize Harald as joint king; had Harald shared his treasure with Magnus, as Einar himself had originally suggested, he would have had no legitimate cause or basis for continued opposition to Harald. The monk-annalist Theodric, too, states that the agreement was that the two men should be joint sovereigns in Norway but that, because Harald failed to share his treasure, Magnus would be the sole king in Denmark.[17]

Snorre Sturlusson, too, seems undecided in his verdict on the divided treasure. His story is that Harald laid out a vast quantity of gold and silver and challenged Magnus to match it. Magnus said his treasury was bare because of the constant wars since 1042 and all he had to offer was a ring. He took it off and showed it to Harald, who examined it quizzically, then remarked it was little enough for a man who claimed two kingdoms, especially as his very ownership of the ring was doubtful. Magnus replied loftily that if he was not the owner of the ring, he could scarcely claim to be owner of anything, since his father Olaf had given it to him. Harald replied with a cynical laugh that he did not doubt it; the ring originally belonged to *his* father, Sigurd Syr, but Olaf had expropriated it: 'In truth it was not a good time for small kings in Norway when thy father was in power.' Significantly, though, there is no definite statement that Harald's treasure *was* divided.[18]

About the reasons for the establishment of the joint sovereignty, however, there is near unanimity. All the powerful magnates and chieftains of Norway were determined not to become embroiled in a fratricidal civil war between too close kin and were as adamant on this point as on their insistence that there should be joint sovereignty rather than division of the realm. From Magnus's point of view three main considerations held. If he denied Harald his claim to kingship, he would have to live in permanent fear of a *coup* from a man who had a large following. How, then, could he ever leave Norway to deal effectively with Svein Estrithson? He could not fight Harald and Svein together and would therefore have to come to an agreement with one of them. Since Svein was insistent on retaining Denmark as the price of any compact, the pluses and minuses clearly indicated an alliance with Harald. Moreover, Svein was as impecunious as he (Magnus) was, and if he was ever to achieve his ambition of conquering England and restoring Cnut's empire, he needed the direct or indirect use of Harald's treasure, to say nothing of the military know-how he had acquired in Byzantium.[19]

Needless to say, the joint kingship agreed in 1046 engendered many problems unforeseen or unresolved in the original compact. Each king had his separate court, courtiers and entourage, but rivalry and jealousy between them bred constant problems. Harald, a natural autocrat, was harsh and uncompromising and soon acquired the title that would stay with him for ever – Hardrada, the hard ruler; he was also known as 'the land ravager' and, more simply, 'Harald the bad'. Magnus, by contrast, was widely perceived to be generous and compassionate and Harald was frequently contrasted with him to the uncle's disadvantage.[20] There was always particular tension whenever the two kings met, especially as the implacable Einar Tambarskjelver, who enjoyed Magnus's protection, openly referred to Harald as a usurper and lost no opportunity to foment discord between him and Magnus.

Two very different stories illustrate the tensions between the joint sovereigns. On one occasion when they were feasting in the same hall, the renowned bard Arnorr Hordarson arose to recite two lays, one for each of the kings. Wrongly choosing to recite for Magnus first, on the ground that the young are more hot-tempered and impatient than their elders, Hordarson recounted a magnificent tale of adventure involving the Orkney earls with a setting ranging across the ocean to Iceland. Harald interrupted to ask Magnus sardonically how he could bear to sit there and listen to the adventures of other men, but Magnus replied that he would be praised in due course, which he was. Hordarsson then recited a song called the 'Black Goose' lay for Harald, which was a much more routine composition. Harald was then asked, as a man reputed to be a shrewd judge of poetry, which of the two lays was better. Ruefully he declared that the Black Goose lay would soon fade into oblivion but that the song composed for Magnus would live for ever.[21]

In the spring of 1047 there was an even more serious clash. The two kings ordered a universal call-up in Norway, hoping to deal once and for all with Svein Estrithson, and agreed a general mustering point. Harald was first at the rendezvous and moored his ships in the part of the harbour reserved for the king. When Magnus arrived and found 'his' berth taken, he flew into a rage and ordered his ships to form battle stations. Harald was obliged to order his ships out of the royal anchorage to avoid a bloody battle there and then. A while later, when Magnus's vessels had supplanted his, he boarded Magnus's ship and remarked wryly that he thought he was among friends at the rendezvous but the events of the past few hours had disabused him. Glancing condescendingly at Magnus, he said witheringly: 'It is a truth that childhood is hasty, and I will only consider it as a childish freak.' Magnus answered coldly that childhood had nothing to do with it; it was a maxim in his family to hold one's own; he pointed out that, while determined to keep to his agreement with Harald, he relinquished none of his royal prerogatives. Harald riposted that the prerogative of the wise was to give way before the foolish, turned on his heel and returned to his ship.[22]

As he brooded on this and other incidents, Harald became more than ever convinced that Magnus was trailing his coat. After all, the 1046 agreement merely stipulated that if the two kings arrived *together* at an anchorage Magnus was to have preference; nothing was said about the situation where Harald arrived *first*. If it now turned out that he had to give up his place to Magnus *whenever* the younger man arrived, what meaning could attach to the so-called sharing of the kingdom? Harald concluded that Magnus was itching to rescind the agreement and that conflict between them was inevitable once they had disposed of Svein Estrithson. But how to bell the cat? No matter how many victories they won against Svein, his hold on the affections of the Danish people seemed unaffected. Clearly 1047 would be a make-or-break year.

In the summer of that year Harald and Magnus campaigned vigorously in Denmark, laying waste Zealand and Jutland and forcing Svein eastwards to Skane; by the end of the year Svein was at his last gasp. Even as he lost the actual battles, Svein was trying to win the propaganda war by asserting that he had been named as successor in England and Denmark by both Harthacnut and Edward the Confessor.

His argument was twofold: that Edward had explicitly named him while he was in England; and that the alleged agreement between Magnus and Harthacnut at the Gotha river had never taken place. The weakness of Svein's argument was that, if he had been nominated as Edward's heir, why had he left England in the first place; and why had he fitted out a fleet to conquer Denmark, when, according to the alleged bequests from Edward and Harthacnut, he had already been named heir in Denmark as well? The truth is that, if Edward, notoriously slapdash with his pledges of the succession, had promised anyone it would have been Magnus, for the very good and prudent reason that it would have headed off his oft-threatened invasion.[23]

But Svein's dauntlessness and his invincible belief in his own star stood him in good stead. On the point of abandoning the hopeless struggle in Denmark and retiring permanently to Sweden, he was unexpectedly heartened by an apparent miracle, for Magnus suddenly died, seemingly in the very moment of total triumph. The details of his death are mysterious: most sources relate that he fell sick and died of an unknown disease while in pursuit of Svein, but cannot agree whether the sickness struck him in Zealand or Jutland. Inevitably in this era, whenever sudden death struck, foul play was suspected, and there were those who said that Harald Hardrada had simply poisoned a turbulent rival. Snorre Sturlusson stated baldly that Magnus drowned, without giving any details. Saxo Grammaticus claimed that he died near the town of Alsted when his horse was startled by a hare and bolted into a tree with spiky branches, which lifted Magnus out of the saddle and threw him to the ground, where he expired from multiple fractures. Some scholars think Saxo's account is allegorical, as it sounds too much like the Old Testament story of Absalom, since the hare is a symbol of doom, and since, anyway, no other source tells this story or places him in Alsted. Whatever the case, Magnus's death was interpreted by Svein and the Danes as a sign from God – an inference strengthened when Thor, Magnus's brother, told Svein that it was Magnus's dying wish that Svein (whose courage he secretly admired) should succeed him in Denmark. The deathbed bequest seems feasible, evincing an entirely plausible hatred of Harald Hardrada.[24]

On Magnus's death Harald immediately held an assembly of all the warriors in his fleet and announced that he would not respect Magnus's deathbed request, as he intended to pursue his claim to the throne of Denmark. A large faction, led by Einar Tambarskjelver, refused to continue the campaign in Denmark, on the ground that the immediate priority was to bury Magnus: Einar indeed declared pointedly that he would rather follow Magnus dead than any king living. Taking a large part of the fleet with him, Tambarskjelver sailed for Nidaros (Trondheim), where Magnus was laid in the tomb in St Clement's church alongside his father, St Olaf. Harald was forced to abandon the pursuit of Svein Estrithson. He proceeded to Viken in southern Norway and summoned a *thing* which proclaimed him king of all Norway; he was then recognized as king in all the districts of the land. At the age of thirty-two, he appeared to have achieved his every ambition.[25]

Harald's first acts as king were shrewd. As half-brother and most important surviving kinsman, he claimed to be the true inheritor of the mantle of St Olaf and wrapped himself in the mystique of Olaf's rapidly developing cult. To show his superiority to Magnus as statesman he settled the long-running crisis in the Orkneys, where Thorfinn had so signally set Magnus's authority at nought. Harald agreed to wipe the slate clean with Thorfinn and to forget his massacre of Magnus's bodyguard, provided Thorfinn accepted Norwegian suzerainty over the Orkneys and made a pilgrimage of repentance. Thorfinn accepted these terms, made a pilgrimage to Rome, visiting the emperor in Germany *en route*, and was ever afterwards a loyal supporter of Harald.[26]

In another clever move, in 1048 Harald made a dynastic alliance with the powerful Arnmodling family by marrying Thora, daughter of Thorberg Arnesson of Giske. This has puzzled some historians, since his wife Elizabeth was still alive, but the Scandinavians still practised polygamy, and indeed this may have been the reason for Yaroslav's reluctance to let his daughter depart for her husband's northern kingdom. On Harald's part, an additional motive for the bigamous match may have been a desire to humiliate Elizabeth, for he was a man who bore grudges and never forgot slights, and may not have truly forgiven Elizabeth's initial rejection of him. Of the bigamy itself there can be no question, since both Elizabeth and Thora were alive in 1066. Elizabeth bore him two daughters, Maria and Ingigerd, while Thora produced two sons, Magnus and Olaf. Some historians have rather lamely objected that a Christian king could not live in open bigamy without protests from the pope, but, as Harald demonstrated in 1061, he cared nothing for the pope's opinion.[27]

Determined to continue the war against Svein Estrithson, Harald built a new war fleet on the Nith river in 1048 and made a great show of steering his flagship galley westward out of the river. But Svein did not engage him in pitched battle, preferring to employ Fabian tactics, avoiding contact and engaging in hit-and-run guerrilla warfare. Fabian tactics were appropriate in more ways than one, for the long fifteen-year war that now commenced and that saw an almost annual invasion of Denmark reminds one of Hannibal's equally long and equally futile campaigns in Italy from 218 to 203 BC. There is something of a mystery about this long war, for Harald's tactics were equally short-term, *ad hoc* and inconsistent with his stated desire to conquer Denmark. Some have speculated that overpopulation was still a problem in Scandinavia and war its natural outlet, but it is more likely that Harald kept Norway on a permanent war footing as a way to solve his internal problems with the Norwegian aristocracy.[28]

In an attempt to cut the Gordian knot both combatants sent ambassadors to England in 1048, Harald to negotiate an alliance, Svein to ask once more for fifty ships. Svein's supporters advanced the absurd argument that Harald had sworn an oath of loyalty to Svein which he had violated by devastating Denmark and sacking churches – this last, presumably, to appeal to the pious Edward. Naturally, the English courtiers realized that Svein was trying to confuse the short-term agreement Harald made with him in 1045, when they were both fighting Magnus, with the very different situation after Magnus's death, and treated the argument with the contempt it deserved. Earl Godwin dearly wanted to intervene in the Scandinavian war on the side of his kinsman Svein, but Edward always opposed this. The Confessor saw clearly enough that, if there was ever a clear victor in the northern war, that king, whether Harald or Svein, would immediately look to England for his next conquest.[29]

In 1049 Harald again invaded Denmark and devastated the country; this time Svein's tactic was to counter-invade Norway. The year's hostilities petered out in stalemate, with Svein proposing a decisive test of strength next year at the Gotha river. In the spring of 1050 Harald arrived at the Gotha river with a large host but found no Svein there. Thinking that Svein would not dare to meet him in pitched battle, the overconfident Harald dismissed most of his *bondermen*, retaining his *hirdmen* and *lendermen* and the *bondermen* from the frontier marches. He then made a systematic sweep through Jutland, ravaging as he went and culminating in a devastating sack of Hedeby, a great centre of trade and Viking art, which never recovered from the destructive treatment meted out by Harald.[30]

As Harald sailed north into the Jutland sea with sixty ships laden with booty, he was suddenly intercepted at Thjoda by Svein with a fleet or more than a hundred vessels. Never one to be daunted by inferiority in numbers, Harald engaged the enemy inconclusively, then stood away north. Finding the wind against them, the Norwegians were compelled to shelter in the lee of Lesso, where they were swathed in a thick fog. Next morning they awoke to find the sea seemingly on fire, then realized it was the torches and flambeaux of the Danes piercing the mist. They weighed anchor and tried to escape north through the drifting fog, but, once clear visibility was restored, the Danish ships, lighter and not laden down with loot, began to gain on them. Harald at first tried to slow down the pursuers by throwing overboard all the booty; the ruse worked, as the Danes scattered to recover it. Then an angry Svein came on the scene, rebuked his men for their folly and sent his ships in pursuit again. Finding that jettisoning his food and liquor supplies did nothing to slow the pursuers down, Harald had all his Danish prisoners thrown into the sea. Faced with the clamour of his men, who begged him to rescue their friends and kinsmen, Svein was finally forced to break off the chase. For all that, he took seven straggling Norwegian vessels captive off Lesso and taught Harald that he was not to be underestimated.[31]

Quite apart from the interminable war with Svein Estrithson, Harald's reign was turbulent and eventful; he was 'the thunderbolt of the North, a pestilence to all the Danish islands', in the words of Adam of Bremen. His Christianity was skin-deep, for he thought nothing of sacking churches, as he notably did in Aarhus and Schleswig, and was unmoved by cries of 'Sacrilege!' when he diverted the funds gathered nationwide and placed as an offering at St Olaf's tomb in Nidaros for his own use as a war chest. His enemies alleged that he was a second Julian the Apostate, who despised Christianity as a religion of cowards, practised the runic arts secretly and would like to have returned Norway to the heroic pagan age of the Aesir and the Volsungs. This is undoubtedly an exaggeration, but it is clear he cared nothing for papal authority. As a result of the Church reforms of the early 1050s, Norway was placed under the canonical authority of Adalbert, Archbishop of Bremen. Harald refused to accept this, appointed his own bishops, and expelled both the bishop appointed from Bremen and the papal legates. When Pope Alexander II wrote to him in 1061, bidding him yield to the authority of the Vatican-appointed bishops, Harald replied blithely that he knew no authority in Norway save himself.[32]

What kept Harald firmly on the throne, proof against all challenges, was the economic prosperity Norway enjoyed under him. This was partly due to the booty brought back from the wars in Denmark, partly the result of the impetus given the domestic economy by the huge demand for war *matériel* of all kinds, but was above all the consequence of the demand-driven inflation engendered by the massive treasure he brought back from Byzantium. Harald regularized the coinage, and the volume of money in circulation in Scandinavia in these years tells its own story. As the noted Byzantine expert Dimitri Obolensky has written: 'The appearance of a series of strikingly accurate imitations of contemporary Byzantine coin types on Danish coins of the mid-eleventh century was almost certainly due to the arrival in Scandinavia of the vast treasure which Harald Hardrada is known to have accumulated while in imperial service.'[33]

Harald's life and career is in many ways the apotheosis of the Norsemen's role as transmission belt and professional middlemen between the societies of northern Europe and the Mediterranean. The network which linked Scandinavia to Asia via Russia and the Mediterranean was the most enduring Viking legacy and as the living embodiment of this process Harald Hardrada was truly the ultimate Viking. The one fixed point in a chaotic foreign policy was unswerving friendship for Byzantium, even though he had left Constantinople under a cloud. With the much more splendid title of king of Norway to his name, he still took pride in the old rank of Spatharocandidatus he had received in imperial service, and noted with sadness that the Varangian guard was becoming less and less Norse in composition, though this was a process that would intensify only after 1066.[34]

Harald also took a great interest in Byzantine affairs in general and had his spies send him regular reports on the personalities he had known there. Constantine IX had scarcely improved in wisdom since 1043. He virtually committed military suicide by his plan to 'Byzantify' the army. The backbone of Constantinople's fighting machine was the corps of Georgians, 50,000 strong, second in calibre only to the Varangians themselves. The absurd Constantine suggested they should buy their way out of military service on payment of a nominal fee, and nearly all the Georgians took him up on his offer, gravely weakening the empire. By 1050 the powerful Seljuks were masters of Baghdad and preparing to move against Constantinople, while in Sicily and southern Italy the family of the Norman Tancred de Hauteville were on the point of dislodging the Byzantines completely. Having gelded the army, Constantine nearly wrecked the economy by debasing the gold coinage. By the time he died in 1055, he had presided over the great religious schism the year before, when Rome and Constantinople squabbled over metaphysics instead of making common cause against the Normans.[35]

Harald's other great foreign policy triumph was the way he integrated Norway's overseas empire. He succeeded in bringing the Orkneys back under the Norwegian aegis, where Magnus had failed, and enjoyed particularly close ties with Iceland, where indeed he was more popular than in his native country. When there was a famine there in 1056, he sent four ships laden with wheat at a giveaway price, sent timber to build a church to St Olaf at Thingwalla and allowed free migration between Norway and Iceland. Fascinated by geography, he sent out expeditions to chart the Baltic minutely and to explore the unknown stretches of the North Sea and the Atlantic. Regular trade routes were established between Norway and Iceland. He knew the secret of avoiding scurvy on his ships by taking the arctic cloudberry (*Rubus chamoemorus*) from the Scandinavian heathlands on his voyages and, in the late 1050s, during a lull in the war with Svein, even went on an expedition himself into the 'ultima thule' region of the Atlantic.[36]

Harald was also a great patron of the arts, an unrivalled judge of poetry and no mean songwriter himself. This sensitive side may at first appear surprising in such a cruel and ruthless warrior, but it is one of many contradictions in the personality of this complex man. Afraid of no one on earth, he was deeply superstitious and was said to have been terrified by the corpse of Ivar the Boneless, the great Viking hero of the ninth century. Of all the kings of Norway he was undoubtedly the finest poet and the man with the profoundest aesthetic sense. He particularly admired the work of Arnorr Hordarson and gave him a spear inlaid with gold for the excellence of his poetry. In return Arnorr promised that if he lived longer than Harald, he would compose a timeless memorial lay about him − which he subsequently did. The one aspect of Arnorr Harald did not care for was his excessive piety: in his lays Arnorr prayed for the soul of the king in terms which suggested he was not convinced Harald would attain heavenly bliss. More to Harald's taste were Bjodolfr and Sneggu-Halli, who composed in the old pagan, heroic style. But a very high level of sophistication was required of Harald's courtiers, who were expected to be able to catch all the abstruse references of the 'kennings' − those euphuisms whereby 'a tribute of Lapps' means 'arrows'.[37]

Harald's comrade-in-arms at Byzantium, Haldor Snorresson, was also a talented poet and liked to go to Iceland each summer for the *Allthing*, where sagas were recited. Harald was fond of Haldor, and particularly prized his unflappability − for Haldor acted exactly the same in good times and bad, always eating and drinking copiously, never losing sleep, always stoical and enduring. A close-mouthed laconic man, Haldor had one great fault: he was blunt, opinionated, and called a spade a spade − on one notorious occasion during the 1038–40 campaign in Sicily he had accused Harald of cowardice. In middle age, Harald developed a taste for sycophancy and grew tired of the plain-spoken Haldor. On the pretext that Haldor had grown immensely stout and was no longer fit for battle, Harald 'suggested' that his old comrade retire permanently to Iceland, which he did. Haldor's banishment opened the way for the elevation of the other old Byzantine comrade, Ulf Ospaksson, who was endowed lavishly with lands and married to Jorun, the sister of Harald's wife Thora.[38]

Yet by far the most significant feature of Harald's twenty-year reign was his strengthening of the institution of the monarchy. Harald continued the policy of centralization begun by Harald Fairhair, whose actions had led to so much emigration in the tenth century: curbing the power of the landed aristocracy and binding the powerful oligarchs to the monarchy by intermarriage.[39] In this regard Harald was immeasurably helped by the cult of St Olaf, for the feedback image from this now most revered of Norwegian icons meant that a strong king was 'natural' and the resistance of the aristocrats was 'unnatural'. Magnus had cleverly steered between being an autocrat and being a figurehead: the oligarchs had given him their qualified support, he was not their puppet, but neither was he their taskmaster. Magnus always treated his nobles with consideration and without arrogance. Such, however, was not Harald's way – he regarded diplomacy and compromise as weakness – and the beginning of his reign saw a spate of expulsions and even murders as he sought to make his arbitrary power unchallengeable.

It was obvious that Harald's first target would be Einar Tambarskjelver, the man who had always opposed him, and the most powerful *lenderman* in the Drontheim province. Kinship ties between him and Harald were not strong enough, since the only link was through Harald's great-niece Sigrid, who was married to Einar's son Eindride, a man almost as popular in his province as Tambarskjelver himself; Einar's chief kinship ties were to Hakon Ivarsson, whose daughter Bergljot he had married. Since Harald's accession in 1047, Einar had continued to speak out against him in council, frequently angering the king by reminding him that, in any conflict between monarchy and law, the law must prevail. Einar knew he was swimming in very dangerous waters and for this reason always kept a bodyguard of picked retainers around him whenever he had dealings with the king. On one occasion he enraged Harald by arriving at a council with nine warships and five hundred warriors.[40]

It was difficult for Harald to find a pretext to eliminate Einar, even though he went to the lengths of sending his secret agents to try to entrap him, pretending to be spies from Svein Estrithson and promising him the crown if he would help to overthrow Hardrada. Einar told them that he was no friend to Harald but would always help him to defend the kingdom against Svein Estrithson. Baulked of his prey, Harald invited Einar to a banquet of reconciliation at Nidaros, and then went out of his way to alienate him, out of a perverse desire to destroy him at all costs. While welcoming him with false bonhomie, Harald confided his true thoughts to his circle of intimates, where one of the court poets recorded them in words which give us the authentic flavour of the man: 'Here is the bold Einar, the earth-shaker, with his company. He knows how to plough the sea. In his pride he looks forward to filling the throne. I have often seen a lesser number of retainers at an earl's heels. He will scheme us out of the land, unless he kiss the thin lips of the axe.'[41]

Finally the wily noble made a false step. When a man arrested for theft turned out to be one of Einar's favourite retainers, Tambarskjelver broke the law by going to the trial at the *thing* and releasing him. To answer the charge of contumacy Harald summoned him to his new palace by the river Nid. Since the venue was in lands controlled by Einar and his sympathizers, he went to the meeting with a smaller bodyguard than usual, taking Eindride with him. Seeing no sign of Harald's warriors in the palace courtyard, Einar assumed he had been summoned for a one-to-one conclave and left Eindride and his men outside. He was shown into a darkened room where a party of armed men lay hidden; they despatched him immediately. When Eindride heard his father's cries of agony, he drew his sword and rushed inside but was himself slain. Harald called out in a voice of thunder that all Einar's men must lay down their arms. Although they greatly outnumbered Harald and his men, without a leader they were indecisive and did not press their advantage. After a while, scenting victory, Harald and his men emerged cautiously, in Roman turtle formation, crept down unopposed to the ships they had anchored in the fiord, and made good their escape.[42]

Einar's widow raised the country in protest against the murder, and Harald faced the prospect of years of blood-feud. To find a settlement he turned to another powerful *lenderman*, Finn Arnesson of Austratt, brother of the Kalv Arnesson forced into exile by Magnus's hostility. Finn was a shrewd choice as peacemaker for he was at once the uncle of Thora, Harald's second wife, close friend of Guttorm Gunhildson, one of Harald's intimates and also an old privateering partner of Hakon

Ivarsson, in whose hands now rested the decision for peace or civil war. But Harald's initial interview with Finn at Austratt was tense: Finn bitterly criticized him for the murder and accused him of having failed to think through the consequences.[43]

Swallowing his pride, Harald accepted the rebuke and pleaded with Finn to go on a mission to Drontheim, to appease the *bondermen* whom Einar's widow was trying to stir up and, crucially, to neutralize Hakon Ivarsson. Finn underscored the dangers of such a mission but in the end reluctantly agreed to go, provided he was made a plenipotentiary and provided his brother Kalv was restored to all the estates he held before his exile. Harald had no choice but to agree. Finn then went to Drontheim in company with his brother-in-law Earl Orm to meet Hakon Ivarsson. At first the negotiations got nowhere: Hakon declared that it was his moral duty to avenge Eindride at the very least. Patiently Finn continued to talk, pointing out the risks of revolt: why risk everything on a rebellion that might well end with forfeiture, exile or even death when Harald had already promised to make him the greatest noble in the land? At this, Hakon changed his mind and agreed to let matters rest, provided Harald gave him Ragnhild, Magnus's daughter, in marriage. The terms were agreed.[44]

Hakon then travelled up to Trondheim to see Harald, who said that he had no objection to the marriage but, since this involved a king's daughter, Hakon must first get Ragnhild's consent. She, however, proved to be a haughty woman who said she could not marry anyone of lesser rank than an earl. Hakon returned to Harald and, claiming that Ragnhild's refusal in effect made his agreement with Harald worthless, demanded to be made an earl. Harald replied that both Olaf and Magnus had established the precedent that there could be only one earl in Norway; to create a second now would in effect be an insult to Earl Orm. A furious Hakon, who had already stayed the hand of the Drontheim men, raged that he had been duped, and accused Harald of compromising his honour. After such fighting talk he had second thoughts and feared for his own head: mindful of Einar's fate, he fled to Svein Estrithson. Svein gave him great estates and made him commander of the coastal defences against the Vendland people.[45]

Hakon was not the only great noble to seek sanctuary with Svein, for Finn Arnesson, too, soon learned it was dangerous to trust Harald Hardrada. At first all was euphoria, as his brother Kalv returned from the Orkneys and retrieved all his estates. But Harald secretly loathed Kalv for his role at Stiklestad just as much as Magnus had.[46] The ruthless monarch soon found a way to destroy him. In 1051, during the annual invasion of Denmark, Harald sent Kalv ahead with an élite corps as the vanguard, with orders to secure a beachhead; the understanding was that he and the main army would come ashore as soon as the beachhead was secure. But when the Danes counterattacked the landing army, Harald found it 'impossible' to come to their immediate aid; Kalv and his comrades were wiped out. A furious Finn rightly accused Harald of having deliberately sacrificed his brother; he too fled to Svein Estrithson and was rewarded with the earldom of Halland. The supremely ruthless Harald meanwhile boasted of his treachery in lines recorded by a court skald:

Now I have caused the deaths of thirteen of my enemies; I kill without compunction and remember all my killings. Treason must be scotched by fair means or foul before it overwhelms me. Oak trees grow from acorns.[47]

By the early 1050s Harald had killed off or driven into exile all the powerful nobles who opposed him: Einar Tambarskjelver and his son Eindride; Hakon Ivarsson; Finn and Kalv Arnesson; even Haldor Snorresson, his old comrade in Byzantium. In the Orkneys Thorfinn had accepted his overlordship, and their alliance held fast, even if this was for prudential motives. Thorfinn's great friend and ally was Macbeth – they had even gone to Rome together on pilgrimage in 1050 – and when Edward the Confessor sent Siward to overthrow him in 1054 and put Malcolm on the throne, Thorfinn felt the cold winds blowing.[48]

In Harald Hardrada's new regime – as close to absolute monarchy as medieval kingship could get – the key figures were Ulf Ospaksson, whom Harald appointed as his marshal, Stump, a blind saga-teller, who was a Rasputin-like figure at the court, and Guthorm Gunhildson, Harald's nephew. Guthorm was both a brave warrior and a shrewd and trusted counsellor, who had the peculiarity of looking fifty when he was in his twenties. Until 1052 he had had a roistering career as a freebooter and pirate in Irish waters before being taken up as a favourite of King Margad Rognvaldsson (known in Irish as Eachmarcach MacRagnall), who ruled Dublin from 1046 to 1052. In 1052 the two friends went on a slave-raiding expedition to Wales, but in Anglesey Sound fell out over the division of the spoils. Margad peremptorily informed Guthorm that he would not after all be splitting the booty equally and that, if he was not prepared to accept a lesser share, he would have to fight to make good his claim. Even though heavily outnumbered, with five smaller ships ranged against Margad's six large galleys, Guthorm gave battle, defeated and killed Margad and made sure that his exploit would be remembered by getting his skalds to note the exact day: 28 July 1052.[49]

It may have been Guthorm who first kindled Harald's interest in the British Isles, of which there are signs in the 1050s, but everything about Hardrada's pre-1066 attitude to England is mired in controversy. Some claim that it was always Harald's dream to restore Cnut's empire, embracing Scandinavia and England. Others assert that the real dynamic behind the accord of 1052 whereby Edward the Confessor bowed his head to the Godwin family was fear that civil war in England would so weaken the realm that Harald would be handed an easy conquest. The only certainty is that in 1058 Harald sent his son Magnus on a large-scale raiding expedition to the British Isles. Again historians are divided on the meaning of this probe. Was it simply a large-scale slave-raiding expedition, was it part of an inchoate alliance with Gruffydd ap Llywelyn or Aelfgar, or was it simple opportunism by a man restless in a lull in the war with Denmark? He may also have sent the fleet as a warning to Edward that he still maintained a claim to the English throne as Magnus's successor and victor over Svein Estrithson or as a warning not to intervene on Svein's side now that Harald was so close to total victory.[50]

Meanwhile the long war with Denmark dragged on. We hear of significant activity in 1054, for Harald campaigned that year in the Elbe and held a moot at Thumla in Gauta-Elf, where he denounced the Danish people in terms that signal his frustration; no matter how many times Svein was defeated, he still kept the loyalty of his subjects: 'The Danes have bartered their honour and their good lord for Svein; this villainy will long be held in mind.' This may have been the campaign when Harald won a lasting reputation for cunning and resourcefulness. Svein apparently tried to trap him in Lymfjord around Livo Bredning, but Harald escaped by portaging his ships overland and then sailing north along the Jutland coast. But although we hear of virtually annual forays into Denmark, Harald cannot have had things all his own way. Some time in the 1050s Harald founded the city of Oslo, so as to be able to defend the country more effectively than from Nidaros. Well supplied by the fertile, food-growing lands around, Oslo may also have featured in Harald's mind as a symbol of his own fame, a base in the south to set against the northerly centre of Nidaros, which was too closely associated with St Olaf for his liking.[51]

In the early 1060s Harald staked all on one last great effort to win the war with Svein. He made the most elaborate preparations, including the construction in Nidaros of a large *buss* – a combined merchantman-warship with thirty-five rowers' benches – and his own great flagship with a dragon's figurehead known as the 'dragonship' with seventy oarsmen. He called out a general levy and launched his new fleet on the river Nid. The year 1061 saw him once again laying waste Jutland, and ended with Harald's challenge to Svein to meet him next year at the Gotha river – scene of so many great encounters in Norwegian history – in a pitched battle to decide the outcome of the war once and for all. There was no confidence that Svein would accept the challenge, for he had ducked such invitations before; the rumour was that, ever since their mauling during the 1048 campaign, Svein's troops preferred to face death by drowning rather than the cold steel of Harald's warriors.[52]

To make sense of the events of 1062, we have to follow the career of the exiled Hakon Ivarsson in Denmark. For a long time Svein had been troubled by the activities of his nephew Asmund, his brother Bjorn's son, a young hothead who ran his own private army of desperadoes and raided royal lands to finance it. Svein tried binding the young man to him by loading him with favours, but Asmund quickly became bored with life at court and raised another warband. When Svein's patience snapped and he sent his bodyguard to arrest him, Asmund managed to escape from his chains and raise the countryside once more. The devious Svein decided to shift the blame on to Hakon Ivarsson. When the landlords whose estates Asmund had devastated complained to Svein, he referred them to Hakon, saying it was clearly his problem as lord of the marches; in an unguarded moment he added the sarcasm that it was a pity Hakon was not doing the job he had been appointed to do and that he was always somewhere else when Asmund struck.

This was reported to Hakon, who marshalled all his resources to deal with Asmund. Catching up with him, he brought his motley warband to battle, defeated it, slew Asmund and cut off his head. Hakon then went to Svein's palace, histrionically threw the severed head on a table in front of Svein and asked him ironically if he recognized it. Svein, pale with shock and shaking with rage, said nothing but soon after sent a message to Hakon, ordering him to leave his service immediately; he added disingenuously that he personally would not harm him, but he could not speak for Asmund's powerful kinfolk. Hakon understood the implicit death-sentence and left Denmark forthwith; he put out peace feelers to Harald and learned that, with Earl Orm now dead, there would be no obstacle to his being appointed to the vacant earlship, which would enable him to marry Ragnhild.[53]

This was the situation when, in the summer of 1062, Harald sailed

south towards the rendezvous at the Gotha river. At Viken the fleet ran
into a heavy storm and had to lie to, but when the weather cleared and
they reached the spot appointed for the decisive battle there was no sign
of Svein. Deprived of his climactic encounter, Harald led the *bondermen*
home and proceeded with 180 ships south to Halland, where he began
laying waste the country. At Laholm Bay, near the modern town of
Halmstad, he anchored at the mouth of the Nissa, one of the five rivers
which rise in the plateaux of Vastergotland and Smaland and flow
westward through Halland to the sea. There, on 9 August 1062, Svein
Estrithson came upon him with a fleet estimated to be at least twice as
large. Harald at last had his decisive battle, but hardly in the
circumstances of his choosing.[54]

Ulf Ospaksson, the marshal, ranged the 180 Norwegian ships in a
wedge-shaped formation behind Harald's 'dragonship'. Facing them
was Svein and, next to him, Finn Arnesson; the Danes lashed all their
ships together, possibly because of low morale among their men, even
now, with a clear numerical advantage. It was about two hours before
sunset; the two armies began showering each other with stones and
arrows, and the battle continued thus as darkness fell. One of the skaldic
poets described the scene with the usual plethora of kennings: 'The
Upland king [sc. Harald] was drawing his elm-bow all that night,
making the arrow-heads hail on the white bucklers; the bloody points
pierced the franklins' mail, what time the Finn's tribute [sc. arrows]
stood thick on the serpent's shields.'[55]

Some time after dark, Hakon Ivarsson arrived and intervened
decisively on Harald's side. He did not lash his ships together, but acted
as a mobile squadron, picking off Danish ships that had worked loose
from Svein's seaborne phalanx. Hakon's sea rovers caused immense
damage, and led to significant early desertions by some of the Danes.
This is reflected in the skaldic comments: 'The king of the Danes would
not have given way (we must speak the truth of him) if the men from
the south of the sea had fought well for him.' Early next morning Harald
ordered a general advance. His warships scythed through the Danish
ranks and he himself boarded Svein's flagship during a general panic
where the Danes were throwing themselves overboard or being felled
by Norwegian axes. A general rout ensued: seventy Danish ships were
captured and others sunk, but many got away up a side channel. Finn
Arnesson was taken prisoner – the result, it was said, of his short-
sightedness – but Svein got away in controversial circumstances. Some
say he was originally taken prisoner, not recognized, and thus able
to steal away in the dark later. Others said that Hakon Ivarsson trapped

him but then let him escape as he did not want to witness his execution at Harald's hands.[56]

The Nissa was a stunning victory for Harald and established him without doubt as the greatest warrior in Europe. Casualties were certainly enormous, though unquantifiable, since Harald had to press the local peasantry into service to bury the mounds of bodies. The disingenuous Svein claimed that he had been beaten only by superior numbers and vowed to continue the war, though he was severely shaken and admitted to his intimates that he would never again make the mistake of meeting Hardrada in a pitched battle. The burning question of the hour was what Harald would do about Finn Arnesson. Brought before him in chains, Finn was offered his life in exchange for loyalty but he contemptuously rejected the offer and compounded his arrogance by insulting the king's wife and son, Thora and Magnus. Harald kept him with him for a couple of days, uncertain what doom to mete out, but eventually tired of Finn's doleful countenance, released him and allowed him to return to Svein.[57]

Hakon was initially the hero of the hour, received his earldom of the Uplands, married Ragnhild, and seemed set fair to displace Ulf Ospaksson as the second man in the land. But Harald's old courtiers, jealous of the triumphant return of a man they had thought safely exiled, began to intrigue against him. They whispered to Harald that Hakon styled himself as the victor of Nissa, claimed Harald could not have won without him, and boasted that he had decided the future of Scandinavia by allowing Svein Estrithson to escape. Eventually the poison worked. One day at court Harald sprang up in a rage and ordered Hakon's immediate execution, but the earl, forewarned, fled to King Steinkel of Sweden.[58]

The zest for fighting seemed to go out of Harald after he had failed to capture and execute Svein. Or perhaps he simply reflected that he had gained enough martial glory and that, however many victories he won over Svein, he could never persuade the people of Denmark to accept him as their overlord. Accordingly, he opened negotiations with Svein for a permanent peace and suspended hostilities pending the outcome. He spent the period of armistice in a lengthy tour of Norway, basing himself at Oslo in the winter of 1062, in Drontheim in the summer of 1063 and in Viken in the autumn. The protracted negotiations were difficult, as both kings were proud and haughty men, prone to brinkmanship and prima donna antics. At last, though, terms were agreed and the two monarchs met at the Gotha river to ratify the peace treaty. It was agreed that Harald was rightful king of Norway and Svein of Denmark and that the peace between them would last as long as they both lived; mighty oaths of friendship were sworn and high-ranking hostages given on each side. There were to be no war damages, and everything was to be settled on an 'as is' basis.[59]

Doubtless the meeting on the Gotha river allowed each man to observe the personal ravages time and the long, fruitless war had wrought on the other. Svein was still handsome and strong, though now very stout. Well-spoken, a natural athlete who had set himself to master skill in weaponry in all its branches, he was, unlike Harald, devout and conformist in his dealings with the Church, quite prepared to be governed in matters ecclesiastical by the Archbishop of Bremen. In Adam of Bremen and Saxo Grammaticus he found propagandists who performed for him the role the Williams of Poitiers and Jumièges played for their namesake the Duke of Normandy, but not even they could disguise Svein's lustful womanizing and the informal harem by which he seemed single-handedly determined to repopulate Denmark.[60]

By this time, too, the personality and character of Harald were known throughout Europe. His great height (six feet six inches at a time when the mean stature for males in Scandinavia was five feet eight inches) was legendary, and in Scandinavian iconography he was a familiar figure, with his yellow hair, short beard, long moustaches, large hands and feet and the peculiarity of one eyebrow higher than the other. Brave, bold, resourceful, ingenious and even lucky in war, he was shrewd and quick-thinking, particularly good at dealing with the pressures of having to make snap decisions. It was generally agreed that his finest attribute was his ability to improvise in time of danger and to choose the course under stress which, in cool retrospect, everyone agreed was the best one that could have been made. Avaricious and greedy for power and possessions, Harald was a natural autocrat who had no more idea than his half-brother St Olaf how to win friends and influence people. It could be said of Harald that he had no middle range, since his two modes were severity and cruelty to those who opposed him and generosity to friends, sycophants and hangers-on who did his bidding. Unlike Olaf, however, he knew how to temper a fanatical vision and firmness of purpose with consummate cunning, so that there was no Stiklestad in his biography.

By 1064 Harald had entered his fiftieth year and must often have thought of the succession. His two sons by Thora were similar in looks though very different in personality. Magnus learned the arts of a warrior but was essentially a peace-loving man. Even more distinctive was his other son, Olaf, later known as 'the quiet'; he was reticent and spoke little in council, seeming to come to life only in his cups, when he was over-loquacious. A man who preferred drink to women, and would later reverse his father's attitude to the Church, Olaf was peaceful and cheerful to the end of his days, no doubt resting on the laurels of his great physical beauty, for contemporary poets described him as a second Balder, with his perfectly proportioned body, thick, yellow silky hair, fair skin and beautiful blue eyes. Harald's daughter, Maria, too was exceptional, described by one contemporary in the following terms, redolent of Malory: 'She was of all women, the wisest, the fairest to look upon and the friendliest.'[61]

7

Harold Godwinson

Edward the Confessor celebrated his fiftieth birthday in 1053, able to console himself that his great tormentor, Earl Godwin, was dead. Some have seen the suspicious death of Godwin as the occasion for Edward's reassertion of regal authority. The argument is that by juggling the earldoms the king achieved a redistribution of power away from the Godwin family; he used the pretext of appointing Harold Godwinson to his father's earldom in Wessex to give Harold's previous earldom in East Anglia to Aelfgar, Leofric's son. But what we do not know is whether this arrangement had Harold's approval, and in many respects it is inconceivable that it could not have had it, since the new earl of Wessex was in some ways an even more titanic figure in the land than his father had been. At the beginning of Edward's reign, Godwin, Leofric and Siward were of roughly equal wealth and influence, but by the time of Godwin's death, his family had far outstripped their rivals.[1]

Some idea of the power Harold Godwinson wielded in England in the 1050s and early 1060s can be derived from his sheer wealth in land. He first witnessed charters as an earl in 1045 but by 1057 his estates alone were worth £2,847; his nearest challenger as a landowner was Morcar, son of Aelfgar, with lands worth £960. To put these figures into perspective it is worth noting the landed wealth of other earls: Siward at the time of his death in 1055 was worth £350, Earl Ralph in the same period was worth £170, and Edwin, the other son of Aelfgar, held lands to the value of £588; by contrast, Tostig Godwinson had estates worth £492, Gyrth was worth £250 and Leofwine £588. In short, both Godwin and his sons were immensely wealthy, lived lavishly and were early exponents of conspicuous consumption.[2]

If we add to the wealth of Godwin's sons the land held by their mother and their sisters and that owned in her own right by Edith, who always took her family's side against the king, and the £1,200 in the hands of thegns loyal to the Godwinsons, by 1066 the family controlled at least £7,500 of real estate, of which the four Godwin sons possessed £5,000. The estates were widespread across England. Sixty per cent of Harold's lands lay south of the Thames – in Surrey, Hampshire, Berkshire, Wiltshire, Dorset, Somerset, Devon and Cornwall – and the rest in Essex, Hertfordshire, Yorkshire and the South Midlands. Tostig's were mainly in Yorkshire, Hampshire and the Midlands; Gyrth's in Norfolk, Suffolk, Cambridgeshire and Bedfordshire; Leofwine's in Kent, Middlesex, Essex, Buckinghamshire, Dorset and Devon; Gytha's in Wiltshire, Somerset and Devon; and her daughter Gunnhild by Godwin had holdings in Somerset. But so far was Harold the dominant landowner, even in his brothers' earldoms, that in Hertfordshire, Buckinghamshire and Essex he owned more than Gyrth and in Yorkshire twice as much as Tostig.[3]

The pattern of acquisition by the Godwinsons was interesting. Edward transferred lands to them not by slicing tranches off the royal demesne or rewarding them with the confiscated estates of particular families but by ceding *ad hoc* those parts of ancient ecclesiastical, ealdormanean and royal estates that were particularly vulnerable militarily or especially important for the defence of the realm. To some extent, therefore, the holdings of the Godwinsons had a geopolitical significance. Since Edward perceived the main threat to England as coming from Flanders or Normandy – rather than Scandinavia – Sussex and Kent increasingly loomed in his calculations. This is the probable explanation of the rise of Godwin and his family, for they were the first South Saxon dynasty to be prominent in Anglo-Saxon politics; hitherto the south-east had been a backwater and all eyes had been on Winchester, Wessex and southern Mercia.[4]

By 1066 Harold and his brothers held 66 per cent of all land in the English earldoms; by contrast, Leofric's family had 31 per cent and Siward's just 3 per cent, and by the time of Edward's death his lands were worth £1,550 less than those of the Godwin family. The

Godwinsons and their thegns controlled over a third of all England's arable land, and their dominance was particularly marked in Sussex, where the Godwin brothers alone had estates worth £850 – a quarter the value of the entire county. In Sussex all the thegns were Harold's men and a similar situation obtained in Essex and Herefordshire. But the tentacles of the Godwinsons stretched far and wide, as Harold alone had land in all but five counties and, in the few where he had no holdings, his brothers were usually prominent, as with Leofwine in Kent.[5]

All this land gave the Godwinsons immense power, for thousands of modest thegns and freemen were sucked into their orbit as clients, as it were spontaneously. Nothing succeeds like success, so that the Godwin family were very soon approached to extend their lordship over many of the wealthiest thegns too. They could attract a huge following, as their vast holdings allowed them to alienate property to land-hungry thegns and housecarls, to support them in courts or protect them from neighbours. The more the Godwinsons acquired, the more they were sought after as patrons. But some scholars have seen the hegemony of the Godwinsons and the weakness of the king as twin factors making late Anglo-Saxon society peculiarly brittle and vulnerable. Edward's tolerance of the Godwinsons, of whom it is known he disapproved, clearly reveals his impotence, but on the other hand the fact that the Godwinsons had come from nowhere and achieved their dominant position within fifty years after Cnut wiped out the old aristocracy meant that the family did not have suffcient time to consolidate and put down strong roots before facing serious external threats.[6]

An important question crying out for resolution is the exact relationship of the Godwin family to the Church, for the traditional 'black legend' portrays them as irreligious despoilers of church property. To an extent the Godwins were unfairly blackened by Norman propagandists for an activity that was common and conventional Anglo-Saxon practice. Godwin himself was probably harsher towards the Church than his sons, and it is perhaps significant that there was no ecclesiastical foundation associated with his name. In his defence it can be said that, having risen from obscurity, he was in a hurry to acquire lands so that he could advance his sons and that market forces played into his hands owing to the financial plight of many monasteries. He had a good reputation among the religious communities of St Augustine's, Canterbury, Worcester and Peterborough, but against this are clearly documented spoliations and appropriations, principally at Canterbury, involving Godwin personally.[7]

Harold Godwinson, on the other hand, presents a much more

nuanced picture. He and his brothers were out of favour with the papacy for supporting the traditional Anglo-Saxon church which Rome regarded as corrupt. And he and his brothers did on occasion go in for outright seizures of church lands, on one famous occasion provoking a major confrontation with the angry Bishop Giso of Wells. A notable example of the power the Godwinsons could wield occurred when Edward under pressure granted Harold the rights to Steyning in Sussex, even though he had already given it to the Norman abbey of Fécamp.[8] It was this kind of riding roughshod over Edward's authority that led one recent scholar to declare: 'The fact that the Godwinsons could permanently alienate land set aside for the endowment of royal officials is a sure sign that the West Saxon monarchy was in serious trouble.'[9]

On the other hand, Harold was a generous benefactor of the Church in some areas, notably at Durham and Waltham Holy Cross in Essex, where he endowed an abbey and later became the focus of a cult. The truth about Harold's 'irreligiosity' is probably that he merely favoured one religious foundation over another and that the losers then traduced him as being an enemy of the Church.[10] It must be remembered that Harold continued his father's policy of favouring one set of ecclesiastical magnates against another, and here too the disadvantaged divines had powerful propagandist voices. The controversial takeover of the Christchurch estates in Kent by the Godwinsons was achieved with the approval and assistance of Stigand, Ealdred and Eadsige, who were family favourites Harold inherited from his father. To the list of Godwin clerical protégés he himself added Wulfstan, the Abbot and later Bishop of Worcester, who became a close friend.[11]

Harold Godwinson was the most powerful man in England during the thirteen years after 1053. Of the three great personalities of 1066, he is probably the most straightforward, lacking the darkest hues of William of Normandy and Harald Hardrada of Norway. From the eulogies of his supporters and the denunciations of his enemies – often, surprisingly, agreeing on the same characteristics – a reasonably trustworthy picture emerges. He was tall, probably around 5 feet 11 inches or 6 feet, remarkably handsome, graceful, and possessed of superabundant strength; in the Bayeux Tapestry he is depicted pulling a Norman knight from quicksands with one hand during the 1064 campaign in Brittany.[12]

Able to endure great hardships and to do without food and sleep for forty-eight hours while campaigning, Harold was a formidable warrior and a shrewd captain in the field. Singularly forbearing and merciful for a great man in such a cruel age, Harold impressed all who met him by his frank and open nature, his sunny temperament, his easygoing self-confidence, his even temper and his ability to take contradiction without flinching. Loyal and, if anything, over-trusting, he provoked contrary opinions from observers on his capability as a decision-maker: some said he was too slow to act and liked to tarry and enjoy himself too much *en route* to an objective; others that he was inclined to be impetuous and rash, to take the first option from the top of his head and make policy on the wing, but always within a general framework of basic shrewdness, which even his Norman enemies acknowledged.[13]

From an early age Harold had made it his business to be fully abreast of political developments on the Continent, and especially in France, to know the rulers and all their strengths and weaknesses. He advocated alliances with Flanders and Denmark, thus flying in the face of Edward's diplomatic orientation, and favoured intriguing with the king of France to keep any latent threat from Normandy dormant. The monk-historian John of Worcester regarded Harold as a second Judas Maccabeus (the Jewish patriot in the struggle against Antiochus of Syria in the second century BC) and William of Malmesbury concurred that love of England was probably Harold's most outstanding characteristic.[14] It is perhaps unfortunate that Godwin's son was taken up in later writings as a hero of the resistance of the 'pure' Saxon race to the yoke of the Normans, but later events were to prove that he was held in genuinely high regard by the thegns of England, who approved of his habit of discussing his policies and battle plans with a wide circle of friends and associates.

Both at the time and ever since observers have been drawn irresistibly to compare and contrast Harold with his younger brother Tostig, another ambitious high-flyer, who signalled his intention to make his mark in Europe by the marriage with Judith of Flanders. Tostig was also courageous and shrewd, though neither as good a general as Harold nor quite as cunning. Although he fought hard to achieve self-restraint, he was quick-tempered, dogmatic and tended to see things in black and white or, as the author of the *Vita Eadwardi* put it, 'was a little overzealous in attacking evil'.[15] Very slow to make up his mind, once he did he was inflexible and acted decisively. Generous and famously a man of his word, he was inclined to be secretive and lacked Harold's gift for living life to the full: Tostig aimed merely at success but Harold felt success should also involve happiness. Tostig did not have Harold's wit – which to his critics sometimes involved allowing his tongue to run away with him – and was, on the face of it, an introvert to Harold's extrovert, except that all who met the brothers remarked that, their very different personalities notwithstanding, it was very hard ever to know what they were really thinking.[16]

There seems no good reason for imagining that before 1065 the two were anything other than devoted siblings. Until he was appointed Earl of Northumbria, Tostig made no significant enemies, perhaps because he curbed his tongue where Harold allowed his full rein, and he largely avoided the ecclesiastical odium in which Harold was held in some quarters. Whereas Edward had hated Godwin and was largely indifferent to Harold, he genuinely adored Tostig, as did his wife Edith, who far preferred him to her other male siblings. Perhaps the devious, circumspect and introverted Edward recognized a kindred spirit, or perhaps the contrary was the case, producing the attraction of opposites, and this essentially passive monarch recognized the driving ambition behind Tostig's pious surface. As for Edith, she may have been drawn to Tostig rather than Harold because of the younger man's notable solicitude for women and his known fidelity to his wife. Harold by contrast was a known hedonist and womanizer. Where Tostig dutifully contracted a dynastic marriage with Judith of Flanders, Harold preferred the twilight state, half wedlock, half concubinage, of the liaison *more danico* with Edith Swan-neck, which brought him further territorial holdings. From this union came five sons, Ulf, Godwin, Edmund, Magnus and Harold, and two daughters, Gytha and Gunnhild.[17]

After 1053 the history of Edward's reign became largely the story of the exploits of the Godwinsons, with a shadowy monarch reduced to figurehead status. Relations with the Celtic fringes occupied much of the king's time, and border warfare became as much an annual and predictable affair as the interminable wars in Scandinavia between Svein Estrithson and Harald Hardrada. The dominant figure in Wales at the time was Gruffydd ap Llywelyn, ruler over the northern and central areas. Known as 'Alexander of Wales', he first attracted notice in 1039 when he annihilated a Mercian force near Welshpool on the upper Severn; the English commander, Eadwine, Earl Leofric's brother, died in the vicious hand-to-hand fighting.[18]

Gruffydd ap Llywelyn was hated by the English and he, more than any man, was responsible for the violent upsurge of anti-Welsh sentiment that would reach an apogee in the following century. The perception of the Welsh, dating from Gruffydd's hegemony, was that they were treacherous and cowardly, craven in face of superior force, bold and merciless when they had the whip hand, but essentially primitive people who worshipped only power and the authority of the sword. What especially irritated the Anglo-Saxons and their successors in England was the way the Welsh surrounded their mayhem and rapine with an aura of legend, so that cattle-thieves, rapists and murderers were presented in Welsh bardic tradition as mythical heroes. The *locus classicus* of this sort of thing was the remark attributed to Gruffydd when accused of executing all actual and potential pretenders to his kingdom. He shrugged and replied: 'I kill no one; I only blunt the horns of Wales lest they wound their mother.'[19]

From 1044 there was another powerful Gruffydd in South Wales, Gruffydd ap Rhydderch, who proved himself as troublesome a scourge as his northern namesake by his defeat of Bishop Ealdred on the Wye in 1049 – the event that set in train Swein Godwinson's murder of Bjorn. Preoccupied as he was with the crisis involving Swein in 1050 and then the near-civil war with the Godwins in 1051–52, Edward was not ready to retaliate until 1053, but when he did so the allegedly saintly Confessor proved he could be as ruthless as any of the other players in the game of power politics. He took his revenge for the depredations of four years earlier by sending a death squad to bring back the head of Gruffydd ap Rhydderch's brother. In retaliation the enraged ruler of South Wales raided across the border and ambushed a large English patrol near Westbury on the Severn.[20]

Once again Edward's attention was distracted elsewhere, for in 1054 Normandy and Scotland occupied his thoughts. Late that year Duke William of Normandy sent John, Abbot of Fécamp, to Edward on a mission whose real purpose is unknown. Ostensibly, John, who had a reputation for piety and sanctity, was supposed to be visiting the abbey's English possessions at Winchelsea and Rye, but the only concrete result of his interview with Edward was a request for further lands at Eastbourne. Since John could have sent one of his deputies on such a trivial errand, the suspicion arises that he was in England for some other purpose. Maybe William wanted some reassurance that his 1051 'understanding' with Edward was still in place after the return of the Godwins. Or maybe the duke, flushed with his great military victory against the French in 1054, was already considering that he might have to fight the Godwins and sent John on a military espionage mission. This is once again an instance of copious sources being long on irrelevant detail but short on pith and moment.[21]

More immediately significant, earlier in 1054 Edward ordered Siward, Earl of Northumbria, to invade Scotland in support of the pretender Malcolm, son of the king Duncan who had been assassinated by Macbeth in 1040 as part of an anti-English reaction north of the border. Since Siward and Duncan had been kinsmen, the Earl of Northumbria accepted with alacrity. This is yet another example of Edward the ruthless aggressor, the angry man who transfers private problems on to the public stage, who loves military solutions but baulks at fighting in the field himself, for Macbeth's reign had been remarkably peaceful and his later evil reputation was entirely the product of the overheated imaginations of fourteenth- and fifteenth-century chroniclers.[22]

With a well-equipped fleet and a contingent of Edward's own housecarls, Siward crossed the border from Northumbria and brought King Macbeth to battle north of the Tay in Perthshire. The result was defeat for Macbeth in a bloody battle (where there were 3,000 Scots casualties and 1,500 English); among the Scots casualties was a sizeable contingent of French mercenaries, formerly men who had been based in Herefordshire but fled to Macbeth when Godwin was restored in 1052. Siward placed Malcolm on the throne, whence he devoted himself to tracking down the elusive Macbeth, who had survived the battle; he finally caught up with him and killed him at the battle of Lumphanan in 1057.[23]

The year 1055 was a period of drama when attention switched back to Wales. Gruffydd ap Llywelyn had his southern namesake assassinated, which enabled him to stand forth as king of all Wales. A united Wales was a serious threat to English security, but the situation was made worse when Siward died, for his son Aelfgar was known to have intrigued with Gruffydd and could scarcely be allowed to succeed in Northumbria. Under pressure from Harold and Edith, Edward outlawed Aelfgar for treason – though the aggrieved son of Siward protested that he was entirely innocent – and appointed Tostig to the earldom, slicing off a tranche so as to be able to favour Gyrth. The charge against Aelfgar, whatever its intrinsic merits, soon became a self-fulfilling prophecy as the banished magnate fled to Gruffydd and made common cause with him.[24]

When Aelfgar, in an action reminiscent of Harold and Leofwine in 1052, returned from Ireland to Wales with eighteen ships and men, he proved a valuable ally for Gruffydd. Together they attacked Hereford in October, only to be intercepted by Earl Ralph two miles outside the city walls. The result was a fiasco: Ralph, overcautious, ordered his Anglo-French troops to mount up and attack as cavalry, but the war cries and ululations from the Welsh warriors and the Irish Norsemen panicked the horses, who stampeded off the field, leaving Ralph's unprotected and outnumbered infantry to be slaughtered. Like sharks in a feeding frenzy, Gruffydd's men then turned on Hereford itself to slake their lust for massacre. The town was sacked and all but razed to the ground; the new cathedral was pillaged and then gutted, its clergy butchered; all male defenders were put to the sword, while women were raped and led off with their children into slavery.[25]

Edward could scarcely ignore this atrocity, since his very credibility was at stake. He summoned levies from all corners of England and gave the command to Harold Godwinson. Harold was the natural choice for this operation, combining as he did the roles of deputy to the king, great territorial magnate and England's finest captain, but it should not be imagined that he accepted the command with anything other than avidity. Having mustered his army at Gloucester, he advanced into Wales, hoping to tempt Gruffydd to an early engagement, but the Welsh melted away before him; some said the cunning Welsh king already knew something of Harold's calibre from his spies and decided not to risk testing his ability on the battlefield. Denied his prey, Harold returned to Hereford, which he partially rebuilt, fortified and surrounded with defence works. Presumably in consultation with Edward, he split the enemy alliance by offering Aelfgar pardon and the recovery of his earldom in East Anglia. For the time being Gruffydd was left in possession of his conquests, except for an enclave to the west of the Dee – an arrangement that saved face on both sides.[26]

Harold's prestige lost nothing from the outcome in Wales, and his position was strengthened by the passing of many of the old guard: Siward died in 1055, Odda in 1056, Leofric and Earl Ralph in 1057. In 1056 Harold was absent from Wales, as he spent a good part of that year on the Continent as a roving ambassador, but it is not easy to keep track of his movements nor to be precise about the aims of his diplomacy. He was certainly in St-Omer in November and visited Flanders to promote the reversal of alliances in favour of Baldwin for which he had always lobbied. He also met Pope Victor II at Cologne and the emperor at Regensburg, but opinion is divided on whether he accompanied the pontiff back to Rome; some even say there was a second Continental visit by Harold in 1058 and it was on that occasion that he went to Rome. But that he already had powerful enemies is certain, for we learn that by his skill and cunning he avoided an ambush that had been set for him: as the *Vita Eadwardi* puts it: 'By God's grace he came home, passing with watchful mockery through all ambushes, as was his way.'[27]

During his absence, most of his good work in Wales was undone. When Aethelstan of Hereford died in February 1056, Edward appointed Leofgar, Harold's clerk, to the vacancy. Leofgar was considered by many to be an unsuitable promotion to the see, for he emulated his master

Harold in wearing long blond hair and moustaches – a fashion habitually decried by the Church as pagan – and yearned to match him in martial glory. Within three months of his consecration, the warrior-bishop of Hereford took the field against Gruffydd, only to be disastrously defeated and slain (together with most of the élite – priests, sheriff and thegns – of Hereford) in June at Glasbury-on-Wye. Further campaigning by the English led nowhere, so Harold on his return patched up another peace with Gruffydd, co-opting as negotiators Bishop Ealdred and Earl Leofric. It was agreed that there would be a formal reconciliation with Edward, with the Welsh king acknowledging fealty.[28]

Tradition says that Edward was most reluctant to agree to this peace – which he saw as a humiliation – favoured continuing the war and was grudgingly talked into it by the triumvirate of Harold, Ealdred and Leofric, whose last significant political act this was. The king was also angry that, having pardoned Aelfgar, he found that troublesome earl continuing to play both sides against the middle and, indeed to be strengthening his Welsh alliance by the marriage of his daughter to Gruffydd. If tradition is correct, and Edward met Gruffydd on the banks of the river Severn near Gloucester, at the ferry crossing, his temper can scarcely have been improved, for Gruffydd started a tiresome wrangle about precedence. He claimed that he was the senior king and Edward should cross the water to meet him, since the Welsh had once conquered the whole of Great Britain; Edward replied that he inherited Britain from its Scandinavian conquerors. Legend has the saintly Edward humbly begin to cross the river, only for Gruffydd to be overcome by the Confessor's sanctity and do him homage.[29]

The year 1057 saw diplomatic activity on another front, or possibly Harold's European trip in 1056 meant that Edward was already putting out tentative feelers. Despite the previous vague half-promises to Svein Estrithson and William of Normandy, the king finally decided on the man he definitely wanted to succeed him. This was Edward the Atheling, son of Edmund Ironside, currently residing in Hungary. For a bare twelve months in 1015–16 Cnut had shared the kingdom of England with Edmund, with Cnut holding the north and Edmund the south. After Edmund's death Cnut, wishing to be rid of any rivals to the throne but seeking to avoid the opprobrium of cold-blooded murder, sent Ironside's infant sons Edmund and Edward to Sweden with instructions that they be quietly put down and the whole thing presented as an accident. But, as in a medieval fairy tale, the king of Sweden took pity on the innocent babes and sent them on to Hungary, out of harm's way. Edmund died young, but Edward married Agatha, a daughter of Emperor Henry II's brother, and sired three children – two daughters, Margaret and Christina, and a son, Edgar the Atheling.[30]

The choice of Edward the Atheling as heir presumptive had been on the Confessor's mind since 1054. In that year he sent Bishop Ealdred to Germany to sound the emperor's reaction to the proposal, but even as Ealdred was *en route* to the imperial court, Baldwin of Flanders once more raised the standard of revolt against Henry III, this time in conjunction with a revolt in Hungary. The patient Ealdred was treated with great consideration by the emperor but left dangling without a reply; in this way he spent an entire year at the imperial court at Cologne. Finally he got his answer. Angry with the Magyar forays into his empire, Henry told Ealdred that the time was not ripe; the unsettled situation in Hungary weighed far more with him than the prospect of seeing his kinsman on the throne of England.[31]

The Magyar kingdom of Hungary had been simmering with revolt since 1046, when the nationalist party took the upper hand, but matters took a more serious turn in 1054 when the Hungarians, in collusion with Baldwin and Kuno, the deposed Duke of Bavaria, invaded Carinthia. Edward the Confessor bided his time and waited for an opportunity to resurrect the atheling succession project. The chance came in October 1056 when the affairs of the empire were again thrown into confusion, by the death of Henry III. Given Harold's presence both in Flanders and Germany the very next month, it is inconceivable that the succession of Edward the Atheling was not again at the head of the agenda.[32]

By 1057 Edward the Atheling, who had been initially reluctant to accept the Confessor's offer, saw his safe refuge in Hungary turning into a cockpit of war as the political situation in central Europe worsened. Ealdred once again set out as the English envoy, and this time he secured the Atheling's return to England; it is even possible that Harold met them and escorted them back across the Channel. By now a universal consensus had formed: Edward the Atheling was the overwhelming favourite to succeed to the English throne, since his candidacy was backed by Edward, by Queen Edith and all the Godwinsons, especially Harold.[33] Norman propaganda notwithstanding, Harold's support for the Atheling makes nonsense of the allegation that he was casting envious eyes on the crown from 1053 on.

Edward the Exile landed in England early in 1057, laden with a vast treasure. But very soon afterwards he was dead, suddenly and mysteriously, and was buried in St Paul's before he had even met

Edward the Confessor. That he was the victim of foul play can scarcely be doubted, and on a *cui bono?* basis the finger of suspicion seems to point at Harold Godwinson, for whom 1057 was a lucky year, in that Leofric and Earl Ralph, two other obstacles to his supreme power, also died. Some have speculated that the absence of any mention of sickness in the Anglo-Saxon Chronicle, coupled with the enigmatic reference to the Exile's not having been admitted to the king's presence, suggests that the Godwinsons had stood between him and the king and then murdered him. But if Harold was the culprit, it seems odd that he should have backed Edward's choice of successor and allowed his protégé Ealdred to spend so much time on the mission to bring him home. The obvious course for a machiavellian Harold would have been to send an assassin to dispose of Edward in Hungary. Since the acclamation of Edward the Atheling as heir would have put paid to William of Normandy's chances, and he had a track record of disposing of rival claimants, it seems more plausible to detect the hand of the Normans in the mysterious death. If Harold did escort Edward back to England, that would explain the ambuscades he was said to have avoided; the one thing the sources do not tell us is who was laying the ambush, but, as with all acts of violence, it is sensible to look for the motive.[34]

The years 1056–58 saw Harold consolidating his hold on England, to the point where he was king in all but name. He increased the territorial holdings of his family, annexed Herefordshire to his earldom, gave East Anglia to Gyrth and created a new earldom for Leofwine which stretched from Buckinghamshire to Kent. With Tostig's appointment to the earldom of Northumbria in 1055 when Siward died (supposedly because Waltheof was still a child), the Godwinson brothers controlled all England, nominally under Edward, except for a reduced earldom possessed by Aelfgar in Mercia. Moreover, after the deaths of Edward the Exile and Earl Ralph in the same year (1057), there was no obvious candidate apart from Harold to succeed the king, unless Duke William's tenuous claim was to be entertained. As a further refinement to his hegemonic status, in 1058 Harold secured the second banishment of Aelfgar, who, until his death in 1062, eked out a precarious existence, part exile, part rebel, forever trying to interest Scandinavian rulers or Gruffydd of Wales in an invasion of England. After his death in 1062, the earldom passed to his son Edwin, who virtually surrendered it to Harold.[35]

Common sense suggests that after 1058 Harold consciously aimed at the succession and already looked forward to the time when he would be hailed as Harold II. Whether under duress, by free will, or out of apathy or fatal resignation, Edward acquiesced in Harold's acquiring the title of *subregulus* or deputy king, and there was a tacit assumption in Anglo-Saxon élite circles that Harold was the Confessor's designated successor. His name was coupled with Edward's in public documents; vassal lords plighted their troth to king and earl; and foreigners referred to Harold not just as earl but as duke or vassal prince. But it is important to be clear that there was no formal act of succession, that Edward did not publicly associate Harold with him as co-ruler, nor did he summon the *witan* to endorse the earl as the next king. This may indicate Edward's angry impotence at his figurehead role or it may simply mean that he was still hoping to beget an heir, though this seems unlikely in view of the elaborate plans for Edward the exile in 1057.[36]

It is plausible to assume also that Harold, secure in England, now began to look across the Channel and assess the possible threat to his future takeover from William of Normandy. There is some evidence that by the end of the 1050s Harold concluded that his policy of friendship with Flanders had been a failure and that the guiding light in Flemish policy henceforth would be a strong alliance with William of Normandy; in this respect the recognition by Pope Nicholas II of the legitimacy of William and Matilda's marriage in 1059 looked ominous. The Godwinsons had been unpopular with the papacy throughout the decade because they held aloof from the ecclesiastical reform movement, but hitherto that factor had been balanced by Rome's hostility towards Normandy. With Pope Nicholas as a pro-Norman pope, and the old entente between empire and papacy in tatters, Harold decided on a twin-track policy. He would make overtures to the emperor so as to constrain Flanders and would also send an embassy to Rome to try to win over Pope Nicholas; at the very least he could hope to secure some advantage by playing off the papacy against Germany.[37]

For this delicate mission Harold selected his brother Tostig, in whose cleverness and guile he had full confidence. As was customary in the heyday of the Godwinson brothers, Tostig was accompanied by Gyrth; as in 1051–52, these two brothers worked closely together, leaving Harold and Leofwine as the other natural pairing. Early in 1061 Tostig and his wife set out for Rome, travelling via Saxony and the upper Rhine. They were accompanied by a numerous party, including Gyrth, Ealdred, Bishop of Worcester, whom Harold had raised to the archbishopric in 1060, Wulfnig, Bishop of Dorchester, Giso, Bishop of Wells, who had accused Harold of expropriating church lands, Bishop Walter of Hereford, and Burehard, a son of the exiled Earl Aelfgar. The public part of Tostig's mission was to get a clean bill of spiritual health for the English Church from a papacy that regarded it as corrupt, and to sort out the mess in England, where bishops were unconsecrated and senior bishops held plural holdings. Quite apart from Stigand, who had received his pallium two years before from a deposed pope (Benedict X), even though he held both Winchester and Canterbury, there was now the issue of Ealdred, who had the livings and benefices of both York and Worcester.[38]

Tostig's embassy was initially a spectacular failure. Pope Nicholas seemed to go out of his way to favour the anti-Godwinson faction in the English Church and humiliate Harold's protégés. Giso of Wells was confirmed in his bishopric, as was Walter of Hereford, but Ealdred was not given the pallium and was deposed from his episcopal rank; moreover, in the dispute over lands between the sees of Dorchester and York, the pope pointedly snubbed Ealdred by deciding in favour of Bishop Wulfnig of Dorchester. Tostig brooded on the consequences of failure. Not only would he lose face in the eyes of Harold, but he realized how dangerously isolated the Godwinsons in England were. Neither of the warring factions in Scandinavia was an ally, while the threat from William of Normandy, now in alliance with the Vatican and Flanders, seemed to go from strength to strength at the very time there was a power vacuum in northern France, with Henry I and Geoffrey Martel both recently dead.[39]

At this juncture Fate played into Tostig's hands in a singular and unexpected way. On the day the English party left the Eternal City, they were ambushed on the Via Cassia (fifteen miles north-west of Rome) at the junction with the Via Clodia by the banks of the river Arrone, in the most desolate part of the Campagna, by what appeared at first to be a robber band. In fact the 'bandit chief' who uplifted their goods and money was a Tuscan nobleman, named Gerard, Count of Galeria, who had a political agenda of his own. He had secured the election in 1058 of Benedict X and protected him a year later when the deposed pontiff fled to Galeria. Gerard's purpose was to make Pope Nicholas a laughing-stock and dent his credibility by a barefaced act of highway robbery within the papal domains.[40]

The wily Tostig at once saw how he could turn this contretemps to his advantage. He stormed back to the Vatican and demanded immediate audience with Nicholas. No doubt feigning more anger than he really felt, Tostig blustered that the hold-up was such an outrage that he would have to withhold the traditional tribute of Peter's Pence. A conciliatory Nicholas asked what he could do to make up to the

English, at which Tostig pounced and insisted on having Ealdred confirmed in the archbishopric of York. He berated the pope for his failure to guarantee the safety of travellers (this was a particular hobbyhorse of Tostig's in his earldom) and underlined the threat to papal credibility: who would fear excommunication in England when the pope's authority was not even respected in the environs of Rome? Nicholas took the hint. In almost his last act before his death later that year, he convoked a full synod and formally excommunicated Gerard for his contumacious highway robbery. Tostig was within an ace of returning defeated and demoralized but in the end he went home to a hero's welcome from his brother.[41]

With Tostig's return from Rome in late 1061, Harold felt reasonably confident that his ecclesiastical and foreign policies were working. It was time to deal decisively with the Welsh problem, for when Aelfgar died in 1062 Gruffydd ap Llywelyn let it be known that the English peace had died with him. Harold counterattacked by having Aelfgar's teenage son Edwin appointed to the earldom of Mercia – a shrewd move which seemed to destroy at a stroke Gruffyd's fifth column in England; a boy earl, even if he had the freedom and inclination, could not deliver to the Welsh the level of armed support Aelfgar was used to providing. But Harold also had the long-term aim of destroying the power base of Aelfgar's teenage sons Edwin and Morcar, by depriving them in the future of any possible Welsh alliance.[42]

At his Christmas court at Gloucester at the end of 1062, King Edward decided to deal with Gruffydd in the same way he had dealt with his southern namesake: he would despatch a commando squad of assassins to surprise him at his palace of Rhuddlan on the river Clywd in North Wales. Harold was put in command of a crack cavalry force, deemed large enough to sweep away any immediate opposition; concentration of Welsh forces would be avoided by using the element of surprise. Harold made a forced march to the north-eastern frontier of Wales, and by the speed of his approach in the depths of midwinter came upon the enemy unawares. By the narrowest of margins Gruffydd escaped the dragnet and Harold had not the military resources to pursue him through snowdrifts and lakes of ice; he contented himself with burning down his palace, destroying his fleet and leaving his ships as blackened hulks before returning to Gloucester.[43]

During the spring of 1063 Harold planned a much more ambitious punitive expedition; this time there would be two invading armies, one of them under Tostig's command, and the navy would play a major role, preventing the escapes by sea which had been so notable a feature of Gruffydd's career. In May Harold sailed with the fleet to Bristol, disembarked his army and invaded South Wales; Tostig entered North Wales, having marched from Northumberland; the fleet ravaged the Welsh coastline and blocked all exit points. The two brothers met in mid-Wales and began a systematic policy of devastation, avoiding pitched battles but wearing the enemy down by a war of attrition. Harold showed his calibre as a captain by his imagination and ingenuity: he had his housecarls lay aside their heavy armour and fight as irregulars or rangers. For three months savage fighting ensued, with no quarter given by either side. When the Welsh sent him severed heads to make it plain that they would take no prisoners, Harold met violence with violence; every Welsh male who resisted by so much as a flicker of an eyebrow was summarily executed.[44]

After three months of this, the Welsh will to fight snapped. Gruffydd's followers turned on him, declared him outlaw, offered hostages to Harold and treated for terms with some desperation. In return for the decapitation of so many of his soldiers Harold demanded of the Welsh that they bring him the head of Gruffydd ap Llywelyn; in August, after pursuing Gruffydd into the wilds of Snowdonia, they brought it to him. Harold then imposed harsh terms: the annexation of large tracts of eastern Wales to England; the giving of hostages and the taking of mighty oaths; and acceptance of an annual tribute. But there were no reprisals once the Welsh accepted these terms, and Harold proved himself well capable of tempering victory with mercy. He divided North Wales between Gruffydd's half-brothers Bleddyn and Rhiwallon, after taking oaths and hostages from them guaranteeing their loyal vassalage to Edward.[45]

Harold's reputation was now at its apogee, and people wondered how the conquest of Wales, hitherto considered an impossibility, had been achieved so easily. Gruffydd's death released the genie of Welsh centrifugalism from the bottle so that a nation, formidable in arms until that point, disintegrated into a confused factionalism of petty princelings and local warlords. Just to make sure Wales would never again threaten Anglo-Saxon England, Harold built himself a primitive castle or 'hunting seat' at Portskewet in Gwent, South Wales. He proposed to the English *witan* a new law whereby any Welshman found in arms on the English side of Offa's Dike should have his right hand chopped off. To balance this, and show that he would be merciful and conciliatory if the Welsh obeyed his rules, Harold tried to make up to Wales for the terrible manpower losses it had sustained in the 1063 war by persuading

Edward to lift the ban on intermarriage between Welsh women and English men. To give an example, Harold announced that he would be taking Gruffydd's widow Ealdgyth as his wife.[46]

Harold's stunning victory in Wales showed clearly that the Anglo-Saxon military machine was in full working order and was in no way inferior in discipline, equipment and technology to any European force it might have to fight against. Anglo-Saxon England was at least as powerful, sophisticated and technologically competent as Normandy. It was better administered than most of the duchies and kingdoms of western Europe, and its political unity, economic growth and stable government made the realm of Edward the Confessor one of the premier states of the mid-eleventh century. Any force of invaders, whether from Scandinavia or the European mainland, was always going to find an army led by Harold Godwinson a tough nut to crack.[47]

The manpower available to an Anglo-Saxon commander-in-chief was normally in the 8,000–10,000 men range, though it is possible, given a total population of two millions, that an exhaustive conscription could have raised as many as 60,000. The troops available to the king and his commander ranged from the élite warriors of his household and those of his earls to the rawest rustic levies. For this reason a ruler tended to make use of the 'selective fyrd' – a force of professional noble warriors – rather than the 'great fyrd' – a kind of eleventh-century equivalent of the *levée en masse*. The monarch would supplement his own forces with those of provincial earls and contingents from bishoprics and abbeys and only in emergency would he call up the county forces composed of the peasantry.[48]

A huge gulf in fighting quality yawned between the raw levies of the 'great fyrd', used for garrisoning boroughs, defending coastlines and purely local operations, and the seasoned troops a general took with him on an offensive campaign against the enemy. This was not just a question of training and morale or professional as against amateur. More saliently, the rising cost of warfare and the expense of armour consolidated the key social division between those who fought and those who laboured on the land. To some extent this distinction correlates with the differences between the personal obligations of lords and thegns to the king and the territorial obligation, based on 'hides', relating land to military service.[49]

The shire levies were set low – in Berkshire, for instance, one soldier was owed for every five 'hides' of land (a hide was 120 acres) – which meant that England's 70,000 'hides' produced just 14,000 men. How low a levy this was can be gauged from an examination of Berkshire, where roughly one soldier was owed for every twelve families. The strict hide system meant that even with a population of two millions, 70,000 hides produced roughly one soldier for every hundred inhabitants. All men liable to military service had to fight on sea or land as required, for in the Anglo-Saxon forces no distinction was made between army and navy (except at the very highest levels, where housecarls were differentiated from sailors or lithsmen), and all 'hosts' were amphibious. It is not hard to see that in a dire emergency this figure of 14,000 could be quadrupled, though in the short term it was very difficult to call out more than 10,000 men.[50]

But the success of the late Anglo-Saxons in battle depended overwhelmingly on the élite caste of warriors attached to king and earls – the housecarls. Originally Scandinavian mercenaries not wholly unlike the Varangians in the service of the emperor at Byzantium, the housecarls first came to prominence under Cnut, when it was estimated there were just under a thousand in the royal service. At first they were mercenaries who were stationed in towns where they carried out garrison duties; later they were used as tax collectors; and finally they became the strong right arm of the noble or royal household. The housecarls were the crack troops of the Anglo-Saxon army and as such were the equivalent in England of the knights in Normandy.[51]

Scholars have puzzled over the nuances of the housecarls' position. Were they a kind of landless thegn? How did they differ, if at all, from the continental type of mercenary? They seem at once personal retainers in a royal household, professional warriors and tax collectors, sometimes appearing as an esoteric masonry of mercenaries with its own guild and rulers, at others beneficiaries of the danegeld and minor landowners. It seems that, though most housecarls were not landowners, some were, so that a purely military/landowning division of housecarl/ thegn will not suffice; the most likely explanation is that 'housecarl' was a word also used to denote a thegn or landowner of foreign (usually Danish) descent. As for the housecarl/mercenary distinction, the key difference was that the housecarl was tied to his employer by the bond of lordship rather than the cash nexus, as with the mercenary proper; housecarls were paid, it is true, but their wages were an accidental rather than essential part of their service. By their lords in turn they were highly prized, even though the expense of feeding, clothing, lodging and arming them was considerable. Two pieces of evidence point to the supreme value put on them. The law ordained that killing a housecarl was a grave offence, which the king could punish by laying waste the lands of the perpetrators. And by 1066 significant portions of the

Crown's regular revenues were being earmarked for the upkeep of the king's housecarls.[52]

The housecarls' traditional method in battle was to fight on foot from behind a shield-wall. It is quite clear that, although Anglo-Saxons rode horses to battle and would mount up after a victory to pursue a routed foe, they did not use them, Norman-style, as warhorses; lacking a policy of selective horse-breeding, they hardly could, since archaeological remains show Anglo-Saxon horses as scarcely larger than ponies. But it would be an egregious error to assume from this that in any armed conflict between Saxon and Norman the latter was certain to emerge victorious; the facile theory of technological supremacy via the warhorse in the eleventh century has been discarded by the best authorities.[53]

It is often said that the shield-wall was based on the Roman *testudo* or turtle and, though true in general, this proposition must be stated with care. The most fearful weapon of the housecarls was their terrible two-handed battle-axe, and if they were standing too close together they could not wield it. In fact the axemen fought in combat groups, protected by swordsmen and javelin throwers. For this reason the housecarls did not lock their shields together as in the *testudo* and for this reason too we may doubt the authenticity of the Bayeux Tapestry when it shows Saxons fighting with kite-shaped shields. Had the housecarls massed together behind a carapace of kite-shaped shields, they would have found the shields too narrow to form a 'wall' and would additionally have been unable to swing their axes. An unbroken front could, on the other hand, have been provided by the use of traditional German wooden shields (some as large as ninety centimetres in diameter), equipped with an iron bar which provided protection for the hand grip on the other side.[54]

The housecarls had learned from the mistakes of previous Anglo-Saxon armies, and especially from the débâcle at Maldon in 991 when Byrhtnoth had been so signally defeated by the Vikings under Olaf Tryggvason. In that battle the Saxons had fought without byrnies or helmets against better-armed opponents and had been forced to avoid close-order combat where swords could be used. Ethelred the Unready seems to have taken his time to deduce the obvious lesson, but in 1008 he ordered the production of helmets throughout England, one for each man eligible to be raised under the hide system. Equipped with helmets, powerful shields and a two-handed axe that could scythe clean through a man with one well-aimed blow, the housecarl in the shield-wall was supremely well placed to acquit himself efficiently in hand-to-hand combat.[55]

Anglo-Saxon tactics depended on adamantine cohesion in the shield-wall, which in turn depended on morale. Victory could turn into defeat if lack of discipline led men to break rank in pursuit of loot, if a contingent deserted or if a leader was killed in battle. Provided none of these things happened and morale held, it was difficult, to say the least, for an enemy to make any inroads. But it would be a mistake to think of the shield-wall as a static, ponderous, bristling porcupine. Anglo-Saxon armies were trained to deploy in open order, each man about six feet from his comrades, to hurl spears, fire arrows or wield axes, then to close up again when a clash with the enemy was imminent. In close-order mêlée the housecarls' main weapons were their shields and long 'winged' thrusting spears, used like poleaxes, and the aim was the disruption of the foeman's line. As death depleted the front ranks, solid formations were prised open, allowing space for warriors to hurl spears, slash with swords or parry thrusts with shields.[56]

Despite the prominence given in traditional battle accounts to the two-headed axe, it was really the thrusting spear that was the housecarls' primary weapon. There were three main kinds of spear: a throwing javelin with a barbed blade (to prevent easy removal); pikes for thrusting and piercing; and the favoured leaf-shaped weapons suitable both for piercing and for lateral blows. Bows and arrows were also available, the bows being cut from a single wooden stave, from yew, dwarf-elm, ash, holly or hazel. Archers were used to soften up an opposing army and, although there was no intrinsic inferiority in their capacity in this area, all the evidence suggests that the Anglo-Saxons neglected archery, though some troops carried bows with which they could reuse the opponent's fallen shafts. It is anachronistic to import the longbow of Crécy and Agincourt into this era: at Hastings and other battles of this period bows were drawn to the chest only, not, as with the later longbow, to the ear. Some say that the need to carry spears cut down on the numbers of arrows the housecarls could carry into battle, and others that there was not yet any tradition of the yeoman archer; those with the economic surplus to learn specialized skills disdained bowman-ship, while the raw levies of the fyrd lacked the margin to learn the craft.[57]

The sword was still the aristocratic weapon *par excellence*. Archaeological evidence from Anglo-Saxon graves shows spears outnumbering swords by about twenty to one, which confirms literary evidence pointing up the sword as *the* symbol of noble status. The Anglo-Saxon sword was a broad double-edged weapon weighing about three pounds, easy to wield and control because of the balance between the length of the blade and the weight of the pommel; with a hard and flexible steel blade about three feet in length, it was wielded with one hand and intended for cutting and slashing rather than thrusts.[58] Sword in hand, Harold Godwinson, together with his brothers and their noble allies, was sanguine that he would always have the numbers, fighting spirit, morale and sheer warrior calibre of their housecarls to see off any enemy that menaced England. And as long as the kingdom remained united, there was every basis for his belief. But at the very end of Edward's reign, a series of unexpected events suddenly changed everything.

8

Tostig

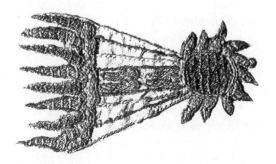

The year 1064 saw the three greatest warriors of Western Europe at their apogee: William of Normandy had conquered Maine, captured le Mans, sacked Mayenne and built castles at Mont Barbet and Ambrières; Harold Godwinson had provided a definitive solution to the military problem of Wales, and Harald Hardrada had won his most shattering victory yet over Svein Estrithson of Denmark. The increasing power of William seemed paralleled by the steady rise of Harold Godwinson, but where the two Harolds looked forward to an era of peace the restless William was already casting envious eyes across the Channel. His conquest of Maine meant there would be no problems in northern France if he launched an adventure overseas: the Angevins were locked in a civil war over the succession, the Capetian king Philip I was a minor and a ward of the Count of Flanders, and the house of Vexin had passed into the tame hands of Ralph of Creps, Count Walter and his wife Biota having died in mysterious circumstances.[1]

Harald Hardrada, however, did not yet have motive or opportunity to turn his attention to England. One of the reasons he ratified the lifetime peace treaty with Svein Estrithson was that he found himself in the years 1064–65 with a major internal revolt on his hands. To display their loyalty to the exiled Hakon Ivarsson, the people of the Oplandene (the Uplands, roughly corresponding to modern Kristian and Hede-marken), where he had been earl, insisted on paying their land dues, scatt and court mulcts to him in Sweden. This was a direct challenge to Harald's authority which he could not ignore, but the king estimated that he could not subdue the Uplands while Hakon was still at large. He therefore decided to invade Sweden in pursuit of him, even if this meant war with King Steinkel.

Harald's plan was to take Hakon by surprise in a winter campaign and ambush him in Gotland. He began by portaging his ships across country to Lake Vaner and then rowed east across the lake, hoping to catch his adversary completely by surprise. At the other side of the lake he left a strong party to guard the ships and advanced overland, trekking through snowdrifts and along frosty narrow paths. Hakon and the Swedes, however, were forewarned, so that the two armies came face to face across an icefield. For most of the day the two hosts stood shivering, waiting for the other to make the first move. Then, one hour before dusk, Harald ordered his men forward; there was a brisk skirmish which the Norwegians won; Hakon's standard was captured but the earl himself got away under cover of night. The next day, messengers came from the ships to report that they were in danger of being iced in for the winter. Harald was forced to retreat to Lake Vaner and with great difficulty free his vessels from the ice; with even more difficulty the Norsemen finally managed to hew a channel in the ice, from which they floated out on to open water. Acknowledging the insuperable problems of winter warfare, Harald admitted defeat and returned to Norway.[2]

In the spring of 1065 he led a strong punitive expedition against the Uplands and implemented a scorched-earth policy, killing, maiming, burning, looting and raping wherever he went. Raumarike, Hadeland, Hedemarken and Ringerike all tasted his wrath. It is incorrect to portray the revolt of the Uplands as a peasants' rising or rebellion by 'primitive rebels', but the ferocity with which it was suppressed shows that Harald regarded it as a serious threat to his position. To those who reproached him for atrocities, he liked to reply that he was acting no differently from St Olaf in similar circumstances. Much blood and treasure had to be expended before the Uplands came to heel, and the revolt took eighteen months (from mid-1064 to late 1065) to put down.[3]

Further uncertainty was engendered when Thorfinn died in the Orkneys in 1065. In the Orkneys proper he was mourned but in the Shetlands and Faroes the news of his demise was greeted with relief; the territories conquered by Thorfinn soon split off under local warlords.

Thorfinn's death worried Harald, for there was always the possibility that his successors would try to repudiate the Norwegian overlordship which Thorfinn had accepted in 1048 – and the possibility was all the more real as his son Paul was married to a daughter of Hakon Ivarsson. Paul, however, was counterbalanced by Thorfinn's other son, Erlend, who objected to the dynastic link with Hakon – this issue was to cause trouble between the brothers later. Since Thorfinn bequeathed his island earldom to both sons and Erlend was disposed to renew the friendship with Harald, Paul had little choice but to acquiesce or face a civil war in which his brother would be supported by Norway. By the beginning of 1066, then, Paul and Erlend had accepted their role as Harald's vassals.[4]

Far more dramatic events were taking place in the south. Some time between spring and summer 1064 the most extraordinary event occurred, whose precise nature has baffled historians ever since: for reasons obscure William and Harold Godwinson came face to face and spent many weeks together. Norman propaganda asserts that King Edward sent Harold to Normandy to promise William the succession; the Anglo-Saxon version is that Harold ended up in Normandy for quite other reasons but was coerced by William into entering into an agreement that was unsatisfactory to him; the most sceptical view is that no visit ever took place at all or that, if it did, it was at an earlier period, possibly in connection with Harold's other European diplomatic ventures.

Those who accept the truth of the visit in 1064 all agree that, whether Harold's real destination was Normandy or somewhere else, he was wrecked on the coast of Ponthieu in north-eastern France, a small, nominally independent enclave, whose ruler owed fealty to William of Normandy. In 1064 the ruler of Ponthieu was Count Guy, brother to the Enguerrand who was killed at the battle of St-Aubin on 25 October 1053; Enguerrand had married Adelaide, an illegitimate daughter of Duke Robert, and was thus brother-in-law to Duke William of Normandy. Guy commenced an incumbency that was prolonged by the standards of the age: he did not die until 1100, by which time Duke William and his successor were both dead. His career can be traced with reasonable accuracy: he became a vassal of William's in 1055, attended the coronation of Philip I of France in 1059 and was infamous as an insatiable plunderer of the abbey of Saint-Riquier.[5]

Ponthieu was also notorious as a centre for wrecking – by the custom of *Lagan*, dating from Charlemagne and practised also in Vimieu and Normandy, the local lord had absolute rights over shipwrecks, the hapless victims and their goods – and there is a suggestion that Harold was a victim of false lights put out by professional wreckers. Sailing from Bosham, Harold's ships were driven by a sudden storm to the coast of Ponthieu, where they ran aground, at the mercy of people who thought nothing of using imprisonment and torture to extract the maximum ransom. A Norman fisherman, who recognized Harold, having seen him once before in one of the fishing ports on the south coast of England, tipped off Guy that among those taken was a man worth a ransom of £100 in his own right. Guy rode to the coast and had Harold imprisoned in fetters at the inland fortress of Beaurain near Hésdin in the Pas de Calais.[6]

One of Harold's party escaped and made his way to William at Rouen, where he explained his master's parlous situation. William at once sent couriers by fast post-horse to demand that Guy of Ponthieu surrender Harold to him, threatening the direst penalties if Guy did not obey. At an earlier stage in his career Guy had sampled the rigours of William's dungeons and had no wish to repeat the experience. He at once released Harold and rode with him to the rendezvous appointed by William at Eu, and was rewarded for his compliance with a gift of money to the putative value of the ransom and a manor on the Eaulne.[7]

From having so recently been a fettered prisoner, Harold was now William's honoured guest and received a splendid reception in Rouen, where a tournament was put on for his honour, and he was introduced to William's family. There was even a legend that William used to retire early to bed, leaving Harold and Matilda alone, so that the guileful duchess could work her wiles on Harold and make him over to the Norman cause. Harold is also said to have promised to marry one of William's daughters when she came of age and to have pledged a sister of his own (previously unknown), named Aelfgifu, to a marriage with a Norman noble. Harold, whether genuinely charmed or only too uncomfortably aware that he was a virtual prisoner, appeared beguiled by all the attention lavished on him and agreed readily enough when William suggested that he accompany him on a campaign against Brittany.[8] It would be of a piece with the psychology of 'making over' if William flattered Harold by saying that the fame of his Welsh victories had preceded him and that the Normans felt privileged to have with them such an expert in subduing Celts by warfare. What was to prevent him repeating against Conan of Brittany the tactics he had used so brilliantly against Gruffydd of Wales?

Brittany at the time was riven by civil war, for Conan was beset by rebels under Rivallon, who seized Dol in William's name, thus allowing the duke to intervene treacherously; Conan was forced to seek the help of Geoffrey of Anjou, nephew of the far greater Geoffrey Martel, and tried to turn the tables by penning Rivallon up in Dol. William's motives were, in the short term, to resolve a continuing struggle for mastery over Mont St-Michel and, in the long term, to make sure there was no powerful enemy in his rear when he finally launched his planned invasion of England. Harold's presence on such a campaign therefore contained more than a little bitter irony, but he swallowed his distaste and even displayed spectacular heroism by rescuing some Norman soldiers from quicksands near Mont St-Michel. As the Norman army approached Dol, Conan raised the siege and retreated to Rennes. The triumph was short-lived, for Rivallon was soon complaining that the Norman army did nothing but waste his substance. After a month William himself pulled out of Brittany, but the war continued. There was a ferocious siege of Dinan, which seems to have ended when the Normans used their old method of circumventing a stubborn defence by shooting blazing arrows into the town.[9]

Harold and William returned to Bayeux, where it was alleged that Harold then took an oath of fealty to the duke. Nothing is more controversial than this so-called oath; it is so mired in argument and obscurity that not even the primary sources can agree where it took place, with some asserting that the venue was Bayeux, others Rouen and still others Bonneville. If an oath was administered, wherever this happened, there is then further controversy about its content and meaning. The only thing that all 'oath' sources can agree on is that Harold promised to marry into William's family; beyond this it is variously asserted that he promised to be William's man in England, to promote his claim to the throne and to receive him as Edward's successor when the Confessor died.[10]

To make sense of this farrago, we have to ask first: why did Harold go to Normandy in the first place? Assuming the story to be true, we are left with three possibilities. Harold may have gone at Edward's prompting and behest to offer the succession to William or to confirm an offer already made. In this case, two further questions arise: when was the alleged offer made: in 1042, 1051 or at some other time? And why would Harold meekly go on such an errand? The second possibility is the so-called 'accident' theory. It is possible that Harold had no intention whatever of visiting Normandy, that he was travelling to the Continent on some other diplomatic mission and was blown to the coast of Ponthieu by a storm. Alternatively, he may simply have been on a fishing trip or pleasure cruise and suffered the same fate. Finally, and most plausibly, it is conceivable that Harold went to Normandy to ransom hostages taken from the Godwin family by William at some time in the past.

There are so many weighty objections to the theory that Harold went to Normandy as Edward's agent to confirm the succession for William that it seems surprising that the idea is still taken seriously. There seem to be only two occasions when Edward could have offered the succession to William: either before his own accession in 1041, when he was still in Normandy, or in 1051 during the crisis with the Godwins, when William is alleged to have visited England. We know that Edward was enraged at his treatment when in exile in Normandy and clearly would not have made such a request out of 'gratitude' and certainly not to an untried fourteen-year-old boy whom Edward scarcely knew. If he made the promise under duress it was invalid, but it would anyway have been meaningless, for he was not king then; furthermore, even if he had been king then, he could not have nominated his successor without the endorsement of the *witan*. If, on the other hand, he made the promise in 1051, and we can get over the almost insurmountable objections to the idea of William's presence in England at the very moment he was fighting for his life in Normandy, where are the charters containing the names of the alleged witnesses and co-guarantors of a Norman succession: Leofric, Stigand, Siward and Godwin? The truth is that the entire story of a succession promise in 1051 is a clumsy and obvious *ex post facto* rationalization by Norman propagandists, who jumbled up a number of names chosen without regard for chronology and plausibility (at the time of the supposed promise Godwin was in exile and could not have been a witness).[11]

Whatever vague promises Edward made in 1051 in the heat of his battle with the Godwin family he soon laid aside, as his choice of Edward the Atheling in 1057 shows plainly. If Edward had wanted William as his indefeasible successor, he had many clear options: he could have announced it formally, he could have invited him to be an associate king, he could have crowned him in his own lifetime, or he could surely have put him in possession of some castle or key stronghold in England. If Edward wanted William as his successor, he would at the very least have exchanged gifts and hostages, and would certainly have surrendered Edward the Atheling to Normandy as an earnest of his intentions. In Edward's eyes, and those of the rest of Europe, he would have been doing William a favour, so where were the gifts and rewards, the oaths and the hostages, *from William to Edward* that we would expect in such a case? Such an exchange would be mandatory if we could but once suspend our disbelief at the notion that Edward's honour would be enhanced by nominating a bastard count as his successor.[12]

Every rational assumption works against the theory of an offer of the succession by Edward to William in 1064. Norman apologists say that Edward made the offer because he felt he was dying, but in 1064 there was no sign that Edward was near death. The only other circumstance that might have made the machiavellian Edward make even a half-promise to Normandy was a threat from Scandinavia, of which there was less sign in 1064 than there had been in the whole of his reign. And every single normal assumption made by this theory turns out to be implausible. It assumes three things, all of them false: that Harold and Edward were on excellent terms, and that Harold would willingly carry out the king's bidding against his own interest; that Harold had no designs on the crown himself; and that Edward thought he had no such designs. Most unfortunate of all for the theory is the evidence from the Bayeux Tapestry which shows Edward imploring Harold not to go to Normandy.[13]

The only interpretation allowing Edward to have offered the succession to William in 1064 and Harold to have played along with his game requires us to impute deep motives of psychopathology to both men. Harold and Edward may simply have been playing games, enjoying making a fool of William. Harold by this time clearly saw himself as Edward's successor, was remarkably devious, and moreover wished to know William's likely reactions in the event of his own coronation. According to one version of the story, Harold was blown off course while fishing, but it may be that he had gone fishing in a metaphorical sense, dangling some vague pledge of friendship before William in order to draw him out and discover how seriously he had set his heart on the English throne.

Edward, for his part, may have colluded with Harold's machiavellian designs out of the bitterness and deep anger of his secret soul. A man of sudden whims and cruel humour, Edward had already revealed his mad streak in 1051 when he demanded of Godwin that he restore his murdered brother Alfred to life. It is not impossible that Edward encouraged Harold to visit Normandy in 1064 out of a mood of sheer malevolence, avenging the 'slights' he had suffered in Normandy by amusedly observing William's raised hopes and eventual discomfiture. Alternatively, he may have been working out his anger against *both* Harold and William by encouraging a mutual hatred that he had triggered in the first place. Some sources say that Edward promised to marry William's sister Adelaide when she was still a child, then jilted her for Edith, daughter of Godwin, which was the original cause of a long latent antagonism between William and the house of Godwin. If all this is rather far-fetched, it represents the only hope of rescuing the Norman story that Harold came from Edward to William with an offer of the throne. As Freeman well remarked: 'The tale that Edward sent Harold or that Harold consented to go, on an errand which shut out himself and every other Englishman from all hope of succession to the crown, is simply absurd and impossible.'[14]

A surprising amount of credence has been given to the 'accident' theory – that Harold found himself in Normandy against his will after a chapter of unforeseen and unwelcome occurrences. In favour of the idea is the circumstantial fact of Harold's imprisonment by Guy of Ponthieu – something he would surely not have dared to do if it was already known that Harold was on his way to Normandy as part of a formal embassy. What, then, was Harold doing according to this version? Some have suggested a fishing or hunting trip that went wrong – Freeman mentions that Harold took hawks and dogs with him – but this makes no sense. In the eleventh century humans (rightly) feared the power of the sea and would not have boarded ship to find hunting terrain they could easily have found by a cross-country journey. Moreover, all the sources indicate that Harold sailed from Bosham, which again makes no sense if he was hunting or fishing; accordingly, it is further suggested that he might have sailed from Wales instead, thus making the story even more improbable.[15]

Much more plausible is the idea that Harold set out on a tour of European states to gauge the likely reaction if he succeeded Edward as king and found himself, as a result of storms and wrecking, in the one court he had had no intention of visiting. In a tricky situation, and knowing William's unsavoury way with state prisoners, Harold would then have extricated himself with difficulty by taking some form of oath to be William's man. An ingenious variant on this is that Harold in 1064 still intended to press the claims to the succession of the fourteen-year-old Edgar the Atheling but, alerted by what he saw in Normandy to the scale of William's ambitions, became concerned that Edgar would not have the authority and strength to resist a Norman counter-claim. The year 1064, then, so far from being a year when Harold furthered his pre-existing designs on the throne, could have been the very moment when Harold decided he had no realistic alternative to seizing the crown for himself.[16]

By far the most likely explanation for Harold's presence in Normandy in 1064 was that he attempted to ransom two of his kinsmen sent as hostages to William by Edward in 1051 during the crisis with Godwin. We have already examined the circumstances in which Wulfnoth, youngest son of Godwin, and Hakon, son of Swein Godwinson, were probably taken to Normandy in 1051, and it is a fair inference that in that case William double-crossed Edward and refused to let him have the hostages back in 1052 when the Confessor was reconciled with Godwin. Wulfnoth certainly passed into Norman hands at some stage, since he was released by William only in 1087 as part of a deathbed amnesty, though it cannot be stated with certainty that it was in 1051. If this was the reason for Harold's journey, his strategy was high-risk, since a request for the return of his kinsmen after such a long period in captivity could presumably mean only that Harold was planning some stroke which would not redound to William's benefit; William was the exact opposite of naïve and would have been alerted by such an embassy.[17]

It is only fair to state that there are serious difficulties with the 'hostage' theory also, to the point where some have considered it a tall story. Wulfnoth and Hakon are shadowy figures who barely exist outside this particular context; Hakon's status is particularly shaky since Swein Godwinson is not known to have had any progeny, though this objection is by no means decisive. The most serious strike against the theory is the initial action by Guy of Ponthieu, though he may not have known the true identity of his prisoners. The waters have been further muddied by writers like Freeman, who made the absurd suggestion that Harold took Wulfnoth and Hakon *with* him in 1064 (for what purpose?). Freeman may, however, have been on firmer ground, in his theory that a sister of Harold's named Aelfgifu was among his party; there is an unexplained cryptological mystery about the presence of a woman named Aelfgifu in the Bayeux Tapestry that no one has been able to clear up satisfactorily.[18]

In the whole of this singular story, where one riddle begets simply another enigma, nothing is more singular than the affair of the oath. There is confusion in the sources about what exactly this bound Harold to, what was its moral, legal, juridical or theological force, and even when and where the alleged oath was administered. As described in the *Carmen de Hastingae Proelio* the famous oath is simply a pact of mutual assistance, such as that previously sworn between Cnut and Edmund or Harthacnut and Magnus. The only common point in all the sources is a possible betrothal of Harold to one of William's kinswomen.

Norman propaganda converted this into a solemn oath of fealty whereby Harold agreed to support William as the next king of England. Various details are adduced: Harold was said to have agreed to be William's proxy at Edward's court, to secure him the succession, and to garrison Dover and other key places against the day of his coronation. The promise was said to have been sealed when William bestowed on Harold the Norman order of knighthood and, in an even more absurd extension of the legend, after Harold had been tricked into swearing a mighty oath on a chest full of holy relics; according to the tall story, these were concealed under a cloth and then revealed to Harold once he had taken the oath.[19]

There is no need to labour the point that the entire story about the oath is a tissue of confusion, a mélange of different propagandist traditions. The Norman 'historians' cannot agree where the oath was supposed to have taken place – whether at Rouen, Bayeux or Bonneville-sur-Touques – or even whether it was administered before the Brittany campaign or after it. Nor can they escape from the dilemma that their story fails once we pose a simple question: was the ceremony public or private? To be binding in any meaningful sense, it would have to have been public, yet we know it cannot have been, for otherwise the 'authorities' would know where it took place. If it was private, it was a meaningless pledge unless backed by the usual exchange of hostages; yet William actually released one of the hostages, Hakon, to Harold instead of demanding further sureties.[20]

The other dilemma from which the propagandists cannot escape is this: either the oath was meaningful, in which case it was taken under duress and thus Harold was relieved of all moral culpability for breaking it; or it was trivial, in which case nobody expected it to be kept. The likelihood is that there was no 'oath' at all, but merely a frivolous gentleman's agreement that Harold would marry William's daughter or some other Norman noblewoman; this was then accompanied by a formal act of homage, which William was later able to present as a full-blooded oath. Any other interpretation stretches credulity to snapping point, especially since oath-taking was unusual in Norman society, with only three oaths by vassals being recorded in the whole of Norman history to 1066. As a noted authority on Norman law has commented: 'William of Poitiers's passage on Harold Godwinson's homage to Duke William is the only extended description of homage and fealty and the only mention at all of investiture in this context.'[21]

To make any sense out of the entire incident we have to look at the psychology of the participants. William may well have been playing a double game – extracting from Harold an oath he knew could not be kept so as to derive a clear propaganda advantage: when he invaded England, he wanted to be able to present his aggression as a 'crusade' against a perjurer. It may well be that the 'oath' was nothing more than a temporary agreement that Harold would be William's man for the duration of the Breton campaign out of gratitude for his release from the clutches of Guy of Ponthieu. Even if the 'oath' was an agreement to marry William's daughter, once Harold went back on that agreement it was open to William to implement a double-cross, by claiming that implicit in the pledge to marry his daughter was Harold's acceptance that he could hold England only as a fief for his intended father-in-law. Harold, we know, had a reputation for being too facile in his approach to oaths and agreements, and his cynicism (or fear of the consequences if he refused) almost certainly led him to an ill-advised informal agreement which played into William's hands.[22]

Several points may be in order at this juncture, in ascending rank of importance. First, early medieval grandees made and unmade promises with great alacrity, seldom in expectation that they would have to be fulfilled; the gentleman's agreement meant little in this era. Harold may well have returned from England and simply forgotten all about his pledge to marry William's kinswoman. Secondly, and allied to this in meaning, is the fact that relations between lords and vassals, even when supposed to be binding, were remarkably fluid, if only because often internally self-contradictory. William himself was at one and the same time in the 1050s supposed to be the man both of Edward of England and Henry of France; Malcolm of Scotland was Tostig Godwinson's sworn brother yet did not find this an impediment to ravaging Northumbria while Tostig was absent; and Herbert of Maine achieved a kind of *pièce de résistance* in the field of feudal obligations by owing simultaneous allegiance to Henry of France, William of Normandy and the Duke of Anjou.[23]

Furthermore, the factor of duress casts a moral shadow over everything done and promised by Harold in Normandy in 1064. Let us leave on one side what he owed to gratitude or normal diplomatic punctilio. Perhaps he should still have held firm and refused to make even the vaguest of promises to William; perhaps he should have yielded neither to the alleged blandishments of Matilda nor the implicit threats of her husband; maybe he should have stood firm and risked the danger of death by poison or in a 'hunting accident' or avoided the temptation to make a fool of William, if that is what his intention was. Yet the moral villain of the story as traditionally related was undoubtedly

William: he achieved a psychological advantage over his guest by the demonstration of the 'road not taken' when he rescued Harold from Guy of Ponthieu; he browbeat him into taking part in a campaign against Brittany in which he had no legitimate interest; and the entire story of trickery over sacred relics, machiavellianism over the oath and overall latent duress is of a piece with the ferocious William of Normandy we know from other sources. For Norman propaganda to attempt to brand Harold as a traitor, villain and perjurer on the basis of evidence that so manifestly does not redound to William's favour is one of the most singular aspects of the entire 1064 incident.[24]

Norman propaganda was hamfisted in every way, as the ludicrous story of Edward's promise of the crown in 1051 makes clear. William of Poitiers and his followers seemed to think that an oath extracted from Harold in some way bound the kingdom of England, even though Harold was not king and even though it was anyway the *witan* and not the monarch that decided on the succession.[25] Perhaps the most risible part of the story is the alleged sequel, when Harold returned to England, allegedly to the reproaches of Edward, who knew that William was a hard bargainer. According to one version, Edward told Harold: 'Did I not tell you I knew William, and that your going might bring untold calamity upon this kingdom?'[26] In what sense he 'knew' a man he had last seen twenty-five years earlier as a fourteen-year-old boy is unclear, but let us assume he meant he had observed the rise and rise of the hard and unyielding duke. Why was Harold's attempt to bring back hostages (which is the explanation this story opts for) likely to bring calamity to the kingdom? Presumably when William detained the hostages illicitly in the first place, Edward would already have been alerted to his true ambition. It must have been clear to all that William intended to press his claim to the throne of England whatever Harold did or did not do.

At all events Harold returned to England, having definitely lost caste. He had been humiliated in Ponthieu and reduced to secondary status in Normandy. Superficially William had honoured him, by the initial release, by taking him on the Breton campaign as a companion of honour, by knighting him, giving him rich gifts on his departure and by releasing his nephew Hakon. But Harold had not secured his major objective, the freedom of his brother Wulfnoth, and the effect of his embassy was to exacerbate tension between England and Normandy. Both Harold and William must have known in their hearts that the issue between them would only ever be resolved by force of arms, and both had seen enough of the other to know what a formidable opponent he was. Yet the task ahead of William still seemed insuperable. To conquer

England he would need a crack in the steely military carapace Harold presented to any would-be invader. By the most incredible good fortune, 'William the lucky bastard', as he has been well dubbed, was about to achieve his dearest wish.

The year 1065 was considered an ill-omened one, for it was thought that the world would come to an end when the Feast of the Annunciation coincided with Good Friday. As the old legend put it:

> *When Our Lord falls on Our Lady's lap*
> *England shall have a dire mishap.*

For all that, the early months of the year seemed uneventful. Much of the spring and summer was taken up with affairs in Wales. Some English traders at Newport refused to pay the customary toll, whereupon Rhiryd, Gruffydd ap Llywelyn's successor, had them roughed up and cut their anchor away. When the merchants reported this to Harold, he invaded Glamorgan and started building a fort at Portskewet, south-west of Chepstow. Then in August there was an even more serious incident when Caradoc, son of Gruffydd ap Rhydderch, attacked Harold's fortress, slew many of the workers and artisans, and carried off the stores and equipment.[27]

Caradoc's action is yet another mystery from the last days of Anglo-Saxon England. Would he really have ventured such a contumacious act against a man who two years before had convulsed Wales, unless he was secretly in league with some other powerful faction? Rumours of plots abounded in 1065, and in the same year there is the sudden banishment by Edward for treason of the wealthy pro-Danish clerk Spirites. The 'D' version of the Anglo-Saxon Chronicle states clearly that the attack on Portskewet was part of a conspiracy, though sceptics reply that this chronicler finds every untoward event as part of a hidden, sinister pattern. Nevertheless, the sequence of events in 1065 suggests strongly that some sort of power struggle was going on in England, and the obvious inference is that the Spirites and Portskewet affairs denote a conflict between Harold and his party on one side and Edward, Edith and Tostig on the other.[28]

We know little of Edward's personal relations with Harold, and the few hints in the sources consistently speak of men at variance on means and ends. It would scarcely be surprising if the king, reduced to a figurehead by Godwin and then further truncated in power by his eldest surviving son, should have resented and even hated the powerful and charismatic Harold. Tostig, on the other hand, he adored only just short of idolatry – an emotion in which he was encouraged by Queen Edith, whose favourite brother Tostig was. Edward's high regard for Tostig may have combined the attraction of opposites – the weak for the ruthless, perhaps – with a genuine regard for his marital fidelity, his refusal to follow his brother Harold into promiscuous womanizing, and the large sums of money he spent on piety and good works. It is not inconceivable that both Edward and Edith played on Tostig's vanity and encouraged him to believe that he would make a more natural successor to the throne than his more vaunted elder brother. Tostig's marriage to Judith of Flanders, kin both to Baldwin and Edward, was the most obvious sign of an early high-flying ambition which the royal couple appear to have worked on assiduously.[29]

But in the struggle with Harold Tostig had a notable weak spot which was to be used against him with devastating effect: the earldom of Northumbria that he had acquired in 1055. Tostig had been made earl for three main reasons: because of the expulsion of Aelfgar for 'treason'; because of intense lobbying by Harold and Edith; and because the obvious successor, Waltheof, Siward's son, was a mere boy. Aelfgar, who bitterly opposed the encirclement of his Mercian family's territory by the encroaching Godwinsons, was totally outwitted by Harold in 1055 and ended up being banished on a spurious charge of treason, though he may well have given hostages to fortune by some unwise intrigues and by wild behaviour that suggested he was another Swein Godwinson. Waltheof, on the other hand, was by no means disgraced and spent his minority full of honours and privileges.[30]

The appointment of Tostig as Earl of Northumbria was a new departure – the first time a scion of a Wessex family had ruled in the north – and was widely considered provocative and tactless. Since the early tenth century the north of England had been ruled by the Bamburgh family virtually on franchise from the kings of England, but since the death of Ethelred the relationship had been uneasy and violent: three of the family members, Uhtred, Eadulf and Ealdred, had been murdered on the orders of Cnut and Harthacnut as part of a continuing struggle to bring Northumbria fully under the control of the monarchs in the south. The position of the Bamburgh family was shaky but it still clung on, heartened by the knowledge that northern earls had always been either Bamburghs or Anglo-Danes and Scandinavians. Tostig's appointment, a manifest sign of the triumphalism of the Godwinsons, changed all that.[31]

Tostig was notoriously strong-willed and inflexible and one of those who believed in the old maxim 'let the heavens fall provided justice be done'. He waged a draconian campaign against the endemic crime and lawlessness of the north, but his opposition to lawlessness and corruption bordered on fanaticism, and it is easy to see how such a 'sea-green incorruptible' soon acquired the reputation of a tyrant. In 1055 Northumbria was in a state of near anarchy, where the only rules were those imposed by local mafias linked to the ruling families, and especially the Bamburghs. Any party of strangers less then thirty strong travelling through the earldom could be certain of ambush, plunder, rape and possibly death, and it was well known that local nobles were involved in this highway robbery and made money out of it. Tostig was adamant and pertinacious in his resolve to root out crime and corruption and was prepared to follow the trail of lawlessness however high it led and deal without mercy with the perpetrators. He began by using death and mutilation against individual offenders and progressed to the use of death squads against recalcitrant local magnates. Most of all, he abolished the laws of Cnut, which allowed blood-feud, in favour of a settled system of law over which he would preside.[32]

Tostig also built up a powerful bodyguard of about two hundred housecarls. This private army, needed for his own protection, added to his new system of justice administration, required money, and the earl added to his reputation for 'tyranny' by the zeal with which he taxed, fined, mulcted and seized church properties. As with Harold, the accusation that he was harsh against the church has to be treated with caution. What happened was that there were winners and losers when it came to Tostig's often generous ecclesiastical benefactions, and the cries of 'Despotism!' by the losing abbeys and monasteries lost nothing in the telling. In trying to equalize the burden of taxation, Tostig naturally offended some, but there can be no doubt that he and his wife Judith were important patrons of the church of Durham. As with his campaign against brigandage on the highways, Tostig's primary concern was justice and it was this that alienated the local élites. The north had traditionally been taxed much more lightly than the rest of the country, and Northumbrian magnates had largely evaded their burden altogether; what irked them now was that Tostig had an efficient system of taxation based on equality.[33]

Tostig's innovations, his new legal system, his taxation, his passion for justice, all helped alienate any putative allies in the north. As his unpopularity grew, so did his taxation demands, for he had to employ more and more men in his household to carry out his fiscal and law enforcement policies. Tostig scarcely increased his standing in North-umbria by his frequent absences from the earldom, largely in response to

Edward's impassioned requests for the presence of his great friend and confidant at his court in the south. The king himself never travelled further north than Shrewsbury, which angered the largely Scandinavian-descended people of the north; here was insult added to injury: not just a king who disdained the north but an earl who was frequently absent from Northumbria at the behest of the selfsame monarch. In his absence Tostig left the task of administration to his deputy Copsig, who was unhappily neither from the house of Bamburgh nor a member of Siward's family. Copsig tried unsuccessfully to conciliate the clerks of Durham and attempted to curry favour with them by deposing the unpopular Bishop Aethelrig. Unfortunately, instead of leaving the choice of successor to the clerks, Copsig referred the matter to Tostig, who nominated Aethelwine, Aethelrig's brother – in the eyes of the clerks the mixture as before and therefore unacceptable.[34]

The final area in which Tostig lost caste was his inability to solve the problem of Malcolm III of Scotland. Despite Edward's support for him in 1054 against Macbeth, Malcolm proved to be a treacherous ingrate and, after he had finally disposed of Macbeth in 1057, ceased to be Edward's tame client king and began raiding across the border into Northumbria, stealing cattle, carrying off men and women as slaves, uplifting goods and garnering booty. From the Scots' point of view Malcolm was merely doing what was expected of a warrior king, but his incursions were worrying, since they challenged the credibility of Tostig at the very moment that he was engaged in a power struggle with the old élites of Northumbria. Encouraged initially by the selfsame fissiparous politics of the earldom, Malcolm began by testing Tostig's intentions with minor military probes. Tostig responded by a series of Fabian campaigns, taking care not to waste his manpower in pitched battles, but intending to wear Malcolm down with a war of attrition; at the same time he put out peace feelers.[35]

In 1059 Tostig's long game paid off, or at least did so in the short run. After the exchange of a number of increasingly important envoys, Tostig journeyed north of the border in company with Aethelwine, Bishop of Durham, and Kynsige, Archbishop of York. Together they persuaded Malcolm to venture into England for a summit meeting with King Edward. The subsequent negotiations were successful. Malcolm asked for the return of Cumberland, which had originally been a Scottish possession seized by the previous earl, Siward, but Edward blunted the thrust of this request with a lavish bestowal of compensatory gifts. Apparently satisfied, Malcolm withdrew, having first sworn blood-brotherhood with Tostig and pledged eternal peace as long as he was Earl of Northumbria.[36]

In 1061 Tostig made his famous journey to Rome to win the pallium for Ealdred, the new Bishop of York. Taking advantage of his absence, and using the spurious argument that his pact with Tostig held good only while the earl was physically present in Northumbria, Malcolm led a powerful army on a deep raid which cut a swathe through the earldom and penetrated as far south as Durham. Having laid waste Lindisfarne, Malcolm swung in an arc and ravaged Cumberland, announcing as he went that he was taking possession of ancient Scottish lands. On his return, Tostig meekly bowed to the *fait accompli*, accepted the loss of Cumberland, made no attempt to retaliate against Scotland and instead signed another peace treaty with Malcolm. Here was a wonderful propaganda for the powerful anti-Tostig faction in the earldom: the absentee earl, it was said, was playing high politics in Rome while grossly neglecting the province he was supposed to be governing; what price the frenzied campaign for law and order and the ordinances against brigandage when Malcolm could devastate the land without let or hindrance; and why were the men of Northumbria supposed to pay for Tostig's burdensome tactics when he could not provide them with the most elementary military security? Tostig might well have replied that it was precisely the lack of support he enjoyed among the grandees of Northumbria that made it impossible for him to campaign against Malcolm.[37]

By 1064 tensions in the earldom were almost at snapping point. A furious vendetta raged between Tostig and the sons of Aelfgar, the nobility of Yorkshire was disaffected, while angry scions of the house of Bamburgh watched from the sidelines awaiting their chance. A powerful anti-Tostig faction had also arisen within the northern Church, based on the clerks of Durham and particularly associated with Bishop Aethelwine and the sacristan Elfred Weston. The overwrought emotions finally found expression in outright murder, for in 1064 two of the powerful northern magnates were assassinated: Gamel, son of Orm, and Ulf, son of Dolin. These were two of the leading lights of Northumbrian separatism and associates of Gospatric, youngest son of the earl Uhtred (son of Ethelred), previously Siward's collaborator in Northumbria, a possible claimant to the throne and, in the eyes of most northerners, the real earl of the province.[38]

Finally, on 28 December 1064, Gospatric himself was murdered at Edward's Christmas court. For all three murders Tostig was held responsible, and in the assassination of Gospatric he was said to have been materially aided (in ways unspecified) by his sister, Queen Edith. These are very deep waters indeed. Some say Edward's agents killed Gamel and Ulf to help Tostig, but without the earl's knowledge, and then slew Gospatric in concert with Edith. Some go further and assert that neither Tostig nor Edith was involved: Edward carried out the killings to remove possibly troublesome pretenders and ensure that his beloved Tostig succeeded to the throne. As one recent scholar has put it: 'We may suspect that Edward himself had a part in the murder which his later reputation whitewashed, leaving Edith with the blame.'[39]

We are left with yet another unsolved mystery: who killed the leading lights of Northumbrian separatism and why? On a *cui bono?* basis the answer must be Tostig: he committed murder to take out the leaders of the opposition to his rule in Northumbria. But Edward too had his reasons for being concerned about the drift of events in the north and, as later events showed, he was implacably opposed to Northumbrian separatism; he could have rationalized his murder of the trio as *raison d'état*. So it is possible that either Tostig or Edward acted alone, that both colluded with Edith, or even that all three conspired together. The difficulty for the historian is that even the simplest incident involving Earl Tostig is susceptible to the most ambiguous interpretations. The Gospatric murdered at Christmas 1064 had a half-nephew, himself later an Earl of Northumbria, whom Tostig had insisted on taking with him on his 1061 pilgrimage to Rome. Does this mean that Tostig and Gospatric the younger were bonded in friendship or does it mean that Tostig took him with him as surety for his uncle's good behaviour?[40]

Even more opaque is the story of Gospatric's exploits on the journey home from Rome. The official story of the ambush outside Rome was that the heroic Gospatric, seeing Tostig's party about to be intercepted, exhorted the earl to gallop away to safety on a fast horse, while he himself impersonated Tostig. Once Tostig had got clear away, Gospatric admitted the truth, which made the robbers so angry they at first resolved to kill him for the deception; finally, however, admiration for his courage got the better of them and they released him with their heartiest best wishes.

But others said that Tostig was not with his ambushed party but, forewarned of Gerard's attempt, remained in Rome on 'urgent business', hoping that Gospatric would resist the highway robbery and be killed. The Northumbrians certainly thought it suspicious that the young Gospatric was nearly killed while supposedly under the protection of Tostig and thought back to the murder of Ealdred Bamburgh by Harthacnut's man Carl in 1038 – a murder which had been preceded by Carl's proposal that the two of them should go on a pilgrimage together.[41]

Given the iron grip of the Godwinsons on England, the events of 1065 make sense only if we postulate a severe divergence in interests and ambitions between Harold and Tostig, with Tostig secretly encouraged and abetted by Edward. We do not know why two brothers, who had collaborated so well hitherto, suddenly fell out; maybe Tostig's contempt for Harold's lifestyle, his envy of his brother's advantages and latent sibling rivalry were already at boiling point when Edward whispered to him that he, Tostig, was his preferred successor. Either Tostig encouraged Caradoc to attack Harold's fort at Portskewet or Harold thought he had and decided to retaliate in the north. Despite many provocations, the anti-Tostig party in Northumbria would not have risen without getting the green light from Harold.[42]

Perhaps, too, it is significant that Harold was hunting with Tostig in Wiltshire in early October 1065 when news came in of a seismic rebellion in the north. On 3 October the standard of revolt was raised in Yorkshire by a formidable coalition of thegns representing Mercia, Northumbria and Yorkshire, regions which had rarely if ever collaborated. An *ad hoc* junta, prominent among which were Gamelbearn, kinsman of the murdered Gamel, Dunstan, the son of Aethelnoth, and Glonicorn, son of Heardulf, began issuing decrees in defiance of Tostig. At a *gemot* in York the thegns utterly repudiated Tostig's authority as earl while stressing their continuing loyalty to Edward; Tostig was declared deposed and outlaw and it was announced that Morcar, son of Aelfgar, would be the new earl. The leaders of Tostig's Danish housecarls, Amund and Reavenswart, saw at once the extreme danger in which they were placed and fled south from York, but were overtaken on the road and summarily executed. Next day there was a bloody purge when all two hundred of Tostig's housecarls were hunted down and massacred, after which the rebels broke open the deposed earl's treasury and plundered it.[43]

Several things became plain after these two tragic days that convulsed the north. Although the flame of Northumbrian independence still burned brightly, the rebellion was a more complex phenomenon than mere localism, as was shown by the choice of Morcar as earl, a man with no obvious connections with the Anglo-Scandinavian society of the north. The obvious choice was Waltheof, Siward's son, who was now in his early twenties and hence highly eligible, but it was plain that the house of Siward enjoyed no great popularity. It has been suggested that

Morcar was a compromise candidate, since Northumbrians would not accept Waltheof nor the men of Yorkshire Oswulf, son of Earl Eadulf, and the current leading scion of the house of Bamburgh. As consolation prizes, both the rejected candidates were given sub-earldoms, Oswulf in Northumbria and Waltheof in Huntingdon and Northampton, with the clear understanding that they held their lands by Morcar's favour.[44]

The rise to prominence of Morcar and his brother Edwin showed that the vendetta waged by the house of Aelfgar against Tostig had finally paid off. The choice of Morcar as the new earl can be further interpreted in a number of different ways. Did the fact that the rebels turned for leadership to another Saxon mean, as has been suggested, that they did not intend a breakaway movement from Edward's England and still considered that their best interests lay in a united England? Or did it mean that the Northumbrians were biding their time, waiting to see what Harold Godwinson and Edward would do before finally revealing their hand? Clearly the basic Northumbrian intention, having snubbed Waltheof, Siward's son, and chosen instead the son of one of his victims (Earl Eadulf), was to return to quasi-independence under a direct descendant of one of their ancient earls. Morcar was important to all the parties: to Oswulf and Waltheof as a means of heading off faction-fighting between their parties, which might allow Tostig to return, and to Harold (with whom Morcar presumably intrigued) as a means of preventing an independence movement in Northumbria.[45]

Nevertheless, it became increasingly difficult for Morcar to allege that the overthrow of Tostig represented conflict within the regime rather than an overt challenge to Edward's authority. The much-vaunted grievances against Tostig should have been rehearsed before Edward and his *witan* or a *witenagemot* of the entire realm, so the decrees of 3 October were unconstitutional, to say nothing about the way the rebels had infringed the severe prohibitions against the killing of housecarls. Moreover, the thegns of Yorkshire had broken into Tostig's treasury and plundered it indiscriminately, whereas, if they were claiming that Tostig's taxes were illegal, they should have handed the money over to the new earl, Morcar, with a petition for a legal refund.[46]

The rebellion soon developed its own momentum. Flushed by the ease of their early successes, the rebels sent for Morcar, confirmed him as earl, and invited him to lead them south on an expedition to root out those enclaves in the vast earldom of Northumbria that were still loyal to Tostig. Morcar's army struck south, bringing a reign of terror to the towns of Lincoln, Nottingham and Derby, killing and plundering as they went, and sweeping into their ranks many volunteers, either those genuinely caught up in the euphoria of booty and rapine, or believers in expediency who joined the winning side. At Northampton, Morcar was joined by his brother Edwin, with a large body of freebooters. Finding Northampton not very sympathetic to his aims, Morcar allowed his army to run amok: Northampton was systematically sacked, hundreds of its citizens were killed or raped, several hundred more were carried off as slaves, houses were gutted, the winter's supplies of corn and wheat committed to the flames, and herds of cattle driven off as the spoils of war.[47]

The presence of large numbers of Welsh adventurers with Edwin forces one to re-examine the role of Wales in the crisis of 1065. Who were these Welshmen: mercenaries, professional desperadoes or the rump of Gruffydd ap Llywelyn's defeated army, thirsting for revenge for the humiliation of two years before? Yet one more mystery presents itself, so that some historians have seen Morcar and Edwin as the prime movers of the crisis of 1065, acting completely independently of Harold. The Welsh alliances of Aelfgar and his sons are well known, so that it would by no means be far-fetched to see the assault on Harold's fort at Portskewet as the action of Caradoc in collusion with Edwin and Morcar. But this would construe the 1065 rising as a frontal challenge to the power and credibility of the Godwinssons as a whole; knowing what we know of Harold, it is inconceivable that he would have ignored a challenge to Tostig if it was really a disguised form of a challenge to his own prestige.[48]

The sequel to the sack of Northampton certainly suggests that Harold had some secret understanding with Morcar and Edwin, if only because his military inertia contrasts so strikingly with the flair and élan he would demonstrate the following year. Harold hastened from his Wiltshire hunting lodge to Northampton with a message from the king: the rebels should lay down their arms forthwith and submit their grievances to a full assembly of the realm. The Northumbrians replied defiantly that they would lay down their arms only if Edward confirmed the banishment of Tostig and the 'election' of Morcar as earl. If ever the Confessor had doubts about the seriousness of the rebellion, he could entertain them no longer; the threat to his authority and the implicit hint of civil war were only too palpable.

The royal council the king assembled at Britford, near Salisbury, quickly turned into an acrimonious affair. Tostig openly charged his brother Harold with having fomented the revolt, but Harold's faction riposted that Tostig had brought all his trouble on his own head, alienating his subjects over a decade out of insensate covetousness for the wealth of the Northumbrian magnates. Harold argued that, with so many powerful external enemies snapping at their heels, the English could not afford civil war, which would be the inevitable outcome if he tried to restore Tostig by force. Tostig, though, was adamant that Harold was duty-bound to support him, come weal or woe, for two reasons: the king's dignity, prestige and sovereignty were at stake; and for Harold, as his brother, to fail him at this stage would be an 'unnatural' act. The more Harold demurred, the wilder grew Tostig's allegations; to quieten the assembly Harold finally swore an oath that he had no part in fomenting or compassing the rebellion.[49]

At this point, in the teeth of the arguments by all his commanders, which ranged from the difficulties of mounting a winter campaign in the north to endorsement of Harold's argument that what they now faced was civil war, Edward intervened to demand the defeat of the rebels by force of arms. Harold could not openly refuse to obey a direct order from the king, but he effectively sabotaged Edward by calling on a number of senior military commanders, all of whom declared to the assembly that an army sufficient for the task could not be assembled until the following spring. At this Edward became almost apoplectic with rage and called down the vengeance of the Almighty alike on those who had rebelled and those who stood in the way of their just punishment.

Harold took the obvious course to camouflage his own reluctance to act against Morcar and Edwin and persuaded the king to summon a general *witenagemot* of the whole realm. Edward agreed, seemingly in hopes that, in the interim, the same fate would strike Morcar and Edwin as had attended Godwin in 1051, and that the rebel army would melt away. Alas for his hopes, no such thing happened. At the meeting of the full assembly at Oxford on 28 October Harold at first fruitlessly tried to reconcile Tostig and the rebels, then conceded their demands at virtually every point: Tostig's laws were annulled and the laws of Cnut reinstated, the illicit acts of the York *gemot* were validated, Morcar declared elected and Tostig deposed. Whether because as an innocent he now feared the fissiparous tendencies engendered in England, or because as a conspirator he sensed Morcar and Edwin slipping from his control, Harold extracted one concession: the shires of Northampton and Huntingdon were to be detached from Northumbria and given to Waltheof. He had now engineered a situation where the rebels were split three ways, between the factions of Morcar, Waltheof and Oswulf.[50]

Edward, who had all along hankered for a military solution, was said to have been so angry that he suffered a succession of minor strokes.

Certainly he was never the same man again, and the humiliation he suffered at the two councils, allied to the grief he felt at having to sign the order for the exile of his beloved Tostig, effectively broke his heart. He took to his bed and never recovered. After an emotional farewell with the king, Tostig and Judith departed for exile at the court of Baldwin in Flanders.

Harold's position is the least clear of the three. His refusal to fight Morcar and Edwin was either consummate statesmanship or part of a devious game. His apologists say that he did not want civil war for two reasons. Unlike Edward, who was always for military solutions, he had actually seen the horrors of war and was reluctant to let more blood unless he had no choice; this is part of the well-known phenomenon whereby veterans opt for peaceful solutions while those who have not experienced combat rattle sabres. Moreover, he saw only too clearly that a protracted civil war between north and south would simply play into the hands of future claimants to the English throne, and perhaps he particularly feared that if he fought the northern rebels William of Normandy would emerge as *tertius gaudens* (lucky third party). In a word, depending on what interpretation we put on his conduct in 1065, he was either egregiously selfish and calculating or a statesman of Solomonic wisdom.[51]

By the end of November 1065 Harold was aware that the king was fading fast and that the crown would soon be his. Since Edward was sick and could not hunt and since, moreover, he wanted to consecrate his new church at Westminster, he did not hold his Christmas court at Gloucester, as originally intended, but in London. The last Christmas court of the Confessor's reign saw the greatest of the land convened in one place; all the various interests in the kingdom were represented, so that if there was significant opposition to Harold as the next king this fact would have emerged. It is probable that at this stage Harold agreed to marry Ealdgyth, widow of Gruffydd ap Llywelyn and sister of Edwin and Morcar, in return for their support for his bid for the throne. It is impossible to claim that Harold's eventual succession represented a kind of *coup d'état*, as the Norman propagandist William of Poitiers asserted.[52]

Edward sank lower on Christmas Eve – it is likely that he had another in a series of strokes – valiantly staggered through the Christmas Day ceremonies, but had to take to his bed the next day. His last public act was to be present at the consecration of the new abbey church of Westminster on 28 December. Once again he took to his bed, where Archbishop Stigand, Harold, Edith, Robert fitzMarch and other royal favourites were in constant attendance. He sank into a coma, regaining consciousness only to relate the details of an apocalyptical vision, in which he had seen England consumed by fire and sword, abandoned to the Devil and his demons because God, in his anger with the Anglo-Saxons, who would not repent of their wickedness, would not grant forgiveness. Queen Edith was greatly distressed at these revelations and thought her husband a true prophet, but the cynical Stigand whispered to Harold that the king was simply raving in a pre-death delirium.[53]

While Edith wept and lamented, Edward made his last will and testament in the form of the *verba novissima* – the last words which under Anglo-Saxon custom were the only universally recognized and valid way to dispose of goods and property. He asked God to repay his wife for her loving and dutiful service, then held out his hand to Harold and spoke as follows: 'I commend this woman and all the kingdom to your protection. Remember that she is your lady and sister and serve her faithfully and honour her as such for all the days of her life. Do not take away from her any honour that I have granted her.' Edward then made Harold protector of all his housecarls and foreign servants, asking him to give them the choice of staying on to serve the new king or returning home with full honours, pay and safe-conduct.[54]

Here surely was the death-knell for William's claim that he was Edward's clearly designated heir. All English sources make it crystal clear that Edward named Harold as his successor, but William's apologists tried (and some do so even today) to deny the obvious, in a number of ways. Some claimed that Edward was not *compos mentis* and others that he was acting under duress from Harold, though what threat could be brought aginst a man already at the point of death is unclear. Still others barefacedly claimed that, in ways unexplained, the 1064 'oath' overrode Edward's deathbed bequest. A modern, quasi-legalistic argument is that Edward made Harold his executor, not his successor, but this poses the obvious question: executor in favour of whom? Edward would scarcely have appointed him an executor for an unknown beneficiary. The only pro-Norman argument with a scintilla of plausibility is the one that stresses a failure to communicate between the two cultures. In Anglo-Saxon culture a verbal promise not accompanied by physical investment did not have the force of a *post obitum* bequest, as it may have done in Normandy. Edward's *verba novissima* bequest could only be overriden by a genuine *post obitum* gift to William, which Edward had not made.[55]

If Edward had wanted to make an irrevocable *post obitum* offer of the throne to William, he would have invited him to the Christmas court, since all such bequests were legitimatized by crowning the heir in the

1. Edward the unsaintly neurotic

2. Harold: a coin from his short reign

3. Earl Godwin's seal – symbol of dynastic power

4. The Anglo-Saxon 'equalizer' was used only by the housecarls

5. The Varangian Guard – often it decided the fate of Emperors

6. Yaroslav: the Wise to the Russians, but the Miserly to the Norsemen

7. A lugubrious Svein Estrithson stares out from one of his 'pennings'

8. St Olaf –
the half-brother
whose legend
Harald Hardrada
co-opted

9. A Viking picture stone –
the Northern version of Trajan's column

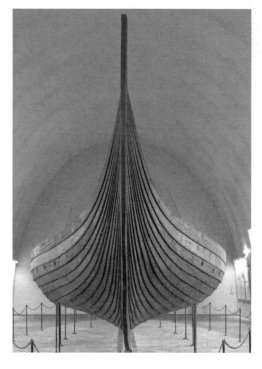

10. The Gokstad ship –
a fine example of the
longships that terrified Europe

11. Viking armour – the missing element at Stamford Bridge

12. Seal of William the Conqueror – even here the warhorse is all-important

13. Norman knights – it was said they could knock down the walls of Jericho

14. Norman propaganda at its apogee; Harold's alleged oath to William

15. For the invasion the Normans built ships – a new experience for them

16. The Norman fleet at sea – they feared the Channel more than
they feared the English

17. By laying waste Hastings and its environs William forced Harold to an early battle

18. The irresistible force and the immovable object: Norman cavalry collide
with Saxon shield wall

19. The Saxons lure the Norman horse into a trap

20. Death of Gyrth and Leofwine. If Harold had been wise, his brothers would not have been at the battle.

21. Death of Harold. Is he stricken with an arrow in the eye?

lifetime of his predecessor, by dividing the kingdom or by shared kingship, such as that of Magnus and Harald Hardrada or Edward and Harthacnut. Edward never formally invested William with kingship, and the statement in the *Carmen* that he sent William a sword and ring as tokens of the succession is transparent Norman propaganda. The Norman case was always based on two things: the alleged promise in 1051 and the oath in 1064. By his offer of the throne to Edward the Exile in 1051 Edward had already rescinded whatever he had said to William in 1051; and the 'oath' of 1064, whatever it was, was overriden by the Confessor's *novissima verba*; as an English herald patiently explained to William in October 1066, for 450 years ever since the days of Augustine of Canterbury, it was settled law and custom in England that a person's last will and testament annulled any previous pledge made by that person.[56]

Having incontestably named Harold as his successor, Edward died on 5 January 1066, after receiving the last rites from Archbishop Stigand, and was buried in Westminster the next day. The *witan* met on 5 January and confirmed Harold as king; Edwin and Morcar were among those voting for him. It is said that a few voices were raised in favour of Edgar the Atheling and someone even mentioned William, but the assembly, without faction or separatist sentiment, overwhelmingly opted for Harold. In terms of *realpolitik* Harold had no sensible alternative but to accept. If Tostig and William were to stake their claim by armed force, as seemed likely, it would be better for England to be ruled by a warrior-king in his prime with strong links to the northern earls rather than see the fifteen-year-old Edgar the Atheling grapple with the problem.[57]

So it was that on 6 January there took place the double ceremony of the burial of Edward and the coronation of King Harold. Norman propagandists asserted that Stigand crowned Harold king and thus increased the element of 'illegitimacy' in his kingship (Stigand had received his pallium from a pope who had been stricken from the records of official pontiffs), but the truth is that to avoid just such an allegation Harold had taken care to see that his friend Ealdred, Archbishop of York, officiated at the coronation ceremony. For similar reasons perhaps Stigand took no part in Edward's funeral, where the master of ceremonies was Abbot Edwin. It has sometimes been suggested that Harold's coronation the day after Edward's death betokened 'unseemly haste,' and this is why the king's funeral is shown *before* his death on the Bayeux Tapestry, but this is an anachronistic judgement. As Professor Barlow has commented: 'It is most unlikely that anyone thought it unseemly for the funeral baked meats to furnish coldly the coronation banquet. Eleventh-century man was a realist: when he required delay it was for a practical reason. There could have been no indecent haste about a coronation.'[58]

Harold immediately tried to show himself the very model of a just and conciliatory king: despite their possible role as fifth columnists, he refrained from expelling the leading Normans William, Bishop of London, and Robert, son of Wymarc. Mindful of the example of Edward, who by over-reliance on the royal demesne had ended up as a figurehead king, he was determined to retain a landed base, so kept the earldom of Wessex in his own hands. His first real headache was the continuing problem of the north. He had no choice but to treat Morcar and Edwin as friends, especially as they had voted for him in the *witan* and he had married their sister Ealdgyth. But he knew they loved him not and harboured continuing plans for dividing the kingdom. Even stronger opposition was evinced by Waltheof and the Bamburgh family – though it remained at the level of passive resistance – but Harold had little room for manoeuvre with his northern problem, since he was even less willing to risk civil war now than in 1065; at least if he had taken the plunge then, Tostig would have been at his side. In this respect Harold can be seen as a man just as consistently unlucky as William of Normandy was lucky, for had Edward died a year earlier the whole of England would still have been in the grip of the Godwinsons.[59]

Displaying remarkable courage, élan and presence of mind, Harold decided to conciliate the north with a frontal diplomatic assault. Accompanied by his trusted friend Bishop Wulfstan, he travelled to York shortly before Easter 1066 and at a *gemot* there exhorted the assembled men of Northumbria and Yorkshire to join him in the common cause of opposition to William and Tostig. Warming to his theme that a house divided against itself must fall, he warned darkly that there were many fifth columnists in the country and may even have hinted that the reason he transacted all his business in London and no longer went to Winchester was that his sister Edith, who openly favoured Tostig and may also have been intriguing with William, had her seat there. He argued that if separatist sentiment was listened to, and the kingdom divided, it would be easy prey for invaders: Tostig and his allies could well dismember an unaided Northumbria while William was doing the same with Wessex.[60]

Harold's eloquence and the patient diplomacy of Wulfstan secured him a major, if temporary, triumph. Secretly displeased with the turn of events, Morcar and Edwin had no choice but to go along with majority opinion and publicly embrace Harold as lord of the entire kingdom. It was in a spirit of some euphoria that the new king was able to hold his Easter *gemot* at Westminster. Yet the breathing-space was short-lived. Already William was on the move in Normandy, while the restless and turbulent Tostig seemed likely to engineer a situation where England might be menaced on four sides simultaneously: in Northumbria by Malcolm of Scotland; on the Saxon coast by Tostig himself; in Wessex by William; and in Yorkshire by a new player who had been coaxed into the drama: the mighty Harald Hardrada of Norway.

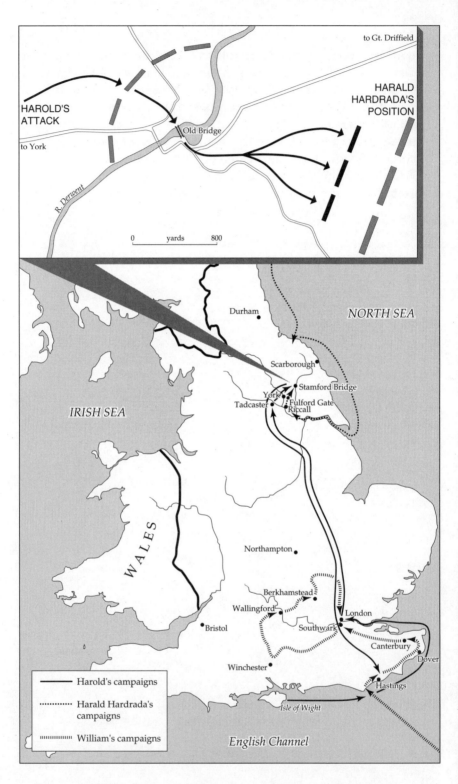

**HARALD
HARDRADA'S
POSITION**

**HAROLD'S
ATTACK**

to Gt. Driffield

Old Bridge

to York

R. Derwent

0   yards   800

Durham

NORTH SEA

Scarborough

Stamford Bridge

York

IRISH SEA

Tadcaster

Fulford Gate
Riccall

WALES

Northampton

Berkhamstead

Wallingford

London

Southwark

Bristol

Canterbury

Dover

Winchester

——— Harold's campaigns

·········· Harald Hardrada's
campaigns

ııııııııı William's campaigns

Hastings

Isle of Wight

English Channel

Stamford Bridge and the campaigns leading to the battle

9

Stamford Bridge

Duke William is said to have heard the news of Harold's coronation as he set out to hunt in his park of Quenilly near Rouen, whereupon, so the legend says, he abandoned the hunt and sat sunk in silence for hours, to be roused only by his strong right arm, William Fitzosbern. We may take leave to doubt this version of events. Both Harold and William were ruthless men who had been planning to seize the throne of England for many years. In Harold's eyes, kingship was his reward for long years of service propping up an inert dog-in-the-manger in the form of Edward; for William the conquest of England was always implicit in the logic of his elaborate kinship network, which meant there had to be new territories to conquer so as to satisfy the aspirations of those who had joined his web of royal clientelism. To start with, he needed to look no further than his own household: he had three sons greedy for land, William Fitzosbern had two, Roger of Montgomery four, and this was the tip of the iceberg.[1]

William began by summoning a council of his great nobles. Present in conclave were all the great names of Normandy: William's brother Robert, Count of Mortain, William Fitzosbern, Odo of Bayeux, Richard of Evreux, Roger of Beaumont, Hugh of Grandmesnil, Roger of Montgomery, Walter Giffard, Hugh of Montfort, William of

Warren. The assembled magnates listened to William's plans for the conquest of England, realized the scope of his ambitions and the magnitude of obstacles to be overcome, and recommended summoning a great meeting of the entire Norman nobility, at which they pledged to back him to the hilt.[2]

While he waited for the summonses to be delivered to his vassals throughout Normandy, William took the first step in the all-important propaganda war with Harold. He began by sending an embassy to England, knowing it was pointless, but hoping to present himself as a peace-loving sovereign forced unwillingly into war. The embassy apparently adverted to the 1064 promise to exchange sisters in dynastic marriages; Harold, who had married the widow of Gruffydd ap Llywelyn, replied tersely that his sister was dead: did William therefore want a corpse shipped over to Normandy? As for William's claim to the throne, the answer was the same as always: Edward had named Harold his successor on his deathbed, this had been ratified by a representative assembly of the entire nobility of England and only this *witan* had the legitimate power to make kings.[3]

With consummate cunning, William decided to take the matter over Harold's head by appealing to the pope in Rome. He realized that the nuances of English law and custom were unknown at the Vatican and, by presenting a case couched in the kind of continental European terms the pontiff would understand, he could easily make a weak case appear a strong, and even unassailable, one. William's envoy to Alexander II, Gilbert, Bishop of Lisieux, made a general case based on notions of hereditary right and the French system of bequest and then introduced the irrelevant matter of Harold's alleged perjury in 1064 – irrelevant because, even if Harold did actually swear the most mighty oath on the most sacred relics, this neither bound Edward in his bequest nor the *witan* in its ratification; whatever Harold said or did not say, it had no binding power in the matter of the succession. Gilbert, however, produced a turgid olio of arguments, in which the oath of 1064, the behaviour of the Godwin family in 1051, the murder of Alfred the Atheling in 1036 and the role of Stigand as 'unlawful' Archbishop of Canterbury all featured.[4]

It was the last proposition that most interested Alexander. William pitched his appeal to the papacy largely on his putative role as the leader of the religious and ecclesiastical reform movement in Normandy and as a man who would clean the Augean stables of church corruption in England; this weighed heavily with Alexander, who, as his joust with Harald Hardrada in 1061 demonstrated, thought the churches of

northern Europe far too remote from papal control. It was the abiding
dream of the new 'reformist' papacy to be universally accepted as the
arbiter of thrones and their succession; William's homage therefore
constituted a valuable precedent. Not surprisingly, Alexander gave the
proposed invasion of England his blessing. It has sometimes been
queried why Harold did not send his own embassy to counter William's
arguments. Almost certainly, the answer is that he thought it a waste of
time on two grounds: the method of electing a king in England had
nothing to do with the pope and was not a proper area for his
intervention; and, in any case, the pope was now the creature of the
Normans in southern Italy and would ultimately do what they ordered
him to do. Harold was right: Alexander II blessed all the Norman
marauding expeditions of the 1060s.[5]

But although papal sanction for William's 'enterprise of England' was
morally worthless, it was both a great propaganda and diplomatic
triumph for the Normans. It was a propaganda victory because it
allowed William to pose as the leader of crusaders in a holy war,
obfuscating and mystifying the base, materialistic motives of his
followers and mercenaries. It also gave the Normans a great psychological boost, for they could perceive themselves as God's elect, and it is
significant that none of William's inner circle entertained doubts about
the ultimate success of the English venture. Normandy now seemed the
spearhead of a confident Christianity, on the offensive for the first time
in centuries, whereas earlier Christendom had been beleaguered by
Vikings to the north, Hungarians to the east and Islam to the south. It
was no accident that, with Hungary and Scandinavia recently Christian-
ized, the Normans were the vanguard in the first Crusade, properly so
called, against the Islamic heathens in the Holy Land.[6]

Alexander's fiat was a diplomatic triumph, too, as papal endorsement
for the Normans made it difficult for other powers to intervene on
Harold's side. William also pre-empted one of the potential sources of
support for the Anglo-Saxons by sending an embassy to the emperor
Henry IV; this, too, was notably successful, removing a possible barrier
to a Europe-wide call for volunteers in the 'crusade'. It seemed unlikely
that William would encounter any obstacles in the French-speaking
world, for France was still a paper tiger, run by Baldwin of Flanders
during Philip's minority. Anjou, too, was out of the reckoning, for
Geoffrey Martel's two nephews (Geoffrey le Barbe and Fulk le Rechin)
were still locked in bitter combat in 1066. There is something almost
supernaturally fortunate in the way William became fortuitously free of
continental enemies at the very moment England was riven with

fratricidal strife between Harold and Tostig. It is hard to resist the conclusion that if Edward the Confessor had died even a few years earlier, or alternatively if Cnut had lived to the age of sixty, as William did, there could have been no Norman invasion of England.[7]

When the second council of the whole Norman nobility met, at Lillebone, there was far less enthusiasm for the invasion of England than at the original conclave of William's inner circle. The meeting is said to have dissolved in uproar when William simply assumed he had the support of his barons and began at once to get down to the question of individual contributions. In some quarters vociferous opposition was expressed, on three main grounds: the enterprise was said to be impossible because of England's military strength, because the necessary army and fleet could not be raised in Normandy alone, and because the nobility lacked the resources to finance such a massive endeavour. The nobility asked for more time to reflect on the proposal.[8]

The meeting was adjourned, but the nobles made the mistake of asking William Fitzosbern to be an intermediary between themselves and the duke; they expressed their terror of the Channel crossing and pointed out that by the terms of their feudal obligation they were not bound to serve beyond the sea. The wily Fitzosbern, whose outstanding quality was his loyalty, agreed to act as go-between provided he were given a *de facto* power of attorney. But first he tried to browbeat his 'clients' by hinting darkly at the duke's capacity for savage reprisals if his will were thwarted. Then he withdrew and planned with William a strategy that would circumvent these objections. When the meeting was reconvened, he stood up and barefacedly double-crossed the nobles by a speech in which he promised that each of them would serve beyond the sea and bring double the contingent due under the feudal bond: the lord of twenty knight's fees would bring forty knights, and so on.

As Fitzosbern and William had foreseen, his two-faced treachery led to cries of protest in the hall and once again the conclave was racked by confusion, with nobles openly baying at the subterfuge and fearful that Fitzosbern had tricked them by sleight of hand into doubling their military obligation. William used the uproar as an excuse to adjourn the meeting once more, and then summoned the barons privately for a personal interview; face to face with the duke, and knowing his uncertain temper, one by one they meekly accepted the obligation Fitzosbern had laid on them, provided that the extraordinary levy should not be taken as a precedent. Fitzosbern and William proved themselves masters of human psychology. No such lavish offer could have been carried by a majority vote or as the result of open debate. Foreseeing this, they had first engineered an adjournment and then browbeaten the recalcitrant nobles by the hint of dreadful retribution in the case of a refusal: at the private interviews, a scribe noted down what was said and recorded each contribution, just to add the right chilling touch to the proceedings.[9]

William now had promises of ships and men, and, of the two, ships were the more vital, for Normandy had no significant standing navy and a fleet would have to be built from scratch. The Norman chroniclers have provided extensive lists of the numbers of craft supplied by each of the great nobles, and in some cases the numbers of knights too. We learn that Robert of Mortain provided 120 vessels, Odo of Bayeux 100, William of Évreux 80, William Fitzosbern, Roger of Montgomery, Roger of Beaumont, Hugh of Avranches and Robert of Eu 60 each; Walter Giffard supplied 30 boats and one hundred knights, Hugh of Montfort 50 boats and sixty knights, Nicholas, Abbot of St-Ouen 20 and a hundred knights, and so on.[10]

How many vessels eventually sailed in William's invasion fleet is a matter of conjecture, for estimates vary from the exact figure of 696 confidently announced by Wace in the *Roman de Rou* to a high of 3,000. Much confusion has arisen because of the tendency to liken the Norman invasion craft to the very different Viking longships; in fact the Norman vessels were simply large open boats with a single mast and sail, about forty feet long, broad in the beam and about four feet deep in the water. The Bayeux Tapestry shows eleven different vessels on the Channel crossing, with eleven also as the highest number of occupants of any boat. Given that the average complement of the boats was seven, and that William probably took 14,000 men with him to England, the correct number is probably around 2,000.[11]

While the forests of Normandy rang with the sound of axes in spring 1066, as tens of thousands of trees were chopped down to build the invasion fleet, the call for volunteers went out across Europe. High wages were promised during the waiting period, and the mouth-watering prospect of plunder, rapine and Saxon women drew in mercenaries by the thousands to a freebooting enterprise made even more attractive by the papal approval, which converted a simple act of aggression into a crusade. Individuals can be identified as having come from Germany, Hungary, Aragon, Apulia and Norman Sicily, though most of the volunteers were French-speaking. While William got no direct help from Baldwin of Flanders, it is certain that individual Flemish mercenaries enlisted, though the number is disputed. Flemings were well known as naval mercenaries – most of Tostig's men came from there – but it is likely that William had to give Baldwin a money-fief in exchange for permission to recruit his subjects.[12]

Whatever room there may be for scepticism about the contribution of non-Francophone troops to William's invasion force, it is clear that within the French-speaking world thousands of non-Normans participated in the 'crusade', including men from France, Brittany, Maine and Aquitaine, which in those days stretched from the Loire to the Pyrenees and from the Atlantic to the Auvergne. The role of Aquitaine seems strange at first sight, since one hundred miles of hostile territory – the provinces of Maine and Anjou – separated it from Normandy, but there were many bonds linking the two territories. In the past, vulnerability to Viking raids had made the Viscounts of Thouars in Aquitaine interested in having a common policy against the raiders with Normandy, so that links were close, and intermarriage made them closer: in 1066 Count Guy-Geoffrey of Aquitaine and William of Normandy were third cousins, and Normans had fought with him against the Saracens in Spain.[13]

One of the great lords of the Aquitaine area in 1066 was Duke William's cousin Aimeri of Thouars, a fortified town which commanded the Thouet river and the main routes between Poitou and Aquitaine. Aimeri was a very powerful viscount, only nominally the vassal of the Comte de Poitou and the lord of seventeen castles, hundeds of square miles of territory and scores of noble vassals. Aimeri was one of the most eager participants in William's enterprise in 1066 and won his place among the fabled 'Companions of the Conqueror'. His commitment was ideological and dynastic, but that of another great Francophone lord was less certain. For Eustace of Boulogne the return of the Godwin family to England in 1052 had been a severe setback, and thereafter he was on the wane while the fortunes of William and Baldwin of Flanders rose and rose. In hopes of making a sudden leap into the premier league Eustace decided in 1066 to throw in his lot with the Normans, even though he disliked William personally and had not been on good terms with him. William never really trusted him and Eustace had to leave his son in Normandy as a hostage before he would give him a command.[14]

At the very last moment there was a hitch in the smooth progress of William's co-option of the major figures in the French-speaking world. Some time in the summer of 1066 William's old foe Conan of Brittany put in his own claim to the throne of England, on the grounds that Duke Robert had entrusted Normandy to his father, Alan III, in 1035, that this trust had never been revoked, and therefore that he had an overriding claim to Normandy and any other domains it might acquire or lay title to. It can well be imagined that this especially infuriated William, as it was a case of someone else playing the kind of diplomatic and propaganda games he liked to specialize in himself. William made no direct answer to this, but by Christmas 1066 Conan was dead. It was widely whispered that William had poisoned him, and the accusation seems plausible. Some have naïvely countered that William would have poisoned him, if that was his intention, before setting out for England, without appreciating the much greater efficacy of a slow-acting poison that would give William the perfect alibi.[15]

In the first six months of 1066 the clear tactical advantage lay with William. He could make his preparations slowly and methodically while Harold was reduced to preparing a still divided kingdom for a blow that might fall on the south coast of England at any time. During this stalemate period of 'phoney war' the third of the four great personalities made his appearance in the drama, for in January 1066 Tostig travelled from Flanders to Normandy to confer with William. Superficially, since Tostig's wife Judith was close kin to his wife Matilda, William could welcome him as a cousin, but, more importantly, William saw that the ex-Earl of Northumbria had powerful propaganda and nuisance value. As a gadfly, raiding the English coast, Tostig could keep Harold in a permanent state of suspense and uncertainty about how many invasion points he would need to cover; while as a propaganda counter Tostig was a gift, for what more convincing confirmation could there be that Harold was a liar and perjurer than the fact that he had treacherously subverted his own brother?[16]

The two men conferred, and William gave his blessing to Tostig's plan for a spring raid on the south coast, to test Harold's defences. However, it seems that the duke's slow and steady military build-up did not suit the impatient Tostig, for soon he was off on a mission to find a ruler who would give him more immediate aid. Tostig set out on an odyssey that took him to the courts of Svein of Denmark and Harald Hardrada of Norway. Some historians object that the chronology of Tostig's rovings is impossibly tight, since he was raiding off the south coast early in May, but there is nothing so difficult about fitting a trip to Scandinavia into the intervening three months. Some have speculated that, after leaving William, Tostig merely sent an ambassador to the Scandinavian courts, but the Norse sources are adamant that Tostig went there in person, and the wealth of circumstantial detail concerning his embassy is unlikely to derive from a totally false tradition.

Leaving his deputy, Copsig, to assemble an army in Flanders, Tostig sailed north to Denmark, where he had an unsatisfactory interview with Svein Estrithson. The king still claimed the English throne but, exhausted by the long war with Harald Hardrada, lacked the resources for an invasion and told Tostig so bluntly. Nevertheless, he seems to have taken to the ex-earl personally for he offered him a position in Denmark similar to that previously occupied by Hakon Ivarsson. Tostig rejected this contemptuously as he did Svein's reasons for inaction; in some sources it is even said that he taunted the king with cowardice. However, Svein did see the danger to his own position if either William of Normandy or Harald Hardrada became king of England and sent volunteers to fight on the side of Harold Godwinson.[17]

Tostig then proceeded to Norway, where he had a notable interview with Harald Hardrada at Viken, in the south-east of the country. He asked him first to restore him to his old earldom in Northumbria, but could raise no interest in the king. Harald said that he still yearned for martial glory, but what Tostig proposed was dangerous and, from his viewpoint, fruitless. Tostig then suggested that Harald should revive the claim to the throne he inherited from Magnus, who got his right from Harthacnut at the Gotha river conference; Harald could be king and Tostig would be content with the role of *subregulus* and Earl of Northumbria. Harald then made three points. First, the English had a reputation for unreliability, so that he did not want an alliance with such people. Secondly, the housecarls had a ferocious reputation and each of them was said to be as good as any two Norwegian warriors. Thirdly, he had no great stomach for an English expedition, with its formidable supply and logistical problems.[18]

Tostig plugged away at Magnus's bequest from Harthacnut. Was a king as great as Hardrada really going to stand idly by while William of Normandy and Harold Godwinson decided who was to rule England? Doubtless nettled by this, Harald asked scathingly how it was that the great Magnus, of whom Tostig seemed so fond, had failed to acquire England when he had so manifest a right to it. Tostig quipped back that Harald had a perfect right to Denmark but had not managed to secure it. Harald then began to boast of how he had killed Danes by the thousand. Smiling at the evasion, Tostig told the king the reason he had failed in Denmark was that the people were wholeheartedly on Svein's side and not on his and for the same reason Magnus had not tried to conquer England, realizing the people preferred Edward. The situation now was very different: Harold was widely disliked and he, Tostig, could guarantee to bring half the population over to the Norwegian side once

Hardrada landed; how could he fail to push at such an open door after fifteen years' pointless campaigning in Denmark?[19]

At first Tostig seemed faced with a Sisyphean task of persuasion, for every point he answered was capped with a fresh objection; Ulf Ospaksson, the marshal, was particularly opposed to an English enterprise. But it seems that Tostig gradually convinced powerful allies among the younger warriors in the king's council. Harald's son Olaf had a very close friend named Skule Konfrostre, who was so eloquent on Tostig's behalf that an absurd legend later arose that he was Tostig's son, though Tostig had never seen him before 1066. We do not know all the stages whereby Hardrada eventually allowed himself to be persuaded. Perhaps he needed new lands with which to reward a too numerous following, or perhaps the lure of one final Viking achievement was too much for him to resist. But it is certain that Tostig gravely misled him about the reception he would get in England and blatantly lied about his brother Harold's unpopularity. At all events, Harald announced a levy of half the able-bodied men in his kingdom and ordered ships built for an invasion of England. He arranged to rendezvous with Tostig in the Humber estuary in July or August that summer.[20]

Early in May Tostig attacked the Isle of Wight with the ships and men Copsig had purchased for him in Flanders. He disembarked his men and, after a show of force, compelled the islanders to provide money and provisions. Then he sailed away eastwards, landing and ravaging all along the south coast as he went, until he made a more permanent landfall at Sandwich. Learning of this, Harold effected a forced march to Sandwich, but Tostig's fleet again stood away, this time north-east into the North Sea, having first recruited more professional sailors with lavish promises of pay and plunder. At the Humber we first get a clue as to the size of his forces, for we learn that Tostig entered the estuary with a fleet of sixty ships. He was apparently ravaging Lindsey in his old earldom when the armies of Morcar and Edwin came upon him and badly mauled his marauders; the defeat was followed by large-scale desertions as the newly recruited adventurers realized that Tostig's vision of booty and treasure was a pipe-dream. Reduced to just twelve ships, Tostig sought refuge with his 'brother' Malcolm in Scotland, determined to wait there until Hardrada sailed from Norway.[21]

Tostig's raid on the Isle of Wight, apparently sponsored by William, may actually have harmed his strategy, since Harold Godwinson read the probe as the prelude to a general Norman assault on the south coast and concentrated his forces there; the Humber landing he dismissed as Tostig's being forced into a *pis aller*. Faced with threats from both

William and Tostig, Harold Godwinson called out both the select and general fyrd; he may also have implemented an emergency draft of other men not normally called up, which would have given him a huge force on paper, for the manpower pool of males aged between fifteen and fifty-four may have been as high as 240,000. Even if he raised only 5 per cent of the male population, this would have given him a force 50,000 strong. Certainly it was the most enormous mobilization England had ever known and many at William's court thought the duke had taken leave of his senses in trying to overcome such a powerful enemy – a sentiment that was apparently echoed by the *grognards* in the ranks.[22]

Just before Tostig's raid on the Isle of Wight, another event occurred to test the nerve of the commanders on both sides, for it seemed to presage disaster: the only question was, for whom? Halley's Comet, seen from Earth once every seventy-six years, appeared in the sky in England in full clarity after 24 April; for those who regard the Bayeux Tapestry as a naturalistic source, this provides another problem, for the Tapestry shows the comet appearing in January. The comet was first seen in Normandy on 26 April, two days later than in England, and is recorded in the annals of every European country for 1066. We cannot know how either Harold or William were affected by this portent, but those who interpreted it favourably for their side thought it indicated Heaven's support for bold action: Gyrth Godwinson proposed that an invasion force be sent *to* Normandy, to harry William and slow him down until Harold could assemble the full military strength of the kingdom.[23]

Harold overruled the suggestion, so that William was free to make his preparations unhindered and then order a general muster of his army at the Channel port of Dives. As the transport vessels neared completion, and the volunteers thronged in during the early summer, William behaved with notable outward calm, devoting much attention to religious matters as if he were a saintly king going on a crusade. A day-by-day reconstruction of his movements at this stage is not possible, but we know that he held another council at Bonneville on 15 June and consecrated the Abbey of the Holy Trinity in Caen three days later. William may also have been keen to show himself to his troops as much as possible, to reassure them that he was in rude health, for at some time during the years 1063–65 he had been seriously ill and had a long convalescence at Cherbourg castle.[24]

There is much we do not know about William's preparations and particularly his method of building the necessary ships to transport an army. It has been objected that the construction of the numbers of ships required by summer 1066 in the time allowed was simply an impossibility, given eleventh-century technology. To be sure, the vast forests of the Seine contained the necessary raw materials, but only if the Norman barons were prepared to see their favourite hunting grounds laid waste. And, even if we discount the costs of tree-felling and the transport of timber to the coast, there is the cost of the shipbuilding itself to consider. One estimate is that it would take 8,400 men three months to build 700 ships, with 6,900 peasants working non-stop to feed them betimes, but this seems an excessive estimate in the light of the small size of the craft. Nevertheless, the overwhelming likelihood is that William simply requisitioned all existing craft in Norman ports and purchased most of the rest of his vessels from Flanders. The clear implication is that William had a healthy cash surplus at the beginning of 1066.[25]

There is a woeful lack of detail in the sources, too, concerning Harold's preparations. The Anglo-Saxon Chronicle relates that he assembled the mightiest force ever seen in England immediately after the appearance of Halley's Comet (24 April) and kept it in being for four months, but we learn nothing of the huge commissariat problems this must have entailed. Harold stationed his fleet of 700 ships, propelled by rowers, at the Isle of Wight, whence it was often absent – otherwise Tostig could not have staged his raid – and kept it cruising up and down the coast, expecting that William's flotilla would emerge on to the Channel unescorted by warships, when it would be an easy prey. Since Morcar and Edwin were disposed to act independently, and the threat from Harald Hardrada had not at this stage materialized, Harold felt that the northern earls could look after themselves, leaving him free to concentrate all his forces in southern England.[26]

At the beginning of August William left his capital for the rendezvous at Dives, having made the final arrangements for the Council of Regency. His queen Matilda would reign in his absence, assisted by the elderly Roger of Beaumont and Hugh, Vicomte of Avranches. Among those who accompanied William to Dives and ultimately to England were Robert of Mortain, Hugh de Montfort, William Fitzosbern, Ralf de Tosny, Hugh de Grandmesnil, Odo of Bayeux, Geoffrey, Bishop of Coutances, Walter Giffard, the two foreign allies Eustace of Boulogne and Aimeri of Thouars and a number of young sons of the Norman aristocracy, such as Robert, son of Roger de Beaumont, and Geoffrey, son of Rotrou, Count of Mortagne.[27]

The Norman army arrived at the mustering point at Dives on 4–5 August. This particular port had been chosen because of the ease of water transport, because there was a plentiful grain supply in the plain of Caen in the hinterland and because the inner harbour (which no longer exists) kept the invasion flotilla safe from storms and any warships Harold might send against it. The choice of Dives was an inspired one and was of a piece with the brilliance in planning, provisioning and general strategy evinced by William during the month of August. Although the desertion level seems to have been relatively high, William did his best for troop morale by provisioning them at his personal expense. That he could make such an offer already suggests a highly centralized system of purchase, requisition, control, storage and distribution, possibly modelled on the commissariat procedures used by the Roman legions. So confident was he that he even released one of Harold's captured spies so that he might report back to his master the scale of the preparations.[28]

William's host remained at Dives for a month, prohibited from plundering or living off the land on pain of death. The size of the army is disputed, but the most likely figure is 14,000, of which 8,000 would be used in battle, 2,000 on garrison duties, another 4,000 sailors and non-combatants (oarsmen, helmsmen, pilots, cooks, armour-bearers, smiths, carpenters, artisans, clerics, monks) and – most tellingly – 3,000 horses. It is worth dwelling for a while on the extraordinary problems faced by such a large mustered army compelled to remain in one spot for so long a time. A ration of four pounds of grain and a gallon of water meant the provision of 28 tons of unmilled wheat and 14,000 gallons of fresh water every day – even if we make the minimum assumption that the army existed on bread and water, whereas we know that it was liberally supplied with meat and wine. To sustain 14,000 men and 3,000 horses for a month the Normans would have needed 2,340 tons of grain (two-thirds of this for the horses) plus 1,500 tons of straw and 155 tons of hay. At a total tonnage of 4,000, this means 8,000 cart-loads at 1,000 pounds per two-horse cart. If, as was likely, the men's grain was baked into bread or cooked to make porridge, this in turn would entail 420 tons of firewood at a rate of two pounds per day per man. Transport of firewood added 840 cart-loads. Moreover, every 125 gallons of wine required one two-horse cart, so that even if each man had just eight ounces of wine a day – a ludicrously small and implausible amount – this would mean another 210 cart-loads during the month at Dives.[29]

Even greater problems were engendered by the warhorses, with which special care had to be taken, since they were perceived as the key to military success. To begin with, they needed shelter if they were to remain in good condition, which meant the construction of lean-tos for the stabling of the beasts. And since the *destriers* weighed on average 1,500 pounds, the minimum daily ration would be twelve pounds of grain (oats or barley) and thirteen pounds of hay per horse. The horses would also require five tons of clean straw each day for bedding and 20,000–30,000 tons of fresh water; if this was not available for even short periods, the steeds would collapse and die. This assumes that there were just 3,000 horses at Dives, but some historians have objected that he must have had almost that number in reserve, as he would not have taken all his cavalry across the Channel. Whatever their numbers, clearly the warhorses had to be in superlative condition if they were to carry 250 lbs of rider and equipment into a battle that might last all day and involve uphill charges.[30]

But the problems of administering men and horses did not end with the food supply. If we assume that a tent housed ten men, 1,000–1,5000 tents required the hides of 36,000 calves and the labour of scores of tanners and leather workers. Care of the 3,000 horses was even more of a headache. To maintain their health, they had to be shod properly, which in turn meant horseshoes and nails. Using fifteen-ounce horseshoes with six nails, ten blacksmiths working a ten-hour day would be occupied for the whole of August in fitting between 8,000–12,000 shoes and hammering 75,000 nails – a total of eight tons of iron previously forged by other blacksmiths. Also, to avoid health problems, 5,000 cartloads of equine waste had to be disposed of – five million pounds of faeces and 700,000 gallons of urine. It says a lot for Norman sanitation engineers that there were no outbreaks of disease at Dives, whereas they encountered dysentery at Dover.[31]

Whoever presided over this nightmare of logistics was clearly an administrative talent of a very high order and, happily, it is possible to identify him by a process of elimination. Since Roger of Beaumont was left behind in Normandy as head of the Regency Council advising Queen Matilda, Count Robert of Eu was in charge of the advance 'springboard' camp at Saint-Valéry and the peerless William Fitzosbern was responsible for logistics once the army reached England, we can infer that the 'genius of Dives' was Roger II of Montgomery. One of the most impressive aspects of the Norman invasion of England in 1066 was the way old quarrels and enmities had been laid to rest, and families who had previously feuded with each other or with Duke William himself collaborated for the common purpose. For the smooth administration of Dives William had the leading scion of the house of Montgomery to thank, but it seems he did not see the fruit of his labours, being left behind in Normandy to assist the Council of Regency.[32]

The month's wait at Dives in August has puzzled some observers, since the official explanation – waiting for favourable winds – does not seem convincing. An August in the Channel without a south wind seems unusual, to say the least, and then there is the telling point that Harald Hardrada, who needed precisely opposite winds for his expedition south, was also delayed in Norway during this month. It is therefore most likely that William had favourable winds in August but deliberately kept his army at Dives, intending all along to launch his invasion from Saint-Valéry, at the mouth of the Somme, further up the coast and nearer to England. The inference is strengthened by William's decision not to keep all his ships at Dives but to disperse some of them to neighbouring ports.[33]

His motive for remaining at Dives was to stretch Harold on the rack, keeping him at full readiness throughout August, knowing that the legal terms of the fyrd's two-month service must soon expire and that, in any case, Harold's men would have to disperse in the harvest season; like all agricultural societies, England would reach a low point in food reserves just before the harvest. Certainly, when Harold was reported as having disbanded the fyrd on 8 September, leaving the south coast of England undefended, William seemed to have won the first round in the campaign. Even worse, when Harold ordered his warships to sail for London, they were caught in a storm and many of them were wrecked.[34]

As soon as he heard the news from England, William ordered his fleet out to sea for the perilous passage up the coast to Saint-Valéry, 160 miles by sea, though only one hundred overland as the crow flies. The Normans employed mariners who knew all about the English coast and its vagaries – there was a vast amount of cross-Channel traffic in Edward the Confessor's reign – and these sailors, mindful of uncertain weather conditions around the equinox, advised him to move further up the coast where the chance of a south wind would be better. They were merely advising William what he had anyway long since decided; for logistical reasons – the denuding of the hinterland of Dives of food and supplies, and particularly the fact that the horses had grazed out the area – he always knew he would have to move on after a month.[35]

The warhorses were taken to the rendezvous overland, to avoid a lengthy period at sea. The Norman fleet set out on 12 September, timing the exit from Dives in low water with a high west wind, and heading for the narrows. Once in the open sea it took a battering from equinoctial gales (south-west winds blow up to Force Eight in the Channel in September), and other ships were wrecked as a result of the well-known navigational difficulties of the Normandy coast; William was said to have buried hundreds of bodies of the drowned secretly, so as not to affect morale. It is probable that the fleet made one or two stopovers during its passage east, maybe near Cap d'Antifer or Fécamp. Once at Saint-Valéry, William incessantly watched the weathercock on the minster tower, which for fifteen days pointed resolutely south, while the Norman troops shivered beneath under a cloudy sky, beset by rain and cold weather.[36]

However, it is possible that William had not after all won the first round so easily and that he was merely being gulled by Harold while he contemplated how to fight a war on two fronts simultaneously. We do not know enough about Harold's dispositions in 1066 to say for certain that he was forced to withdraw the fyrd because of the expiry of its legal term or because the harvest had to be brought in; it is possible that in his emergency decrees Harold had called out the fyrd on an indefinite basis, and we should beware of imagining that William alone could trick his followers into serving beyond the limit of their natural obligations. One theory is that Harold deliberately withdrew his army inland because he got word that Harald Hardrada's fleet had sailed from Norway, hoping at once to tempt William over and keep him hemmed in by the troops he had stationed in strength in the inland areas of Sussex. Harold's best bet, given that he lacked the manpower to fight on both fronts, was to play for time, concentrating on the northern invasion and gambling that a cautious William would not move from the southern coast until he (Harold) was ready to deal with him.[37]

This seems plausible, for at the end of August Harald Hardrada left Norway on a favourable northerly wind, taking with him a huge armada of longships. Once again there is dispute about the size of the fleet, with scholars opting for anything between a low of 200 to a high of 1,000, with around 300 being the most likely number. Viking longships were of four main kinds: the 13-bench with 26 oars; the 15-bench with 30 oars; the 20-bench with 40 oars, and the 30-bench with 60 oars. The most common variety was the 20-bench vessel with 40 oars (two men to each oar) and a total crew of ninety. The Gokstadt ship excavated in Norway is $76\frac{1}{2}$ feet long and had a crew of 70 (including 64 rowers); not especially large, she provides a fair average. The Danish ships which ravaged England in the early eleventh century were believed to have carried 40–50 men, but shipbuilding technology in Scandinavia had improved since then. Harthacnut's ships averaged 50–80 men each, Olaf Tryggvason's famous ship *The Long Serpent* had a crew of 300, and some of the 30-bench leviathans were known to have housed 260 men. Even if each of Hardrada's ships had a crew of 40 men (the lowest possible estimate), 300 longships meant a total force of 12,000. If we more reasonably posit that many of the ships were larger, Hardrada may have taken as many as 18,000 warriors on his invasion of England.[38]

Hardrada had made more serious preparations for the conquest of England than historians have usually given him credit for; like Harold Godwinson in 1066, they assume that the expedition was either a large-scale raid or an ill-thought out exercise in quixotry. According to some sources, he intended to emulate Cnut and transfer his seat of government to England once he had conquered it; this makes sense of his curious action in going to St Olaf's tomb in Nidaros, unlocking it, clipping his hair and nails (an old Viking custom), locking up the tomb again and then throwing the keys into the river Nid. Also curious is his behaviour in regard to his wives: he took Elizabeth and his daughters Maria and Ingigerd with him as far as the Orkneys and left Thora in Norway with her son Magnus, whom he appointed as regent. Does this mean there was acute jealousy between the wives, that he dared not leave the foreign-born Elizabeth behind lest some harm come to her?[39]

Harald also took with him a number of warhorses, though nothing like on the scale of Duke William's expedition; he knew all about the problems of transporting the beasts by sea, as he had observed them minutely during the invasion of Sicily in 1038. But the Norsemen did not set off on the great adventure in an especially good state of morale. Many remembered the forebodings of the marshal Ulf Ospaksson, who had spoken out against Tostig in the spring council and since died. When Hardrada called a general muster of his forces at the Solund Islands at the mouth of the Sogne fiord (near present-day Bergen), many gloomy portents were reported and several people recounted dire premonitory dreams. One of Harald's colonels, named Gyrd, had a terrifying nightmare of a demon woman and the king himself dreamed that St Olaf appeared and told him he was doomed. Yet Harald was in good spirits: he was confident that Magnus would prove a good regent in his absence and at his side in England he would have his son Olaf and the new favourite, a young warrior named Eystein Orri, son of Throlberg Arnesson, to whom he had promised in marriage his beloved daughter Maria.[40]

The armada sailed south, to the Shetland Islands, then mustered again in the Orkneys. Here Harald was joined by his principal allies, Paul and Erlend, Thorfinn's sons, and Godfrey Crovan, son of Harald the Black of Iceland, later to be king of the Isle of Man; there were also other contingents from Iceland and Ireland. A council was held at which Tostig's ideas were discussed and in particular his argument that the

Norsemen would find allies in northern England. This seemed plausible, for the region had close links with the Viking world and York, an independent Norse kingdom until 954, had once been as much a Viking town as Trondheim, Copenhagen or Dublin. The Scandinavian empire of Cnut had been popular in northern England and in 1042, when Edward became king, there had even been support for a Scandinavian candidate. Harald's spies were competent and he knew there was no great love for Harold Godwinson in the north of the kingdom he hoped to conquer. But he made the mistake of believing Tostig, of imagining that it was Morcar and Edwin who were the unpopular ones north of the Wash not Tostig himself; had his political intelligence been truly first-rate, he might have considered that his best interests were served by an alliance with the sons of Aelfgar.[41]

From the Orkneys Hardrada's great fleet sailed south, putting in at various points for food and water, ravaging the coastline of Scotland without opposition, and thence to the north-east of England. The first major landfall was at Cleveland, where the Norsemen raided Scarborough, gutted the town and slaughtered or enslaved the inhabitants; all local levies sent against them were routed in short order, including a sizeable detachment of Morcar and Edwin's men sent against them at Holderness. According to the sagas, however, the superstitious Norwegians took less notice of these easy victories and more of the supposed bad omen when Harald, on setting foot on English soil for the first time, allegedly stumbled and fell – allegedly, as such stories are a staple experience of would-be conquerors.[42]

Sailing on, the Norse fleet doubled Ravenspur and entered the Humber estuary, where, in accordance with the plan previously agreed, Tostig met them with his reduced fleet and the hard core of Flemish pirates and mercenaries. The ships of the Northumbrian Earl Morcar did not dare engage Harald's host and retreated before him up the Ouse, then turned into the inland waters of the Wharfe to Tadcaster. Morcar's tactics evidently were to wait until the invaders had passed the turn-off of the Wharfe at Canood, then drop down the tributary on the last of the ebb to take them in the rear. But Hardrada disappointed him. Convinced that he did not need his full strength, he anchored at Riccall, a mile *above* the junction of the Ouse and Wharfe, on the left bank of the river and some nine miles from York as the crow flies (much longer via the winding river). The spot was well chosen, as the Viking fleet could now stop up the Ouse and bar the descent of its tributary, thus neatly bottling up Morcar's fleet in Tadcaster.[43]

Leaving Olaf and Eystein Orri with a substantial force to guard the fleet – safeguarding the longships was always of primary concern in Viking warfare – Harald and Tostig set out for the march on York by foot, probably taking no more than 6,000 men. There were two roads from Riccall to York, and the invaders used both. One hugged the Ouse via Stillingfleet and Naburn and the other diverged from the river through Escrick and rejoined the first road at Water Fulford, about two miles south of York, from which point the single road ran parallel with the Ouse into York. As Harald's army joined up again at Water Fulford, they saw signs of activity ahead. It was Morcar and Edwin with their troops; the brothers had finally decided that there was nothing for it but a pitched battle. From Harald's point of view there was at least some clarification of the current situation in England for his political intelligence was out of date and, as Freeman put it: 'Harald Hardrada must have set sail, hardly knowing whether he would find the shores of Northumberland guarded by the axes of England or the lances of Normandy.'[44]

Half a mile from York, at Fulford Gate on 20 September, Edwin and Morcar's men formed rank for the first of the year's three great battles. Roughly equal in numbers with the Norsemen, and consisting partly of the earl's housecarls and partly the local levy, Morcar's army was drawn up across the road with its right flank resting on the river and the left on a boundary ditch, beyond which there was broad and deep boggy ground. We may well imagine that Morcar and Edwin felt trepidation, for they liked to avoid battle if possible, and this time they were faced with the flower of Scandinavia, and not merely two hundred of Tostig's housecarls outnumbered and taken by surprise. We may surmise that the brothers did not like the odds but, in light of the Saxons' notorious hopelessness in defending their towns, they had no choice.

From Harald's position, his left sloped gently away to the river, while his right stretched across rising ground as far as the ditch, with the marsh beyond. The weak spot in Harald's position was the right wing, and it was there, whether by accident or design, that the English launched their first attack. A vigorous Saxon charge at first carried all before it, but then the seemingly victorious English were taken in the flank by Harald and the Norwegian left, who seem to have rolled up the enemy right in a trice. With the royal standard, the Land-Ravager, Harald and his picked praetorians smashed into the thick of battle. For perhaps ten minutes there was ferocious hand-to-hand combat, then the enveloped Saxons broke and fled. Trying to escape the pincer movement, the English veered away into the marsh, where they floundered in the bog until cut down or sucked into quicksands; those who tried flight on the other side mostly drowned in the Ouse. Soon the marsh and the ditches were clogged with human bodies, to the point where the Norwegians waded in blood and marched over the impacted corpses as if on a solid causeway.[45]

The pitiful remnants of the English army followed Morcar and Edwin back to York, which formally surrendered on 24 September. The city agreed to feed the Norwegian host, to join Harald on his march south and to give hostages at an agreed location next day. Harald's mild treatment of the town belied his ferocious reputation but he was, after all, trying to win hearts and minds and he noted with satisfaction that there was a great deal of latent pro-Norwegian feeling in the city. So far the strategy recommended by Tostig was working out well, for after Fulford Bridge the whole of northern England seemed with him in his attempt to conquer England, showing how much hatred of the West Saxons still remained. Morcar and Edwin appear to have made their peace with the king, protesting that they had done all, and more, that was owed to loyalty to Harold by their efforts on the battlefield.[46]

Suspicion about the attitudes of Morcar and Edwin may well have been the reason why Harold Godwinson took his samurai-like decision to proceed north by forced marches and take the Norwegians by surprise. No other explanation really fits the chronology of the campaign, for, if Harald had waited until he had word of the Viking landfall at Riccall, he could not have been at York by 25 September. Harold must have guessed, from the sack of Scarborough and the dispersal of Morcar's levies at Holderness, that this was no raid and required the kind of energetic action he could not trust the new Earl of Northumbria to take. He still regarded the threat from Normandy as the greater one, but reckoned it might be possible to steal north, defeat Hardrada, and still be in time to deal with William. He made his dispositions on two possible scenarios: on the best case, he would defeat the Norwegians and return south before the Normans could cross the Channel; on the worst case, he would keep enough troops in Sussex to bottle William up near his beachhead until he could return to deal with him.[47]

Taking his brother Gyrth with him, and with his housecarls and such other troops as he could spare from the defence of the south, Harold marched north in seven divisions, pressing volunteers as he went. The speed of his advance has always drawn superlatives from historians used to the ponderous pace of medieval warfare, but it may be that a good deal of his force was on horseback and that, as was the custom with

Anglo-Saxon armies, they dismounted before fighting. There have always been those who maintain that the precipitate march north was a bad mistake, that a more machiavellian man might have allowed Hardrada to crush Morcar and Edwin definitively and so scotch for ever the myth of the viability of an independent Northumbria. Others claim that he should have withdrawn and allowed Hardrada and William to fight over the kingdom, himself ready to intervene at the right time as *tertius gaudens*. Certainly the stress of having to make snap decisions on such crucial matters took its toll on Harold. There are extant sources which suggest he was ill for much of 1066. During the march north, particularly, he was said to have been up all one night with a violent pain in his leg; when praying at dawn for release from the malady, he fell into a trance and had a vision of victory over the Norwegians.[48]

Hardrada meanwhile agreed to a handover of 150 children from the prominent families of Yorkshire as surety for their loyalty and offered to exchange hostages of his own to seal the bargain. On the evening of the 24th the Norwegians returned to their ships at Riccall, laden with vast amounts of booty uplifted from York as a 'peace offering'. But Harald's most pressing problem was his food supply, for his mighty host was running into the same shortages that Roger of Montgomery surmounted so brilliantly for the Normans at Dives. The burghers of York pledged themselves to bring in food from a wide catchment area, but pointed to the exiguous supplies in York itself. It was therefore agreed that the formal handover of the hostages would take place at Stamford Bridge on the Derwent, a tributary of the Ouse, seven or eight miles to the north-east, which was a suitable point for assembling the cattle and grain of the county and for bringing in mounts for the move south. The venue was doubtless chosen as a nodal point for magnates from the important population centres – the Wolds, the Vale of Pickering, the east side of the Vale of York – to make their submission.[49]

Monday 25 September was one of the most dramatic days in English history. The morning was bright, clear and sunny and in the broiling heat Harald made two bad decisions. First, he allowed his men to proceed to the Stamford Bridge rendezvous dangerously underequipped; they left behind on the ships their shields, helmets, coats of mail and spears, taking only their swords and a few bows and arrows. Then, supremely overconfident, Harald decided that only one in three of the army should accompany him, so that only about 5,000 troops were on the march with him and Tostig; Olaf, Eystein Orri, Paul Thorfinsson and his brother Erlend were left behind on shipboard. Harald's men set off in high spirits, their previous misgivings apparently laid to rest, tracing a route running through Escrick, Wheldrake, Elvington and Kexby, keeping on the right bank of the river and following a low ridge about fifty feet above sea-level. Near the bridge they found a convergence of several Roman roads: from York to Bridlington via Gate Helmsley; to Thornton-le-Street and Newcastle; and two separate roads to Malton, one of which crossed the York–Bridlington road about a mile from Stamford Bridge.[50]

That very morning Harold Godwinson, who had arrived at Tadcaster late on the 24th, was approaching York on a converging route, having been brought up-to-date about Fulford Gate and the surrender of York. The speed of his advance was rivalled only by its unexpectedness: the Norse intelligence system was evidently lamentable – perhaps they had grown complacent after their defeat of Morcar and Edwin – and, even more remarkably, none of the citizens through whose towns Harold's army had passed thought of making himself a small fortune by riding to the Norsemen with a warning. Harold probably left Tadcaster around 6 a.m. and arrived in York three hours later. The arrival of this large force from the south must have caused a sensation in York, doubtless eliciting an ambivalent response; we do not know how Harold was greeted in the city, only that there was no resistance.

Pausing briefly for rest in York, Harold considered his options. He could build a rampart at York and await attack, but Saxons were useless at resisting sieges, there was not enough food and water in the city for his army, and he was anyway greatly outnumbered by the combined forces of the Norwegians. He could attack the Viking fleet at Riccall, but he lacked the ships for a successful amphibious assault. That left him with the option that most appealed to him personally: to attack the smaller Norse force at Stamford Bridge. Getting his men into line once more, Harold pressed on, following the Roman road via Gate Helmsley to Stamford Bridge. The first indication the Norwegians had of the enemy was when the English came over the brow of the gradual slope running down from Gate Helmsley to Stamford Bridge.[51]

The Norsemen were collecting cattle on the right side of Stamford Bridge, having thrown no scouts out on the Gate Helmsley road; there may have been a few units lounging desultorily on the left-hand bank and the bridge itself was certainly guarded. Suddenly they were aware of a great cloud of dust, then they began to make out the distinct shapes of soldiers, whom Hardrada at first foolishly thought had been sent on as an afterthought by his son Olaf. Once they learned the truth, Tostig was all for a fighting retreat back to Riccall and reinforcements, even though the English occupied the only viable route back, but Hardrada was determined to stand his ground; he did, however, send his best riders back to the fleet to ask Eystein Orri to come with all speed. Then he formed a circular shield-wall with Land-Ravager in the centre.[52]

Before battle was joined, there were a number of verbal skirmishes – some of them doubtless apocryphal – eagerly recorded by the saga writers. Hardrada was said to have been thrown when his horse became skittish (yet another alleged stumble!) and to have passed off the incident with the remark that a fall is lucky for a traveller. Harold Godwinson, seeing a man fall from a black horse, is said to have asked who was the rider and, when told it was Harald, to have remarked that Hardrada's luck had deserted him.[53] We are on firmer ground when it comes to the details of the preliminary horse-trading, for the sources have the circumstantial ring of truth. Interestingly, it is Tostig who emerges as the knight *sans peur et sans reproche*.

Harold and twenty of his housecarls rode up to the foot of the bridge on the left bank of the Derwent to parley; Harald, Tostig and a small bodyguard rode over to meet them. Harold, posing as his own herald, promised Tostig that if he returned to the Godwinson fold he would be rewarded not just with the return of his earldom but with one-third of all England. Tostig asked what would happen to Harald Hardrada. 'We will give him seven feet of ground or as much more as he is taller than other men,' was the uncompromising reply. Tostig answered that it would never be said of him that he brought the king of Norway to England only to betray him. He turned on his horse and rode away; Hardrada, who understood very little English but followed the 'herald's' body language very well, followed him and asked who it was who had spoken so boldly. Tostig answered that it was his brother Harold. Hardrada said that if he had known he would have killed him on the spot. Tostig answered, that he could also never be the murderer of a brother who had offered him friendship and dominion; if one of them had to die, he preferred Harold to kill him. Harald grunted, then remarked rather patronizingly that Harold stood very well in his stirrups for such a small man. Since Harold Godwinson was at least 5 feet 11 inches tall, we may take this as an instance of Hardrada's vanity about his great height.[54]

The battle began on the York side of the river, with the English trying to get possession of the bridge and the valiant Norse vanguard fighting a delaying action to allow Hardrada to deploy his men most effectively on the right bank. It is clear that the Horatius-like stand at the bridge held the English up far longer than expected, and we hear of a single giant Norwegian warrior who is supposed to have slain forty Saxons with a battle-axe. If Harold had archers, it is surprising that he did not take this defender out with long-range arrow fire, but perhaps this option clashed with his notion of chivalry; this would be consistent with the story that the defender was offered clemency by the English as a mark of their admiration for his valour, but he refused it and taunted his foes with being a pack of cowards. In the end the attackers lost patience and all thoughts of chivalry were thrown to the winds. The English launched a boat and one of them stood in the vessel and thrust a long pike up through the wooden planking of the bridge, dealing a mortal wound to the Viking hero.[55]

It was 3 p.m. by the time the English poured across the bridge to get to grips with Hardrada's main force, three hundred yards from the right bank of the river. Harald had tried to take advantage of a slight slope by drawing his men up in a more linear formation than usual, long but not deep, only too aware that he was badly outnumbered. His best hope was to knock the English off balance by a sudden counterattack, as at Fulford Gate, where he had secured his flanks in difficult terrain. As a further refinement, he kept his personal retinue of axemen at a distance from the main body but bent the line round on itself to form a circle that could not be outflanked. This was cumbersome, restricted mobility, revealed a kind of siege mentality and invited a Cannae-style encirclement, but Viking warfare was marked by an obsession with vulnerable flanks.[56]

Furious hand-to-hand combat now ensued, housecarl against berserker, sword against sword, axe against axe. Outnumbered, without their armour and most of their weapons, the Norsemen stood little chance and were soon being cut down in their hundreds. The shield-wall was then breached, which provoked Hardrada to rush out into the open in berserker fury, only to be slain almost immediately, possibly, as the sagas relate, by an arrow in the windpipe. In his last moments on earth, Harald had not lost his taste for heroic poetry. As the English poured across the bridge, he dictated a poem to his scribe: 'We march forward in battle-array without our corselets to meet the dark blades; helmets shine but I have not mine, for now our armour lies down on the ships.' Then Harald decided this was a bad poem and would not inspire his men. In a singsong voice he yelled out a composition richer in kennings and metrically superior, which was recorded thus: 'We do not creep in battle under the shelter of shields before the crash of weapons; this is what the loyal goddess of the hawk's hand [sc. Woman] commanded us. The bearer of the necklace told me long ago to hold the prop of the helmet [sc. the head] high in the din of weapons, when the valkyrie's ice [sc. sword] met the skulls of men.'[57]

Harald's death was the perfect ending to the career of a great Norse warrior, utterly befitting the man who was the last of the Vikings. As always when a great leader was killed in medieval warfare, there was a lull as his followers hesitated about what to do next. Seeing a chance to avoid further loss of life – he could not afford casualties with William still to deal with – Harold offered terms to the Norsemen if they would surrender. But when Tostig ostentatiously took his stand by Land-Ravager, his men roared their defiance and the Norwegians announced their resolve to die around their slain lord. The second act of the battle then commenced, with combat bloodier than ever; soon Tostig himself was dead along with the unnamed king from Ireland, and only Godred Grovan remained of the luminaries. The English cut down their foemen by the hundreds, driving many into the Derwent to drown there, all the time taking heavy casualties themselves. It may be, as has been suggested, that the main victims in the second phase of the battle were Tostig's Flemish mercenaries, since the only prominent Norseman recorded as falling then was the Icelander Brand. But whether the dead were largely Tostig's men or Harald's berserkers, soon there were few left of the 5,000 who had marched out from the longships so cheerfully that morning.[58]

Harold and his men were left in possession of the battlefield for only a matter of minutes before the final, and most ferocious, act of the battle took place. Eystein Orri proved a worthy choice as Harald's would-be son-in-law. As soon as Harald's messengers reached the longships at Riccall, Eystein and his warriors donned their heavy coats of mail and set off for Stamford Bridge at the double, sweltering in the afternoon sun. It must have taken them three hours to reach the battlefield, for Eystein had to work out a new line of march: had he followed Hardrada's route of that morning, he would have found himself in the English rear, on the wrong side of the bridge. Improvising rapidly and doubtless with the help of local guides pressed into service at swordpoint, Orri found a route that took him through Wheldrake to the bridge at Kexby, where the Norwegians crossed and made their way across country via Catton or Wilberfoss to the Stamford Bridge–Gagfoss road; they then formed up in battle order and came crashing in on the enemy right from a southerly direction.[59]

Tired from the long march and sweltering in the heat, the Norsemen yet gave a good account of themselves. Their fearsome charge – later made legendary as 'the storm of Orri' – nearly succeeded in breaking the English, but Harold's men stood firm and fought them to a standstill. The dreadful, close-combat slaughter continued until nightfall, by which time Eystein Orri and most of his lieutenants were all dead. Under cover of darkness the rank and file stole away, leaving Harold in possession of the field after almost an entire day's continuous fighting. Harold took severe losses – far more than he could afford – but the most shocking aspect of Stamford Bridge was the near-annihilation of the huge Norwegian army. The loss of life cannot be as great as in the sagas, where it is related that only twenty-four longships returned to Norway (perhaps this means there were only twenty-four vessels that had not sustained fatalities), but Monday 25 September was an utter disaster for Norway, from which it took years to recover.[60]

The English pursued the defeated Norsemen to Riccall, and fired some of the longships. At Stamford Bridge the body of Tostig was found (and buried at York) but most of his comrades were never formally laid to rest; the bones of the slain lay bleaching for years, along with the skeletons of dead horses and their iron horseshoes. Among the few Viking grandees to escape was Hardrada's new marshal, Styrkar, appointed a few months before on the death of Ulf Ospaksson. Styrkar stumbled away from the evening slaughter in his shirt and encountered an English carter who was wearing a leather coat. Styrkar offered to buy it, but the man taunted him with being a defeated Norwegian, whereupon Styrkar cut off his head, took the coat and horse and rode to the Humber estuary.[61]

The twenty-year-old Olaf Haraldsson, the notable man of peace, was now in command of the battered remnants of the Norsemen. He at once asked for terms from Harold and was allowed to depart in peace with his ships; Harold realized that the Norwegians would not pose a threat again for a generation, and that to wage war to the knife on a cornered foe would simply result in further heavy casualties to his army – which he could ill afford. Olaf also asked for leave to bury his father's body, but for some reason this was not immediately surrendered and Skule Kongfroste had to return from the Orkneys for it later. Olaf stood away from Spurn Head at the mouth of the Humber, wintered in the Orkneys with Paul and Erlend, then, having received Harald's corpse from Skule, took it with him to Norway in the spring of 1067 and buried it in St Mary's church, Nidaros (Trondheim). Magnus, who had ruled wisely as regent, reigned peacefully with his brother until his early death in 1069. Olaf the Quiet then reigned until 1093. Hardrada's wife,

Elizabeth, and his daughter Ingigerd returned to Norway, but his favourite daughter, Maria, died suddenly in September 1066 – legend said in the very hour of her father's death.[62]

Stamford Bridge confirmed that Harold Godwinson was a general of great talent. Even if we concede that he was lucky to catch Hardrada with only a third of his army, and lightly armed, and that he was able to defeat the Norwegians piecemeal, this was surely a case of fortune favouring the brave. His forced march north was an outstanding exploit in itself, whatever judgement we form on its ultimate wisdom. But while he rested for two days in York, he could allow himself only temporary euphoria. At a council held the day after Stamford Bridge, all agreed he must start for the south at once to deal with the Norman menace. The army with which he had fought Hardrada was in no shape for another battle, so Harold set off south with just his housecarls.[63]

Two decisions taken by Harold at York were to have serious consequences. First, he announced, even as he called for volunteers, that there would be no distribution of the plunder taken from the Norwegians and that it would be left in the care of Archbishop Ealdred. Two interpretations of this ill-judged action are possible. It may simply be that Harold's coffers were empty, that he needed money for the war against the Normans, and could not be lavish with treasure. Or possibly the explanation is that most of the loot was in the form of captured ships and naval impedimenta with which he intended to rebuild his fleet. Whatever the explanation, his refusal to implement some form of prize money caused dismay in the ranks; many men deserted instantly, others declared they would never serve such an ungrateful lord.[64]

Secondly, Harold made the egregious mistake of both trusting and not trusting the sons of Aelfgar. He trusted them in the sense that he exhorted them to follow him south at all speed with their housecarls and levies and counted on their support, but did not trust them in the sense that he appointed his man Meruleswegen as his deputy in the north, with the title of acting sheriff. Morcar and Edwin took the appointment as an insult, but it is doubtful in any case if they intended following Harold to London. Still obsessed with their separatist schemes for an independent Northumbria, they considered their best interests would be served by a Norman victory, so did not take their forces to the muster in the south. Their foolish idea that William would divide England with them reveals their breathtaking naïvety.[65]

Harold got his housecarls mounted and started south, passing through Stamford and accomplishing the journey to London in eight days. Somewhere on the way south, he heard the news he had been dreading.

Three days after Stamford Bridge the Normans had landed on the south coast and were now ravaging Sussex. Harold is said to have exclaimed that it would have been better if he had given Tostig all he wanted, both in 1065 and at Stamford Bridge, rather than drink this chalice. In his heart he knew he was faced with his greatest crisis yet.

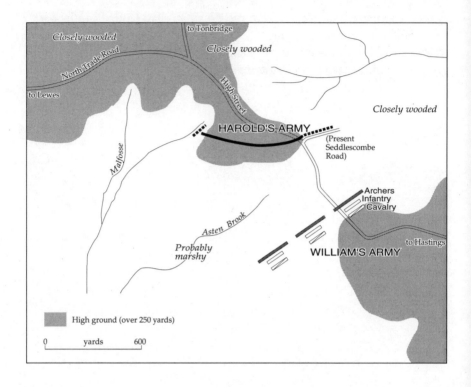

The site of the Battle of Hastings

10

Hastings

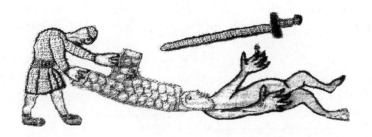

Whether we accept the story of William's watching the weathervane at Saint-Valéry with alternating moods of inchoate elation and tearful despair, or believe he observed the weather with a more glacial stoicism, it is certain that on 27 September 1066, two days after the battle of Stamford Bridge, the Norman duke finally got the south wind he had been hoping for. As soon as the wind was favourable, William ordered his fleet to put to sea. To avoid frequent collisions and to maintain formation during the overcast and moonless night, each ship was equipped with lanterns, flambeaux and signalling devices. Making full use of the high tide, the Normans left at nightfall on the evening of the 27th and landed at Pevensey the next morning, having experienced favourable winds all the way.[1]

The voyage across the Channel was uneventful and William, always supernaturally lucky, avoided the worst risk to his armada: that it would be caught by a full gale on the high seas. His own flagship, *Maria*, lost contact with the rest of the fleet early on, possibly because, unencumbered by horses, it could make easier way, but William had ordered a mid-Channel rendezvous and ordered all his vessels to display lanterns. The statement that the fleet actually *anchored* halfway across must be taken with a pinch of salt, as this would have required massive lengths of anchor warp. There is no reason, though, to doubt the story that as dawn broke *Mora* found itself alone on the open sea and that William's sailors became jittery. He ordered a sailor to shin up the mast to see if there was any sign of their comrades, but there was none; William then calmly ordered his men to prepare breakfast. About half an hour later he ordered his agile sailor to climb the mast again; this time he reported four sail in sight and very soon the entire armada was visible.[2]

After arriving off the south coast of England around 10 a.m. on the morning of 28 September, the Normans waited for the change of tide shortly after 11 a.m., landed on the shingle beach of Pevensey Bay and found it undefended. They ran the ships up on the beach, cast anchors and lowered masts. Only two of his boats had been lost on the crossing and the only other casualties were sustained by some Normans who landed by mistake at Sandwich and were attacked (presumably killed) by the locals. Once again William was lucky. Harold had spotted the potential of the Hastings area for an invader earlier in the summer and the Pevensey area had been heavily guarded, but when he became preoccupied by the threat from Hardrada in the north, he garrisoned Romney and Dover but pulled his troops out of Hastings. Just a little later or a little earlier William would have been met at the beachhead with overwhelming force.[3]

However, Harold cannot be absolved from all blame, for his naval dispositions that summer were singularly inept. He made no attempt to singe William's beard at Dives, as a Drake would have done, or to keep a fleet in being to intercept the Normans in mid-Channel, though some sources do speak vaguely of a number of unspecified fleet engagements. Even if we accept, as some have argued, that such actions were beyond the naval technology of the time, the level of seamanship in Harold's fleet does not seem high, arguing for a rapid decline of the navy since the 1040s, when it was still imbued with the Viking spirit of Cnut. On paper, Anglo-Saxon society was far superior to Norman in naval strength, reflecting the greater impact of recent Scandinavian culture on England. There is a profound irony in the way Harold, with a long tradition of sea power behind him, failed to use this option effectively, whereas the Normans, who had to build a fleet from scratch, and whose culture emphasized horses rather than warships, performed so well in this virgin territory.[4]

Inevitably, the story of the Norman landing had to be embroidered by the mandatory stumble. This time it was William who was said to have lost his footing and to have passed off the bad omen by claiming that he had deliberately seized his rightful kingdom in both hands. He ordered the ships anchored close together, as if expecting counterattack, began releasing the horses and commanded the bulk of his men to unload arms and supplies while he sent an advance guard of archers and infantry cautiously inland on reconnaissance. Finding no one there to resist him, William grew more confident and sent his knights to demand the surrender of Hastings, which would solve immediate problems of food supply. With none of Harold's troops close to them, the burghers of Hastings had no option but to bow the head. Just twenty-four hours after landing the Normans were already engaged in garrisoning both Hastings and Pevensey, where they built a trench and a mound surmounted with a wooden castle.[5]

Pevensey had powerful fortifications dating from Roman times, enclosed by a stone wall with a perimeter of about seven hundred yards; additionally, there was a network of docks used by the Saxon navy and merchant shipping. The entire complex was sufficiently sophisticated to allow William to land 3,000 battle-ready troops in a single afternoon. He then built walls to protect the horse transports from landward attack, and strengthened and modified the Roman fortifications. The enlargement of fortifications at Pevensey and Hastings had manpower implications, for a garrison of 1,000 men was required at each location; in this concern for the safety of his fleet William was being atavistic, harking back to the concerns of his Norse forebears. He was being overcautious, for the local fyrd commander was evidently not a man of any military talent. It has been estimated that he could have raised a force of 1,500–1,600, which could have been a serious menace to the garrisons once William moved inland, but the Pevensey landing was notable for the absence both of opposition at the beachhead and of a counterattack thereafter.[6]

It was probably at Hastings on the 29th that William first learned the news of Stamford Bridge – traditionally the news was said to have been brought to him by Robert, son of Wymarc, who had held office under King Edward – so that he now knew it was Harold Godwinson not Harald Hardrada he would be facing. William immediately saw that it was in his interest to fight a tired Harold as soon as possible, while his foe's strength was diminished and before he could assemble fresh forces. While he sent his armies to ravage Harold's lands in Sussex to tempt him to an early battle, his propaganda machine got into full swing. Harold's victory at Stamford Bridge was presented as being in some sense contrary to the natural order and much use was made of Lucan's phrase in the *Pharsalia*, dealing with the civil war between Julius Caesar and Pompey, where he says that some battles go beyond even civil war in their wickedness. William encouraged his propagandists to popularize the idea that the campaign against Harold was in part a war of revenge for their 'kith and kin' slain at Stamford Bridge; what he would have said about the Norsemen had he had to face them in battle is a moot point. But the most obvious propaganda ploy was to portray Harold as a fratricide for the death of Tostig – an indictment that was embellished with the ludicrous charge that Harold had beheaded Tostig's corpse.[7]

After building an inner rampart at Pevensey, William moved his base of operations to Hastings, as it provided a haven for the fleet he had to keep in contact with constantly before he could engage Harold in battle. So far things had gone to plan, for the peninsula of Hastings, fifty miles square, made an ideal short-term base for an invader, as cattle could be penned there and reinforcements brought in by sea. William completed his fort at Hastings and sent out his men to plunder and lay waste everything not of immediate use to the Normans, pursuing a scorched-earth policy and concentrating particularly on lands known to be Harold's, especially those at Steyning seized from the abbey of Fécamp. This was England's first taste of the 'harrying' mentality that had already made the Normans dreaded in Europe and would later make their name a byword for barbarism and savagery. The Bayeux Tapestry shows houses and huts being burnt to the ground while terrified occupants cower outside. There was method in the brutality, for unless he could dent Harold's prestige, authority and credibility there seemed no way the vital early battle could be fought. On the other hand, Harold was almost bound to rise to the bait, for contemporary notions of honour demanded immediate retaliation in such a case, or the entire notion of lordship would fail.[8]

Harold arrived in London on 6 October, having taken eight days to retrace the 190 miles from York. His first action was to go to pray at Waltham Abbey; then he returned to London, to find an ambassador from William besetting him with all the hoary old arguments about the Norman right to the succession. The envoy was Hugh Margot, a monk from Fécamp, who seems to have gone about his business so undiplomatically that Harold lost his temper and was with difficulty restrained from killing the monk on the spot. After rejecting all William's pleas to have their rival claims assessed by an independent commission, Harold consulted with his advisers and principally with his brothers Gyrth and Leofwine. From this conclave came the absurd Norman propaganda story that Harold lost his nerve and had his sinews stiffened only after a talking-to from Gyrth. What actually happened was that Gyrth made the very sensible suggestion that, if Harold was so set on a quick battle with the Normans, he, Gyrth, should lead the English into the field so that, if he lost, Harold could gather another army and fight again; but if they gambled all on a single cast of the die and lost, the result would be utter disaster for the realm.[9]

In assessing Harold's generalship in 1066, there is a particular temptation to adopt an all-or-nothing approach: either to view him as a peerless commander and gallant hero who was the victim of an incredible run of bad luck or as a man who was constantly outwitted by William. The truth lies between the two extremes. Harold had lost the first round, both by stationing his fleet at the Isle of Wight until 8 September and choosing to fortify Dover. The thinking was that William would probably either cross from Normandy to Wessex to march on Winchester or would take Eustace's 1051 route towards Dover. He was about to lose the second round by a similar failure to think through all possible scenarios. On the other hand, Harold's actions in the second week of 1066, though wrong-headed, contained more rationality than he is sometimes credited with. The task is to disentangle the rational from the irrational in his thinking, to distinguish the strategic from the tactical, perceptions from reality and courage from stupidity. Certainly no account of his 'mindset' is satisfactory which views him as a hot-headed creature of impulse with a short fuse, who burst into anger if opposed and kicked his mother for urging caution; these are simply the vanishing echoes of ancient Norman propaganda.[10]

In arguing for a rapid advance on Hastings and an early battle, Harold was probably influenced by four main points. First, he could not be sure that William was not receiving reinforcements from the Continent and thus growing stronger every day. Secondly, as lord and king he felt morally bound to rescue his lands from the 'wrath of God' treatment to which the Normans were subjecting them. Thirdly, he felt overconfident after Stamford Bridge and may have dreamed of a second victory which would place him in the annals of the great conquerors of all time, alongside Alexander the Great, Hannibal and Julius Caesar. Fourthly, his strategy depended on bottling up William in the Hastings hinterland (which was in those days a peninsula with a narrow isthmus as the only means of access); it was October, very soon forage for the Norman warhorses would dry up and, if confined on the peninsula, William would have no choice but to surrender. His commissariat problems were compounded by the exhaustion of local supplies by Tostig's raid in May and the demands of the fyrd before 8 September. As for re-embarkation to Normandy, Harold hoped to rule that option out by sending his fleet to take William in the rear.

These were all weighty considerations, but all depended on being able to bell the cat and, as Gyrth pointed out, the manpower currently available to Harold did not make an early battle seem a feasible option. Gyrth proposed adopting Fabian tactics: wait until all available manpower had come in before offering battle and in the meantime scorch the earth, burn all the land between Hastings and London, leaving the Norman army to march through a wilderness. Too many men had been lost at Stamford Bridge, he urged, and a breathing-space was needed before another battle. The advice was sound: just a few more days would have given Harold a much more formidable army, and many of his northern units would have come in, including the corps of archers who had been left behind. Even if William and some of his men could have struggled through the man-made desert, his horses would not have survived, and he would have been easy meat for the Saxon housecarls. There is the further point that Gyrth was successfully second-guessing William's strategy of a Viking campaign with victory in months rather than a lengthy war.[11]

Harold would have none of it. He insisted that he would never let any man face danger while he avoided it, no matter what the reason; he was therefore duty-bound to go the aid of his vassals in Sussex, and he could not consent to stand idly by while the Normans ravaged without let or hindrance. Insisting on his 'bottling up' strategy, he argued that the scorched-earth policy was impracticable. Even if reluctant peasants could be forced to destroy their own livelihood, where was Gyrth's *cordon sanitaire* to be drawn? To speak of the land between Hastings and London was all very well, but once William escaped from the neck of the Hastings peninsula he was free to roam anywhere; he could provision himself and keep his army in being by taking a looping itinerary, north and then west. Harold therefore gave orders for an immediate march and sent his fleet round the Saxon shore to Sandwich to cut off the Normans' retreat.[12]

There is no question but that Gyrth's advice was correct. Fabian tactics do not necessarily require scorched-earth policies as well. If Harold had waited a week or two, he could have met William with a massive superiority in numbers, especially if his fleet had blockaded Hastings and prevented reinforcements from arriving. Morcar and Edwin would have been forced off the fence and obliged to appear in the field with their housecarls, and Harold would have had archers and even horses, had he chosen to use them. As it was he went to meet William with an army that was certainly no more than half, and possibly only a third, the size he could have taken with him had he only been patient. Even greater folly was evinced by his insistence that Gyrth, Leofwine and all the great names of Wessex and southern England accompany him to Hastings; this meant that if they were defeated, the English would be left with no leaders who could rally them.[13]

Harold set off for Hastings with a motley array of armed men. The core of his force were the housecarls who had fought with him at Stamford Bridge; then there were the thegns he had recruited in London, including sheriffs and abbots from Oxfordshire and Kent; next in importance were the mercenaries, including those sent by Svein Estrithson; then there were the men raised by the fyrd, mainly from southern England, but with a sprinkling from Norfolk and Suffolk. There were not many freemen or genuine volunteers properly so called, and the idea of a Saxon *levée en masse* or nation in arms is anachronistic, if only because in this era men fought for lords rather than the country or the nation. The legend of the last of the Saxons fighting for hearth and home is an attractive and seductive one, but it does not accord with historical fact.[14]

Even more amazing than Harold's disinclination to wait until he had marshalled the full strength of the kingdom was his refusal to wait even twenty-four hours to receive the levies on their way to him from the home counties; he simply left word that they were to follow him to Hastings with all speed. By accepting battle at the earliest possible moment with diminished numbers and resources (for example, the horses he and his men had ridden south from York were not fresh enough for further military use), Harold played into William's hands. Flushed by the signal victory he had won over Harald Hardrada, Harold never stopped to wonder whether Harald and Tostig had not simply let their attention wander and dropped their guard, thus handing him victory on a plate. Instead, intoxicated by his success, he thought that he could simply repeat his method of forced marches followed by a surprise attack. A more prudent man, having been smiled on once by the gods, would not have pushed his luck by assuming that Fortune would favour him so easily a second time; perhaps he was simply a victim of that common human arrogance that attributes sheer luck to God-given talent. The only real result of his overweening confidence was that he wore his men out by a gruelling 58-mile forced march over three days. The army that reached the eastern edge of the South Downs late on the night of Friday 13 October (and possibly as late as 2 a.m. on the 14th) was an exhausted army.[15]

If Harold hoped to surprise William as he had surprised Hardrada, he was soon disabused, for Norman scouts detected his approach and alerted the duke, who had his men stand to all night in expectation of attack. There is confusion in the Norman sources, for William of Jumièges speaks of Harold's army marching all night and arriving at dawn – which would have ruled out the possibility of a nocturnal attack – and the Bayeux Tapestry seems to suggest that the Norman foragers *were* almost surprised but spotted an English scout at the last moment. It makes most sense to assume a Saxon arrival anywhere from 11 p.m. to 2 a.m. There is some evidence that Harold did intend a night attack but rethought his position once he knew the Normans were on to him. But there is absolutely no truth in the absurd propaganda story that the English spent the night of 13–14 October carousing and feasting while the Normans spent it in prayer and silent vigil.[16]

We may assume that both sides passed a tense and nervous night, only too aware of the ordeal to come next day. William intended at first light to try to break out of the isthmus, while Harold, apparently thinking the Normans were short of food and would still be sending out foragers, determined to take out these advance parties in hopes of affecting Norman morale. It is clear that Harold did not intend to advance against William's main force until his own expected reinforcements had come up, and meanwhile was quite content to take up a defensive position on Caldbec Hill near the 'hoary apple tree' which had been agreed in London as the rendezvous point for later reinforcements and units not proceeding directly with Harold. The location was at the southern exit from the wooded hills, and some scholars even think the subsequent battle was fought there and not on Battle Hill, the traditional site. But such a reading means that William must have surprised Harold right at the rendezvous point, which does not accord with the best evidence. What did happen was that William tried to break out of the peninsula and that, to forestall this, Harold had to send his men to seize Battle Hill; this forward position then forced them to fight the Normans there and then.[17]

At first light the Norman advance guard on Telham Hill saw the Anglo-Saxon standards on Caldbec Hill, with more men coming out of the Weald forest, what looked like a large army behind them, and the whole scene seemingly a-glitter with spears. They raced back to inform William, who stood for a moment pensively, then ordered his archers forward in an attempt to stop the English seizing Battle Hill. The signs are, not least from the coiffed knights on the Bayeux Tapestry, that his mounted men were not yet ready but he hoped the archers could delay the English vanguard until his knights were ready to charge and seize the hill. The grim-faced archers advanced, crossbowmen in the middle, and fired a fusillade at the enemy's faces. Their orders were to harass the Saxons in hopes of throwing them into confusion, but not to be sucked into premature combat; if too hard pressed, they were to fall back where they would be supported by the knights, who should by that time have donned their armour and mounted their horses. If, on the other hand, the archers succeeded according to William's best hopes, his cavalry would then charge and take the hill.[18]

Harold spotted the manoeuvre and sent his men in large numbers to get to Battle Hill first. First to the hill were the mounted infantry, followed by the slower foot-soldiers proper. This race for the summit makes sense of otherwise enigmatic remarks in the sources, such as that Harold began the battle before all his army had arrived and that William hoped to 'establish his knights in the rear of the foot'. The English won the race for the hill and drove off the Norman archers, but not before being badly disconcerted by a cloud of arrows launched towards them. It is said that wounds from the terrifying crossbow quarrels sustained by some of the fyrdsmen shattered their morale, convinced them they were up against some new miracle weapon, and made them desert; in this way William's first movements in the battle may have had important long-term consequences.[19]

The initial skirmishes were now over, and a long period of 'phoney war' ensued as both sides made ready for the battle proper. William may have attempted to draw Harold down from Battle Hill to attack him on Telham but this was a forlorn hope with a general as good as Harold, for he knew very well that this would give the Norman cavalry an advantage. The battle of Hastings was a more prolonged affair than most medieval battles, but some historians have made it absurdly long by stating that the first serious clashes occurred at 9 a.m. and that the final Norman attack did not take place until 7.30 p.m. Because of the initial hostilities on Battle Hill, it is unlikely that the first clash of the assembled force of both armies took place until about 11 a.m. and the conflict must have been over by 5.30 p.m., for (before Daylight Saving Time) that is the hour of dusk in these latitudes in mid-October.[20]

The English took up their positions on the entire crest of the ridge facing south towards the Normans. All of the horsemen dismounted to fight on foot. The battle front was about half a mile wide: four hundred yards to the west or right of Harold and his standards and 200–400 yards to the east or left. On the crown of the hill, where the ground began to slope away to the south-east, Harold placed his two standards: the Dragon of Wessex and the Fighting Man, his personal ensign. Then he pondered his position. Both armies contained roughly 7,500–8,000 men, though William had more seasoned professionals and a more varied force, with heavy cavalry, archers and crossbowmen; moreover, they were better armed. Harold's housecarls wore full armour, helmets and coats of mail, with round shields and javelins to hurl at the beginning of the action, and swords and axes as the follow-up weapons. To stiffen his weak spot, the fyrdmen, Harold partly amalgamated them with the housecarls, putting them in the rear ranks, and partly located them to the south-west of the hill, beyond the isthmus. His army was now in close formation, protected in the front and at the flanks by the shield-wall of the housecarls.[21]

Harold had an ideal defensive position for his housecarls to fight off the Norman knights and archers, though the location was not without disadvantages. The ranks would have to stand in close order so that the dead would scarcely be able to fall, and the wounded could not detach themselves from the action. Also, the shield-wall would have to part to allow the housecarls to wield their dreaded two-handed axes. Even though a warrior was momentarily (and dangerously) exposed while wielding it, his warriors had practised this manoeuvre time after time, and Harold felt confident. The fyrdmen were more of a worry, for some were frightened by the initial fusillade from Norman crossbows and others deserted when they saw the narrow space in which they would have to fight. Initially this did not trouble Harold, for he knew he had only to hold out until nightfall when reinforcements were certain to arrive; he could play for a draw but William had to have a win. None the less, he was always alert to the issue of morale and decided to exhort his men, stressing their invincibility if they stood firm, and telling them that they were fighting effete aliens who had won only flukey victories in France and could not stand against their axes; he added, however, that if they broke rank, they were lost.[22]

William's speech to his men seems to have been more prolix, if we may credit the chroniclers. He began by saying that great courage was needed, for an outright victory alone would suffice this day. Retreat was impossible, and defeat would mean death of a particularly horrible kind; William's version of the bloodbath at Stamford Bridge lost nothing in the telling. He dwelt on Harold's broken oath, the murder of Alfred the Atheling, and the victorious record of their kin, the Norsemen, in all battles fought against the English. Pointing to the papal banner in their midst and displaying the relics, hung about his neck, on which Harold was supposed to have sworn falsely two years before, he reminded them that God was on their side and that the pope had blessed their crusade. He wound up by recalling the unparalleled martial record of the

Normans in Apulia, Calabria and Sicily. He then made a public vow that if he was granted victory he would build a church on the site of the battle.[23]

There may have been further inconsequential parleys during this period of lull, and certainly there was much blowing of trumpets. William then ordered his army drawn up prior to the advance. In the centre were William and the Normans, with a picked force of Evreux archers. By his side rode Robert of Mortain and Odo of Bayeux, together with Toustain of Bec, the standard-bearer. This was a right that belonged by tradition to Ralph of Tosny and Walter Giffard but they had waived it so as to be in the thick of the fighting. Other Normans in this central group included Roger of Bigod, William Malet and William Patry. On the left wing were the Bretons, Poitevins and men from Maine under Alan of Brittany, with Aimeri of Thouars as his second-in-command, and Ralph of Norfolk as his deputy. On the right the French troops and the foreign mercenaries were under William Fitzosbern, with Eustace of Boulogne, whom William did not entirely trust, and Robert de Beaumont, in senior positions.[24]

When the army reached the bottom of Telham Hill, the knights put on their armour and mounted their horses. William's coat of mail was at first put on back to front, which his men were inclined to take as a bad omen, but he shrugged it off, saying the reversal of the hauberk meant he would that way be turned from a duke into a king. His Spanish warhorse, a gift from King Alfonso, was then brought out, and William mounted up, choosing the mace as his weapon for the day. All three divisions of the army were ranged in a threefold order; first came the archers, slingers and bowmen, then the infantry and finally the knights. The cavalry bore heavy swords, long lances, maces and kite-shaped shields, but the horses had no artificial defence of any kind, and the infantry and archers were not in much better case. William's intention was for the Bretons, considered his weakest troops, to attack Harold's supposed weak spot on his right, while the right wing attempted the difficult east and north-east corners of the hill and he himself in the centre aimed straight for Harold's standard.[25]

For the first assault on the shield-wall William used the unsupported infantry and archers, partly to test the calibre of the opposition, but also to delay using the shock tactics of the mounted charge until the enemy was more weary. But he was worried about morale in his army, which was noticeably jittery, so called for a volunteer who would open proceedings by challenging a Saxon to single combat. What he was really calling for was a man willing to undertake a suicide mission, and the request was understood as such. Up rode a man named Taillefer, a military adventurer who had also made his living as a juggler and *jongleur*. Taillefer is himself a battleground, with one group of scholars accepting him as a real person and another as a mythical accretion: 'the mountebank Taillefer seemed a figure of romance rather than of history' is one typical remark, and we may well believe that subsequent accounts of the battle added ever more colour to his biography. But the basic idea of a man sacrificing himself to give his comrades heart at a critical moment contains nothing essentially false.[26]

Taillefer, then, whoever he was or whatever his real background, challenged a Saxon to single combat on horseback and killed him – whether through superiority as a warrior or simply as a horseman is not revealed; he then charged the shield-wall, where he was killed instantly. There is no need to believe the later stories that he killed three men in single combat before dying at the point of a lance – as though Harold would obligingly send man after man out of the ranks for a purpose that was not his – to appreciate that his self-sacrifice might have been just the spur needed to get demoralized and shaky men to charge uphill against a strong defensive position. It seems plausible that the Norman infantry were maddened by the loss of their champion and forgot their fear in an outburst of rage. They were said to have marched determinedly up the slope, singing the Song of Roland in his honour.[27]

When both sides came within range, there was a fusillade of missiles on both sides: arrows shooting uphill and javelins, hatchets and stone fastened on pieces of wood hailing down. The Norman archers could make no impact on the enemy as, shooting from a lower level, their arrows either struck the housecarls' shields or passed over their heads. Once within stabbing range of the shield-wall, the Normans were skewered, impaled and scythed down in dozens. The Normans yelled their war cries, especially *dieu aide* (assist us, God), but could make little impression. The Saxons worked out a kind of land shanty as they went about their grisly work; anyone gaining a toehold anywhere near the adamantine barrier of shields was run through and the corpse thrown back with an exultant cry of 'Out, out!'[28]

The infantry assault lasted perhaps half an hour before petering out. There was now nothing for it but sending in the cavalry, on which such great hopes rested. It says something for the calibre of the Norman *destriers* that they were able to charge uphill carrying 250 lb of rider and equipment, but the velocity on impact with the shield-wall cannot have been great and was easily withstood. This time the English took some casualties, but not nearly so many as the Normans. The advantages of height and the sheer physical strength of the terrifying axemen broke up this mounted attack in turn. The Bretons on the Norman left took a terrible mauling; their nerve cracked, they broke and began streaming down the hill. In defiance of strict orders, those fyrdsmen who were not hemmed within the human stockade of the shield-wall – perhaps the ones Harold had posted on his right flank – rushed after the Bretons, thinking the battle already won.[29]

Some of the pursuers got too far ahead of their comrades and were easy meat when the Breton cavalry wheeled round and picked them off. But this minor skirmishing was soon subsumed in a general engagement as Harold ordered a widespread advance. The chaos and confusion on the Norman left was his great chance and he knew it. Whereas the Norman knights had been able to isolate the handful of Saxons who had scattered in the pursuit, they were powerless against the shield-wall advancing in formation, for there was no opening in the ranks through which they could ride. The battle had reached its climactic moment, and at this very point William was thrown from his horse – the first of three unhorsings this day – leading to a rumour that he was dead. Had this really been the case, the Normans would have disintegrated; the cavalry might have got away but the infantry would certainly have been slaughtered.[30]

Why, then, did Harold fail to score a decisive victory at this moment just when the Normans were on the point of being routed? Two separate incidents explain why Harold was unable to press his advantage. In the first place, William, mounted on a new horse, took off his helmet and showed himself to his troops, proving beyond doubt that he was not dead. He is said to have yelled that they were all madmen, that victory was in front of them and only death behind them, but whether he could be heard above the din is doubtful. The important thing was that the rumour of his death was laid by the heels. Grabbing a spear, and ignoring the protestations of Eustace of Boulogne that retreat might be the best policy, William whacked at his fleeing men. His half-brother Odo and some of the other Norman nobles did likewise, so that very soon the Bretons were shamed and browbeaten into facing about.[31]

But a Norman rally still does not explain why there was not the most colossal shock of arms as the advancing English smashed into them. Somehow, mysteriously, the general advance ordered by Harold was halted, and the logical presumption must be that it was halted by the death of his brother Leofwine, which occurred about this time. This is borne out by the evidence of the Bayeux Tapestry and also, indirectly, by William of Jumièges, who says that Harold was killed early in the battle; clearly he was confused and meant Harold's brother. If Leofwine was leading the counterattack (he is shown in the Tapesty wielding a battle-axe) and was struck, perhaps by an arrow, in front of the Saxon army just as their advance was hitting its stride, it would not be surprising if the sudden loss of leadership stayed the pulse of the onslaught. It is also possible that the fyrdmen on the wings, who broke rank to pursue the Bretons and were picked off, did so at this point, unaware that Leofwine had died and the advance had been called off.[32]

The English had lost the vital impetus – for in battle minutes, and even seconds, count. Quickly rallying his men, William headed a charge which drove the Saxons back up the hill with heavy losses. Forming up their shield-wall again, Harold's men prepared to sustain another furious Norman attack. Despite their losses, they were still in good heart, their discipline was unbroken and they continued to maintain close order. A terrible hand-to-hand combat now ensued, with some inroads being made on the Saxon left by Robert, son of Roger of Beaumont. William was again unhorsed, but soon afterwards the spear-wielding Gyrth was killed – another bad blow to Harold. There is no need to accept the obvious *Iliad*-inspired story that Gyrth first unhorsed William and that William then slew Gyrth; the chaotic fighting on the hill did not allow for that degree of heroic precision. More plausible is the version that William called to a knight of Maine to give up his horse and, when the knight refused, the furious duke struck him from the charger and mounted up himself, only to be again unhorsed almost immediately and half stunned by the 'son of Helloc', who was himself slain by the duke's bodyguard. It seems that Eustace of Boulogne made up for his earlier lapse into cowardice by rescuing William in the thickest maelstrom of the battle.[33]

By now it was about two o'clock in the afternoon and the contest was still a stalemate. Both sides paused to rest, recuperate and consider options. Harold must have been concerned by the gradual depletion of his manpower and to have prayed, to amend the words of Wellington at Waterloo nearly eight hundred years later: 'Give me nightfall or give me reinforcements.' William must by now have been confident of the outcome, if only the daylight hours would last long enough. He knew that the next attack on the shield-wall would be the crucial one: secure a breakthrough and victory would be his; fail, and the advantage would shift to Harold. William realized that if the Saxon strength could be diminished incrementally, eventually their lack of numbers would allow a breach to be made in the defence. It was time to dig into the deep resources of Norman battlecraft.

It seems clear that, although William was good at improvising in the heat of battle, he was not a particularly original captain and did not innovate in the manner of the great military geniuses of the ages. His tactics at Hastings were based on a store of knowledge dating back to the behaviour of Richer of Rheims at the battle of Montpensier in 892 and of the Bretons against Fulk Nerra of Anjou at Conquerer one hundred years later. Included in this corpus was the stratagem of the feigned retreat, a particular favourite of the Normans, who used it at Arques in 1053, at Messina in 1060 and at Cassel in 1071. The most controversial claim of the Norman historians is that William won the battle of Hastings by luring the English off the brow of the hill by a pretended flight, then turning and destroying them. Is this credible, or is the entire story of a feigned retreat simply a device to mask the real rout of the Bretons early in the battle?[34]

As traditionally told, the story is obvious nonsense. The bulk of the shield-wall never was lured from the crown of the hill, as William of Poitiers admits when he speaks of this stage of the conflict as being 'an unknown sort of battle, in which one side launched attacks and manoeuvres, the other stood like rocks fixed to the ground'. There are other obvious objections to the traditional story, which have been put with great force over the years. The Bayeux Tapestry gives no support to the idea. In the heat of battle it would be impossible to carry out such a manoeuvre on a large scale since it would require every man to know exactly when to retreat, how far to retreat, when to turn back and fight again, and would need perfect synchronization if chaos was not to result. Moreover, how could William's orders be conveyed over the din and clangour of more than 14,000 men in combat, many clad in reverberating metal and wielding clanging metal weapons? Military experts add the point that soldiers once committed to attack cannot be made to change direction. Others say it is not psychologically credible that, having with difficulty extricated his men from a real flight, William should then have involved them in a simulated one. Most telling of all is the objection that stories of feigned retreats occur in the military annals of all medieval nations – the Byzantines, the Saracens, the Mongols – that the stratagem was widely known and was particularly associated with the horsemen of the steppes – the Alans, the Huns, the Visigoths, the Magyars.[35]

Historians have tended to take up rigid positions on the alleged 'feigned retreat' at Hastings, with one side asserting the manoeuvre's impossibility on a confined battlefield like Hastings, and others simply reiterating that it 'must have' taken place because the sources tell us so, and anyway the Norman knights were superlatively trained.[36] The entire confusion has arisen because of William of Poitiers's tendency to hyperbole, first by pretending that the initial rout of the Bretons was faked, and secondly by implying that it was a stratagem involving the whole army. The overwhelming probability is that William gradually whittled away the manpower of the fyrdsmen on the English right who had been placed by Harold on outcrops of the hill to prevent the shield-wall being outflanked. Groups of Norman and Breton knights, no more than twenty strong, almost certainly tempted the men of the fyrd out of their protected positions, then wheeled round and slaughtered them, and these isolated incidents were then built into a ludicrous story involving the entire army. William would have used the Breton cavalry on his left for two main reasons: they had already fled in a genuine panic, so English suspicions would be lulled; and the Bretons were uniquely versed in the technique of the feigned flight, having learned it centuries earlier from the Alans in Armorica.[37]

William's ruse worked. The Bretons rode up to the fyrdmen and, after a brief and furious combat, turned and fled. The Saxons sprang after them like hounds but all too soon the Bretons turned and began scything them down. Now it was the turn of the English to flee, but some of the fugitives reached a small outlying hillock, where there was already a garrison; the men on the hill showered the Bretons with missiles, forcing them to sheer off. Yet the best Saxon exploit was yet to come. Another party of English fugitives fled in the direction of ground to the west of the hill known to be treacherous because of the deep gulleys and then made a stand by the steep and thickly wooded banks of a hidden ravine; when the cavalry came charging after them, dozens of horses lost their footing, broke their legs or plunged to their doom in the hidden chasm, taking their riders with them.[38]

Although the fyrdsmen had acquitted themselves well, they had fallen into William's trap by losing sight of their primary objective. While they and the Bretons were pursuing their mixed fortunes, the Normans seized the vantage points on the Saxon right and began making their way to the top of the hill via the gentle slope to the west. Harold had all but lost his crucial advantage of ground and was, moreover, now vulnerable to attack from two directions: from the initial point of attack, straight up the hill, and from the west, whence the Normans could charge directly against the Saxon standard. It was now about 4.30 in the afternoon, and at last Saxon spirits began to droop; around this time there were significant desertions from the fyrd.[39]

William gathered his cavalry for a final effort and this time, with a broader front on which to operate, he was able to co-ordinate his horse and foot. He ordered his archers to work out a high-angle plunging trajectory for their arrows, so that they fell on the defenders' heads. The purpose was not to achieve significant fatalities this way – unlikely, since the arrows would lose their force on the descent – but to irritate the housecarls, who would instinctively raise their shields in Roman *testudo* (turtle) formation, giving the cavalry an opportunity to charge. Whereas previously the defenders could either blunt the arrows of the archers on their shields or withstand the mounted charge of the *conrois*, now they had to do both simultaneously, at the very time there were gaps in the shield-wall from the repeated earlier attacks and they were tired with an unprecedently long day's fighting. It is also likely that as the arrows from the longbows whistled overhead, the Saxons started to take casualties from the crossbowmen, who were finally close enough to make their powerful shafts tell; hitherto, Harold had been able to keep these sharpshooters at a safe distance, but now his densely packed and reduced ranks provided an easy target.[40]

This time the Norman charge succeeded in punching a hole in the defence, but not before terrible, sanguinary hand-to-hand fighting had taken place around the Saxon standard. The victorious heroes of previous encounters closed with each other: there was a notable combat between a French knight and a pair of Saxon sworn comrades who had already distinguished themselves by killing large numbers of men and horses; this time it was the Frenchman who prevailed. The Norman Robert Fitzerneis was cut down as he tried to seize the English standard. One gigantic Saxon captain proved himself a veritable Ajax, slaying all around him in heaps and on one occasion scything down both horse and rider from a single swing of his battle-axe; but eventually he was outnumbered and was run through by the lance of a Norman knight. William himself was allegedly in the thick of the fighting, lost his third horse of the day, and was almost killed in single combat before being rescued by his men.[41]

Terrible scenes of carnage took place as wounded men screamed in agony, sometimes being trampled to death as they fell under the ever-diminishing shield-wall. Others ran around in mortal distress, clutching at arrows in their eyes. More and more holes were made in the defence and soon the shield-wall collapsed altogether, leaving pockets of defenders fighting back to back, perhaps twenty strong against an enemy now present on the hill in overwhelming force. Once victory was assured, many of the French and Normans broke off the fight to plunder the dead and dying. But William knew the battle was not over while

Harold still lived. Suddenly he saw him on the top of the hill, with the remnants of his housecarls still grouped around the Golden Dragon and the Fighting Man. Even though William claimed to have been willing to meet Harold in single combat, now that he saw the lion at bay and remembered his superhuman strength from the Brittany campaign, he thought better of it.[42]

Instead, he summoned Eustace of Boulogne and told him to assault Harold with the best knights available. Eustace took with him Hugh of Ponthieu, son of the man who had held Harold prisoner two years before, Walter Giffard and Hugh de Montfort. A furious fight was raging round the standard, as twenty picked knights were trying to wrest it from the housecarls. Taking advantage of the confusion, William's four-man hit squad found it an easy matter to slay Harold. Eustace ran him through the chest with a lance, drenching the earth with spurting blood, one of the others cut off his head, a third disembowelled him, and a fourth cut off his leg; some say the severing of the leg is a euphemism, that Harold was castrated. There has also been voiced the dark suspicion that William himself took part in the slaying. He later claimed to have been disgusted at the unchivalrous treatment of his enemy and to have broken the knight who cut off Harold's leg (or gelded him), but this story is likely to be an *ex post facto* rationalization of his chroniclers.[43]

As when Byrhtnoth fell at Maldon and his followers considered it their duty to perish with their lord, Harold's housecarls did not even ask for quarter and went down fighting to the last man. Among the heaps of slain were names well known in the Godwinson household: Thurkill, Godric and Aelfwig. The only survivors were the wounded who, assumed to be dead, were thrown on to the pile of corpses, but who later recovered enough strength to crawl away under cover of darkness. Even so, not many of them lived: one of Harold's favourite thegns, Leofric, survived the battle but died of his wounds on 1 November. Ironically, the housecarls probably fought even harder in the last half-hour of daylight than they had done all day, for now they knew they would see the sun no more on this earth. It was otherwise with the men of the fyrd – such few as had not already deserted. They were signally cast down by the death of their king and began slinking away off the battlefield even before dusk fully hid their movements. Some went on foot, and a lucky few on stolen horses; some followed the road to London and others cut across country, thinking themselves safer from pursuit that way.[44]

As so often when a grimly fought, close-run battle finally inclines decisively to one side (Waterloo is a case in point), the initial flight became a rout, and the rout a slaughter, which went on well after nightfall until William recalled his men for a general muster. Many fugitives were cut down or trampled by horses, and others expired from their wounds in the deep cover of the woods or simply dropped dead from exhaustion. But the pursuit cost the Normans very dear, for they ran into very difficult terrain just as English reinforcements finally began to reach Caldbec Hill, and the result was minor catastrophe. Six hundred yards north of Caldbec Hill, the newly arrived housecarls took up a strong defensive position and encouraged many of the fleeing Saxons to join them. They took up station on the edge of a ravine at a place identified as Oakwood Gill, just on the edge of Duniford Wood, and ever afterwards bearing the name 'the Malfosse'.[45]

The Malfosse was a deep gully enclosing a series of ditches with steep banks, whose precipitous nature was largely disguised by brambles and undergrowth. Pursuing fugitives in the gathering gloom, the Norman cavalry plunged into the steep descent on the north side of the hill; those behind them who could not see what had happened followed into the death-trap, until the entire ravine was a seething mass of dying men and whinnying horses. Many riders broke their necks and were killed outright; others who lay sprawling and broken-backed were despatched by the waiting Saxons. Eventually the slaughter came to an end when the pursuers were brought up short by the sheer volume of the dead in front of them. The Normans dismounted and sent scouts forward, who reported the English present in battalion strength. Leading a group of fifty pursuing knights was Eustace of Boulogne. Eustace allegedly panicked at this point and sent word back to William that a fresh English army had arrived. As the opposition was no more than a strong rearguard – as would have been discovered in the morning – Eustace might well have fallen into the duke's disfavour once more, but he was rescued from his dilemma by a happy accident. Struck by a blow from a missile in the shoulder, he was carried off wounded, with blood pouring from his nostrils, able thus to pass himself off as one of the 'heroes of the Malfosse'.[46]

William camped for the night among the carnage of the fallen, deliberately pitching his tent amid the heaps of slaughtered. It was long after dusk before he took off his armour, received the plaudits of his troops and at last sat down to eat and drink. At dawn the Normans began burying their dead, and meanwhile Saxon women came to the camp, asking for the bodies of their husbands, sons and brothers. William allowed them to be removed for burial, then ordered Harold's

dismembered corpse assembled for burial. There was great difficulty at
first in recognizing the body, but Harold's old mistress, Edith Swan-
neck, had hurried to the battlefield and was able to identify it by
distinguishing marks which only she knew. Her devotion was in sharp
contrast to the behaviour of the late king's recently married wife, who
was already on her way north to seek the protection of her brothers
Morcar and Edwin.[47]

Harold's mangled limbs were wrapped in a purple robe and taken to
the beach for burial. At this moment a message arrived from his mother,
Gytha, asking William for the boon of her son's body and promising to
pay as ransom Harold's weight in gold. An angry William refused
indignantly: his prickly sense of honour was outraged by the offer of
money and he was all the more irritated since, as a notably greedy man,
he would probably have liked to accept but could not bear the loss of
face in his soldiers' eyes. Moreover, he told his intimates that he did not
want to grant Harold the honour of Christian burial since so many good
men had died because of him; more likely, his fear was that a cult would
form around the dead king, which happened anyway. The Norman
knight William Malet was given responsibility for the bizarre burial of
Harold, which some have seen as an atavistic throwback to the Norse
paganism of William's ancestors. Harold was laid to rest under a mound
of stones at the foot of a sea cliff. Perhaps taking pity on the dishonoured
king, Malet had a lapidary inscription engraved on a large headstone,
and the legend read: 'By the duke's command, Harold, you rest here, to
guard the sea and shore.'[48]

The battle of Hastings was one of those rare conflicts that actually
merits the overused accolade 'decisive battles of world history', though
it was not immediately apparent that such was the case. Harold's
insistence that his two brothers and all the senior nobility of Wessex
should be at Hastings, with no contingency plan in case of failure, was
shown to be reckless folly. As well as being one of the longest of
medieval battles, it was also one of the bloodiest. No exact figures on
casualties are possible – hardly surprisingly when the number of
combatants on each side is disputed – but if the Normans were 7,500
strong, they must have taken about 2,500 casualties; in an era when
septicaemia meant battle wounds were usually fatal, such a tally
represents also the number of deaths. Given the fight to the death by the
housecarls and the slaughter of the fugitives afterwards, English casualties
must have been far higher, perhaps 4,000. Certainly most European
contemporaries, hardly squeamish or with a great feeling for the sanctity
of life in this era, were shocked by the bloodshed and the casualty lists,

and William himself felt the need to do penance for the slaughter he had wrought.[49]

There was nothing inevitable about the outcome of the battle. In recent years there has been a tendency to stress the alleged superiority of Norman technology, military science and expertise, to insinuate that England was up to three centuries behind Normandy, to misunderstand and underrate the Anglo-Saxon fighting potential and to conclude that Harold, on his march to Hastings, was engaged in a forlorn quest. The Norman troika of castles, archers and heavy cavalry has been overrated; it was effective in some cases but could make little impact against irregulars and guerrillas or in mountainous terrain, as events after 1066 show very clearly. Others have mistakenly inferred, by extrapolating from the peculiar circumstances of Hastings, that the Anglo-Saxon shield-wall had to remain rooted to the spot and was thus bound to fall victim to mobile archery and the charge of heavy cavalry.[50]

It cannot be too strongly emphasized that Hastings was a remarkably near-run affair whose outcome was for a long time in doubt and which the Normans won by luck as much as anything else. If Harold had been able to hold out for one hour longer, the balance would have swung in his favour the next day, for William's force would get no bigger but his would; the Normans meanwhile were in a hostile country with their rear menaced by the Saxon fleet. They themselves had the grace to admit that they came within an ace of defeat and that only divine intervention could explain their ultimate success. Had William been killed, or if he had failed to rally his troops after the Breton left collapsed, the result would have been catastrophe. Harold was unlucky in that his reinforcements did not reach him in time but foolish to trust Morcar and Edwin, for if their housecarls had come to Hastings, as promised, there could only have been one result. Some of the shrewder observers saw that the failure of the Northumbrians to appear in the field was in some ways *the* great act of treachery in a story not short on perfidy. And of course if Harold had lived to fight again another day, Hastings would not have been a decisive battle but only the Fulford Gate preceding a Stamford Bridge, fought near London and with who knows what result.[51]

The death of Harold and his brothers and all the great pre-1066 Wessex magnates was, in effect, the death of Anglo-Saxon England. But Harold was destined to win in legend the place denied him in history. According to twelfth-century tradition at Waltham Abbey, Harold's body was eventually brought there for Christian burial, and a cult grew up around the last Saxon king according to which he, and not Edward the Confessor, was the true saint. In time rumours arose that Harold had not died at Hastings but had survived: the story was that he had been knocked unconscious, thrown into the heap of the dead, then found, still breathing, by peasant women, who nursed him back to health in a nearby cottage. He was then taken to Winchester, where he hid in a cellar for two years before escaping to Germany. The anonymous *Vita Haroldi* makes even more sensational claims: that he survived and then conducted guerrilla warfare against the Normans for many years, after which he 'got religion' and became a hermit. After a pilgrimage to Rome, he settled down as an anchorite in a remote part of England and lived out the rest of his life far from the stress of wars and high politics. A lost cause, it seems, will always win a last victory in the human imagination.[52]

Epilogue

From 15 to 20 October William remained at Hastings, resting his troops, sending for reinforcements and hoping for submissions to come in from all over England; he was confident that, without leaders, England would soon surrender to him. But the expected overtures did not materialize: instead, Archbishop Ealdred, together with Morcar and Edwin, who had belatedly arrived in the capital, got the *witan* to elect the sixteen-year-old Edgar the Atheling as the new king, with the proviso that the coronation be delayed until Christmas. But the treacherous brothers then left Edgar high and dry by marching north to Northumbria with their housecarls. They took with them the dubious record of having betrayed two kings within a single month through their fanatical desire for an independent Northumbria.[1]

Disappointed by the lack of response, William got his army on the march again on the 20th. First stop was Romsey, which he had earmarked for revenge for the attack on the handful of his men who had landed there by mistake on 28 September. Executions and maimings showed the 'Christian' spirit in which this papal paladin intended to proceed. Next on his list was Dover. Despite its defences, the town surrendered without a fight, cowed into submission by the terrifying example of Romsey. William told his followers that clemency should be offered to all towns surrendering without opposition, but his loot-crazy troops took matters into their own hands and gutted Dover none the less. Canterbury was the next to surrender, on 29 October, and soon Winchester followed, persuaded by ex-Queen Edith. William's rapid progress was made easier by the absence of castles in England, which would have made his conquest a laborious affair.[2]

At Canterbury William and the Normans were delayed for a month, suffering from dysentery; once again it is said that the duke came close to death. Then, at the end of November, he advanced on London. There was a minor engagement outside the city between the Saxon defenders and five hundred Norman knights, which made William decide not to attack immediately. Keeping on the south bank, he cut a swathe of devastation through Surrey, Hampshire and Berkshire, finally crossing the Thames at Wallingford (where Stigand made his submission) and looping back towards London from the north-west, thus effectively encircling the city with devastated terrain. Hearing that the Normans intended to invest them with siege engines, and seeing themselves facing a long war of attrition which they could not hope to win without the help of the traitorous Morcar and Edwin, the opposition party in London finally accepted the inevitable. Edgar the Atheling, Bishop Ealdred, Ansgardus the Staller (commander of the Saxon garrison) and the other English notables came out to meet William at Berkhamstead to make formal obeisance and hand over hostages. To palliate his wrath they begged him to accept the crown.[3]

William summoned a council of his followers to sound their views; they advised him to become king at once. William sent a party of armed men into London to build a fort, later to be the Tower, and arranged to be crowned at Christmas. So it was that on Christmas Day 1066 William, Duke of Normandy, became King William I of England, and was anointed by the great friend of the man he had defeated, Archbishop Ealdred. But the terrible destruction caused by the Normans in the year 1066 was not yet over. Although he had given strict orders against systematic looting, William's troops were out of control and he had to turn a blind eye to their depredations. They were still in the mood for killing and plundering when they heard the great shouts of acclamation coming from Westminster Abbey and 'inferred' that an anti-Norman riot had broken out. Oddly enough, instead of rushing to the abbey to protect their king, they decided instead to set fire to neighbouring houses and slaughter a few Saxons. It was entirely appropriate that a man who had waded in blood to become king of England should have been crowned while flames licked and roared around the abbey.[4]

William reigned until 1087, and was engaged in a never-ending series of rebellions in England and wars in France. For those who claim him as a peerless warrior it is significant that after 1071 he never won a major victory. He survived plots and conspiracies by Eustace of Boulogne, Odo of Bayeux and even his eldest son, Robert Curthose. Svein Estrithson invaded England in 1069, together with Malcolm of Scotland, but re-embarked before facing William in battle. The punishment for northern England's support of Svein was the infamous 'harrying', whereby William systematically destroyed the local economy of the north and left the people to starve. In 1071 Morcar and Edwin joined Hereward the Wake in a famous revolt in Ely. When this failed, Morcar was imprisoned and died in jail, then Edwin was killed while trying to rescue his brother. The two men who, by their machiavellianism and treachery, had sabotaged Anglo-Saxon England more effectively than anyone else did not enjoy the fruits of their duplicity. Without them there would have been no disaffection of Tostig, no invasion by Harald Hardrada, no battle of Hastings and no Norman Conquest. Tolstoy, who famously argued that great men do not affect history but was obsessed by the influence of evil men, would have found in the story of Morcar and Edwin a notable moral example.

Appendix

The story that Harold Godwinson was killed at Hastings by an arrow in the eye is part of the historical legacy that every Macaulayan schoolboy is supposed to know. But is it any more than a story and does it deserve credence at any higher level than that of Alfred with the burnt cakes, Canute commanding the sea or Robert the Bruce and the spider? Until recently historians accepted the story of Harold and the arrow in an alarmingly uncritical way, doubtless concurring with the tradition in the spirit of Aristotle of an event which, even if it did not happen, could have happened, might have happened and even *should* have happened. But history is not drama: it obeys the laws of contingency not necessity; it goes its own stubborn and irreducible way regardless of plausibility. The historian, as opposed to the novelist, playwright or romancer, needs to ask, not is this the way Harold's life should have ended, or does this lend the battle of Hastings an extra patina of glamour, but only: did it actually happen? As soon as we ask this question, the difficulties inherent in the story begin to proliferate.

There are three main views on the battle of Hastings and the death of Harold. The most credulous is that the Normans won the battle by a feigned retreat of the entire army and that Harold was killed with an arrow in the eye. The middle view, which I espouse, is that the battle was a more complex and nuanced affair than that and that Harold was killed by Norman knights. But it is only fair to mention a third view, what we might call the standpoint of Humean scepticism or, as they say nowadays in the media, 'nobody knows anything'. A very good example is this statement by the great scholar of eleventh-century England, Professor Frank Barlow: 'There is no acceptable story of how the Normans won the battle. The simple truth may be that they were still losing it, or at least had achieved no decisive advantage, when, to their surprise, the English fled, Harold having fallen, unrecognized by his foes, in some skirmish.'

The initial problem is one of sources. By far the best source for 1066 is the Anglo-Saxon Chronicle, but this tell us very little about the battle of Hastings other than that the Normans were victorious. Space does not permit one to delve into the provenance and authenticity of manuscripts and other materials, but suffice it to say that there is near-unanimous agreement among students of the battle of Hastings that the prime sources are fivefold: the *Gesta Guillelmi Ducis Normannorum et Regis Anglorum* of William of Poitiers; the *Gesta Normannorum Ducum* of William of Jumièges; the *Historia Ecclesiastica* of Ordericus Vitalis; the *Carmen de Hastingae Proelio* of Guy, Bishop of Amiens; and the Bayeux Tapestry. These are the only five artefacts composed by contemporaries of the events described.

William of Poitiers's work is thought to be particularly valuable, for he was chaplain to William the Conqueror. Born about 1028, he did not accompany the Normans on their cross-Channel invasion in 1066 but spoke to those who had fought there when compiling his 'official biography' of William (written between 1074 and 1077), which is ill-concealed hagiography. Jumièges's work, too, which is about Norman history in general and not specifically about William, dates from the 1070s.

The works of William of Poitiers, Jumièges, Ordericus and Guy of Amiens all describe the death of Harold but say nothing whatever about an arrow in the eye, or anywhere else for that matter. Jumièges and Ordericus also introduce a massive complication into the story by saying that Harold died, not as night was falling, as William of Poitiers would have it, but in the morning, during the first Norman assault on the English shield-wall. The first writer to state that Harold was killed by an arrow is Baudri of Bourgueil, author of a work entitled the *Adelae Comitissae*, written between 1099 and 1102, but even he says nothing about an arrow *in the eye*. The first appearance of *that* story is not until 1125 (i.e. sixty years on from the battle), in William of Malmesbury's *De gestis regum Anglorum*, an entertaining but not particularly accurate history of the English kings from Alfred the Great to 1125.

There is general agreement that the Bayeux Tapestry is an important source for the Norman Conquest, though far less unanimity on what that importance consists in. The so-called tapestry is 20 inches high and 230 feet in length and contains seventy-three scenes forming a more or less linear narrative. On a backing of bleached linen embroiderers worked in five colours of wool over a pre-sketched series of tableaux with stem and outline stitches. It is usually considered that the tapestry originally contained a further nine feet of post-Hastings scenes, dealing with William the Conqueror's entry into London and his coronation. The consensus among scholars is that the tapestry was made by English embroiderers at Canterbury to a commission by Odo of Bayeux, William's half-brother, to show him and his friend Eustace of Boulogne in the best possible light. It was probably completed in the late 1070s and may even have been ready for the dedication of Bayeux Cathedral in 1077.

It has often been alleged that the Bayeux Tapestry shows clearly that Harold died with an arrow in his eye. Plates 71 and 72 show two figures, one with an arrow in his eye, another being hacked down by a Norman horseman with a sword. The words 'interfectus est' (was killed) appear over the figure being scythed down. The common-sense interpretation of this would seem to be that the figure with the arrow in his eye is one of Harold's last defenders and that Harold is the man falling under the sword. To get round this objection, those who are determined to adhere to the old story that Harold was killed with an arrow in his eye have advanced a number of ingenious arguments. Some of these revolve around arcane theories to do with the stitching of the tapestry: one plausible version is that there may be vestigial stitch marks by the head of the second figure, suggesting that the tapestry has been tampered with and that these allegedly phantom stitches originally represented the shaft of an arrow in the eye of the second, falling figure also. A popular argument of the arrow-in-the-eye faction is that *both* figures are Harold. To quote a recent apologist for this point of view: 'It is a sort of cartoon strip representation of him being first hit by an arrow and secondly being finished off by a cavalryman.'

The *Carmen de Hastingae Proelio* is at the core of the entire argument about the arrow in the eye, for much depends on the value we place on it as a source. The most convincing view is that it was written by Guy, Bishop of Amiens, and is a product of the years 1070–71, thus making it the earliest of all sources and one drawn on by both William of Poitiers and the Bayeux Tapestry. This is a view that has been argued persuasively by the editors of the most scholarly edition of the poem, Catherine Morton and Hope Munz, by the doyen of scholars of eleventh-century England, Professor Frank Barlow, and the distinguished Cambridge academic Elizabeth van Houts. Those of the anti-*Carmen* school, led by R. H. C. Davis, want to date the poem to about

1100, to claim that the author was not Guy of Amiens, and to make it derivative from William of Poitiers and not vice versa. This might be the place to say that I personally can see no validity in any of their ideas and objections.

The importance of the *Carmen* is that it does not just, like Poitiers, Jumièges and Ordericus, say nothing about an arrow in the eye; it tells us in detail exactly how Harold died. When the Normans finally broke through the Saxon shield-wall at around 4.30 p.m. on that fateful Saturday, 14 October 1066, some of them dispersed to plunder even before the battle was finally won. William, though, saw Harold and a few housecarls still holding out at the top of Battle Hill. While ordering a charge by his knights on the housecarls, he handpicked a 'hit' squad to kill Harold. Although William had previously boasted that he would meet Harold in single combat, he knew from his Brittany campaign in 1064 of Harold's phenomenal physical strength; baulking at the task, he sent four of his most prominent knights instead. These were Walter Giffard, Guy de Montfort, Hugh of Ponthieu and Eustace of Boulogne. They fell on Harold and overpowered him: one struck him in the breast after piercing his shield; another cut off his head; the third ran him through the belly with a lance; and the fourth cut off his leg (which may well be a euphemism for castration).

Given the barbarity of the age, this seems a very plausible ending for Harold. What do the defenders of the arrow-in-the-eye version have to say about the *Carmen* version? Mainly, it seems, they try to discredit the story by discrediting the *Carmen* itself: the principal argument is that the poem cannot be by Guy of Amiens (even though Ordericus Vitalis specifically mentions that a poem sounding very like the *Carmen* was written by Guy of Amiens) since it contains legendary and allegedly *chanson de geste* material that must come from a later era. All of the detailed points adduced can be refuted quite easily, but what concerns us here is what is said specifically about Harold's death. The best thing is to cite a leading arrow-in-the-eye theorist about the *Carmen* version. Here is R. Allen Brown: 'Had William, duke of the Normans with only three companions, attacked the heavily defended headquarters of the English army – which is what the alleged exploit amounts to – to kill the king and thereby take the crown, far from being hushed up as Morton and Munz will have it, the feat of arms would have been bruited abroad in every court and *chanson* in Latin Christendom and beyond. Meanwhile, as it seems to me, the whole improbable incident recorded by the *Carmen* goes far to condemn that source itself.'

Here is an amusingly tendentious defence of traditional orthodoxy.

Note the phrase 'heavily defended headquarters' (the last word in particular insinuating a prepared position instead of the tattered remnants of a shield-wall). As is made very plain in the *Carmen*, in his last moments on earth Harold, far from being 'heavily defended', had with him a handful of housecarls who were sustaining crossbow fire and cavalry attacks at the very time William's quartet beset Harold. William would certainly not have wanted 'bruited abroad' the fact that he had shirked single combat with Harold and that it had taken the Normans four picked men to kill the Saxon king. The final sentence is a classic of *petitio principii*. The incident is only 'improbable' in the light of a hidden premise: that the *Carmen* is a later work, adulterated by mythical accretions from jongleurs and others. The 'improbability' of the incident – itself a proposition based on the unacceptability of the *Carmen* as a major source – is then used circularly to argue for the unacceptability of the *Carmen* as a source.

Since this is not a learned article about the credentials of the *Carmen*, I can only add the 'anecdotal' point that my own researches and those of others continue to underline the high credibility of the *Carmen*. To take just one example, in a ground-breaking 1993 article in *Mariner's Mirror*, designed to show the difficulties in William's cross-Channel operation in 1066 from the viewpoint of the professional mariner, Christine and Gerald Grange comment: 'As we have worked on this study, we have become increasingly convinced of the status of the *Carmen* as source . . . the author of the *Carmen* understood the importance of wind force and direction to people whose main way of travel was by water, and the sailor's obsession with this if he is going out to sea. Above all, the *Carmen* is not only consistent with other contemporary accounts of the crossing, it is also consistent with the weather conditions which may be expected to have prevailed that summer and gives an insight into Duke William's mind at a time of considerable stress. Only the *Carmen* recognizes the danger of a lee shore; only the *Carmen* describes a weather pattern which would be consistent with a period of unfavour-able winds, followed by a weather system which would have brought the required southerly wind; only the *Carmen* records the moonless night of the crossing. Finally, while both William of Poitiers and the *Carmen* give an insight into the Duke's mind during that crucial wait following the disaster of Saint-Valéry, only the *Carmen* recognizes the depth of despair which he must have felt.'

If the best source for the battle of Hastings tells us in detail how Harold was killed, the next best (William of Poitiers) says nothing about an arrow in the eye, and the two other prime sources (Ordericus and

William of Jumièges) say nothing about an arrow, this leaves only the Bayeux Tapestry to be acounted for. As we have seen, some commentators, notably C. H. Gibbs-Smith, have used the Bayeux Tapestry as their principal evidence for arguing that Harold was *not* killed with an arrow in the eye. The entire argument from the visual evidence of the Bayeux Tapestry is inconclusive, but the argument at this level is anyway misconceived, for it assumes that the tapestry is a work of naturalistic representation, whereas it is very clear that many scenes in the 73-plate sequence are iconographic rather than documentary.

The Bayeux Tapestry becomes more mysterious the more one looks at it. To treat it naturalistically is absurd, for at one point the Norman soldiers on their boat seem to be bigger than the boat itself. Among the many unsolved questions arising from the tapestry are: who is the lady Aelfgifu who seems involved with a sexual scandal with a priest; why do Harold and Edward the Confessor appear more kingly than William himself; why are the English in the shield-wall shown with kite-shaped shields when this would have made it impossible for them to swing their two-headed battle-axes? Most importantly there is the problem of the animal motifs. For most of the tapestry there are top and bottom margins which contain illustrations of birds and mammals, both real and mythical, sometimes linked to fables of the Aesop type, but sometimes more enigmatic. It is assumed that these are cryptic comments on the main action, but the exact hermeneutics of these animal figures has proved elusive. What we can say with certainty is that there is a very clear allegorical slant to the tapestry.

If there are no good sources for the arrow-in-the-eye story, how did it get started in the first place? Here I would tentatively like to advance a threefold argument. The first part has to do with Harald Hardrada, who led a Norwegian invasion of England, which was defeated by Harold Godwinson on 25 September 1066 at Stamford Bridge near York. The orthodox view is that we know far less about Stamford Bridge than about Hastings, but, bearing in mind Professor Barlow's comment above, it may be that the reverse is the case. There has long been controversy about the precise historical value of the Icelander Snorre Sturlusson's *Heimskringla* or Sagas of the Norse Kings. It is true that Snorre often makes silly mistakes of detail, but I have found him to be surprisingly accurate. The main outlines of Snorre's account of Harald Hardrada's sojourn in Byzantium from 1034–43 are confirmed in sources on which all Byzantine scholars place a high value, notably the history by Cedrenus and the *Chronographia* of Michael Psellus. Even more impressive is the history of Hardrada as king of Norway from 1045–1066, where Snorre is confirmed in detail by other saga sources. Snorre is particularly good at making sense of confused sequences of events where the other saga writers veer off into fantasy.

It is usually considered that Snorre Sturlusson's account of the battle of Stamford Bridge contains confused material unconsciously imported from accounts of Hastings. I think this is a misreading of the evidence. It is just as likely that William of Malmesbury's account of Hastings contained transmogrified aspects of Stamford Bridge. In this connection Snorre's statement that Harald Hardrada was killed by an arrow in the windpipe comes to the fore. What more natural than that a twelfth-century chronicler like Malmesbury should have heard the story that in 1066 'King Harold' was killed by an arrow and should then have seen the story apparently confirmed in the Bayeux Tapestry?

The second part of the argument concerns the baffling statements by Ordericus and William of Jumièges that Harold was killed early in the battle of Hastings. We know that Harold's brother Leofwine was so killed and, again, it is conceivable that he was struck down with an arrow. In the confusion between Harold and Leofwine the arrow motif may have survived to resurface later in bowdlerized form. We need not take seriously the scene in the Bayeux Tapesty showing Leofwine and Gyrth falling together; this is simply the neat symmetry of two brothers falling together beloved of an allegorist. The *Carmen* makes it clear that Gyrth was slain in a separate encounter, and indeed says it was William who killed him – unlikely from the documentary point of view but understandable 'compensation' from a French author who would show William in a bad light over the death of Harold but did not want to be accused of anti-Norman propaganda in general.

My final argument concerns the Bayeux Tapestry. If we accept that this is iconographic rather than naturalistic, we may even allow that the tapestry shows Harold with an arrow in his eye and still maintain comfortably that this is not how he died. It was a staple of medieval lore that kings were often miraculously blinded by an an arrow for offending against the divine order. In the Old Testament Nebuchadnezzar blinds the Jewish king Zedekiah for breaking his oath. Harold's blinding therefore could either represent in general his punishment for 'perjury' in 1064 – when he supposedly took an oath to back William as next king of England when Edward died – or more narrowly divine vengeance for the alleged role of the Godwin family in blinding Edward's brother Alfred in 1036. Such an interpretation fits the meaning of the tapestry at every point. The similarity of the tapestry images to those in the Roda Bible and other early-eleventh-century sources supports this idea, as does the main motif of the tapestry story: that the English defeat at Hastings was punishment for Harold's perjury. The moral is an 'eye for an eye' in an almost literal sense.

The blinding of Harold as shown in the tapestry – and *if* this is what is shown – would not be intended to denote an actual event but would be meant to inculcate a moral lesson: that God punishes those who do not keep oaths. My contention is that William of Malmesbury heard stories of a King Harold being killed by an arrow in 1066, misread Harold Godwinson for Harald Hardrada, conflated the death of Leofwine (who may also have been killed with an arrow) at Hastings, then saw the story apparently confirmed on the Bayeux Tapestry. Such was the *fons et origo* of the story every schoolboy used to know. In following William of Malmesbury's uncritical lead, later historians have unwittingly embraced the credo of the most unscrupulous kind of journalist: 'Never let the facts interfere with a good story.'

Notes

AHR   *American Historical Review*
ANS   *Anglo-Norman Studies*
ASC   *Anglo-Saxon Chronicle*
BIHR   *Bulletin of the Institute of Historical Research*
B.T.   *Bayeux Tapestry*
CPB   *Corpus Poeticum Boreale*
EHR   *English Historical Review*
PP   *Past & Present*
TRHS   *Transactions of the Royal Historical Society*

1   Edward the Confessor

1 William of Malmesbury, *De gestis regum Anglorum*, ed. W. Stubbs, Rolls Series (1887), i, pp. 185–9, 207–15; D. Hill, ed., *Ethelred the Unready* (Oxford, 1987)

2 Anglo-Saxon Chronicle (hereinafter ASC), 980, 981, 982, 991

3 See the epic poem *Maldon* reproduced in Janet Cooper, ed., *The Battle of Maldon. Fiction and Fact* (1993), and D. Scragg, ed., *The Battle of Maldon* (Oxford, 1991)

4 M. A. S. Blackburn, 'Aethelred's coinage and the payment of tribute,' in Scragg, ed., *The Battle of Maldon*, op. cit., pp. 156–69; M. K. Lawson, 'The collection of Danegeld and Heregeld in the reign of Aethelred II and Cnut', *EHR* 99 (1984), pp. 721–38; Lawson, '"Those stories look true"': levels of taxation in the reigns of Aethelred II and Cnut', *EHR* 104 (1989), pp. 385–406; Lawson, 'Danegeld and Heregeld once more', *EHR* 105 (1990), pp. 951–61

5 Sten Korner, *The Battle of Hastings, England and Europe, 1035–1066* (Lund, 1964), pp. 7–10

6 ASC, 1011, 1016; S. D. Keynes, 'A tale of two kings: Alfred the Great and Aethelred the Unready', *TRHS* 36 (1986), pp. 195–217; Keynes, 'The declining reputation of King Aethelred the Unready', in Hill, ed., *Ethelred*, op. cit., pp. 227–53

7 Cooper, ed, *Battle of Maldon*, op. cit., p. 16; T. M. Andersson, 'The Viking policy of Ethelred the Unready', *Scandinavian Studies* 59 (1987), pp. 285–95

8 P. H. Sawyer, 'Ethelred II, Olaf Tryggvason and the conversion of

Norway', *Scandinavian Studies* 59 (1987), pp. 299–307; J. A. Green, 'The last century of Danegeld', *EHR* 96 (1981), pp. 245–52

9 Frank Barlow, *Edward the Confessor* (1970) pp. 30, 308. Godgifu married twice, the first time with Drogo, Count of the Vexin, who accompanied Duke Robert on his pilgrimage to Jerusalem but did not survive. Her second husband was Eustace of Boulogne, of whom we shall hear much more.

10 ASC, 1016, 'C' 'D' 'E' versions; *Historia Norwegiae* in Gustav Storm, ed., *Monumenta historica Norwegiae* (Christiana, 1880), p. 123; M. K. Lawson, *Cnut. The Danes in England in the Early Eleventh Century* (1993), pp. 16–48

11 M. W. Campbell, 'Queen Emma and Aelfgifu of Northampton: Canute the Great's Women', *Medieval Scandinavia* 4 (1971), pp. 66–79

12 David Douglas, 'Some problems of early Norman chronology', *EHR* 65 (1950), pp. 289–303; Lawson, *Cnut*, op. cit., pp. 109–12; L. M. Larson, 'The political policies of Cnut as king of England', *AHR* 15 (1910), pp. 720–43; Eric Christiansen, 'Canute: model of Christian kingship or brigand Dane made good?', *History Today* 36 (November 1986), pp. 34–9

13 Snorre Sturlusson, *The Olaf Sagas*, trans. Samuel Laing, ed. & notes by John Beveridge (1915), pp. 266–348; Alexander R. Rumble, *The Reign of Cnut. King of England, Denmark and Norway* (1994)

14 *Encomium Emmae Reginae*, ed. and trans. A. Campbell, Camden Series 3, vol. 72 (1949), pp. 32–4

15 Ibid., p. 41; Pauline Stafford, *Unification and Conquest* (1989), pp. 77–9

16 William of Poitiers, *Gesta Guillelmi*, ed. and trans. Raymond Foreville (Paris, 1952), pp. 4–6; Guillaume de Jumièges, *Gesta Normannorum Ducum*, ed. Jean Marx (Paris, 1914), pp. 120–1

17 ASC, 1036, 'C' 'D' versions; C. Plummer & J. Earle, *Two of the Saxon Chronicles Parallel* (1899), pp. 221–2; *Encomium Emmae*, op. cit., pp. 41–7; Florence of Worcester, *Chronicon ex chronicis*, ed. B. Thorpe (1849), i, pp. 191–2; *Vita Eadwardi* or *The Life of Edward the Confessor*, ed. F. Barlow (Oxford, 1992), p. 32; William of Poitiers, *Gesta Guillelmi*, op. cit. (hereinafter Poitiers), pp. 6–12; *The Gesta Normannorum Ducum of William of Jumièges, Orderic Vitalis and Robert of Torigni*, ed. E. M. C. van Houts, 2 vols (Oxford, 1995), ii, p. 106; *The Chronicle of John of Worcester, ii, 450–1066*, ed. R. R. Darlington & P. McGurk (Oxford, 1995), pp. 522–4; Henry of Huntingdon, *Historia Anglorum*, ed. Diana Greenaway (Oxford, 1996), pp. 370–1

18　Jumièges, *Gesta Normannorum Ducum*, ed. Marx, op. cit. (hereinafter Jumièges), pp. 135–6; Poitiers, pp. 10–13; Van Houts, ed. *Gesta Normannorum Ducum*, op. cit. (hereinafter GND), ii, p. 106

19　*Encomium Emmae*, op. cit., pp. 42–3

20　Florence of Worcester, *Chronicon ex chronicis* (hereinafter Florence), i, p. 195

21　S. Keynes, 'The aethelings in Normandy', *ANS* 13 (1991), pp. 173–205 (at p. 195)

22　ASC, 1036, 'C' version; F. Barlow, *Edward the Confessor* (1970), pp. 44–6

23　Snorre Sturlusson, *Heimskringla or Sagas of the Norse Kings*, trans. Samuel Lang, revised and ed. Peter Foote (1961), pp. 141–2; Snorre Sturlusson, *The Olaf Sagas*, op. cit., pp. 364–76

24　*Monumenta Historica Norwegiae*, ed. G. Storm, op. cit., p. 46

25　ASC, 1040, 'C' version; Florence, i, p. 194

26　He was drinking at the wedding feast of Gytha, daughter of Osgod Clapa and Tofig the Proud. ASC, 1042, 'C' 'D' 'E' versions; Florence, i, p. 196. For wedding feasts of this period see Matthew Paris, *Matthaei Parisiensis Chronica Majora*, 7 vols, ed. H. R. Luard, Rolls Series 57 (1883), i, pp. 514–15, and *L'Estoire des Engleis by Geffrei Gaimar*, ed. A. Bell (Oxford, 1960), vv, 4753–6

27　ASC, 1041, 'C' 'D' versions; Florence, i, p. 196; *Encomium Emmae*, op. cit., pp. 52–3; Saxo Grammaticus, *History of the Danes*, ed. Eric Christiansen (1980), Books X–XI, i, p. 210; Adam of Bremen, *History of the Archbishops of Hamburg-Bremen*, trans. Francis J. Tschan (New York, 1959), pp. 124–5; Korner, *Battle of Hastings*, op. cit., pp. 64–7; Pauline Stafford, *Queen Emma and Queen Edith* (1997), pp. 244–7

28　For this party see T. J. Oleson, *The Witenagemot in the Reign of Edward the Confessor* (Oxford, 1955), *passim*

29　E. K. Heningham, 'The life of King Edward who rests at Westminster', *Albion* 7 (1975), pp. 24–40; Barlow, *Edward the Confessor*, op. cit., pp. 54–72

30　Barlow, *Edward the Confessor*, p. 157

31　N. K. Chadwick, *Celt and Saxon: Studies in the Early British Border* (Cambridge, 1963), *passim*; cf. also for pointers W. M. Aird, 'St Cuthbert, the Scots and the Normans', *ANS* 16 (1993), pp. 1–20; N. Higham, *The Kingdom of Northumbria, AD 350–1100* (Stroud, 1993)

32　For full details see F. W. Maitland, *Domesday Book and Beyond* (1960); Eric John, *Land and Tenure in Early England* (1960); J. H. Round, *Feudal England* (1895); P. Clemoes & K. Hughes, eds,

England before the Conquest (Cambridge, 1971); Caroline Hicks, *England in the Eleventh Century* (Stamford, 1992)

33 ASC, 1051, 'D' version; J. Gillingham, 'The most precious jewel in the English Crown. Levels of Danegeld and heregeld in the early eleventh century', *EHR* 104 (1989), pp. 373–84; M. A. S. Blackburn, *Anglo-Saxon Monetary History* (Leicester, 1986)

34 P. Vinogradoff, *English Society in the Eleventh Century* (1908), p. 140; Round, *Feudal England*, op. cit., pp. 25–30

35 Richard P. Abels, *Lordship and Military Obligation in Anglo-Saxon England* (Berkeley, 1988), *passim*

36 H. R. Loyn, 'Gesiths and Thegns in Anglo-Saxon England from the seventh to the tenth century', *EHR* 70 (1955), pp. 529–49

37 Eric John, *Land Tenure in Early England*, op. cit, pp. 57–8

38 J. C. Holt, ed. *Domesday Studies* (Woodbridge, 1987); P. H. Sawyer, ed., *Domesday Book: A Reassessment* (1985); J. McDonald & G. D. Snooks, *Domesday Economy: A New Approach to Anglo-Norman History* (Oxford, 1986)

39 F. M. Stenton, 'The thriving of the Anglo-Saxon *ceorl*' in D. M. Stenton, *Preparatory to Anglo-Saxon England* (Oxford, 1970), pp. 388–9; W. G. Runciman, 'Accelerating Social Mobility: the case of Anglo-Saxon England', PP104 (1985) pp.3–30

40 Pauline Stafford, *Unification and Conquest*, op. cit., p. 210

41 Naomi D. Hurnard, 'Anglo-Norman franchises', *EHR* 64 (1949), pp. 289–327; 433–60

42 M. Biddle, 'Towns', in D. M. Wilson, ed., *The Archaeology of Anglo-Saxon England* (1976), pp. 99–150; J. Tait, *The Medieval English Borough* (Manchester, 1936); P. Nightingale, 'The origin of the Court of Husting and Danish influence in London's development into a capital city', *EHR* 102 (1987), pp. 559–78

43 M. A. S. Blackburn, *Anglo-Saxon Monetary History*, op. cit., pp. 137, 141

44 John S. Moore, 'Quot homines? The population of Domesday England', *ANS* 19 (1996), pp. 307–34; H. C. Darby, *Domesday England* (Cambridge, 1977), p. 89

45 Stafford, *Unification and Conquest*, op. cit., p. 207

46 Robert H. Davies, 'The lands and rights of Harold, son of Godwine, and their distribution by William I: a study in Domesday evidence' (unpublished M. A. dissertation, UC, Cardiff (1967), pp. 3–4

47 Barlow, *Edward the Confessor*, op. cit., pp. 143–8

48 H. H. Lamb, *The Changing Climate* (1966), pp. 208–10; H. Bertil Petersson, *Anglo-Saxon Coinage* (Lund, 1969), pp. 226–32

49 Brian K. Davison, 'The origin of the castle in England: the institute's research project', *Archaeological Journal* 124 (1967), pp. 202–11

50 Barlow, *Edward the Confessor*, pp. 144–5

51 *Encomium Emmae*, op. cit., pp. 82–7; *Vita Eadwardi*, op. cit., pp. 8–10; E. A. Freeman, *The History of the Norman Conquest*, 5 vols (1875), i, pp. 722–5; Frank Stenton, *Anglo-Saxon England* (1970), p. 417; L. M. Larson, *Canute the Great* (1912); M. K. Lawson, *Cnut: The Danes in England in the early Eleventh Century* (1993), p. 91

52 Freeman, *Norman Conquest*, op. cit., ii, pp. 552–55

53 D. J. G. Raraty, 'Earl Godwine of Wessex: Origins of his power and his political loyalties', *History* 74 (1989), pp. 3–19 (at pp. 4–5); S. Keynes, 'Cnut's Earls', in A. Rumble, ed., *The Reign of Cnut, King of England, Denmark and Norway* (1994), pp. 43–88 (at pp. 70–3); R. Fleming, *Kings and Lords in Conquest England* (1991), pp. 92–6

54 *Vita Eadwardi*, op. cit., pp. 5–6; ASC, 1025, 'E' version; Henry of Huntingdon, *Historia Anglorum*, ed. T. Arnold, Rolls Series 74 (1879), p. 187; William of Malmesbury, *De gestis regum Anglorum*, ed. W. Stubbs, Rolls Series 90 (1889), pp. 220–1; Lawson, *Cnut*, op. cit., pp. 96–9; Ann Williams, *The English and the Norman Conquest* (Woodbridge, 1995), p. 11

55 M. W. Campbell, 'The rise of an Anglo-Saxon "kingmaker": Earl Godwin of Wessex', *Canadian Journal of History* 13 (1978), pp. 17–33

56 A. Wilmart, 'La légende de Ste Edith en prose et vers par le moine Goscelin', *Analecta Bollandiana* 56 (1938), pp. 5–307; Pauline Stafford, *Queen Emma and Queen Edith*, op. cit., pp. 257–9

57 *Vita Eadwardi*, pp. 22–5; cf. also K. E. Cutler, 'Edith, queen of England, 1045–1066', *Medieval Studies* 35 (1973), pp. 222–31; Pauline Stafford, *Queens, Concubines and Dowagers: the King's Wife in the Early Middle Ages* (1983), p. 82

58 *Vita Eadwardi*, pp. 59–60; Eric John, 'Edward the Confessor and his celibate life', *Analecta Bollandiana* 97 (1979), pp. 171–8; Stafford, *Unification and Conquest*, op. cit., p. 92

59 Freeman, *Norman Conquest*, ii, pp. 526–31

60 Stafford, *Queen Emma and Queen Edith* (1997), pp. 260–1; Freeman, *Norman Conquest*, ii, pp. 531–5; Susan J. Ridyard, *The Royal Saints of Anglo-Saxon England* (Cambridge, 1988); B. W. Scholz, 'The canonization of Edward the Confessor', *Speculum* 26 (1961); Christine E. Fell, 'Anglo-Saxon saints in old Norse sources and vice versa', in H. Belker-Nielsen, P. Foote & O. Olsen, eds, *Proceedings of the 8th Viking Congress* (Odense, 1981), pp. 95–106. Stafford's warning is well taken: 'It is futile to speculate on the sex lives, sex

drives or sexuality of eleventh-century kings from such sparse and partial evidence' (*Queen Emma and Queen Edith*, p. 261)

61 *Vita Eadwardi*, pp. 17–19; Michael Winterbottom, 'Notes on the life of Edward the Confessor', *Medium Aevum* 56 (1987), pp. 82–4

62 Barlow, *Edward the Confessor*, p. 38

63 Simon Keynes, 'The aethelings in Normandy', *ANS* 13 (1990), pp. 173–205

64 M. W. Campbell, 'Emma, reine d'Angleterre: mère dénaturée ou femme vindictive?', *Annales de Normandie* 23 (1973), pp. 97–114; F. Lishitz, 'The Encomium Emmae Reginae: a political pamphlet of the eleventh century?' *Haskins Society Journal* 1 (1989), pp. 39–50; O. Lindquist, 'Encomium Emmae', *Scandia* 33 (1967), pp. 175–81; E. John, 'The Encomium Emmae Reginae: a riddle and a solution', *Bulletin of the John Rylands Library* 63 (1981), pp. 58–94; M. W. Campbell, 'The Encomium Emmae Reginae: Personal panegyric or political propaganda?' *Annuale Medievale* 19 (1979), pp. 27–45

65 Frank Barlow, 'Two notes: Cnut's second pilgrimage and queen Emma's disgrace in 1043', *EHR* 73 (1958), pp. 651–6

66 Stafford, *Queen Emma and Queen Edith*, pp. 248–51

67 Freeman, *Norman Conquest*, ii, pp. 24–8; cf. also E. K. Heningham, 'The genuineness of the Vita Eadwardi Regis', *Speculum* 21 (1946), pp. 419–56

68 This was one of the reasons Svein was so angry with Edward later when he failed to punish Swein Godwinson adequately. Saxo Grammaticus, ed. Christiansen (1980), i, p. 210; Adam of Bremen, ed. Tschan (1959), pp. 124–5

69 *Codex diplomaticus aevi Saxonici*, ed. J. M. Kemble, 6 vols (1848), IV pp. 74–110

70 ASC, 1046, 1047, 'D' version; Adam of Bremen, p. 123

71 Florence, i, p. 200

72 Barlow, *The Norman Conquest and Beyond* (1955), pp. 72

73 ASC, 1048, all versions; P. Grierson, 'The relations between England and Flanders before the Norman Conquest', *TRHS*, 4th series 23 (1941), pp. 71–112

74 Ordericus Vitalis, *Historia Ecclesiastica*, ed. M. Chibnall, 6 vols (Oxford, 1980); R. Latouche, *Histoire du comté du Maine pendant les Xe et XIe siècles* (Paris, 1810), p. 34

75 Barlow, 'Edward the Confessor's Early Life', *EHR* 80 (1965) (at pp. 237–8)

76 T. Hearne, ed., *Hemingi Chartularium ecclesiae wigorniensis* (1723), i, pp. 275–6

77 T. J. Oleson, *The Witenagemot* (Oxford, 1955), op. cit., p. 117; F. E.

Harmer, *Anglo-Saxon Writs* (1952), p. 563; Barlow, *The English Church 1000–1066* (1963), p. 58

78 ASC, 1046, 'C' version; Florence, i, p. 201; H. L. Maund, *Ireland, Wales and England in the Eleventh Century* (Woodbridge, 1989), pp. 126–30; Lynn H. Nelson, *The Normans in South Wales, 1070–1171* (Austin, 1966), p. 16

79 ASC, 1047, 'E' version; Freeman, *Norman Conquest*, ii, p. 90

80 Florence, i, pp. 201–2; Plummer & Earle, *Two Chronicles Parallel*, op. cit., pp. 229–31; Henry of Huntingdon, *Historia Anglorum*, ed. Diana Greenaway (Oxford, 1996), pp. 374–5

81 ASC, 1049, 'E' version; Florence, i, p. 203; J. E. Lloyd, *A History of Wales* (1939), ii, p. 362

82 ASC, 1049, 'C' D' versions; Florence, i, p. 202

83 John of Worcester, *Chronicle*, ed. R. R. Darlington & P. McGurk (Oxford, 1995), ii, pp. 550–3; Freeman, *Norman Conquest*, ii, pp. 105–6

84 ASC, 1049, 'C' 'D' 'E' versions; Barlow, *Edward the Confessor*, pp. 100–1

85 ASC, 1049, 'C' version; 1050 'E' version

86 Vanessa King, 'Ealdred, Archbishop of York. The Worcester years', *ANS* 18 (1995), pp. 123–37; Janet M. Cooper, *The Last Four Anglo-Saxon Archbishops of York* (York, 1970), pp. 23–9; Barlow, *The English Church*, op. cit., pp. 87–90

2   *Duke William of Normandy*

1 E. M. C. van Houts, 'The origins of Herleva, mother of William the Conqueror', *EHR* 101 (1986), pp. 399–404; H. Prentout, 'De la naissance de Guillaume le Conquérant', in *Études sur quelques points d'histoire de Normandie* (Caen, 1927), pp. 73–89

2 William of Malmesbury, *De gestis regum*, op. cit., ii, p. 285; Benoît, *Chronique des ducs de Normandie*, ed. F. Michel, 3 vols (Paris, 1843), ii, pp. 555–7; H. Prentout, *Guillaume le Conquérant. Légende et histoire* (Caen, 1927), pp. 20–32

3 David C. Douglas, *William the Conqueror* (1964), pp. 379–82

4 Eleanor Searle, 'Possible history', *Speculum* 61 (1986), pp. 783–4; Jumièges, op. cit., pp. 157–71; Searle, *Predatory Kinship and the Creation of Norman Power, 840–1066* (Berkeley, 1988), pp. 154–5

5 Wace, *Le Roman de Rou*, ed. A. J. Holden, 3 vols (Paris, 1973), 11, 3212–14; William of Malmesbury, op. cit., i, pp. 211–12; J. Laporte,

ed., *Inventio et miracula Sancti Vulfranni* (Rouen, 1938), p. 41; C. H. Haskins, *Norman Institutions* (Harvard, 1918), p. 268

6 For Herluin see D. Bates & V. Goseau, 'L'abbaye de Grestain et la famille d'Herluin de Conteville', *Annales de Normandie* 40 (1990), pp. 5–30; D. Bates, 'Notes sur l'aristocratie Normande. Herluin de Conteville et sa famille', *Annales de Normandie* 23 (1973), pp. 21–38. For Herlève's sons see J. Boussard, 'Le comte de Mortain au XIe siècle', *Le Moyen Age* 58 (1952), pp. 253–79; Brian Golding, 'Robert of Mortain', *ANS* 13 (1990), pp. 119–44

7 C. Potts, 'Normandy and Brittany', *ANS* 12 (1989), pp. 135–56; David Bates, *Normandy before 1066* (1982), pp. 70–1

8 Jumièges, op. cit., pp. 97–114; D. C. Douglas, 'The earliest Norman Counts', *EHR* 61 (1946), pp. 129–56; D. Bates, *Normandy before 1066*, op. cit., pp. 68–73; C. H. Haskins, *Norman Institutions*, op. cit., pp. 265–8

9 A. le M de la Borderie & B. Poquet, *Histoire de Bretagne*, 6 vols (Rennes, 1914), iii, p. 9

10 Jonathan Sumption, *Pilgrimage: An Image of Medieval Religion* (New York, 1975), pp. 118–23; L. Musset, 'Recherches sur les pèlerins et les pèlerinages en Normandie jusqu' à la première Croisade', *Annales de Normandie* 12 (1962), pp. 142, 150

11 Wace, *Roman de Rou*, op. cit., vv, 2987–3240; J. Laporte, ed., *Inventio et miracula Sancti Vulfranni*, op. cit., pp. 40–1; Adam of Bremen, *History of the Archbishops of Hamburg-Bremen*, ed. Francis J. Tschan (New York, 1959), p. 92; Rodolfus Haber, *The Five Books of Histories*, ed. J. France (Oxford, 1989), pp. 202–4; *Brevis Relatio de origine Wilhelmi Conquestoris* in J. A. Giles, ed., *Scriptores rerum gestarum Wilhelmi Conquestoris* (1845), pp. 1–2. For contacts between Normandy and Byzantium see E. M. C. van Houts, 'Normandy and Byzantium in the Eleventh Century', *Byzantion* 55 (1985), pp. 544–59; Krijnie Ciggaar, 'Byzantine marginalia to the Norman Conquest', *ANS* 9 (1986), pp. 43–69

12 Gwyn Jones, *A History of the Vikings* (1984), pp. 182–203; P. H. Sawyer, *Kings and Vikings* (1982), pp. 78–97; L. Musset, 'Les deux âges des Vikings', *Medieval Scandinavia* 2 (1969), pp. 187–93; Searle, *Predatory Kinship*, op. cit., pp. 15–40; J. Renaud, *Les Vikings et la Normandie* (Rennes, 1989)

13 D. C. Douglas, 'Rollo of Normandy', *EHR* 57 (1942), pp. 418–32; R. McKittrick, *Frankish Kingdoms under the Carolingians 751–987* (New York 1983), pp. 237, 307–8; P. Lauer, ed., *Recueil des actes de Charles III le Simple, roi de France, 893–923* (Paris, 1940), No. 92

14 For Dudo of St Quentin and his work see L. Shopkow, 'The Carolingian world of Dudo of St Quentin', *JMH* 15 (1989), pp. 19–37; E. Habn Hanawalt, 'Dudo of St Quentin: the heroic past imagined', *Haskins Society Journal* 6 (1994), pp. 111–18; E. Searle, 'Fact and pattern in heroic history: Dudo of St Quentin', *Viator* 15 (1984), pp. 75–86; V. B. Jordan, 'The role of kingship in tenth-century Normandy: Hagiography of Dudo of St Quentin', *Haskins Society Journal* 3 (1991), pp. 53–62

15 D. C. Douglas, 'The earliest Norman Counts', *EHR* 61 (1946), pp. 526–45; E. Searle, Frankish rivalries and Norse warriors', *ANS* 8 (1985), pp. 198–213

16 Searle, *Predatory Kinship*, op. cit., p. 58

17 D. C. Douglas, *Time and the Hour* (1977), pp. 95–119; Searle, *Predatory Kinship*, op. cit., pp. 79–90

18 J. Le Patourel, *The Norman Empire* (Oxford, 1976), pp. 3–27; C. W. Westup, 'Le mariage des trois premiers ducs de Normandie', *Normannia* 6 (1933), pp. 411–26

19 G. A. Loud, 'The Gens Normannorum', *ANS* 4 (1981), pp. 104–116; cf. also F. Lishitz, *The Norman Conquest of Pious Neustria* (1995); Lauren Wood Breese, 'The persistence of the Scandinavian connection in Normandy in the tenth and eleventh centuries', *Viator* 8 (1977), pp. 47–61; Jean Adigard des Gautries, *Les Noms de personnes Scandinaves en Normandie de 911 à 1066* (Lund, 1954); Michel de Bouard, ed., *Documents de l'histoire de la Normandie* (Toulouse, 1972)

20 H. R. Loyn, *Vikings in Britain* (1977), p. 107

21 K. S. B. Keats-Rohan, 'William I and the Breton contingent in the non-Norman conquest', 1060–1087, *ANS* 13 (1990), pp. 157–72 (at p. 161); R. McKitterick, *The Frankish Kingdoms under the Carolingians, 751–987* (1983), pp. 236–7

22 Cassandra Potts, '*Atque unum ex diversis gentium populum effecit*. Historical tradition and the Norman identity', *ANS* 18, pp. 139–52 (at pp. 141–2); M de Bouard, 'La Hagne, camp retranché des Vikings?', *Annales de Normandie* 3 (1953), pp. 3–14; Bouard, 'De la Neustrie Carolingienne à la Normandie féodale: continuité ou discontinuité', *BIHS* 28 (1955), pp. 1–14

23 Flodoard, *Annales*, ed. P. Lauer (Paris, 1906), p. 84; F. Lot, *Fidèles ou Vassaux* (Paris, 1940), pp. 177–92; Searle, *Predatory Kinship*, p. 121; D. C. Douglas, 'The Rise of Normandy', *British Academy Proceedings* 33 (1947), pp. 101–31; cf. also in general J. F. Lemarignier, *Le Gouvernement royal aux premiers temps capétiens (987–1108)* (Paris,

1965); E. M. Hallam, *Capetian France 987–1328* (1980); J. Dunbabin, *France in the Making, 843–1180* (1985)

24 D. C. Douglas, *William the Conqueror*, op. cit., p. 18; L. Musset, *Normandie Romane: la Basse Normandie* (Paris, 1975)

25 J. le Patourel, 'The Norman succession, 996–1135', *EHR* 86 (1971), pp. 225–50; Jean Yver, 'Les premières institutions du duché de Normandie', in *I Normanni e la loro espansione in Europe nell'Alto Medioevo* (Spoleto, 1969), pp. 299–366; F. Lifshitz, 'Dudo's historical narrative and the Norman succession of 996', *JMH* 20 (1994), pp. 101–20; G. Garnet, '"Ducal" succession in early Normandy', in G. Garnett & J. Hudson, eds, *Law and Government in Medieval England and Normandy. Essays in Honour of Sir James Holt* (Cambridge, 1994), pp. 80–110

26 Bates, *Normandy before 1066*, op. cit., pp. 99–100, 156–58; J. Yver, 'Les châteaux-forts en Normandie jusqu'au milieu du XIIe siècle', *Bulletin de la Société des Antiquaires de Normandie* 3 (1955–6), pp. 28–115 (at pp. 36–8)

27 M. Arnoux, 'Classe agricole, pouvoir seigneurial et autorité ducale. L'évolution de la Normandie féodale d'après le témoignage des chroniqueurs Xe–XIIe siècles', *Le Moyen Age*, 5th series 6 (1992), pp. 35–60 (at pp. 45–51)

28 V. H. Galbraith, 'Monastic foundation charters of the eleventh and twelfth centuries', *Cambridge History Journal* 4 (1934), pp. 205–22; cf. also Donald Matthew, *Norman Monasteries and their English Possessions* (Oxford, 1962); David Knowles, *The Monastic Order in England* (Cambridge, 1940)

29 ASC, 1002, 'C' version; William of Malmesbury, *Memorials of St Dunstan*, ed. W. Stubbs, Rolls Series 63 (1874), p. 322; Henri Prentout, 'Le règne de Richard II, duc de Normandie 996–1027. Son importance dans l'histoire', *Mémoires de l'Académie nationale des sciences, arts et belles-lettres de Caen*, NS 5 (1929), pp. 57–104

30 C. Pfister, *Étude sur le règne de Robert le Pieux* (Paris, 1885), pp. 214–15

31 For the guardians in general see Ordericus Vitalis, *Historia Ecclesiastica*, ed. M. Chinall (Oxford, 1980), 6 vols, iii, p. 86; iv, p. 82. For Osbern the Steward see M. Fauroux, *Recueil des actes des ducs de Normandie* (hereinafter RADN), *Mémoires de la Société des Antiquaires de Normandie* 36 (Caen, 1961), Nos. 43, 93, 99; D. C. Douglas, 'The ancestors of William Fitzosbern', *EHR* 59 (1944), pp. 62–79. For Gilbert of Brionne see RADN No. 97; Ordericus Vitalis, *Historia*

Ecclesiastica, op. cit., iii, p. 88. For the obeisance to Henry see Rodulf Glaber, *Francorum Historia* (Paris, 1886), p. 108

32 Searle, *Predatory Kinship*, op. cit., pp. 193–8. For the love of Herlève see William of Malmesbury, *De gestis regum Anglorum*, op. cit., ii, p. 333

33 Ordericus Vitalis, op. cit., iv, p. 80; Georges Lepelley, 'La jeunesse de Guillaume le Conquérant', *Études normandes* 59 (1966), pp. 57–64

34 Poitiers, GG, op. cit., pp. 12–14

35 'The notion that the duke was frequently snatched from his chamber for fear of his kinsmen and taken to cottages of the poor is a flourish of Orderic's to enliven the duke's supposed deathbed speech' (Searle, *Predatory Kinship*, op. cit., p. 196)

36 *Inventio et miracula sancti Vulfranni*, ed. J. Laporte, op. cit., pp. 47–9

37 Ordericus Vitalis, op. cit., ii, p. 240–2. For the Beaumonts see David Crouch, *The Beaumont Twins* (Cambridge, 1936)

38 Fauroux, RADN, op. cit., No. 97; Ordericus Vitalis, iii, p. 88

39 RADN, Nos. 88, 89, 94, 115; Ordericus Vitalis, iii, p. 130; Crouch, *Beaumont Twins*, op. cit., pp. 106–7; *The Complete Peerage of England and Ireland*, revised V. Gibbs et al. (1959), 13 vols, vii, pp. 522–3

40 Jumièges, p. 119; Douglas, *William the Conqueror*, pp. 40–1

41 Ordericus Vitalis, ii, p. 40

42 Michel de Bouard, 'Sur les origines de la Trève de Dieu en Normandie', *Annales de Normandie* (1959), pp. 169–89; de Board, 'Nouvelles remarques sur l'introduction de la Trève de Dieu en Normandie', *Revue historique de droit français et étranger*, 4th series 38 (1960), pp. 481–2; E. J. Cowdrey, 'The Peace and the Truce of God in the eleventh century', *PP* 46 (1970), pp. 42–67; G. Duby, *The Chivalrous Society*, trans C. Postan (1977), pp. 123–33; T. Head and R. Landes, eds, *The Peace of God. Social Violence and Religious Response in France around the year* 1000 (1992)

43 Freeman, *Norman Conquest*, ii, pp. 199–200; F. M. Powicke, *The Loss of Normandy* (Manchester, 1913), pp. 14–15

44 For Gilbert Crispin see Fauroux, RADN, op. cit., Nos. 105, 110, 128, 137, 156, 188–9, 194; J. A. Robinson, *Gilbert Crispin* (Cambridge, 1911); J. Green, 'Lord of the Norman Vexin', in J. Gillingham & J. C. Holt eds., *War and Government in the Middle Ages. Essays in Honour of J. O. Prestwich* (Woodbridge, 1984), pp. 47–61 (at pp. 49–50).

45 Jumièges, pp. 117–18. For Thurston Goz and his son Richard (who restored his father to William's favour) see Fauroux, RADN, Nos. 85, 100, 104, 110, 159, 199

46 William of Malmesbury, *De gestis regum*, op. cit., ii, p. 286; Henry of Huntingdon, *Historia Anglorum*, ed., T. Arnold (1879), pp. 189–90

47 Douglas, *William the Conqueror*, p. 45

48 Bates, *Normandy before 1066*, op. cit., pp. 61–2

49 Poitiers, pp. 14–20; Jumièges, pp. 122–4

50 Wace, *Roman de Rou*, vv 3737–4194. For the likely accuracy of Wace for this campaign see M. Bennett, 'Poetry as history? The *Roman de Rou* as a source for the Norman conquest', *ANS* 5 (1982), pp. 21–39 (at pp. 25–6)

51 For Taison see Bates, *Normandy before 1066*, p. 153; Michel de Boaurd, *Guillaume le Conquérant* (Paris, 1984), p. 122; cf. Wace, *Roman de Rou*, vv, 3737–4194

52 Freeman, *Norman Conquest*, ii, p. 255

53 Poitiers, pp. 18–20; Jumièges, p. 123

54 F. Taylor, trans. & ed., *Master Wace, his Chronicle of the Norman Conquest from the Roman de Rou* (1837), pp. 18–27; William of Malmesbury, *De gestis regum*, ii, p. 286; E. Edwards, ed. *Chronica monasterii de Hilda juxta Wintoniam*, Rolls Series (1866), pp. 283–321 (at p. 286)

55 Ordericus Vitalis, iv, pp. 82–4; Poitiers, p. 20

56 Poitiers, pp. 22–6.

57 J. O. Prestwich, 'The military household of the Norman kings', *EHR* 96 (1981), pp. 1–35

58 Michel Bouard, 'Sur les origines de la Trève de Dieue en Normandie', *Annales de Normandie* (1959), pp. 172–87

59 For the Montgomerys see J. F. A. Mason, 'Roger de Montgomery and his sons, 1067–1102', *TRHS*, 5th series 13 (1963), pp. 11–28; K. Thompson, 'The pre-conquest aristocracy in Normandy: the example of the Montgomerys', *Historical Research* 60 (1987), pp. 251–63

60 For Odo see David Bates, 'The character and career of Odo, bishop of Bayeux, 1049/50–1097', *Speculum* 50 (1975), pp. 1–20. For Robert of Mortain see Brian Golding, 'Robert of Mortain', *ANS* 13 (1990), pp. 119–44; C. Potts, 'The earliest Norman counts revisited: the lords of Mortain', *Haskins Society Journal* 4 (1992), pp. 22–35

61 Jumièges, p. 127

62 Jean Dhont, 'Henri Ier, L'Empire et l'Anjou (1043–1056)', *Revue belge de Philologie et d'Histoire* 25 (1946), pp. 87–109; P. Grierson, 'The relations between England and Flanders before the Norman Conquest', *RHS Transactions*, Series 4, 23 (1941), pp. 71–113 (at pp.

95–8); Leon Vanderhindere, *La Formation territoriale des principautés belges* (Brussels, 1981), i, pp. 108–11

63 ASC, 1049, 'C' 'D' 'E' versions; cf. Plummer & Earle, *Two of the Saxon Chronicles Parallel*, op. cit., ii, pp. 229–31

64 *Pope Urban II* (Oxford 1996), pp 285–89

65 O. Delarc, *Saint Grégoire VII* (Paris, 1889), i, pp. 101–63; A. Fliche, *La Réforme grégorienne* (Paris, 1924), i, pp. 136–40

66 C. J. Héféle, ed. Leclerc, *Histoire des Conciles* (Paris, 1911), iv, pp. 1011–28

67 Delarc, *Saint Grégoire*, op. cit., p. 163; Fliche, *La Réforme grégorienne*, op. cit., i, p. 140

68 Georges Lepelley, 'La jeunesse de Guillaume le Conquérant', *Études Normandes* 59 (1966), pp. 57–64 (at p. 59); Michel de Bouard, *Guillaume le Conquérant*, op. cit., p. 10; Paul Chesnel, *Le Cotentin et l'Avranches sous les ducs de Normandie, 911–1204* (Caen, 1912), p. 169

69 T. Stapleton, 'Observations in disproof of the pretended marriage of William de Warren, Earl of Surrey, with a daughter of Matilda, daughter of Flanders, by William the Conqueror', *Archaeological Journal* 3 (1846), p. 20; W. H. Blaauw, 'Remarks on Matilda, queen of William the Conqueror and her daughter Gundrada', *Archaeologia. Society of Antiquaries of London* 32 (1817), p. 124; Chester Waters, 'The parentage of Countess Gundrada', *The Academy* (1878), p. 597; (1879), p. 457; E. Freeman, 'The parentage of Gundrada, wife of William of Warren', *EHR* (1888), p. 680. The arguments are concisely summed up in Sten Korner, *Battle of Hastings*, op. cit., pp. 168–73

70 Korner, op. cit., pp. 173–81; M. Gibson, *Lanfranc of Bec* (Oxford, 1978), pp. 109–110; Bates, *Normandy before 1066*, op. cit., pp. 200–1; Duby, *The Knight, the Lady and the Priest: the Making of Modern Marriage in Medieval France* (New York, 1983), p. 35

71 William of Malmesbury, *De gestis regum*, ii, p. 327; H. Prentout, 'Le mariage de Guillaume', *Mémoires de l'académie nationale de Caen* NS 6 (1931), pp. 29–56; D. Bates, *William the Conqueror* (1989), p. 100

72 A. Giles, ed. *Beati Lanfranci Archiepiscopi Cantuariensis Opera Omnia* (Oxford, 1844), 2 vols, i, pp. 286–9; A. A. Porée, *Histoire de l'abbaye du Bec*, 2 vols (Evreux, 1901); A. J. MacDonald, *Lanfranc: A Study of his Life, Work and Writing* (Oxford, 1926); R. W. Southern, 'Lanfranc of Bec & Berengar of Tours', in R. W. Hunt, ed., *Studies in Medieval History presented to Frederick Maurice Powicke* (Oxford, 1948), pp. 27–48

73 William of Malmesbury, *De gestis regum*, ii, p. 327; J. P. Migne, ed.

Patrologiae cursus completus: Patrologia latina, op. cit., containing Milo Crispin, *Vita beati Lanfranci*, p. 151; Margaret Gibson, *Lanfranc of Bec* (Oxford, 1978), pp. 30–2

74 Fauroux, RADN, No. 120; Korner, *Battle of Hastings*, op. cit., p. 166
75 Frank Stenton, *William the Conqueror and the Rule of the Normans* (1908), p. 105
76 Jumièges, p. 181; cf. also Maylis Bayle, *La Trinité de Caen* (Paris, 1979); M. de Bouard, *Le Château de Caen* (Caen, 1979)
77 Ordericus Vitalis, iii, pp. 102–10; Douglas, *William the Conqueror*, pp. 394–5; P. E. Schram, *History of the English Coronation* (1937), p. 29; Pauline Stafford, *Queens, Concubines and Dowagers* (1983)

3 *Harald Hardrada*

1 Johannes Bronsted, *The Vikings* (1965), pp. 24–7, 252–3; Gwyn Jones, *A History of the Vikings* (1984), pp. 182–203; Birgit & Peter Sawyer, *Medieval Scandinavia. From Conversion to Reformation, c. 800–1500* (1993), pp. 33–4, 157–65. Else Roesdahl, *Viking Age Denmark* (1982), estimates the population of Denmark under Svein Estrithson as 700,000, while Sawyers (*Medieval Scandinavia*, op. cit., p. 42) provides a low of 500,000 for Norway and two million for the *whole* of Scandinavia. Sawyer, it is true, was well known for 'downsizing' all population figures, sizes of armies, etc., but such absurdly low figures mean that Harald Hardrada could not conceivably have mounted a credible invasion force in 1066.
2 Jones, *A History of the Vikings*, op. cit., pp. 2–3, 99–103, 153–81, 250–64, 301–2; Sawyers, *Medieval Scandinavia*, op. cit., pp. 34–5, 144–65; Birgitta Hardl, 'Trade and money in Scandinavia in the Viking age', *Meddelanden fran Lunds universitets historiska museu* 2 (1978), pp. 157–71; Klaus Ransborg, *The Viking Age in Denmark* (1980), *passim*
3 Jones, *A History of the Vikings*, pp. 90–1; Sawyers, *Medieval Scandinavia*, pp. 129–42
4 Sawyers, *Medieval Scandinavia*, pp. 80–99
5 L. Musset, 'La pénétration chrétienne dans l'Europe du Nord et son influence sur la civilisation Scandinave', in *Settimane di studio del Centro Italiano di Studi sull'alto medioevo* 14 (Spoleto, 1967), pp. 263–325, 527–35; H. G. Leach, *Angevin Britain and Scandinavia* (Harvard, 1921); Oluf Lolsrud, *Noregs Kyrkjesoga* (Oslo, 1958)
6 P. H. Sawyer, 'Ethelred II, Olaf Tryggvason and the conversion of

Norway', *Scandinavian Studies* 59 (1987), pp. 299–307; Birgit Sawyer, Peter Sawyer and Ian Woods, eds, *The Christianisation of Scandinavia* (Alingas, 1987)

7 Snorre Sturlusson, *The Olaf Sagas*, trans. Samuel Laing, ed. John Beveridge (1915), pp. 118–183; G. Turville-Petre, *The Heroic Age of Scandinavia* (1951), pp. 140–6

8 O. A. Johnsen, *Olav Haraldssons ungdom indtil slaget ved Nesjar* (Oslo, 1922); Sigurdur Nordal, *Om Olaf den helliges saga* (Copenhagen, 1914); O. A. Johnsen & J. Helgason, eds., *Den store saga om Olav den bellige* (Oslo, 1941)

9 Snorre Sturlusson, *The Olaf Sagas*, op. cit., pp. 266–348; Jones, *A History of the Vikings*, op. cit., pp. 383–6; L. G. Jerlow, ed. *Ordo Niderosiensis Ecclesiae* (Oslo, 1968), p. 124–8

10 *The Olaf Sagas*, op. cit., 324–8, 348–50

11 Ibid., p. 141. The *Olaf Sagas* show Sigurd Syr notably henpecked and Aasta egregiously shrewish, ibid., pp. 117, 137–9

12 *The Olaf Sagas*, pp. 183–4. Harald's brother Guttorm chose corn and his brother Halfdan cattle. When speaking of his putative warriors Harald added: 'I would like to have as many as would eat up my brother Halfdan's cows at a single meal.' For other such tales of the young Harald see G. Vigfusson, trans. G. W. Dasent, *Icelandic Sagas* (1894). For Ringerike see James Graham-Campbell, *The Viking World* (1970); P. Anker, *The Art of Scandinavia* (1970); D. M. Wilson & O. Kundt-Jensen, *Viking Art* (1966)

13 G. Vigfusson & F. York Powell, *Corpus Poeticum Boreale*, 2 vols (1883), ii, p. 229; C. R. Unger & C. R. Keyser, *The Shorter St Olaf's Saga* (Christiana, 1849), pp. 64–95; *The Olaf Sagas*, p. 350; Paddy Griffith, *The Viking Art of War* (1995), p. 191

14 *Fornmanna Sogur*, Latin version, *Scripta Historica Islandorum*, 12 vols (Copenhagen, 1846), x, p. 399; F. Jonsson, ed., *Fagrskinna* (Copenhagen, 1903), pp. 178–83; *Orkneyingsaga*, eds. G. Vigfusson & G. W. Dasent, Rolls Series 88 (1887), i, p. 47; *The Olaf Sagas*, pp. 364–78

15 *Orkneyingsaga*, ed. Hermann Palsson & Paul Edwards (1978), p. 55; *Orkeyingsaga*, Rolls Series 88, i, pp. 36–7; *Fagrskinna*, op. cit., p. 217; *Flateyjarbok*, eds. G. Vigfusson & C. R. Unger (Christiana, 1869), ii, pp. 408–9

16 For Yaroslav see S. H. Cross & O. P. Sherbowitz-Wetzor, trans. and ed., *The Russian Primary Chronicle* (Cambridge, Mass., 1953); Vladmir Volkoff, *Vladimir the Russian Viking* (1984), pp. 292–303; S. H. Cross, 'Yaroslav the Wise in Norse tradition', *Speculum* 4 (1929), pp. 177–97; F. Braun, 'Die historische Russland im Nordischen

schriftum des X–XIV Jahrunderts', in *Festschrift Eugen Mogk* (Halle, 1924), pp. 150–96; G. Vernadsky, *Kievan Russia* (1973); B. Rybakov, *Kievan Rus* (Moscow, 1989); S. Franklin & J. Shepard, *The emergence of Rus 750–1200* (1996)

17 *The Olaf Sagas*, pp. 392–6; Snorre Sturlusson, *Heimskringla*, trans. Samuel Laing, revised and ed. Foote (1961), p. 161; *Flateyjarbok*, ed. G. Vigfusson & C. R. Unger (Christiana, 1869), ii, p. 290; P. A. Munch, *Samlede Afhandlinger*, ed. G. Storm (Christiana, 1873), i, p. 534; F. Jonsson, *Skjald Edigtning der Norsk-Islandske Skjaledigtning* (Copenhagen, 1915), p. 355

18 J. L. Teall, 'The grain supply of the Byzantine empire', *Dumbarton Oaks Papers* 13 (1959), pp. 105–34; R. S. Lopez, 'The silk industry in the Byzantine empire', *Speculum* 20 (1945), pp. 1–42; D. A. Miller, *Imperial Constantinople* (1969), p. 119

19 J. Eberzolt, 'Mélanges d'histoire et d'archaeologie byzantines', *Revue d'Histoire des Religions* 76 (1917), pp. 1–23; G. Wright, 'The Automata in the Byzantine Throne of Solomon', *Speculum* 29 (1954), pp. 477–87; F. A. Wright, ed., *The Works of Lintprand of Cremona* (1930), containing *Antapodosis*, v, pp. 21, 190, 207–8

20 Michael Psellus, *Fourteen Byzantine Rulers*, trans. & ed. E. R. A. Sewter (1966), pp. 27–49; M. Ostrogorsky, *History of the Byzantine Empire*, ed. & trans. M. Hussey (1968); M. J. Angold, *The Byzantine Empire, 1025–1204. A Political History* (1984); A. P. Kazhdan, ed., *The Oxford History of Byzantium* (1991)

21 Psellus, *Fourteen Byzantine Rulers*, op. cit. (hereinafter Psellus), pp. 53–9; D. Obolensky, *Six Byzantine Portraits* (Oxford, 1988); Ostrogorsky *History of the Byzantine State* (1966) pp. 283–94

22 Psellus, pp. 63–83; G. Cedrenus, *Ioannis Scylitzae Ope*, ed. I. Beker, ii, p. 505

23 Vihelm Thomsen, *The Relations between Ancient Russia and Scandinavia and the Origin of the Russian State* (New York, 1877), pp. 37–86; George Vernadsky, *The Origin of Russia* (1959), pp. 174–209; G. S. Lebedev & V. A. Nazarenko, 'The Connections between Russians and Scandinavians in the 9th–11th centuries', *Norwegian Archaeological Review* 6 (1973), pp. 4–9; Omeljan Pritsak, *The Origin of Rus. Old Scandinavian Sources other than the Sagas* (Cambridge, Mass., 1982); Henry Paskzkiewicz, *The Origin of Russia* (1954); A. Stender-Petersen, *Varangica* (Aarhus, 1953); M. W. Thompson, *Novgorod the Great* (1967); D. Obolensky, 'Byzantium, Kiev and Moscow: a study in ecclesiastical relations', *Dumbarton Oaks Papers* 11 (1957), pp. 21–78; J. Martin, *Medieval Russia, 1980–1584* (Cambridge, 1995)

24 G. Vernadsky, *A History of Russia* (New Haven, 1969), i, pp. 275–6; A. A. Vasilev, *The Russian Attack on Constantinople in 860* (Cambridge, Mass., 1946); John Scylitzes, *Synopsis Historion*, ed., H. Thun (New York, 1973), p. 367

25 M. Canard & H. Berberian, eds, *Aristakes, Histoire* (1973), pp. 23–4; M. F. Brosset, *Histoire de la Georgie* (St Petersburg, 1851), i, pp. 308–9; J. Gay, *L'Italie méridionale et l'empire byzantin* (Paris, 1909), p. 183; F. Chalandon, *Histoire de la domination normande en Italie et Sicilie* (Paris, 1907), i, pp. 54–5

26 R. J. H. Jenkins, *Byzantium. The Imperial Years* (1966), p. 302; B. S. Benezikz, 'The evolution of the Varangian regiment in the Byzantine army', *Byzantinische Zeitschrift* 62 (1969), pp. 20–4; R. M. Dawkins, 'Greeks and Northmen', in *Custom is King: Essays presented to R. R. Marett* (1936), p. 41; T. Kolias, *Byzantische Waffen: ein Beitrag zur byzantischen Waffennhunde von den Anfangen bis zur lateinischen Eroberung* (Vienna, 1988), pp. 162–72; Mark Harrison, *Viking Hersir, 793–1066* (1993)

27 *Flateyjarbok*, op. cit., ii, p. 380; S. Cross, *The Russian Primary Chronicle*, op. cit., p. 93; A. Harvey, *Economic Expansion in the Byzantine Empire, 900–1200* (Cambridge, 1989), p. 264

28 M. Izedin, 'Un prisonnier arabe à Byzance au XIe siècle: Haroun Ibn Yahya', *Revue d'Études islamiques* 15 (1946), pp. 41–62; F. A. Wright, *The Works of Lindprand of Cremona* (1930) including *Antapodosis*, vi, pp. 10, 211; H. W. Haussig, *A History of Byzantine Civilization* (1971), p. 193

29 R. Guillard, 'Études sur l'hippodrome de Byzance', *Byzantinoslavica* 27 (1966), pp. 289–307; A. Vogt, *Le Livre de cérémonies*, 2 vols (Paris, 1955), ii, p. 119; G. Schlumberger, *L'Épopée byzantine* (Paris, 1905), ii, pp. 280–1; D. A. Miller, *Imperial Constantinople* (1969), p. 30

30 Zonaras, *Annales*, ed. M. Pinder & T. Buttner-Wobst (Bonn, 1897), iii, p. 763; R. Guillard, *Études de topographie de Constantinople byzantine* (Berlin, 1869), pp. 14, 41; S. Blondal, *Vaeringjasaga* (Reyjkavik, 1954), p. 360; B. G. Niebuhr, ed., *The Book of Ceremonies* (Bonn, 1829), i, pp. 692–3; F. A. Wright, trans. & ed., *The Works of Lindprand of Cremona* (1930), pp. 12, 42

31 B. Vasilievsky & V. Jernstadt, *Cecaumeni Strategicon et incerti scriptoris de officiis regiis libellis* (St Petersburg, 1896), pp. 246–97; H. R. Ellis Davidson, *The Viking Road to Byzantium* (1976), pp. 205–6

32 S. Blondal, 'Nabites the Varangian', *Classica et Medievalia* 2 (1939), pp. 145–67; *Formanna Sogur*, eds C. F. Rafn & S. Egilsson, 12 vols (Copenhagen, 1837), vi, pp. 147–8; *Morkinskinna*, ed. F. Jonsson

(Copenhagen, 1932), pp. 59–60; F. Jonsson, *Skjaldedigtning* (Copenhagen, 1915), p. 355; Cedrenus, *Scylitzae Ope*, ed. I. Bekker (Bonn, 1839), op. cit. (hereinafter Cedrenus), ii, pp. 511–13; Schlumberger, *Épopée*, op cit., iii, p. 192

33 *Fornmanna Sogur*, op. cit., vi, p. 148

34 Zonaras, *Annales*, op. cit., iii, p. 589; *Morkinskinna*, op. cit., p. 60; Cedrenus, op. cit., ii, pp. 511–12; Schlumberger, *Épopée*, op. cit., iii, pp. 184–200

35 Adam of Bremen, *History of the Archbishops of Hamburg-Bremen* ed. and trans. Francis J. Tschan (New York, 1959), p. 159; *Heimskringla* op. cit., p. 169; Cedrenus, ii, p. 515; Schlumberger, *L'Épopée*, op. cit., iii, pp. 202–4

36 Matthew of Edessa, *Chronique*, trans. E. Dulaurier (Paris, 1858), p. 352; Michael Glycas, *Annales*, ed. I. Bekker (Bonn, 1836), i, p. 586; M. Canard & H. Berberian, *Aristakes, Histoire* (Brussels, 1973), pp. 36–7; H. R. Ellis Davidson, *The Viking Road to Byzantium* (1976), op. cit., pp. 188–9

37 Cedrenus, ii, p. 517; Schlumberger, *Épopée*, iii, p. 227

38 Scylitzes, *Synopsis historicon*, op. cit., p. 425; Zonaras, *Annales*, iii, p. 591; Schlumberger, *Épopée*, iii, p. 235. For the Byzantine navy and amphibious operations see John H. Pryor, *Geography, Technology and War: Studies in the Maritime History of the Mediterranean, 649–1571* (Cambridge, 1988), pp. 104–11; A. Toynbee, *Constantine Porphyrogenitus and his World* (1973), pp. 343–5

39 Psellus, op. cit., p. 193; Scylitzes, op. cit., p. 406; Cedrenus, ii, p. 500; Schlumberger, *Épopée*, iii, p. 88; *Heimskringla*, p. 163. For Maniakes see Lucio Melazzo, 'The Normans through their languages', *ANS* 15 (1992), pp. 243–50

40 *Cecaumeni Strategicon*, eds Vasilievsky & Jernstadt, op. cit., p. 282; *Heimskringla*, pp. 165–8; Ellis Davidson, *The Viking Road to Byzantium*, op. cit., pp. 215–17

41 *Morkinskinna*, p. 76; *Flateyjarbok*, iii, p. 302; H. Cam, 'The legends of the incendiary birds', *EHR* 31 (1916), pp. 98–101

42 *Heimskringla*, pp. 167–8

43 Cedrenus, ii, pp. 522–3, 544–6, 720; Schlumberger, *Épopée*, iii, pp. 243, 247, 250; William of Apulia, *Gesta Roberti Wiscardi*, ed. D. R. Wilmans (Hanover, 1851), p. 250

44 Aimé, *Ystoire de li Normant*, ed. O. Delarc (Rouen, 1892), ii, pp. 23–5; O. Delarc, *Les Normands en Italie* (Paris, 1895), p. 94; Gay, *L'Italie méridionale et l'empire byzantin* (Paris, 1909), op. cit., p. 457; G. H. Pertz, ed., *Annales Barenses* (Hanover, 1844); F. Chalandon, *Histoire de la domination normande en Italie et Sicilie* (Paris, 1907), op.

cit., p. 98; J. France, 'The occasion of the coming of the Normans in southern Italy', *Journal of Medieval History* 17 (1991), pp. 185–205; E. Joranson, 'The inception of the career of the Normans in Italy', *Speculum* 23 (1948), pp. 353–90; R. H. C. Davis, *The Normans and their Myth* (1976), pp. 88–92; Donald Matthew, *The Norman Kingdom of Sicily* (Cambridge, 1992)

45 Psellus, pp. 109–16; S. Blondahl, *The Varangians of Byzantium*, trans., revised, rewritten by Benedikt S. Benedicz (Cambridge, 1978), p. 74; R. Browning, *Byzantium and Bulgaria: A Comparative Study across the Early Medieval Frontier* (Berkeley, 1975)

46 *Cecaumeni Strategicon*, op. cit., pp. 296, 96–7; S. Blondal, *Vaeringja-saga* (Reyjkavik, 1954), pp. 134–5; H. G. Beck, *Vademecum des byzantischen Aristokraten* (Cologne, 1964), pp. 138–41, 164; M. F. Hendy, 'Michael IV and Harald Hardrada', *The Numismatic Chronicle*, series 7, 10 (1970), pp. 187–97; W. Ennshin, 'The Byzantine army', *Cambridge Medieval History* 4, ii, p. 19; Ostrogorsky, *The History of the Byzantine State* (New Brunswick, 1969), pp. 317–18

47 Cedrenus, ii, p. 547; Psellus, pp. 193–4

48 *Flateyjarbok*, iii, pp. 302–3; *Morkinskinna*, pp. 68, 77; Ellis Davidson, *The Viking Road to Byzantium*, p. 222

49 *Morkinskinna*, pp. 12, 79; *Heimskringla*, p. 170

50 *Flateyjarbok*, iii, pp. 304–5; *Morkinskinna*, p. 79; Saxo Grammaticus, *History of the Danes*, ed. & trans. Eric Christiansen (1980), Bk 11, p. 54; William of Malmesbury, *De gestis regum*, ii, p. 318

51 Cedrenus, ii, pp. 536–7; Psellus, pp. 134–6

52 Psellus, pp. 138–41; Schlumberger, *Épopée*, iii, pp. 369–70

53 Cedrenus, ii, p. 539; Glycas, *Annales*, p. 592; George Finlay, *The History of the Byzantine Empire* (1906), p. 389

54 Psellus, pp. 144–51; *Heimskringla*, p. 171; Jonsson, ed., *Skjaldedigtining*, op. cit., p. 368; S. Blondal, 'The last exploit of Harald Sigurdsson in Greek service', *Classica et Medievalia* 2 (1939); Sigfur Blondal, *The Varangians of Byzantium*, trans., revised, rewritten by Benedict S. Benedikz (Cambridge, 1978), p. 95. Some recent writers have doubted whether Harald personally carried out the blinding, but the weight of tradition in the sagas is overwhelming. Scepticism about Harald's cruelty is of a piece with the recent tendency to play down alleged Viking atrocities. See R. Frank, 'Viking atrocity and skaldic verse: the rite of the Blood-Eagle', *EHR* 99 (1984), pp. 332–43

55 Psellus, pp. 155–62; Cedrenus, ii, p. 542; *Flateyjarbok*, iii, p. 418;

CPB, ii, p. 212; Blondal–Benedicz, *Varangians of Byzantium*, op. cit., pp. 183, 229, 231

56 Psellus, pp. 180–97; Cedrenus, ii, pp. 547–9

57 *Heimskringla*, pp. 171–2; R. Guillard, *Études de topographie de Constantinople Byzantine* (Berlin, 1969), ii, p. 121; Blondal–Benedicz, *Varangians of Byzantium*, pp. 99–100; Gustav Storm, 'Harald Haalraade og Vaeringerne in de Graeske Keiseres Tjeneste', *Historisk Tidsskrif* (Christiana), 2nd series (1884)

58 Psellus, pp. 199–203; Cedrenus, ii, pp. 551–3

59 Schlumberger, *Épopée*, iii, pp. 460–76; J. R. Partington, *A History of Greek Fire and Gunpowder* (Cambridge, 1960); J. Haldon & M. Byrne, 'A possible solution to the problem of Greek fire and gunpowder', *Byzantinische Zeitschrift* 70 (1977), pp. 91–9; H. R. Ellis Davidson, 'The secret weapon of Byzantium', *Byzantinische Zeitschrift* 66 (1973), pp. 61–74

60 G. Vernadsky, 'The Byzantine-Russian war of 1043', *Sudost Forschungen* 12 (1953), pp. 47–67; F. Braun, 'Das historische Russland im nordischen Schrifttrum des 10 bis 14 Jahrundert', in *Festschrift Eugen Mogk* (Halle, 1924), p. 150–96

61 *Heimskringla*, pp. 172–3; V. Lazanev, *Old Russian Murals and Mosaics* (1966), p. 47; G. Turville-Petre, *Haraldr the Hard Ruler and his Poets* (1968), p. 19; N. de Baumgarten, 'Généalogies et mariages occidentaux des Rusikides russes', *Orientalia Christiana*, IX, 35 (1927), pp. 1–95

4 *Earl Godwin*

1 Frank Barlow, 'Edward the Confessor's early life, character and attitudes', *EHR* 80 (1965), pp. 225–51 (at p. 237)

2 ASC, 1051, 'E' version; J. Stevenson, ed., *Chronicon Monasterii de Abingdon*, Rolls Series (1858), i, pp. 462–4; Florence, i, p. 204; Barlow, *The English Church*, pp. 85–6; C. Morris, *The Papal Monarchy* (Oxford, 1991), p. 87

3 *Vita Eadwardi*, op. cit., pp. 30–1; N. Brooks, *The Early History of the Church of Canterbury* (Leicester, 1984), p. 304

4 ASC, 1051, 'E' version; Barlow, *The English Church*, pp. 116–17, 154

5 Bertie Wilkinson, 'Freeman and the crisis of 1051', *Bulletin of the John Rylands Library* 22 (1938), pp. 368–87

6 Ann Williams, 'The king's nephew: the family and career of Ralph,

Earl of Hereford', in Christopher Harper-Bill, Christopher J. Holdsworth & Janet L. Nelson, eds, *Studies in Medieval History presented to R. Allen Brown* (Woodbridge, 1989), pp. 227–43

7 C. P. Lewis, 'The French in England before the Norman Conquest', *ANS* 17 (1994), pp. 123–44; J. H. Round, 'The Normans under Edward the Confessor', *Feudal England* (1895), pp. 317–31; Pauline Stafford, *Unification and Conquest*, op. cit., pp. 90–3; R. G. L. Ritchie, *Normans in England before Edward the Confessor* (Exeter, 1948)

8 Margaret Ashdown, *English and Norse Documents relating to the Reign of Ethelred the Unready* (1930), p. 152; C. E. Wright, *The Cultivation of Saga in Anglo-Saxon England* (1939), p. 67; F. Barlow, *The Norman Conquest and Beyond* (1983), pp. 70–1

9 ASC, 1051, 'E' version; Plummer & Earle, *Two of the Saxon Chronicles Parallel* (Oxford, 1899), ii, pp. 235–6; Korner, *Battle of Hastings*, op. cit., pp. 36–42; Barlow, *Edward the Confessor*, pp. 109, 307–8

10 For Eustace see Edmond Rigaux, 'Recherches sur les premiers comtes de Boulogne', *Bulletin de la société académique de l'arrondissement de Boulogne-sur-mer* (1894), pp. 151–77; H. J. Tanner, 'The expansion of the power and the influence of the Counts of Boulogne under Eustace II', *ANS* 14 (1992), pp. 264–8

11 ASC, 1051, 'E' version; Florence, i, p. 204

12 William of Malmesbury, *De gestis regum*, RS90i (1887) p. 24; Freeman, *Norman Conquest*, ii, p. 132

13 *Vita Eadwardi*, pp. 17–20; Florence, i, pp. 205–6

14 ASC, 1051, 'E' version; Plummer & Earle, *Two of the Saxon Chronicles Parallel*, p. 237; William of Malmesbury, *De gestis regum*, p. 242

15 ASC, 1051, 'D' version; Florence, i, p. 206

16 Barlow, *Edward the Confessor*, p. 112

17 *Vita Eadwardi*, pp. 35–7; ASC, 1051, 'D' 'E' versions; Plummer & Earle, *Two of the Chronicles*, op. cit., p. 237

18 Mary Frances Smith, 'Archbishop Stigand and the eye of the needle', *ANS* 16 (1993), pp. 199–219; N. Brooks, *The Early History of the Church of Canterbury* (Leicester, 1984), pp. 388–9; Barlow, *English Church*, op. cit., pp. 77–81, 302–10

19 *Vita Eadwardi*, p. 36

20 ASC, 1051, 'D' 'E' versions; Florence, i, p. 206; *Vita Eadwardi*, p. 37; Freeman, *Norman Conquest*, ii, pp. 150–7

21 For the Godwinsons in Ireland see *The Annals of Ulster to AD 1131*,

eds S. MacAirt & G. MacNiocaill (Dublin, 1983); B. Hudson, 'The family of Harold Godwin and the Irish Sea Province', *Journal of the Royal Society of Antiquaries of Ireland* 109 (1979), pp. 92–100; Patrick F. Wallace, 'The English presence in Viking Dublin', in M. A. S. Blackburn, *Anglo-Saxon Monetary History* (Leicester, 1986), pp. 201–21 (at p. 205); M. Richter, 'The first century of Anglo-Irish relations', *History* 59 (1974), pp. 195–210; D. Bethell, 'English monks and Irish reform in the eleventh and twelfth centuries', *Historical Studies* 8 (1971), pp. 111–35; A. Gwynn, 'Ireland and Rome in the Eleventh Century', *Irish Ecclesiastical Record* 57 (1941), pp. 213–32; D. O. Corrain, *Ireland before the Normans* (Dublin, 1972); C. Haliday, *The Scandinavian Kingdom of Dublin* (Shannon, 1969); Therese Flanagan, *Irish Society, Anglo-Norman Settlers, Angevin Kingship* (Oxford, 1989), pp. 57–8; K. L. Maund, *Ireland, Wales and England in the Eleventh Century* (Woodbridge, 1991), p. 165; T. Jones, trans. & ed., *Brut y Tywysogyon. Red Book of Hergest Version* (Cardiff, 1973); *The Annals of Tigernach* trans. Whitley Stokes (Llanerch, 1993); *The Annals of Inisfallen*, ed. S. MacAirt (Dublin, 1977); *The Annals of Ulster*, ed. S. MacAirt & G. MacNiocaill (Dublin, 1983)

22 ASC, 1051, 'E' version; Florence, i, p. 205; *Chronicon Monasterii de Abingdon*, Rolls Series (1858), i, p. 463

23 ASC, 1051, 'D' 'E' versions; Florence, i, p. 207; Pauline Stafford, *Queen Emma and Queen Edith*, op. cit., p. 11; Kenneth E. Cutler, 'Edith, queen of England 1045–1066', *Medieval Studies* 35 (1973), pp. 222–31; Barlow, *Edward the Confessor*, pp. 105, 116

24 R. Allen Brown, *The Normans and the Norman Conquest* (Woodbridge, 1985), pp. 102–7; Miles Campbell, 'The anti-Norman reactions in England in 1052', *Medieval Studies* 38 (1976), pp. 428–41

25 Stafford, *Queen Emma and Queen Edith*, op. cit., p. 264

26 *Vita Eadwardi*, op.cit.; Barlow, *Edward the Confessor*, pp. 97–9

27 Adam of Bremen, *History of the Archbishops of Hamburg-Bremen*, trans. Francis J. Tschan (New York, 1959), pp. 124–5; Saxo Grammaticus, *Danorum Regum Heroumque Historia* or *The History of the Danes*, Books 10–16, 2 vols, ed. Eric Christiansen (Oxford, 1980), i, p. 210; cf. for background Else Roesdahl, *Viking Age Denmark* (1982); Klaus Randsborg, *The Viking Age in Denmark* (1980); Jean Dhondt, 'Henri Ier, l'empire et l'Anjou', *Revue belge de philologie et d'histoire* 25 (1947), pp. 87–109

28 Heather Tanner, 'The expansion of the power and influence of the

counts of Boulogne under Eustace II', *ANS* 14 (1991), pp. 251–86 (at p. 266); Korner, *Battle of Hastings*, op. cit., pp. 188–9

29 Korner, *Battle of Hastings*, op. cit., pp. 184–8

30 Poitiers, *GC*, p. 64

31 David Douglas, 'Edward the Confessor, Duke William of Normandy and the English succession', *EHR* 68 (1953), pp. 526–45; David Bates, *William the Conqueror* (1989), p. 34. It is worth mentioning, however, that other reputable authorities accept the reality of the visit. See Barlow, *Edward the Confessor*, p. 116; Korner, *Battle of Hastings*, pp. 158 63

32 Barlow, *Edward the Confessor*, pp. 301–6. A close reading of William of Poitiers does indeed suggest that the hostages were sent to Normandy before the return of Godwin and his sons in 1052. See K. E. Cutler, 'The Godwinist hostages: the case for 1051', *Annuale Mediaevale* 12 (1971), pp. 70–7

33 Poitiers, pp. 30–2, 174–6

34 Barlow, *Edward the Confessor*, pp. 107–8, 117

35 *Vita Eadwardi*, pp. 41–5

36 J. E. Lloyd, *A History of Wales* (1939), ii, p. 363–4. Walker, *Harold, the Last Anglo-Saxon King*, op. cit., p. 46, suggests, reasonably enough, that Leofric and Siward were alarmed by the ease with which Edward had exiled Godwin and feared that what he had done to him he might easily do to them in turn.

37 ASC, 1052, 'C' version; Florence, i, pp. 209–10

38 ASC, 1052, 'E' version; *Vita Eadwardi*, pp. 41–3; R. Fleming, *Kings and Lords in Conquest England* (Cambridge, 1991), p. 58

39 ASC, 1052, 'C' 'D' 'E' versions; Florence, i, p. 208; *Vita Eadwardi*, p. 43; Freeman, *Norman Conquest*, ii, p. 316

40 ASC, 1052, 'E' version; *Vita Eadwardi*, pp. 41–3; Stafford, *Unification and Conquest*, op. cit., p. 91; N. Hooper, 'Some observations on the Navy in late Anglo-Saxon England', in C. Harper-Bill, ed., *Studies in Military History for R. Allen Brown* (1989), pp. 203–13

41 ASC, 1052, 'C' 'D' 'E' versions; Florence, i, pp. 208–9; Plummer & Earle, *Two of the Saxon Chronicles Parallel*, ii, pp. 239–41

42 Korner, *Battle of Hastings*, pp. 36–42; Freeman, *Norman Conquest*, ii, pp. 322–3

43 ASC, 1052, 'C' 'D' 'E' versions; Florence, i, p. 210; Mary Frances Smith, 'Archbishop Stigand and the eye of the needle', *ANS* 16 (1993), pp. 199–219

44 *Vita Eadwardi*, pp. 42–5

45 Stafford, *Queen Emma and Queen Edith*, p. 265; William of Malmesbury, *De gestis regum*, p. 239

46 John of Worcester, *Chronicle*, eds R. R. Darlington & P. J. McGurk (Oxford, 1995), p. 576; Stafford, *Unification and Conquest*, p. 87

47 T. J. Oleson, 'Edward the Confessor's promise of the throne to Duke William of Normandy', *EHR* 72 (1957), pp. 221–8

48 Korner, *Battle of Hastings*, p. 193

49 ASC, 1058, 'D' 'E' versions; N. Brooks, *The Early History of the Church of Canterbury* (Leicester, 1984), pp. 304–10; Mary Frances Smith, 'Archbishop Stigand and the eye of the needle', loc. cit., pp. 199–219 (esp. p. 213)

50 ASC, 1053, 'C' 'D' 'E' versions; *Vita Eadwardi*, op. cit.; Florence, i, p. 211

51 R. Twysden, ed., *Historiae Anglicanae scriptores X* (1652), 2 vols, cols 294, 395; H. R. Luard, ed., *Annales Monastici*, Rolls Series (1865), ii, p. 26

5 The Conqueror

1 For the Giroie family see J. M. Maillefer, 'Une famille aristocratique aux confines de la Normandie: les Geré au XIe siècle', in L. Musset, J. M. Bouvris & J. M. Maillefer, eds, *Autour du pouvoir ducal normand, X–XIIe siècles* (Caen, 1985), pp. 175–206

2 J. Boussard, 'L'éviction des tenants de Thibaut de Blois par Geoffrey Martel, comte d'Anjou, en 1044', *Le Moyen Age* 18 (1963), pp. 141–9; O. Guillot, *Le Comte d'Anjou et son entourage au XIe siècle* (Paris, 1972), pp. 57–72; Louis Halphen, *Le Comte d'Anjou* (Paris, 1906), pp. 70–80

3 G. Louise, *La Seigneurie de Bellême, X–XIe siècles*, 2 vols (Flens, 1992); K. Thompson, 'Family and influence to the south of Normandy in the eleventh century: the lordship of Bellême', *Journal of Medieval History* 11 (1985), pp. 215–16; J. Boussard, 'La Seigneurie de Bellême au X et XIe siècles', in *Mélanges Louis Halphen* (Paris, 1951), pp. 43–54; G. H. White, 'The first house of Bellême', *TRHS*, 4th series, 22 (1940), pp. 67–99; Henri R. du Motey, *Le Champion de Normandie. Robert III de Bellême* (Paris, 1923)

4 R. Bouet, 'Les Domfrontais de 1050 à 1150 d'après les historiens normands contemporains', in J. C. Payers, ed., *La Légende arthurienne et la Normandie* (Condé-sur-Noireau, 1983), pp. 73–94; Henri R. du Motey, *Origines de la Normandie et du duché d'Alençon* (Paris, 1920)

5 Bates, *Normandy before 1066*, op. cit., pp. 255–7; Douglas, *William the Conqueror*, op. cit., pp. 58–67; Freeman, *Norman Conquest*, ii, pp. 280–6. Freeman wrongly dates this campaign to 1048–9.

6 Poitiers, op. cit., pp. 42–4; Jumièges, op. cit., p. 126; Searle, *Predatory Kinship*, op. cit., p. 209

7 Ordericus Vitalis, ii, pp. 46–8; iii, pp. 134–8

8 J. Dhondt, 'Les relations entre la France et la Normandie', *Normannia* 12 (1939), pp. 465–86. Cf. E. James, *The Origins of France* (1982)

9 For William of Arques see Fauroux, RADN, op. cit., Nos. 67, 112, 124–6

10 For the Counts of Ponthieu see *Hariulf. Chronicon Centulense ou Chronique de l'Abbaye de Saint-Riquier*, ed. F. Lot (Paris, 1894), pp. 193, 204, 230, 282

11 Freeman, *Norman Conquest*, iii, pp. 127–9

12 Fauroux, RADN No. 114; M. Bur, *La Formation du comte de Champagne 950–1150* (Nancy, 1977), pp. 212–13

13 Ordericus Vitalis, iii, p. 254; Catherine Morton & Hope Muntz, *The Carmen de Hastingae Proelio of Guy, Bishop of Amiens* (Oxford, 1972), pp. xxx–xxxii

14 Ordericus Vitalis, iv, p. 85; Wace, *Roman de Rou*, vv. 4565–618

15 Ordericus Vitalis, iii, pp. 254–60; Poitiers, pp. 52–64; Jumièges, pp. 119–20

16 Jumièges, p. 130; Freeman, *Norman Conquest*, iii, pp. 150–4

17 Wace, *Roman de Rou*, vv. 4929–40

18 Ibid., vv. 4565–902

19 Ibid., vv. 4927–8

20 Freeman, *Norman Conquest*, iii, p. 163

21 Poitiers, pp. 66–78

22 F. Soehnée, *Catalogue des actes d'Henri I, roi de France, 1031–1060* (Paris, 1907), Nos. 106–7

23 M. Bur, *La formation du comté de Champagne, 950–1150* (Nancy, 1977), pp. 138–9. Intermarriage often produced strange and unexpected results. See also J. Richard, *Les Ducs de Bourgogne et la formation du duché du Xie au XIVe siècle* (Paris, 1954)

24 Poitiers, pp. 80–2

25 Wace, *Roman de Rou*, vv. 5223–42

26 Ibid., vv. 5174–99

27 Freeman, *Norman Conquest*, iii, p. 179; Douglas, *William the Conqueror*, p. 74

28 M. Prou, ed., *Recueil des actes de Philippe I, roi de France, 1059–1108*

(Paris, 1908), pp. xv–xxiii, xxvii–xxviii; E. M. Hallam, 'The king and the princes in eleventh-century France', *BIHR* 53 (1980); J. Dunbabin, *France in the making,* 843–1180 (1985)

29 L. Halphen, *Le Comte d'Anjou,* op. cit., p. 12

30 Ordericus Vitalis, ii, pp. 105–6; Jean Dunbabin, 'Geoffrey of Chaumont, Thibaud of Blois and William the Conqueror', *ANS* 16 (1993), pp. 101–16 (at p. 110)

31 Ordericus Vitalis, ii, p. 18; Poitiers, pp. 77–80, 98–100; Bates, *Normandy before 1066,* pp. 78–9

32 R. E. Barton, 'Lordship in Maine: transformation, service and anger', *ANS* 17 (1994), pp. 41–63; R. Latouche, *Histoire du comté du Maine pendant les Xe et XIe siècles* (Paris, 1910); André Bouton, *Le Maine, histoire économique et sociale des origines au XIVe siècle* (Le Mans, 1962)

33 O. Gillot, *Le Comte d'Anjou et son entourage au XIe siècle,* 2 vols (Paris, 1972), i, pp. 457–8

34 For Fitzosbern's career see V. Gibbs, ed., *Complete Peerage,* 13 vols (1959), vi, pp. 447–51; cf. also Christopher Lewis, 'The Norman settlement of Herefordshire under William I', *ANS* 7 (1984), pp. 195–213 (esp. p. 211). For the Tosny family Fitzosbern married into see L. Musset, 'Aux origines d'une classe dirigeante: les Tosny', *Francia* 5 (1977), pp. 45–80

35 Searle, *Predatory Kinship,* op. cit., p. 233. For some of these families see S. Deck, 'Le Comté d'Eu sous ses ducs', *Annales de Normandie* 4 (1954), pp. 99–101; Andrew Wareham, 'The motives and politics of the Bigod family *c.* 1066–1177', *ANS* 17 (1994), pp. 223–42; cf. also Fauroux, *RADN* No. 18; Freeman, *Norman Conquest,* iii, p. 288

36 J. O. Prestwich, 'War and finance in the Anglo-Norman state', *TRHS,* 5th series, 4 (1954), pp. 19–43; L. Musset, 'A-t-il existé en Normandie au XI siècle une aristocratie d'argent', *Annales de Normandie* 9 (1959), pp. 285–99

37 For the castle as one of the keys to William's dominance see Le Patourel, *Norman Empire,* op. cit. pp. 65–7, 303–18, 351–3. Castles, indeed, virtually merit an entire volume to themselves. The Normans may originally have got this key idea from Fulk Nerra, Count of the Angevins. See Bernard Bachrach, 'Enforcement of the Forma Fidelitatis: the techniques used by Fulk Nerra, count of the Angevins, 987–1040', *Speculum* 59 (1984), pp. 796–819; Bachrach, *Fulk Nerra, the neo-Roman consul, 987–1040* (Berkeley, 1993). Some scholars make castles all but definitional of feudalism. See R. Allen Brown, *The Origins of English Feudalism* (1973), pp. 30–1; Roger

Antenas, 'Les Châteaux forts des Xe et XIe siècles: contribution à l'étude des origines de la féodalité', *Revue historique de droit français et étranger*, 4th series, 17 (1938), pp. 54–86. Others emphasize the way the existence of castles made a quick campaign like that of 1066 impossible in Europe and stress the absence of castles in England as a key factor in the Norman conquest. See Ordericus Vitalis, ii, p. 218; Matthew Strickland, *War and Chivalry: The Conduct and Perception of War in England and Normandy, 1066–1217* (Cambridge, 1996), p. 207

38 Georges Duby, *Rural Economy and Country Life in the Medieval West*, trans. Cynthia Portan (Columbia, SC, 1968), p. 185

39 L. Musset, 'Le satiriste Garnier de Rouen et son milieu (début du XIe siècle)', *Revue du Moyen Age Latin* 10 (1954), pp. 237–66 (at p. 254); Searle, *Predatory Kinship*, op. cit., p. 164

40 D. C. Douglas, 'The Norman episcopate before the Norman Conquest', *Cambrige Historical Journal* 13 (1957), pp. 101–15

41 Cassandra W. Potts, 'Les Ducs normands et leur nobles: le patronage monastique avant la conquête de l'Angleterre', *Études Normandes* 35 (1986), pp. 29–37

42 Margaret Gibson, *Lanfranc of Bec* (Oxford, 1978), pp. 98–108

43 Cassandra Potts, '*Atque unum ex diversis gentibus populum effecit*. Historical tradition and Norman identity', *ANS* 18 (1995), pp. 139–52 (at p. 150)

44 C. Harper-Bill, 'The piety of the Anglo-Norman knightly class', *ANS* 2 (1979), pp. 63–79; J. Fournée, *La Spiritualité en Normandie au temps de Guillaume le conquérant* (Rouen, 1987)

45 Emily Z. Tabuteau, *Transfers of Property in Eleventh-century Norman Law* (Chapel Hill, NC, 1988), pp. cit., p. 189; Robert Norbert Sauvage, *L'Abbaye de Saint-Martin de Troarn au diocèse de Bayeux des origines au seizième siècle: histoire et développement économique d'un monastère normand au Moyen Age* (Caen, 1911), pp. 61–2; Donald A. Matthew, *The Norman Conquest* (New York, 1966), p. 51

46 For the entire complex story see vol. 1 of F. Chalandon, *Histoire de la domination normande en Italie et en Sicile*, 2 vols (Paris, 1907)

47 A. Fliche, *La Réforme grégorienne*, 2 vols (Paris, 1924), i, p. 325

48 H. Leclerc, ed., *Hefele, Histoire des conciles*, 11 vols (Paris, 1952), iv, pp. 1139–79; Fliche, *La Réforme grégorienne*, i, pp. 214–316

49 Margaret Gibson, *Lanfranc of Bec*, op. cit., pp. 109–10

50 Jean-François Lemarignier, 'Political and monastic structures in France at the end of the tenth and beginning of the eleventh century'. in F. Cheyette, ed., *Lordship and Community in Medieval France* (New York, 1968), pp. 100–27; Georges Duby, 'Evolution of

juridical institutions: Burgundy in the tenth and eleventh centuries',
trans Cynthia Portan (Berkeley, 1980), pp. 15–58; Thomas
Bisson, 'Feudal Revolution', *PP* 142 (1994), pp. 6–42; Jean-Pierre
Poly & Eric Bournazel, *The Feudal Transformation, 900–1200* (New
York, 1991). The model is of discontinuity between the centralized
Carolingian *pagi* and centrifugal fiefs. But others say the old *pagi*
were not actually very well integrated and were fairly lawless; that
both the 'old' and 'new' systems depended on kinship, patronage,
and clientelism; and therefore that continuity, not disjuncture,
marked the passage from Carolingian society to that of eleventh-
century France. See Dominique Barthélémy, 'La Mutation feodale
a-t-elle eu lieu?', *Annales* ESC 47 (1992), pp. 776–7; cf. also
Barthelemy, *La Société dans la comté de Vendôme de l'an Mil au XIVe
siècle* (Paris, 1993); Dominique Iogua-Prat, *La France de l'an Mil*
(Paris, 1990)
51 D. C. Douglas, *The Norman Achievement* (1969); L. Musset, 'Les
deux âges des Vikings', *Medieval Scandinavia* 2 (1969), pp. 187–92
52 Krijnie Ciggaar, 'Byzantine marginalia to the Norman Conquest',
ANS 9 (1986), pp. 43–69 (at p. 54)
53 Douglas, *William the Conqueror*, pp. 83–104
54 From the vast literature on this subject one might select L. Musset,
'L'Aristocratie normande au XIe siècle', in P. Contamine, ed., *La
Noblesse au Moyen Age* (Paris, 1976), pp. 71–96; P. van Luyn, 'Les
milices dans la France du Xie siècle. Examen des sources narratives',
Moyen Age 77 (1971), pp. 5–51, 193–238; Sally Harvey, 'The knight
and the knight's fee', *PP* 49 (1970), pp. 3–43; R. H. Hilton, *Peasants,
Knights and Heretics: Studies in Medieval English Social History*
(Cambridge, 1976), pp. 133–73; R. Allen Brown, 'The status of the
Norman knight', in J. Gillingham & J. C. Holt, *War and Government
in the Middle Ages: Essays in Honour of J. O. Prestwich* (Woodbridge,
1984); J. Gillingham, 'The introduction of knight service into
England', *ANS* 4 (1981), pp. 53–64
55 The classic work on feudalism is Marc Bloch, *Feudal Society*, trans. L.
A. Manyon, 2 vols (Chicago, 1961). See also Lynn White, *Medieval
Technology and Social Change* (Oxford, 1962)
56 Bates, *Normandy before 1066*, p. 172
57 Emily Z. Tabuteau, 'Definitions of feudal military obligation in
eleventh-century Normandy', in Morris S. Arnold, ed. *On the Laws
and Customs of England: Essays in Honor of Samuel E. Thorne* (Chapel

Hill, NC, 1981), pp. 18–59, and, more generally, Zabuteau, *Transfers of Property*, op. cit.

58 C. H. Haskins, *Norman Institutions* (Harvard, 1918), pp. 5–30; F. M. Powicke, *The Loss of Normandy* (1961), p. 40; Michel de Bouard, *Guillaume le Conquérant* (Paris, 1958), *passim*

59 Marjorie Chibnall, 'Military service in Normandy before 1066', *ANS* 5 (1982), pp. 65–77 (esp. p. 77)

60 Ordericus Vitalis, ii, pp. 234–7. For the Anglo-Saxon forty-day service see Eric John, 'Edward the Confessor and the Norman Succession', *EHR* 94 (1979), pp. 241–67

61 J. F. Verbruggen, *The Art of Warfare in Western Europe during the Middle Ages* (Amsterdam, 1977), pp. 16–17; cf. Verbruggen, 'La tactique militaire des armées des chevaliers', *Revue du Nord* 29 (1947)

62 R. H. C. Davis, 'The warhorses of the Normans', *ANS* 10 (1987), pp. 67–82; cf. Davis, *The Medieval Warhorse. Origin, Development and Redevelopment* (1989)

63 N. P. Brooks, 'Arms, status and warfare in late Anglo-Saxon England', in D. Hill, *Ethelred the Unready* (1978), pp. 81–103; J. Gillingham, 'Thegns and knights in eleventh-century England: who was then the gentleman?' *TRHS*, 6th series, 5 (1995), pp. 129–53; J. Bradbury, *The Medieval Archer* (Woodbridge, 1985), esp. pp. 12–16, 71–75; J. Manley, 'The archer and the army in the late Saxon period', *Anglo-Saxon Studies in Archaeology and History* 4 (1985), pp. 222–35; R. Hardy & M. Strickland, *The Great War Bow* (1997)

64 BT, Plates 47, 57, 68; G. Pierce, 'The knight, his arms and armour in the eleventh and twelfth centuries', in C. Harper-Bill & Ruth Harvey, eds, *The Ideals and Practices of Medieval Knighthood* (1986)

65 F. Buttin, 'La Lance et l'arrêt de cuirasse', *Archaeologia* 99 (1965), pp. 77–178; D. Nicolle, 'The impact of the European couched lance on Muslim military tactics', *Journal of Arms and Armour Society* 10 (1980), pp. 6–40; J. Flori, 'Encore l'usage de la lance', *Cahiers de civilisation médiévale* 31 (1988), pp. 213–40

66 E. R. A. Sewter, ed., *The Alexiad of Anna Comnena* (1969), p. 416; G. Buckler, *Anna Comnena* (Oxford, 1929), p. 378

67 M. J. Strickland, *War and Chivalry* (Cambridge, 1996), op. cit., pp. 144–6; David R. Cook, 'The Norman military revolution in England', *ANS* 1 (1978), p. 94–102 (at p. 98)

68 Jumièges, pp. 145–9 containing *De obitu Willhelmi* by an unknown monk of Caen; Poitiers, pp. 196–9; William of Malmesbury, *De gestis regum*, p. 335; C. Hippeau, *L'Abbaye de Saint-Etienne de Caen*

(Paris, 1855), pp. 169–82; de Bouard, *Guillaume le Conquérant*, op. cit., p. 124; L. J. Engels, 'De obitu Willhelmi ducis Normannorum regisque Anglorum: textes, modèles, valeur, origines', in *Mélanges Christine Mohrmann* (Utrecht, 1973), pp. 209–55

69 Jumièges, p. 145; Freeman, *Norman Conquest*, iii, pp. 79–80
70 Frank Barlow, *William Rufus* (1983); G. Slocombe, *The Sons of the Conqueror* (1960); F. Barlow, *The Feudal Kingdom of England, 1042–1216* (1962)
71 Freeman, *Norman Conquest*, iii, p. 162; Walter Fröhlich, 'St Anselm's special relationship with William the Conqueror', *ANS* 10 (1987), pp. 101–10
72 ASC, 1086, 1087, 'E' version
73 Douglas, *William the Conqueror*, p. 372; Freeman, *Norman Conquest*, iii, pp. 263–6
74 Douglas, *William the Conqueror*, pp. 408–15
75 Ordericus Vitalis, ii, pp. 252, 269, iii, p. 225; Jumièges, pp. 193–4
76 Ordericus Vitalis, ii, p. 259; R. Latouche, *Comte du Maine* (Paris, 1910), p. 34
77 Jumièges, pp. 172–3

6: *Svein Estrithson*

1 Adam of Bremen, *History of the Archbishops of Hamburg-Bremen*, ed. Tschan, op. cit., p. 159; P. A. Munch, *Samlede Afhandlinger*, ed. G. Storm (Christiana, 1873), i, pp. 506–54; Freeman, *Norman Conquest*, ii, pp. 578–82; K. Gjerset, *History of the Norwegian People* (1915), i, p. 678
2 Frank Stenton, *Anglo-Saxon England* (1971), pp. 420–3; Gwyn Jones, *A History of the Vikings* (1984), pp. 398–400; *Heimskringla*, pp. 127–30; Philip Pulsiano, ed., *Medieval Scandinavia: An Encyclopedia* (1993)
3 F. Jonsson, ed., *Agrip af Noregs Konunga Sogum* (Halle, 1929), p. 36; *Monumenta Historica Norwegiae*, containing *Theodric Monachi Historia de Antiquitate Regum Norwagiensium*, ed. G. Storm (Christiana, 1880), pp. 46, 48; *The Roskilde Chronicle. Scriptores Minores Historiae Danicae medii aevi* (Copenhagen, 1918), ed. M. Gertz, i, p. 22; *Orkneyingsaga*, eds Palsson & Edwards (1978), op. cit., p. 61; Korner, *Battle of Hastings*, pp. 142, 147
4 *Heimskringla*, pp. 138–41
5 *Fagrskinna*, p. 202; *Flateyjarbok*, iii, p. 285; ASC, 1045, 'D' version;

Plummer & Earle, *Two of the Saxon Chronicles Parallel*, i, p. 167; *Regsta Norwegiana* (Christiana, 1898), pp. 2–4; Korner, *Battle of Hastings*, p. 147

6 *Fornmanna Sogur*, v, p. 141; *Fagrskinna*, p. 201

7 *Orkneyingsaga*, Rolls Series 88, i, pp. 35–6; *Flateyjarbok*, ii, pp. 408–20

8 *Orkneyingsaga*, eds Palsson & Edwards, pp. 65–8

9 Adam of Bremen, op. cit., p. 108; Saxo Grammaticus, ed. Christiansen, op. cit., p. 47; J. H. Ramsey, *The Foundation of England*, 2 vols (1898), ii, p. 3; F. Stenton, *Anglo-Saxon England* (1971), p. 594; *Heimskringla*, p. 144

10 *Fagrskinna*, pp. 206–8; *Agrip*, op. cit. p. 36; *The Roskilde Chronicle*, op. cit., i, p. 22; *Heimskringla*, p. 145; E. Arup, *Kong Svend* (Copenhagen, 1931)

11 *Corpus Poeticum Boreale*, eds G. Vigfusson & F. York Powell, op. cit., ii, pp. 200–1; *Heimskringla*, pp. 146–8

12 Saxo Grammaticus, op. cit., p. 49; *Corpus Poeticum Boreale* (hereinafter CPB), pp. 201–2; *Heimskringla*, pp. 150–6

13 ASC, 1045, 'D' version; Earle & Plummer, *Two of the Saxon Chronicles Parallel*, i, p. 167; *Regesta Norvegica* (Christiana, 1898), pp. 2–4

14 *Monumenta Historica Norvegiae. Theodrici Monachi Historia de Antiquitate Regum Norvagiensium*, ed. G. Storm (Christiana, 1880), p. 50; F. Jonsson, *Den old norske og oldislandske litteraturs historie*, 2 vols (Copenhagen, 1923), i, pp. 609–13; G. Storm, 'Harald Hardraade og Voeringerne; de graeske Keiseres', *Norsk Historisk Tidsskrift* (1884), p. 354; J. Schreinder, 'Harald Hardrade og oplandene', *Festschrift til Finnur Jonsson* (Copenhagen, 1928), p. 157

15 CPB, ii, p. 217; Peter Foote & D. M. Wilson, *The Viking Achievement* (1980), p. 67; Ruth Mazo Karras, *Slavery and Society in Medieval Scandinavia* (1988)

16 *Heimskringla*, pp. 175–6; *Flateyjarbok*, iii, pp. 251–441

17 *Morkinskinna*, ed. F. Jonsson (Copenhagen, 1932), p. 94; *Monumenta Historica Norvegiae. Theodrici Monachi Historia*, op. cit., p. 54; *Agrip*, p. 39; *Fagrskinna*, p. 234

18 *Heimskringla*, pp. 177–9

19 *Morkinskinna*, ed. C. R. Unger (Christiana, 1867), p. 44; *Flateyjarbok*, iii, pp. 326, 400; *Fornmanna Sogur*, x, pp. 405–8; *Orkneyingsaga*, Rolls Series 88, i, p. 347; Jonsson, *Den old norske*, op. cit., i, p. 615

20 Saxo Grammaticus, p. 58; Peter Foote & D. M. Wilson, *The Viking Achievement* (1980), p. 213

21 *Morkinskinna*, ed. Jonsson, pp. 116–18; Turville-Petre, *Haraldr the Hard Ruler*, op. cit., p. 6

22 *Heimskringla*, pp. 180–1

23 *Agrip*, p. 39; Saxo Grammaticus, p. 52; Adam of Bremen, pp. 108, 123; E. Arup, *Kong Svend* (Copenhagen, 1931); Korner, *Battle of Hastings*, pp. 143, 150–1, 155–7

24 Saxo Grammaticus, pp. 51, 215; *Heimskringla*, pp. 181, 183

25 *Flateyjarbok*, iii, p. 400; *Heimskringla*, p. 182; L. Gjerlow, ed. *Ordo Nidrosiensis Ecclesiae* (Oslo, 1968), pp. 124–8

26 B. Dickins, 'The cult of St Olave in the British Isles', *Sagabook of the Viking Society* 12 (1937–45), pp. 53–80; *Flateyjarbok*, ii, pp. 182, 420–1; *Orkneyingsaga*, ed. Palsson & Edwards, pp. 70–1

27 Gustav Storm, 'Harald Haardraades Paastaades Dobbeltgifte', *Historisk Tidsskrift* 3 (1883), p. 424; E. Eames, 'Mariage et concubinage légal en Norvège à l'époque des Vikings', *Annales de Normandie* 2 (1952), pp. 196–208; Barlow, *Edward the Confessor*, p. 22

28 CPB, ii, pp. 208–9; Turville-Petre, *Haraldr the Hard Ruler*, p. 18

29 ASC, 1048, 'D' version; Florence, i, p. 200; Adam of Bremen, p. 124; Barlow, *Edward the Confessor*, pp. 92–3

30 CPB, ii, p. 218; James Graham-Campbell, *The Viking World* (1980), p. 94; Peter Foote & D. M. Wilson, *The Viking Achievement* (1980), p. 213

31 *Heimskringla*, pp. 185–7

32 Adam of Bremen, pp. 128–9; J. P. Migne, *Patrologia Cursus Completus. Series Latina* (Paris, 1864), 146, p. 1281; P. A. Munch, *Det norske Folks Historie* (Christiana, 1862), ii, p. 208

33 P. Grierson, 'Harald Hardrada and Byzantine coin types in Denmark', *Byzantinische Forshungen* 1 (1966), pp. 124–38; Grierson, 'Byzantine coins as source material', *Acts of the 13th International Congress of Byzantine Studies* (Oxford, 1967), pp. 317–25; Grierson, *Byzantine Coins* (Berkeley, 1982); M. A. S. Blackburn & D. M. Metcalf, eds, *Viking Age Coinage in the Northern Lands* (1981); C. Morrison, 'Le Rôle des Varanges dans la transmission de la monnaie byzantine en Scandinavie', in *Les Pays du nord et Byzance (Scandinavie et Byzance). Actes du colloque nordique et internationale de byzantinologie* (Uppsala, 1981), pp. 134–6; Dimitri Obolensky, *The Byzantine Commonwealth* (1971), p. 235

34 R. M. Dawkins, 'The later history of the Varangian Guard: some notes', *Journal of Roman Studies* 37 (1947), p. 43; A. Vasiliev, 'The opening stages of Anglo-Saxon immigration to Byzantium in the eleventh century', *Seminarium Kondakovianum* 9 (1937), pp. 39–70;

L. Rogers, 'Anglo-Saxons and Icelanders at Byzantium. With special reference to the Icelandic saga of St Edward the Confessor', *Byzantine Papers* (Canberra, 1981), pp. 82–9; J. Shepard, 'The English and Byzantium; a study of their role in the Byzantine army in the late eleventh century', *Traditio* 29 (1973), pp. 53–92; J. Godfrey, 'The defeated Anglo-Saxons take service with the Eastern Emperor', *ANS* 1 (1978), pp. 63–74; J. Shepherd, 'The use of the Franks in eleventh-century Byzantium', *ANS* 15 (1992), pp. 275–305

35 Cedrenus, ii, pp. 547–610; Psellus, pp. 204–60; J. C. Cheynet, *Pouvoir et Contestation à Byzance, 963–1210* (Paris, 1990); A. A. Vasiliev, *Byzance et les Arabes* (Brussels, 1950); S. Vryonis, *The Process of Islamization from the eleventh through the fifteenth century* (Berkeley, 1971)

36 Adam of Bremen, pp. 194, 220; *Heimskringla*, p. 188; Beasley, *The Dawn of Modern Geography*, ii, p. 525; Haldor Hermansson, *The Book of Icelanders* (Ithaca, 1930)

37 Turville-Petre, *Haraldr the Hard Ruler*, pp. 5, 9–11; M. Olsen, ed., *Ragnars saga. Volsung saga ok Ragnars saga Lodrokar* (Copenhagen, 1908), p. 169

38 Henry Howorth, 'Harald Fairhair', *Saga Book of the Viking Society*, 9–10 (1920–29), p. 245; *Heimskringla*, p. 189; Peter Foote & D. M. Wilson, *The Viking Achievement*, op. cit., p. 425

39 Jenny M. Jochem, 'The politics of reproduction: Medieval Norwegian kingship', *AHR* 92 (1987), pp. 327–49

40 *Heimskringla*, pp. 190–1

41 CPB, ii, p. 230

42 *Heimskringla*, p. 192

43 *Fornmanna Sogur*, vi, pp. 283–6; x. p. 406

44 *Heimskringla*, pp. 193–5

45 Ibid., pp. 195–6

46 *Fagrskinna*, p. 197; *Fornmanna Sogur*, v, p. 127; vi, p. 37

47 *Heimskringla*, pp. 198–9

48 *Orkneyingsaga*, eds Palsson & Edwards, op. cit.; Peter Ellis Davidson, *Macbeth* (1980) pp. 53, 58, 68–72; G. Henderson, *Norse Influence on Celtic Scotland* (1910), pp. 18–29; W. F. Skene, *The Highlanders in Scotland* (1890), i, p. 113

49 CPB, ii, pp. 221–2, 228; *Flateyjarbok*, ii, p. 379; *Fornmanna Sogur*, v, p. 135; *Monumenta Historica Norvegiae*, op. cit., pp. 133–4; J. O'Donovan, ed., *Annals of the Kingdom of Ireland by the Four Masters* (Dublin, 1854), ii, pp. 851, 861

50 Earle & Plummer, *Two of the Saxon Chronicles Parallel*, i, p. 188;

Florence, i, p. 217; 'Annals of Tigernach', *Revue Celtique* 17 (1896), pp. 354–406 (esp. p. 398); *Annales Cambriae*, ed. J. W. ab Ithel, Rolls Series 20 (1860), p. 25; B. G. Charles, *Old Norse Relations with Wales* (Cardiff, 1934), p. 48; Korner, *Battle of Hastings*, pp. 151–4; Stenton, *Anglo-Saxon England*, p. 575; Larson, *Cnut*, p. 212; E. Bromberg, 'Wales and the medieval slave trade', *Speculum* 17 (1942), pp. 263–9

51 CPB, i, p. 365; ii, pp. 209–10; Saxo Grammaticus, p. 52; *Heimskringla*, pp. 202–3
52 CPB, ii, pp. 208–9, 595; Saxo Grammaticus, pp. 54–5; *Heimskringla*, p. 203
53 *Heimskringla*, pp. 196–7
54 E. A. Kock, ed. *Den Norsk-Islanska Skaldediktningen* (Lund, 1949), i, pp. 172–4, 187–8
55 CPB, ii, p. 206
56 *Heimskringla*, pp. 206–8; Saxo Grammaticus, p. 56; CPB, ii, pp. 223–4
57 Saxo Grammaticus, p. 57; *Fagrskinna*, p. 273; *Fornmanna Sogur*, x, p. 407
58 *Orkneyingsaga*, eds Palsson & Edwards, p. 75; *Fagrskinna*, p. 278
59 CPB, ii, pp. 210–11; *Fagrskinna*, p. 278; *Heimskringla*, pp. 213–15
60 Saxo Grammaticus, op. cit. p. 58; Adam of Bremen, op. cit. pp. 124–25
61 *Heimskringla*, pp. 241–2; *Fagrskinna*, p. 295

7:   *Harold Godwinson*

1 Fleming, *Kings and Lords*, op. cit., p. 101
2 Peter Sawyer, ed., *Anglo-Saxon Charters: An Annotated List and Bibliography* (1968), No. 1008; Peter A. Clarke, *The English Nobility under Edward the Confessor* (Oxford, 1994), pp. 13–14; J. P. Migne, *Patrologia* (Paris, 1864), op. cit., vol. 155
3 Clarke, *English Nobility*, op. cit., pp. 24–5
4 Ann Williams, 'Land and power in the eleventh century: the estates of Harold Godwineson', *ANS* 3 (1980), pp. 171–87; R. Fleming, 'Domesday estates of the king and the Godwinesons: a study in late Saxon politics', *Speculum* 58 (1983), pp. 987–1007
5 Clarke, *English Nobility*, op. cit., p. 149; Fleming, *Kings and Lords*, pp. 63–71; D. Hill, *An Atlas of Anglo-Saxon England* (Oxford, 1981), p. 103
6 Fleming, *Kings and Lords*, pp. 48, 65–74, 91–103
7 Freeman, *Norman Conquest*, ii, pp. 32–3; Fleming, *Kings and Lords*,

pp. 82–3; David Bates, 'The land pleas of William I's reign: Penenden Heath revisited', *BIHR* 51 (1978), pp. 14–16

8 For Harold's rapacity and seizures see ASC, 1052, 'C' version; Earle & Plummer, *Two of the Saxon Chronicles*, op. cit., ii, p. 241; H. Ellis, *A General Introduction to Domesday Book* (1833), 2 vols, i, p. 313. For the quarrel with Giso see J. Hunter, ed., *The Autobiography of Giso of Wells*, Camden OS 8 (1840), pp. 15–20; Freeman, *Norman Conquest*, ii, pp. 542–52; J. R. Green, 'Earl Harold and Bishop Giso', *Somerset Archaeological and Natural History Society Proceedings*, 12 (1864), pp. 148–57. For Giso see Simon Keynes, 'Giso, bishop of Wells, 1061–1088', *ANS* 19 (1996), pp. 203–71

9 Fleming, *Lords and Kings*, p. 102

10 W. de Gray Birch, ed., *Vita Haroldi* (1885), pp. 122–7; M. Swanton, *Three Lives of the Last Englishmen* (1984), pp. 7–10; Joseph Stevenson, ed., *Liber Vitae Ecclesiae Dunelmensis* (1841), p. 146; W. Stubbs, ed. *De Inventione Sanctae Crucis nostrae . . . . apud Waltham* (Oxford, 1861), pp. 40–9; D. Giles, ed., *Original Lives of the Anglo-Saxons and Others*, Caxton Society 16 (1854), pp. 50–1; W. Winters, *The History of the Ancient Parish of Waltham Abbey, Essex* (1888), p. 138; Ann Williams, 'Land and Power in the eleventh century: the estates of Harold Godwineson', *ANS* 3 (1980), pp. 171–87 (at p. 182)

11 R. R. Darlington, ed., *The Vita Wulfstani of William of Malmesbury*, Camden Society 3rd series 40 (1928), pp. 13, 18; M. Rule, ed., *Eadmer, Historia Novorum in Anglia* (1884), p. 5; David Douglas, 'Odo, Lanfranc and the Domesday Survey', in J. G. Edwards, V. H. Galbraith & E. F. Jacob, eds., *Essays in Honour of James Tait* (Manchester, 1993), pp. 47–57

12 BT, Plate 20; Ian W. Walker, *Harold. The Last Anglo-Saxon King* (1997), pp. 121–7. On the other hand, there are repeated suggestions in the sources that Harold suffered from periodic bad health, including an incident of temporary paralysis. M. Swanton, *Three Lives of the Last Englishmen* (1984), pp. 5–7

13 For favourable opinions of Harold see R. R. Darlington, ed., *Vita Wulfstani*, op. cit., p. 13; E. Mason, *St Wulfstan of Worcester c. 1008–1095* (Oxford, 1990), pp. 65–7, 219–21; David Rollason, *Saints and Relics in Anglo-Saxon England* (Oxford, 1989), pp. 217–20. For hostile views see W. Stubbs, ed., *Memorials of St Dunstan, Archbishop of Canterbury*, Rolls Series (1874), i, p. 57; Henry of Huntingdon, *Historia Anglorum*, ed. Diana Greenaway (Oxford, 1996), pp. 378–9; M. Rule, ed., *Eadmer. Historia Novorum in Anglia* (1884), pp. 8–9

14 William of Malmesbury, *De gestis regum*, i, p. 380; William of

Malmesbury, *De gestis pontificum Anglorum*, ed. N. E. S. A. Hamilton, Rolls Series (1870), p. 207; Freeman, *Norman Conquest*, ii, p. 38; Martin Brett, 'John of Worcester and his contemporaries', in R. H. C. Davies & J. M. Wallace-Hadrill, eds, *The Writing of History in the Middle Ages* (Oxford, 1981), pp. 101–26 (at p. 123)

14 *Vita Eadwardi*, pp. 48–9
15 Ibid., pp. 50–6
16 Saxo Grammaticus, ed. Christiansen, pp. 228–9; Freeman, *Norman Conquest*, ii, pp. 652–6, iii, pp. 790–3; Ross M. Clunies, 'Concubinage in Anglo-Saxon England', *PP* 108 (1985), pp. 3–34; Walker, *Harold, The Last Anglo-Saxon King*, op. cit., pp. 127–30; C. Fell, *Women in Anglo-Saxon England and the Impact of 1066* (1984), pp. 13–40; M. Meyer, 'Women's estates in later Anglo-Saxon England: the politics of possession', *Haskins Society Journal* 3 (1992), pp. 111–29. Curiously, we know more about Harold's daughters than his sons. Gytha married Prince Vladimir of Smolensk and Kiev, after fleeing from England in 1068 via Flanders and Denmark, while Gunnhild is said to have become a nun (Eleanor Searle, 'Women and the legitimization of the succession at the Norman Conquest', *ANS* 3 (1981), pp. 166–9). There is a particularly good summary of the later lives of Harold's children in Walker, *Harold*, op. cit., pp. 187–98
17 ASC, 1039, 'C' version; Florence, i, p. 193; T. Hearne, ed., *Hemingi Chartularium ecclesiae Wigorniensis* (1723), i, p. 278
18 Thomas Wright, ed., *Walter Mapes, de Nugis Curialium*, Camden Society (1850), pp. 99–104
19 ASC, 1053, 'D' version; J. E. Lloyd, *History of Wales* (1939), ii, p. 357; J. E. Lloyd, 'Wales and the coming of the Normans, 1039–93', *Transactions of Cymmrodorion 1899–1900* (1901), pp. 122–79
20 J. Leclerc & J. P. Bonnes, *Un Maître de la vie spirituelle au XIe siècle: Jean de Fécamp* (Paris, 1946), pp. 14, 17; J. Mabillon, *Annales Ordinis Sancti Benedicti Occidentalium Monachorum Patriarchae* (Paris, 1739), iv, p. 547; Donald Matthew, *The Norman Monasteries and their English Possessions* (1962), pp. 19–21
21 ASC, 1054, 'C' 'D' versions; Joseph Stevenson, ed., *Chronicle of Melrose* (Edinburgh, 1835), pp. 50–1; W. M. Hennessy & B. MacCarthy, eds, *Annals of Ulster*, 3 vols (Dublin, 1895), i, p. 594; Kapelle, *The Norman Conquest of the North* (1979), pp. 46–7. For Macbeth see Peter Beresford Ellis, *Macbeth* (1980); R. J. Steward, *Macbeth. Scotland's Warrior King* (1988)

22 A. O. Anderson, ed., *Scottish Annals from English Chroniclers* (1908), pp. 85–6; W. Stokes, ed., 'Annals of Tigernach', *Revue Celtique* 17 (1896), pp. 395–8; Florence, i, p. 212; William F. Skene, ed., *Johannes Defordun, Chronica Gestis Scotorum* (1871), i, pp. 188–205

23 ASC, 1055, 'C' 'D' versions; *Lives of Edward the Confessor*, Rolls Society 3, p. 408; F. Michel, *Chroniques Anglo-Normandes* (Rouen, 1840), ii, pp. 110–11; K. L. Maund, 'The Welsh Alliances of Earl Aelfgar of Mercia and his family in the mid-eleventh century', *ANS* 11 (1989), pp. 181–90; D. Walker, *Medieval Wales* (Cambridge, 1990), p. 17

24 ASC, 1055, 'C' 'D' 'E' versions; Florence, i, pp. 212–14; J. Williams ab Ithel, *Annales Cambriae*, Rolls Series (1860), pp. Walker, *Harold*, op. cit., pp. 79–80

25 ASC, 1055, 'C' version; Florence, i, pp. 213–14; Richard P. Abels, *Lordship and Military Obligation in Anglo-Saxon England* (1988), p. 174; Freeman, *Norman Conquest*, ii, p. 399

26 P. Grierson, 'A visit of Earl Harold to Flanders in 1056', *EHR* 51 (1936), pp. 90–7; Barlow, *The Feudal Kingdom of England, 1042–1216* (1955), p. 69; M. de Bouard, *Guillaume le Conquérant* (Paris, 1958), p. 72; T. Reuter, *Germany in the Early Middle Ages, 800–1056* (Harlow, 1991), p. 255; *Vita Eadwardi*, p. 52

27 ASC, 1056, 'C' 'D' versions; Florence, i, pp. 214–15; Lloyd, *History of Wales*, op. cit., p. 135; Lloyd, 'Wales and the coming of the Normans', loc. cit., p. 135

28 Ordericus Vitalis, ii, pp. 138, 216; Freeman, *Norman Conquest*, ii, pp. 398–400; T. Wright, ed., *Walter Map. De Nugis Curialium*, Camden Society 50 (1980), p. 99

29 Florence, i, p. 181; D. M. Dumville, 'The atheling: a study in Anglo-Saxon constitutional history', *Anglo-Saxon England* 8 (1979), pp. 1–33; N. Hooper, 'Edgar the atheling: Anglo-Saxon prince, rebel and crusader', *Anglo-Saxon England* 14 (1985), pp. 197–214; Simon Keynes, 'The Crowland Psalter and the sons of King Edmund Ironside', *Bodleian Library Record* 11 (1985), pp. 359–70; Sandor Fest, 'The sons of Eadmund Ironside, Anglo-Saxon king, at the court of St Stephen', *Archivum Europae Centro-Orientalis* (Budapest), 4 (1938), pp. 115–46; Z. J. Koztolnyik, *Five Eleventh-Century Hungarian Kings* (New York, 1981), p. 75; R. L. Graeme Ritchie, *The Normans in Scotland* (1954), pp. 389–92

30 *Chronicle of John of Worcester*, eds Darlington & McGurk, op. cit., ii, pp. 574–5; *Vita Wulfstani of William of Malmesbury*, ed. R. R.

Darlington, op. cit., pp. 15–16; Korner, *Battle of Hastings*, pp. 196–205; Vanessa King, 'Ealdred, Archbishop of York. The Worcester Years', *ANS* 18 (1995), pp. 123–37

31 Korner, *Battle of Hastings*, pp. 204–6

32 Florence, i, p. 215; Eric John, 'Edward the Confessor and the Norman Succession', *EHR* 94 (1979), pp. 241–67 (at p. 257); Pauline Stafford, *Queen Emma and Queen Edith*, op. cit., p. 269

33 ASC, 1057, 'D' 'E' versions; Florence, i, p. 215; Alfred of Rievaulx, *De genealogia regum Anglorum* in J. P. Migne, ed., *Patrologiae cursus completus; patrologia latina*, op. cit., 145, colls 715, 734; William F. Skene, ed., *Johannes de Fordun. Chronica gentis Scotorum*, i, pp. 206–8; R. L. G. Ritchie, *The Normans in Scotland*, op. cit., p. 8; Freeman, *Norman Conquest*, ii, pp. 410–13

34 ASC, 1055, 'E' version; ASC, 1058, 'D' version; William of Malmesbury, *De gestis regum*, op. cit., i, p. 245; Henry of Huntingdon, *Historia Anglorum*, Rolls Series 74 (1879), p. 196; K. L. Maund, 'The Welsh alliances of Earl Aelfgar of Mercia and his family in the mid-eleventh century', *ANS* 11 (1988), pp. 181–90

35 Freeman, *Norman Conquest*, ii, pp. 417–27. Walker, *Harold*, op. cit., pp. 114–19, sees Harold making the decision for kingship only at the moment of Edward the Confessor's death

36 H. Bohmer, *Kirche und Staat im XI und XII Jahrundert* (Leipzig, 1899), p. 79; Korner, *Battle of Hastings*, pp. 211–12

37 ASC 'D' version; Plummer & Earle, *Two of the Saxon Chronicles Parallel*, op. cit., ii, pp. 249–50; *Vita Wulfstani*, ed. R. R. Darlington, op. cit., pp. 16–17; Florence, i, p. 218; William of Malmesbury, *De gestis pontificum Anglorum*, ed. Hamilton (1870), op. cit., pp. 251–2

38 *Vita Eadwardi*, pp. 54–5; D. C. Douglas & G. W. Greenaway, *English Historical Documents* (Oxford, 1981), ii, pp. 599–60; Korner, *Battle of Hastings*, p. 217

39 *Vita Eadwardi*, pp. 54–5; *Vita Wulfstani*, pp. 16–17; Franz Herberhold, 'Die Angriffe des Cadalus von Parma auf Rom in den jahren 1062 und 1063', *Studi Gregoriani* 2 (1947), pp. 477–503; F. Gregorius, *History of the City of Rome*, trans. A. Hamilton, iv, Pt. 1 (1896), pp. 111–15

40 Emma Mason, *St Wulfstan of Worcester c. 1008–1095* (Oxford, 1990), pp. 72–87; Freeman, *Norman Conquest*, ii, pp. 452–9

41 K. L. Maund, 'The Welsh alliances of Earl Aelfgar of Mercia and his family in the mid-eleventh century', *ANS* 11 (1989), pp. 181–90 (at p. 188)

42 ASC, 1063, 'D' 'E' version; Florence, i, pp. 221–2; Plummer & Earle, *Two of the Saxon Chronicles Parallel*, op. cit., ii, pp. 250–1

43 Giraldus Cambrenis, *Descriptio Kambriae* in J. F. Dimock, ed., *Opera Omnia*, Rolls Series (1868), vi, p. 217; Clement C. J. Webb, ed., *Johannis Saresberiensis Episcopi Carnotensis Policraticus*, Bk 6, ch 6, ii, pp. 19–20; M. Chibnall, ed., *The Historia Pontificalis of John of Salisbury* (1956); Freeman, *Norman Conquest*, ii, pp. 466–76

44 John Williams ab Ithel, ed., *Brut y Tywysogion*, Rolls Series (1860), p. 45; *Vita Eadwardi*, pp. 64–5; *The Annals of Ulster*, eds S. MacAirt & G. MacNiocaill (Dublin, 1983); K. L. Maund, 'Cynan ap Iago and the killing of Gruffydd ap Llewelyn', *Cambridge Medieval Celtic studies* 10 (1985), p. 65; J. E. Lloyd, 'Wales and the coming of the Normans, 1039–93', *Transactions of Cymmrodorion* (1899–1900), pp. 122–47; J. E. Lloyd, *A History of Wales* (1939), ii, pp. 358–371

45 *Vita Haroldi*, op. cit., p. 117; Ordericus Vitalis, ii, pp. 138, 216; R. R. Davies, *Conquest, Coexistence and Change: Wales 1063–1415* (Oxford, 1987), pp. 24–5; Davies, *The Age of Conquest: Wales 1063–1415* (Oxford, 1991), p. 26; C. N. L. Brooke, *The Church and the Welsh Border in the Central Middle Ages* (Woodbridge, 1986), pp. 11, 93; D. Walker, *Medieval Wales* (Cambridge, 1990), pp. 18–19

46 J. Campbell, 'Observations on English government from the tenth to the twelfth century', *TRHS*, 5th series 25 (1975), pp. 39–54. Cf. also Campbell, 'Some agents and agencies of the late Anglo-Saxon State', in J. C. Holt, ed., *Domesday Studies* (Woodbridge, 1986), pp. 201–18, and Campbell, 'Was it infancy in England? Some questions of comparison', in M. Jones & M. Vale, eds, *England and her Neighbours, 1066–1453* (1989), pp. 1–17

47 C. Warren Hollister, *Anglo-Saxon Institutions on the Eve of the Norman Conquest* (1962); Michael Powicke, *Military Obligations in Medieval England* (1962)

48 N. Brooks, 'Arms, status and warfare in late Saxon England', in D. Hill, ed., *Ethelred the Unready* (Oxford, 1978), pp. 81–103

49 J. C. Russell, *British Medieval Population* (Albuquerque, 1948), p. 54; John S. Moore, 'Quot homines? The population of Domesday England', *ANS* 19 (1996), pp. 307–34

50 P. Vinogradoff, *English Society in the Eleventh Century* (1908), pp. 19–22; Hollister, *Anglo-Saxon Institutions*, op. cit., p. 12; Lawson, *Cnut*, op. cit., p. 183

51 N. Hooper, 'The housecarls in England in the eleventh century', *ANS* 7 (1984), pp. 161–76 (esp. p. 174); Florence, i, pp. 195–6;

Richard Abels, *Lordship and Military Obligation in Anglo-Saxon England* (1988), pp. 167–8

52 John Langdon, *Horses, Oxen and Technological Innovation* (Cambridge, 1986), p. 18; R. H. C. Davis, 'Did the Anglo-Saxons have warhorses?' in S. C. Hawkes, *Weapons and Warfare in Anglo-Saxon England* (Oxford, 1989), pp. 141–4; Matthew Bennett, 'The myth of the military supremacy of knightly cavalry', in M. J. Strickland, ed., *Armies, Chivalry and Warfare* (Stamford, 1997); A. Hyland, *The Medieval Warhorse from Byzantium to the Crusades* (Stroud, 1994)

53 N. Hooper, 'Anglo-Saxon warfare on the eve of the Conquest; a brief survey', *ANS* 1 (1978), pp. 84–93; Eric John, 'War and society in the tenth century; the Maldon campaign', *TRHS*, 5th series, 27 (1977), pp. 173–95

54 ASC, 1008; Nicholas Brooks, 'Weapons and armour', in Donald Scragg, ed., *The Battle of Maldon* (Oxford, 1991), pp. 208–17

55 Scragg, *Battle of Maldon*, op. cit., pp. 143–55; R. Glover, 'English warfare in 1066', *EHR* 67 (1952), pp. 1–18

56 S. Pollington, *The English Warrior from earliest times to 1066* (1996), pp. 127–35, 236–44

57 John Manley, 'The archer and the army in the late Saxon period', *Anglo-Saxon Studies in Archaeology and History* 4 (1985), pp. 222–35; J. Bradbury, *The Medieval Archer* (Woodbridge, 1985); pp. 12–16, 22–32, 71–5; R. Hardy, *The Longbow: A Social and Military History* (Yeovil, 1992); R. Hardy & M. J. Strickland, *The Great War Bow* (1997)

58 M. J. Swanton, *The Spearheads of Anglo-Saxon Settlements* (1973); H. R. Ellis Davidson, *The Sword in Anglo-Saxon England* (Oxford, 1962); N. Hooper, 'The Anglo-Saxons at War', in S. Hawkes, ed., *Weapons and Warfare in Anglo-Saxon England* (Oxford, 1989), pp. 191–202

8: Tostig

1 Poitiers pp. 91–3; H. Prentout, *Études sur quelques points de l'histoire de Guillaume le Conquérant* (Caen, 1930), pp. 149–53

2 *Heimskringla*, pp. 215–17; CPB, ii, pp. 206–7, 220; *Flateyjarbok*, iii, pp. 365–7

3 *Heimskringla*, p. 218; *Orkneyingsaga*, eds Palsson & Edwards, p. 75; CPB, ii, pp. 191–2

4 *Orkneyingsaga*, Rolls Series 88, i, pp. 58, 239; *Orkneyingsaga*, eds Palsson & Edwards, p. 71; *Flateyjarbok*, ii, pp. 421–7; E. Crawford,

'Birsay and the early earls of Orkney', *Orkney Heritage* 2 (1983), pp. 97–118

5 Morton & Muntz, *Carmen de Hastingae Proelio*, op. cit., xxxi, xxxiv, xl; F. Lot, ed., *Chronicon Centuleuse ou Chronique de l'Abbaye de Saint-Riquier* (Paris, 1894), pp. 230, 239; C. Brunel, *Recueil des actes des comtes de Ponthieu, 1026–1279* (Paris, 1930), p. iv; Le Patourel, *Norman Empire*, op. cit., p. 39

6 *Carmen*, op. cit., vv 50–1, p. 4; Arnold Taylor, 'Belrem', *ANS* 14 (1991), pp. 1–23; C. H. Haskins, *Norman Institutions*, op. cit., p. 39

7 Jumièges, pp. 132–3; Poitiers, pp. 100–6; John Gillingham, 'William the Bastard at war', in S. Morillo, *The Battle of Hastings* (1995), pp. 96–112 (at p. 109)

8 D. C. Douglas & G. W. Greenaway, *English Historical Documents* (1981), ii, p. 231; Wace, *Roman de Rou*, vv 5663–4

9 Poitiers, pp. 110–12; H. S. B. Keats-Rohan, 'William I and the Breton contingent in the non-Norman Conquest, 1060–1087', *ANS* 13 (1990), pp. 157–72 (esp. pp. 164–70); J. C. Potts, 'Normandy or Brittany? A conflict of interest at Mont St-Michel, 966–1066', *ANS* 12 (1986), pp. 135–56; J. Smith, *Province and Empire: Brittany and the Carolingians* (Cambridge, 1992)

10 Poitiers, pp. 100–4; *Carmen*, vv. 239–40, 291–300, pp. 16–20; William of Malmesbury, *De gestis regum*, i, p. 279; ii, p. 294; Henry of Huntingdon, *Historia Anglorum*, ed. Diana Greenaway (Oxford, 1996), pp. 380–1

11 *Carmen*, p. 67; Freeman, *Norman Conquest*, ii, pp. 667–71; C. N. L. Brooke, *The Saxon and Norman Kings* (1963), pp. 28–58; M. Campbell, 'Earl Godwin of Wessex and Edward the Confessor's promise of the throne to Duke William', *Traditio* 28 (1972), pp. 141–58

12 D. C. Douglas, 'Edward the Confessor, Duke William of Normandy and the English succession', *EHR* 68 (1953), pp. 526–45; T. J. Oleson, 'Edward the Confessor's promise of the throne to Duke William of Normandy', *EHR* 72 (1957), pp. 221–8; Eric John, 'Edward the Confessor and the Norman succession', *EHR* 94 (1979), pp. 241–67

13 G. Garnett, 'Coronation and propaganda: some implications of the Norman claim to the throne of England in 1066', *TRHS*, 5th series, 36 (1986), pp. 91–116; N. P. Brooks & H. E. Walker, 'The authority and interpretation of the Bayeux Tapestry', *ANS* 1 (1978), pp. 1–34 (at p. 11); Allen Brown, *The Normans and the Norman Conquest*

(1969), p. 132; Anne Williams, 'Problems connected with the English royal succession, 860–1066', *ANS* I (1978), pp. 144–67

14 Barlow, *William I and the Norman Conquest* (1965), p. 111; Korner, *Battle of Hastings*, pp. 213–17; Freeman, *Norman Conquest*, iii, p. 671; Lewis Thorpe, *The Bayeux Tapestry and the Norman Invasion* (1973), p. 9; Charles H. Gibbs-Smith, *The Bayeux Tapestry* (1973), pp. 10–11

15 William of Malmesbury, *De gestis regum*, i, pp. 278–9; Pauline Stafford, *Unification and Conquest*, p. 97; Freeman, *Norman Conquest*, iii, p. 222

16 Korner, *Battle of Hastings*, p. 137; Barlow, *Edward the Confessor*, p. 227; Stafford, *Unification and Conquest*, p. 97

17 G. Bosanquet, ed. & trans., *Eadmer. History of Recent Events in England* (1964), p. 6; Florence, ii, p. 20; Barlow, *Norman Conquest*, pp. 73–6, Barlow, *William Rufus* (1983), pp. 67–8

18 Korner, *Battle of Hastings*, pp. 126–31; Freeman, *Norman Conquest*, iii, pp. 671–80, 699; BT, plates 4, 17, 18; J. B. McNulty, 'The Lady Aelfgyva in the Bayeux Tapestry', *Speculum* 55 (1980), p. 659–68; M. W. Campbell, 'Aelfgyva: the mysterious lady of the Bayeux Tapestry', *Annales de Normandie* 34 (1984), pp. 127–45; D. J. Bernstein, *The Mystery of the Bayeux Tapestry* (1986), p. 19; D. M. Wilson, *The Bayeux Tapestry* (1985), p. 178; R. D. Wissolik, 'The Saxon statement: code in the Bayeux Tapestry', *Annuale medievale* 19 (1979), pp. 81–8

19 *Carmen*, p. 70; Freeman, *Norman Conquest*, iii, p. 242; Wace, *Roman de Rou*, vv. 5581–604; 5673–724

20 Ordericus Vitalis, ii, pp. 134–7; Poitiers, pp. 102–7; Barlow, *Edward the Confessor*, pp. 220–1; Korner, *Battle of Hastings*, pp. 115–19; H. E. J. Cowdrey, 'Towards an interpretation of the Bayeux Tapestry', *ANS* 10 (1987), pp. 49–65 (at p. 50)

21 Poitiers, p. 230; Ordericus Vitalis, ii, p. 136; iii, p. 114; Barlow, *William Rufus*, op. cit., pp. 42–3; Tabuteau, *Transfers of Property*, op. cit., pp. 55, 122

22 Freeman, *Norman Conquest*, iii, pp. 228–47, 689–92

23 The complexity of feudal obligations can be reconstructed from pointers in a number of recent books: F. L. Cheyette, ed., *Lordship and Community in Medieval Europe* (New York, 1968); T. Reuter, ed., *The Medieval Nobility* (Amsterdam, 1978); W. Davies & P. Fouracre, eds, *The Settlement of Disputes in Early Medieval Europe* (Cambridge, 1986); George S. Duby, *The Chivalrous Society* (Berkeley, 1980)

24 Freeman, *Norman Conquest*, iii, p. 252

25 Oleson, *Witenagemot*, op. cit., pp. 82–90

26 G. Bosanquet, ed. & trans., *Eadmer. History of Recent Events in England* (1964), p. 8; Richard D. Wissolik, 'The monk Eadmer as historian of the Norman succession: Korner and Freeman examined', *American Benedictine Review* 30 (1979)

27 ASC, 1065, 'C' 'D' versions; Florence, i, pp. 222–3; W. J. Rees, ed., *Lives of the Cambro-British Saints* (Cardiff, 1853), pp. 153–4; A. W. Wade-Evans, *Vitae sanctorum Britanniae et genealogiae* (1944), pp. 184–6

28 ASC, 1065, 'D' version; Barlow, *English Church*, op. cit., pp. 131–2, 35, 156, 174–5; Barlow, *Edward the Confessor*, pp. 229, 233–4

29 *Lives of Edward the Confessor*, Rolls Series 3, p. 404; G. H. Pertz, ed. *Monumenta Germaniae Historica* (Hanover, 1909), 5, p. 66

30 William of Malmesbury, *De gestis regum*, ii, p. 245; Henry of Huntingdon, *Historia Anglorum*, Rolls Series 74, p. 196; Ordericus Vitalis, ii, p. 262; Freeman, *Norman Conquest*, ii, p. 560; P. H. Sawyer, *Anglo-Saxon Charters* (1968), Nos. 1033, 1481

31 Dorothy Whitelock, 'The dealings of the kings of England with Northumbria in the tenth and eleventh centuries', in Peter Clemoes, ed., *The Anglo-Saxons: Studies in Some Aspects of their History and Culture presented to Bruce Dickins* (1959), pp. 70–88; Hodgson Hinde, ed., *Symeonis Dunelmensis Opera et Collectanea*, Surtees Society, 51 (1868), pp. 212–13, 156–7, 91–3

32 Freeman, *Norman Conquest*, ii, pp. 380–1. For details on Cnut's laws see Dorothy Whitelock, 'Wulfstan and the laws of Cnut', *EHR* 63 (1948), pp. 533–52; Whitelock, 'Wulfstan's authorship of Cnut's laws', *EHR* 69 (1954), pp. 72–85

33 ASC, 1065, 'C' version; Florence, i, p. 223; William Kapelle, *The Norman Conquest of the North: the Region and its Transformation, 1000–1135* (1979), pp. 86–106 (esp. pp. 96–7); Whitelock, 'Dealings', loc. cit., pp. 72–87; VCH, Lancashire, i, p. 272

34 Symeon of Durham, *Historia Ecclesiae Dunhelmis*, ed. T. Arnold, in *Symeonis Monachi Opera Omnia*, Rolls Series 75 (1882), i, pp. 92, 97; Kapelle, *Norman Conquest of the North*, op. cit., p. 89

35 Geoffrey Gaimar, *L'Estorie des Engles*, trans. & ed. T. D. Hardy & C. T. Martin, Rolls Series 91, 2 vols (1888), 11. 5085–6; Kapelle, *Norman Conquest of the North*, pp. 90–1

36 *Symeonis Monachi Opera Omnia. Historia Ecclesiae Dunhelmenis*, ed. T. Arnold, ii, p. 174; G. H. Pertz, ed., *Monumenta Germaniae Historica* (Hanover, 1866), 19, p. 508; Gaimar, *L'Estorie*, op. cit., ll.

5085–99; Plummer & Earle, *Two of the Saxon Chronicles Parallel*, pp. 25–6

37 *Symeonis Monachi Opera Omnia*, ed. T. Arnold, op. cit., pp. 174–5: Gaimar, *L'Estorie*, op. cit., II. 5115–22; H. W. C. Davis, 'Cumberland before the Norman Conquest', *EHR* 20 (1905), pp. 61–5

38 Symeon of Durham, *Historia Regum* in *Symeonis Dunelmensis Opera et Collectanea*, ed. Hodgson Hynde (1868), pp. 91–3, 156–7, 212–13; Bertie Wilkinson, 'Northumbrian separatism in 1065 and 1066', *Bulletin of the John Rylands Library* 35 (1938), pp. 368–87; Kapelle, *Norman Conquest of the North*, p. 98

39 C. J. Morris, *Marriage and Murder in Eleventh-century Northumbria, a Study of the 'De Obsessione Dunelmi'* (York, 1992); Kapelle, *Norman Conquest of the North*, pp. 94–5; Freeman, *Norman Conquest*, ii, pp. 477–8; Pauline Stafford, *Queen Emma and Queen Edith*, p. 271; Ann Williams, *The English and the Norman Conquest* (1995), p. 69

40 Stafford, *Queen Emma and Queen Edith*, pp. 45–6, 269–72

41 *Vita Eadwardi*, pp. 54–7; Symeon of Durham, *Symeonis Dunelmensis Opera et Colectanea*, ed. Hodgson Hynde, op. cit., p. 156

42 Barlow, *Edward the Confessor*, p. 238; Stafford, *Unification and Conquest*, pp. 96–9

43 ASC, 1065, 'D' 'E' versions; Florence, i, p. 223; Freeman, *Norman Conquest*, ii, p. 479

44 Wilkinson, 'Northumbrian separatism', loc. cit., pp. 368–87; W. H. C. Davis, 'Cumberland before the Conquest', loc. cit.; Kapelle, *Norman Conquest of the North*, pp. 100–1

45 Symeon of Durham, *Historia Ecclesiae Dunhelmensis*, op. cit., pp. 87–9; W. M. Aird, 'St Cuthbert, the Scots and the Normans', *ANS* 16 (1993), p. 1–20

46 Freeman, *Norman Conquest*, ii, pp. 479–84; M. W. Campbell, 'Tostig displaced', *Annales de Normandie* 23 (1973); cf. in general M. R. Godden, 'Money, power and morality in late Anglo-Saxon England', *Anglo-Saxon England* 19 (1990), pp. 41–65

47 ASC, 1065, 'D' 'E' versions; *Vita Eadwardi*, pp. 76–9; Hollister, *Anglo-Saxon Military Institutions* (Oxford, 1962), op. cit., p. 16

48 Ian W. Walker, *Harold the Last Saxon King* (1997), pp. 110–14

49 Florence, i, pp. 223–4; *Vita Eadwardi*, pp. 78–81

50 *Vita Eadwardi*, p. 81; Barlow, *Edward the Confessor*, pp. 236–9; Freeman, *Norman Conquest*, ii, pp. 485–97. For the implications

of the change in laws see Pauline Stafford, 'The laws of Cnut and
the history of Anglo-Saxon royal promises', *Anglo-Saxon England* 10
(1982), pp. 173–90

51 Walker, *Harold*, op. cit., pp. 118–19; Barlow, *Edward the Confessor*,
pp. 238–9
52 B. W. Scholz, ed., *Sulcard of Westminster. Prologus de Constucione
Westmonasterii*, *Traditio* 20 (1964); Ordericus Vitalis, ii, p. 138;
Poitiers, p. 146. For the list of those present see Barlow, *Edward the
Confessor*, pp. 244–6
53 *Vita Eadwardi*, op. cit; Barlow, 'The Vita Aedwardi. The Seven
Sleepers; some further evidence and reflections', *Speculum* 40 (1965),
pp. 385–97
54 *Vita Eadwardi*, pp. 123–5; Stafford, *Queen Emma and Queen Edith*,
pp. 44–5, 273; Barlow, *Edward the Confessor*, p. 249
55 Poitiers, pp. 172–3, 266–8; Raymond Foreville, 'Aux origines de la
renaissance juridique', *Moyen Age* 58 (1952), pp. 63–72; J. le
Patourel, 'The Norman succession, 996–1035', *EHR* 86 (1971), pp.
231–6
56 *Carmen de Hastingae Proelio*, op. cit., pp. 20, 70; J. S. Beckerman,
'Succession in Normandy, 1087, and in England, 1066; the role of
testamentary custom', *Speculum* 47 (1972), pp. 258–60; Ann Williams, 'Some notes and considerations on problems connected with
the English royal succession, 860–1066', *ANS* 1 (1978), pp. 144–67
(esp. p. 165); Poitiers, pp. 172–3
57 ASC, 1066, 'C' 'D' 'E' versions; Florence, i, p. 224; M. Rule, ed.,
Eadmer. Historia Novorum in Anglia (1884), p. 8; Jumièges, p. 133; W.
Dunn Macray, *Historia Ramesiensis*, Rolls Series 83 (1886), p. 178
58 Jumièges, p. 133; *Lives of Edward the Confessor*, Rolls Series 3, pp.
433–4; F. Michel, *Chroniques Anglo-Normandes* (Rouen, 1840), ii, pp.
223–54; R. Drogereit, 'Memerkungen zum Bayeux Teppick',
Mitteilungen des Osterreichischen Instituts für geschichts forschung 70
(1962), pp. 261–76 (at p. 264); Freeman, *Norman Conquest*, iii, pp.
29–49, 576–97; Barlow, *Edward the Confessor*, pp. 254–5
59 Freeman, *Norman Conquest*, iii, pp. 49–61; Stafford, *Queen Emma and
Queen Edith*, pp. 272, 274; William of Malmesbury, *De gestis regum*,
ii, p. 306
60 Florence, i, p. 228; William of Malmesbury, *Vita Wulfstani*, ed., R.
R. Darlington (1928), i, pp. 16–23; J. H. F. Peile, ed. & trans.,
William of Malmesbury's Life of St Wulstan (Oxford, 1934), pp. 34–5;
Freeman, *Norman Conquest*, iii, pp. 61–7

9:    Stamford Bridge

1 Jumièges, p. 133; Searle, *Predatory Kinship*, op. cit., pp. 193–229, 232
2 Poitiers, p. 149; Ordericus Vitalis, ii, pp. 140–1; Wace, *Roman de Rou*, vv. 5841, 6024, ii, pp. 103–9
3 Freeman, *Norman Conquest*, iii, p. 262
4 Ordericus Vitalis, ii, p. 122; Poitiers, p. 152
5 P. Jaffe, ed., *Monumenta Gregoriana* (Berlin, 1865), pp. 414–16; Catherine Morton, 'Pope Alexander II and the Norman Conquest', *Latomus. Revue des Études Latines* 34 (1975), pp. 362–82
6 D. C. Douglas, *The Norman Achievement* (1969); J. Le Patourel, *The Norman Empire* (Oxford, 1976); John Julius Norwich, *The Normans in the South* (1967)
7 L. Halphen, *Le Comte d'Anjou au XIe siècle* (Paris, 1906), p. 133; Korner, *Battle of Hastings*, p. 219; Lawson, *Cnut*, pp. 211–12
8 Wace, *Roman de Rou*, vv. 6069–86, ii, p. 111
9 Ibid., vv. 6110–62, ii, pp. 112–14; Freeman, *Norman Conquest*, iii, pp. 293–9
10 Elizabeth van Houts, 'The ship list of William the Conqueror', *ANS* 10 (1987), pp. 159–83; Freeman, *Norman Conquest*, iii, pp. 379–83; C. Warren Hollister, 'The greater Domesday tenants-in-chief', in J. Holt, ed., *Domesday Studies Novocentenary Conference* (Wodbridge, 1987), pp. 219–48; P. Banbury, *Man and the Sea: From Ice Age to Norman Conquest* (1975), pp. 223–4
11 Wace, *Roman de Rou*, vv. 6417–32, ii, p. 123; Ordericus Vitalis, ii, p. 144; William of Malmesbury, *De gestis regum*, ii, p. 314; Poitiers, p. 180; BT, Plates 42–4; W. Spatz, *Die Schlacht von Hastings* (1896), pp. 28–30; J. Williamson, *The English Channel. A History* (1959), p. 83
12 Ordericus Vitalis, ii, pp. 134, 144–5; Poitiers, p. 190; Wace, *Roman de Rou*, vv. 7657–60; Spatz, *Die Schlacht*, op. cit., p. 27; Stenton, *Anglo-Saxon England*, p. 577; R. H. George, 'The contribution of Flanders to the conquest of England', *Revue belge de philologie et d'histoire* 5 (1926), pp. 81–97; B. Lyon, *From Fief to Indenture* (Cambridge, Mass., 1957), p. 33; J. O. Prestwich, 'War and finance in the Anglo-Norman state', *TRHS*, 5th series, iv (1954), pp. 19–44; Stephen D. B. Brown, 'Military service and monetary reward in the eleventh and twelfth centuries', *History* 74 (1989), pp. 20–38; David Nicholas, *Medieval Flanders* (1992)
13 Korner, *Battle of Hastings*, pp. 228–36, 254; Jumièges, pp. 34–5; Poitiers, pp. 64, 78; Marcel Garaud, 'Les incursions des Normands en Poitou et leurs conséquences', *Revue historique* 37, pp. 241–68; R. H.

C. Davis, 'William of Poitiers and his history of William the Conqueror', in *The Writing of History in the Middle Ages. Essays presented to Richard Williams Southern* (Oxford, 1981), pp. 71–100

14 George Beech, 'The participation of Aquitanians in the conquest of England, 1066–1100', *ANS* 9 (1986), pp. 1–24; J. Verdon, *La chronique de Saint-Maixent, 751–1140* (Paris, 1979), pp. 104, 112, 170, 176, 192; Jane Martindale, 'Aimeri of Thouars and the Poitevin connection', *ANS* 7 (1984), pp. 224–43; Shirley Ann Brown, 'The Bayeux Tapestry: why Eustace, Odo and William?' *ANS* 12 (1989), pp. 7–28

15 Jumièges, pp. 193–4; C. Fahlin, ed., *Chronique des ducs de Normandie*, 2 vols (Upsala, 1854), ii, p. 489; Ordericus Vitalis, ii, p. 312; A. de la Borderie, *Histoire de Bretagne*, 6 vols (Paris, 1914), iii, pp. 14–23; Douglas, *William the Conqueror*, pp. 408–15; Freeman, *Norman Conquest*, iii, pp. 714–16

16 Ordericus Vitalis, ii, pp. 138–42

17 E. Edwards, ed., *Chronica monasterii de Hilda juxta Wintoniam*, Rolls Series (1866), pp. 283–321 (at p. 292); Poitiers, p. 186

18 *Monumenta historica Norvegiae*, ed. G. Storm, op. cit., p. 56; *Flateyjarbok*, op. cit., iii, pp. 386–8; *Morkinskinna*, op. cit., p. 111; *Agrip*, op. cit., p. 41

19 *Fagrskinna*, op. cit., p. 281; *Fornmanna Sogur*, op. cit., v, p. 142; vi, pp. 402, 430; x, p. 407; *Morkinskinna*, p. 262; *Heimskringla*, p. 222

20 *Fagrskinna*, pp. 301–2; *Fornmanna Sogur*, vi, pp. 431–2; *Flateyjarbok*, iii, pp. 398–9; *Heimskringla*, p. 223

21 ASC, 1066, 'C' version; Plummer & Earle, *Two of the Saxon Chronicles Parallel*, i, pp. 194–6; Geoffrey Gaimar, *Estorie des Engles*, eds T. Hardy & C. T. Martin, op. cit., vv. 5191–4; A. O. Anderson, *Scottish Annals from English Chronicles* (1908), p. 87; Symeon of Durham, *Opera Omnia* (1885), op. cit., ii, p. 174

22 J. C. Russell, *Late Ancient and Medieval Population* (Philadelphia, 1958), pp. 96–8; Philip Contamine, *War in the Middle Ages* (Oxford, 1984), p. 52; C. Warren Hollister, *Anglo-Saxon Military Institutions* (Oxford, 1962), pp. 25–37; Poitiers, p. 156; William of Malmesbury, *De gestis regum*, ed. W. Stubbs, op. cit., iii, p. 300

23 P. Lancaster-Brown, *Halley and his Comet* (Poole, 1985), p. 113; F. Stevenson & C. B. F. Walker, *Halley's Comet in History* (1985), p. 57; Fauroux, RADN, No. 229; ASC, 1066, 'D' 'E' versions; Freeman, *Norman Conquest*, iii, pp. 71–3, 645–50; Wace, *Roman de Rou*, vv. 6905, 7897

24 Freeman, *Norman Conquest*, iii, pp. 382–3; Fauroux, RADN, No. 224

25 G. M. Gillmor, 'Navy logistics of the cross-Channel operation, 1066', *ANS* 7 (1984), pp. 105–31; L. Musset, 'A-t-il existé en Normandie au XIe siècle une aristocratie d'argent?' *Annales de Normandie* 9 (1959), pp. 285–94

26 ASC, 1066, 'C' 'D' versions; Plummer & Earle, *Two of the Saxon Chronicles Parallel*, i, p. 194; Freeman, *Norman Conquest*, iii, p. 337; Gillmor, 'Navy logistics', loc. cit., p. 125

27 Poitiers, pp. 39, 182, 192, 194, 204, 260; Douglas & Greenaway, *English Historical Documents*, op. cit., pp. 237–8; D. C. Douglas, 'Companions of the Conqueror', *History* 28 (1943), pp. 130–47; J. F. A. Mason, 'The companions of the Conqueror', *EHR* 66 (1956), pp. 61–9; Brian Golding, 'Robert of Mortain', *ANS* 13 (1990), pp. 119–44 (at p. 121)

28 R. N. Sauvage, *L'Abbaye de Saint-Martin de Troarn* (Caen, 1911), pp. 245–52; Poitiers, pp. 150–2; J. Verdon, ed., *La Chronique de Saint-Maixeunt, 751–1140* (Paris, 1979), p. 136

29 Bernard S. Bachrach, 'Some observations on the military administration of the Norman Conquest', *ANS* 8 (1985), pp. 1–25; Wace, *Roman de Rou*, vv. 6166, 6474, 6509, 6544, 6557, 6629, 7024; Poitiers, pp. 160, 164, 182; *Carmen de Hastingae Proelio*, op. cit., p. 8; Ordericus Vitalis, ii, p. 172

30 C. H. Lemmon, 'The campaign of 1066', in C. T. Chevallier, ed., *The Norman Conquest* (New York, 1966), p. 85; J. F. C. Fuller, *The Decisive Battles of the Western World* (1954), p. 372; J. Laporte, 'Les opérations navales en Manche et Mer du Nord pendant l'année 1066', *Annales de Normandie* 17 (1967), pp. 9–10; Bernard S. Bachrach, 'Cabalus et Caballarius in medieval warfare', in H. Chickering, ed., *Approaches to the Teaching of Chivalry* (Kalamazoo, Michigan, 1986); Poitiers, p. 198; Wace, *Roman de Rou*, vv. 6486, 6888, 7498, 7561; P. Contamine, *War in the Middle Ages*, op. cit., pp. 69–70, 96–7; R. Allen Brown, 'The status of the Norman knight', in J. Gillingham & J. C. Holt, *War and Government in the Middle Ages* (Woodbridge, 1984), pp. 28–9

31 Bachrach, 'Some observations', loc. cit.; Poitiers, pp. 160, 212

32 For Roger of Montgomery see Ordericus Vitalis, ii, pp. 20–2, 48, 210, 262; iii, pp. 136, 142; Jumièges, p. 322; David Howarth, *1066* (1977), p. 124

33 Poitiers, p. 160; Freeman, *Norman Conquest*, iii, pp. 389–93; Gillmor, 'Navy logistics', loc. cit.

34 ASC, 1066, 'D' version; J. Neumann, 'Hydrographic and ship-

hydrodynamic aspects of the Norman invasion, AD 1066', *ANS* 11 (1988), pp. 221–43 (at p. 223)

35 J. Williamson, *The English Channel. A History* (1959), p. 80; Gillmor, 'Navy logistics', loc. cit.; Neumann, 'Hydrographic aspects', loc. cit.

36 *Carmen de Hastingae Proelio*, op. cit., vv. 53, 59, 63–4, p. 6; Poitiers, p. 160; Ordericus Vitalis, ii, p. 170; J. Laporte, 'Les opérations navales en Manche et Mer du Nord pendant l'année 1066', *Annales de Normandie* 17 (1967), pp. 2–36; David Bates, *William the Conqueror* (1989), p. 65

37 Korner, *Battle of Hastings*, pp. 264–6

38 P. H. Sawyer, *The Age of the Vikings* (1971), pp. 66, 228; F. Lot, *L'Art militaire*, i, p. 283; L. M. Larson, *Cnut* (1912), op. cit., p. 177. Cf. also A. W. Brogger & H. Shetelig, *The Viking Ships* (1971); O. Olsen & O. Crumlin-Pedersen, *Five Viking Ships from Roskilde Fjord* (1970); I. Atkinson, *The Viking Ships* (Cambridge, 1979)

39 *Heimskringla*, pp. 223, 225; Marianus Scottus, *Chronicon* in G. H. Pertz, ed., *Monumenta Germaniae Historica Scriptores* (Hanover, 1844), v, pp. 495–565; J. P. Migne, *Patrologia Latina* (Paris, 1853), op. cit., pp. 147, 623–796; Jacqueline Simpson, *The Northmen Speak* (1965)

40 James Graham-Campbell, 'Anglo-Scandinavian equestrian equipment', *ANS* 14 (1991), pp. 77–89; F. Chalandon, *Histoire de la domination normande en Italie et en Sicilie*, op. cit., i, pp. 90–2; CPB, ii, p. 211; *Heimskringla*, p. 224

41 *Flateyjarbok*, ii, p. 423; *Orkneyingsaga*, Rolls Series 88, i, p. 61; *Orkneyingsaga*, eds Palsson & Edwards, p. 73; *Chronicle of Man*, ed. Goss, 2 vols (Douglas, 1874), i, p. 50

42 *Morkinskinna*, p. 112; *Flateyjarbok*, iii, pp. 389–90; *Heimskringla*, p. 225; Bjarni Adalbjarnarson, *Om de Norsk. Kongers Sagaer* (Oslo, 1937); Svenda Hoj, *Studier over den eldste norrone historierskrivning* (Copenhagen, 1965)

43 ASC, 1066, 'D' 'E' versions; Plummer & Earle, *Two of the Saxon Chronicles Parallel*, p. 196; John of Worcester, eds R. R. Darlington & P. McGurk (Oxford, 1995), ii, p. 602

44 Paddy Griffith, *The Viking Art of War* (1995), p. 101; F. W. Brooks, *The Battle of Stamford Bridge* (East Yorkshire Local History Society, 1956), p. 11; Freeman, *Norman Conquest*, iii, p. 342; Kapelle, *Norman Conquest of the North*, op. cit., pp. 103–4

45 ASC, 1066, 'C' 'D' 'E' versions; Plummer & Earle, *Two of the Saxon Chronicles Parallel*, p. 196; CPB, ii, pp. 192, 225, 227; John of Worcester, op. cit., p. 602; *Heimskringla*, p. 226

46 Florence, i, pp. 225–6. For York see A. P. Smyth, *Scandinavian York*

and Dublin, 2 vols (Dublin, 1979); R. A. Hall, *Jorvik, Viking Age York* (York, 1979)

47 Brooks, *Battle of Stamford Bridge*, p. 12; Marianus Scottus, *Chronicon* in Pertz, ed. *Monumenta*, op. cit., v, p. 559; Ian W. Walker, *Harold the Last Saxon King*, op. cit., p. 160

48 R. Glover, 'English Warfare in 1066', *EHR* 67 (1952), pp. 1–18; R. H. C. Davis, 'Did the Anglo-Saxons have warhorses?' in S. C. Hawkes, ed., *Weapons and Warfare in Anglo-Saxon England* (1989), pp. 141–4; *Vita Haroldi*, op. cit., pp. 156–7; W. Stubbs, ed., *De Inventione* (Oxford, 1861), op. cit., pp. 47–8; W. Stubbs, ed., *The Foundation of Waltham Abbey* (Oxford, 1861), p. 125

49 CPB, i, pp. 192–3; *Monumenta Norvegiae Historica*, ed. G. Storm, op. cit., pp. 56–7; Brooks, *Battle of Stamford Bridge*, p. 13

50 *Fagrskinna*, p. 286; *Fornmanna Sogur*, vi, p. 411; *Morkinskinna*, p. 115

51 Florence, i, pp. 225–6; John of Worcester, p. 602; Brooks, *Battle of Stamford Bridge*, p. 14

52 Geoffrey Gaimar, *L'Estoire des Englais*, ed. A. Bell (Oxford, 1960), vv. 522–4; J. Stevenson, *The Church Historians of England*, 5 vols (1858), ii, 2, p. 793; John of Worcester, p. 602

53 *Fornmanna Sogur*, x, pp. 407–8; *Monumenta Norvegiae Historica*, ed. G. Storm, op. cit., p. 57

54 *Heimskringla*, p. 230

55 Henry of Huntingdon, *Historia Anglorum*, Rolls Series 74, pp. 199–200; Huntingdon, *Historia Anglorum*, ed. Greenaway (1996), pp. 387–9; William of Malmesbury, *De gestis regum*, Rolls Series 90, ii, p. 81; B. Dickins, 'The late addition to the Anglo-Saxon Chronicle, 1066', *Proceedings of the Leeds Philosophical and Literary Society* 5 (1940), pp. 148–9

56 Brooks, *Battle of Stamford Bridge*, p. 20; Paddy Griffith, *The Viking Art of War*, op. cit., pp. 191–3; I. Atkinson, *The Viking Ships*, op. cit., p. 26

57 *Heimskringla*, p. 232; Turville-Petre, *Haraldr the Hard Ruler*, op. cit., pp. 19–20

58 CPB, ii, p. 192–3; C. R. Unger, ed., *Frisbok* (Christiana, 1871), pp. 245–6; A. H. Burne, *More Battlefields of England* (1952), pp. 83–95

59 *Flateyjarbok*, ii, p. 423; *Orkneyingsaga*, Rolls Series 88, i, pp. 61–2; Brooks, *Battle of Stamford Bridge*, pp. 21–2

60 ASC, 1066, 'D' version; Plummer & Earle, *Two of the Saxon Chronicles Parallel*, p. 197; *Fagrskinna*, pp. 287–95; John of Worcester, p. 604

61 Ordericus Vitalis, ii, p. 168; D. Howarth, *1066. The Year of Conquest* (1977), p. 106; *Heimskringla*, p. 233

62 *Heimskringla*, pp. 234–9; *Fornmanna Sogur*, vi, p. 143; x, p. 408; *Morkinskinna*, p. 122; *Flateyjarbok*, iii, pp. 399; ii, p. 423; *Fagrskinna*, p. 295; *Monumenta Norvegiae Historica*, ed. G. Storm, p. 58; *Orkneyingsaga*, Rolls Series 88, i, p. 383

63 Korner, *Battle of Hastings*, pp. 260–1; Freeman, *Norman Conquest*, iii, pp. 419–21; Hollister, *Anglo-Saxon Military Institutions* (Oxford, 1962), p. 151

64 Gaimar, *L'Estoire des Englais*, op. cit., v. 5251; Brooks, *Battle of Stamford Bridge*, p. 16

65 Florence, i, p. 228; William of Malmesbury, *De gestis regum*, Rolls Series 90, ii, pp. 306–7; Korner, *Battle of Hastings*, pp. 282–4

10: Hastings

1 Poitiers, pp. 160–2; *Carmen*, vv. 58–75, pp. 6–8; ASC, 1066, 'D' version; Douglas, *William the Conqueror*, p. 396; Neumann, 'Hydrographic aspects', *ANS* 11 (1988), pp. 221–43, loc. cit. (at p. 236)

2 Poitiers, p. 164; BT, Plates 9, 10; Christine Grainge & Gerald Grainge, 'The Pevensey expedition: brilliantly executed plan or near disaster?' *Mariner's Mirror* 79 (1993), pp. 261–73; C. M. Gillmor, 'Naval logistics of the cross-Channel operation', *ANS* 7 (1984), pp. 105–31, loc. cit.

3 BT, Plate 10; Poitiers, p. 210; *Carmen*, vv. 601–11, p. 38; J. R. Lamby, *The Chronicle of Henry Knyghton*, Rolls Series 92 (1889), i, p. 54; J. Beeler, *Warfare in England, 1066–1189* (Cornell, 1966), p. 12

4 ASC, 1066, 'E' version; J. Haywood, *Dark Age Naval Power* (1991), p. 4; R. Allen Brown, 'The Battle of Hastings', *ANS* 3 (1980), pp. 1–21; Stephen Morillo, *The Battle of Hastings* (Woodbridge, 1995), p. 202; Ann Williams, *The English and the Norman Conquest* (Woodbridge, 1995), p. 19

5 William of Malmesbury, *De gestis regum*, ii, p. 300; Wace, *Roman de Rou*, vv. 6483–8, 6573–90, ii, pp. 127–8; R. Allen Brown, *The Normans and the Norman Conquest*, p. 133; A. Taylor, 'Evidence for a pre-Conquest origin for the chapels in Hastings and Pevensey castles', *Château-Gaillard. European Castle Studies* 3 (1969), pp. 144–51

6 Stephen Johnson, *Late Roman Fortifications* (Totowa, NJ 1983), pp.

204–6; Bachrach, 'Some observations on the military administration of the Norman conquest', *ANS* 8 (1985), pp. 1–25; Poitiers, p. 210

7 BT, Plate 51; Poitiers, p. 170; Elizabeth van Houts, ed., *Gesta Normannorum ducum* (Oxford, 1995), pp. 170–1; *Carmen*, vv. 137–8, p. 10

8 BT, Plate 50; Poitiers, pp. 168, 180; W. Spatz, *Die Schlacht von Hastings* (1896), pp. 23, 25; H. Delbruck, *Geschichte der Kriegkunst im Rahmen des politische Geschichte* (Berlin, 1920), iii, p. 160; J. F. A. Mason, 'The Rapes of Sussex and the Norman Conquest', *Sussex Archaeological Collections* 102 (1964), pp. 75–7; D. Matthew, *The Norman Monasteries and their English Possessions* (Oxford, 1962), pp. 19–21; Freeman, *Norman Conquest*, iii, pp. 728–9

9 W. Stubbs, ed., *De Inventione*, op. cit., pp. 48–9; *Vita Haroldi*, p. 127; Wace, *Roman de Rou*, vv. 6983–7050; Freeman, *Norman Conquest*, iii, pp. 427–34

10 Hollister, *Anglo-Saxon Military Institutions*, p. 151; Brown, 'Battle of Hastings', loc. cit.; Morillo, *Battle of Hastings*, pp. 202, 205; Ordericus Vitalis, ii, p. 172

11 Ordericus Vitalis, *Historica Ecclesiastica*, ed. & trans. Thomas Forester (New York, 1968), i, p. 482; William of Malmesbury, *De gestis regum*, ii, p. 301; Wace, *Roman de Rou*, vv. 6905, 7743–4, 7897, ii, p. 173; Jim Bradbury, *The Battle of Hastings* (1998), pp. 167–8; J. A. Williamson, *The English Channel* (1959), pp. 72–80; C. H. Lemmon, *The Field of Hastings* (St Leonards, 1970), pp. 20–2

12 Poitiers, p. 180; Ordericus Vitalis, ed. Chibnall, ii, p. 172; *Carmen*, vv. 319–21, p. 20; Freeman, *Norman Conquest*, iii, pp. 433–7

13 ASC, 1066, 'E' version; Florence, i, p. 227; John of Worcester, p. 604

14 *Domesday Book*, ii, pp. 409, 449; Poitiers, p. 186; William of Malmesbury, *De gestis regum*, i, p. 182; J. Stevenson, ed., *Chronicon Monasterii de Abingdon*, Rolls Series (1858), ii, p. 3; Korner, *Battle of Hastings*, pp. 200, 260–1; Abels, *Lordship and Obligation*, op. cit., pp. 143–4, 179, 185; Clarke, *English Nobility*, op. cit., pp. 87–8; Freeman, *Norman Conquest*, iii, pp. 729–31

15 Elizabeth van Houts, ed., *Gesta Normannorum ducum* (Oxford, 1995), ii, p. 168; James Graham-Campbell, 'Anglo-Scandinavian equestrian equipment in eleventh-century England', *ANS* 14 (1991), pp. 77–89 (at p. 89)

16 BT, Plate 57; Jumièges, pp. 134–5; Poitiers, p. 180; Ordericus Vitalis, ii, p. 172; Wace, *Roman de Rou*, ii, pp. 156–7; William of

Malmesbury, *De gestis regum*, ii, p. 302; Williamson, *English Channel*, op. cit., p. 88

17 ASC, 1066, 'D' version; Nicholas Hooper, 'The Anglo-Saxons at war', in S. C. Hawkes, ed., *Weapons and Warfare in Anglo-Saxon England* (Oxford, 1989), pp. 191–202 (at p. 198); Jim Bradbury, *Battle of Hastings*, op. cit., p. 173; Brown, 'Battle of Hastings', loc. cit.; Morillo, *Battle of Hastings*, op. cit., p. 200

18 BT, plates 57, 63, 67; Jumièges, p. 135; *Carmen*, vv. 261–8, 314, 343–4, pp. 18–22; Williamson, *English Channel*, p. 79

19 *Carmen*, vv. 341–2, 363–8, 381–2, p. 24; ASC, 1066, 'D' 'E' versions; Florence, i, p. 227

20 Stephen of Rouen, *Draco Normannicus*, ed. R. Howlett (1885), ii, vv. 1415–20; Morillo, *Battle of Hastings*, pp. xxiii–xxx

21 Poitiers, pp. 192–4; Spatz, *Die Schlacht von Hastings*, op. cit., pp. 30, 33, 34–6; F. Lot, *L'Art militaire et les armées au Moyen Age en Europe et dans le Proche Orient*, 2 vols (Paris, 1946), i, p. 285; Barlow, *The Feudal Kingdom of England* (1955), p. 83; Fuller, *Decisive Battles*, op. cit., pp. 376–7

22 C. H. Lemmon, 'The campaign of 1066', in D. Whitelock, ed., *The Norman Conquest: Its Setting and Impact* (1966), pp. 77–122 (at p. 100); Wace, *Roman de Rou*, vv. 7771–4, 8607–13; Florence, i, p. 227; *Carmen*, vv. 177–88, pp. 12–13

23 Poitiers, p. 182; Henry of Huntingdon, *Historia Anglorum*, ed. Greenaway, pp. 389–93; Eadmer, *Historia Novorum in Anglia*, ed. M. Rule (1884), p. 9; William of Malmesbury, *De gestis regum*, ii, p. 302; *Brevis Relatio* in J. A. Giles, ed., *Scriptores rerum gestarum Willelmi Conquestoris* (1845), pp. 1–23; Wace, *Roman de Rou*, vv. 7403–41

24 M. A. Lower, ed., *Chronicon monasterii de Bello* (1846), p. 4; Poitiers, pp. 182–4; Douglas, 'Companions of the Conqueror', *History* 28 (1943), pp. 129–47; J. F. A. Mason, 'Barons and their officials in the later eleventh century', *ANS* 13 (1990), pp. 243–62; C. P. Lewis, 'The early earls of Norman England', *ANS* 13 (1990), pp. 207–23

25 BT, Plates 14, 44–6; Spatz, *Die Schlacht*, op. cit., p. 31

26 *Carmen*, vv. 395–402, p. 26; Gaimar, *L'Estoire*, ed. Bell (1960), op. cit., vv. 5261–300; Henry of Huntingdon, *Historia Anglorum*, ed. Greenaway, pp. 392–3; G. H. White, 'The companions of the Conqueror', *Genealogists' Magazine* 9 (1944), pp. 417–24 (at p. 423); E. Faral, *Les Jongleurs de France* (1910), pp. 56–7

27 Wace, *Roman de Rou*, vv. 8035–43; P. Abrahams, ed., *The Carmen of Baudri of Bourgeuil* (Paris, 1926), vv. 405–8; William of Malmesbury, *De gestis regum*, ii, p. 302; D. C. Douglas, 'The Song of Roland and

the Norman Conquest of England', *French Studies* 14 (1960), pp. 99–116

28 Poitiers, p. 188; *Carmen*, vv. 409–12, p. 26; Wace, *Roman de Rou*, vv. 8057–8, ii, p. 184; Spatz, *Die Schlacht*, p. 50; Douglas & Greenway, *English Historical Documents*, ii, pp. 226–9

29 *Carmen*, vv. 413–20, p. 26; Poitiers, pp. 188–90; Spatz, *Die Schlacht*, p. 50; David R. Cook, 'The Norman military revolution in England', *ANS* 1 (1978), pp. 94–102 (at p. 98)

30 *Carmen*, vv. 421–4, p. 28; Poitiers, p. 190; Ordericus Vitalis, ii, p. 174; Spatz, *Die Schlacht*, p. 52; Fuller, *Decisive Battles*, pp. 374–82; Stephen Morillo, 'Hastings: an unusual battle', *Haskins Society Journal* 2 (1990), pp. 95–104; Morillo, *Warfare under the Anglo-Norman Kings, 1066–1135* (Woodbridge, 1994)

31 Poitiers, p. 190; *Carmen*, vv. 439–61, pp. 28–30; Morillo, *Battle of Hastings*, p. 169

32 BT, Plates 64–5; van Houts, *Gesta Normannorum ducum*, p. 168; Ordericus Vitalis, ii, p. 176; Morillo, *Battle of Hastings*, p. 224

33 *Carmen*, vv. 439–44, 471–526, pp. 28, 34, 94; Poitiers, p. 192; BT, Plates 64–5; William of Malmesbury, ii, p. 302; Spatz, *Die Schlacht*, pp. 40–1; Fuller, *Decisive Battles*, op. cit., p. 376

34 J. France, 'La Guerre dans la France féodale à la fin du IX et Xe siècles', *Revue belge d'histoire militaire* 23 (1979), pp. 185–96; J. F. Verbruggen, *The Art of Warfare in Western Europe during the Middle Ages* (Oxford, 1877); Matthew Strickland, *War and Chivalry: The Conduct and Perception of War in England and Normandy, 1066–1217* (Cambridge, 1996), p. 130; Poitiers, p. 194; Wace, *Roman de Rou*, vv. 8189–208, ii, p. 190; William of Malmesbury, *De gestis regum*, ii, pp. 302–3; Jumièges, p. 120; A. Fliche, *Le Règne de Philippe I, roi de France* (Paris, 1912), pp. 258–9; D. P. Waley, 'Combined operations in Sicily, AD 1060–1078', *Papers of the British School at Rome* 22 (1954), p. 123; F. Barlow, 'The Carmen de Hastingae Proelio', in K. Bourne & D. C. Watts, eds, *Studies in International History: Essays presented to W. Norton Medlicott* (1967), pp. 35–67

35 Spatz, *Die Schlacht*, op. cit., pp. 55, 61–2, 67; C. H. Lemmon, *The Field of Hastings* (St Leonards, 1956), p. 44; Lemmon, *The Norman Conquest* (1966), pp. 109–10; Hans Delbruck, *Geschichte der Kriegskunt im Rahmen des politische Geschichte* (Berlin, 1907), iii, p. 162; Alfred H. Burne, *The Battlefields of England* (1950), pp. 31, 42, 43; Eric John, 'The Battle of Hastings', in James Campbell, ed., *The Anglo-Saxons* (1982), p. 235; G. Köhler, *Die Entwicklung des Kriegwesens und der Krieg Führung in der Ritterzeit von Mitte des 11*

Jahrhunderts bis zu den Hussitenkriegen (Breslau, 1886), i, p. 39; John
Beeler, *Warfare in England, 1066–1189* (Ithaca, NY, 1966), pp. 21–2;
R. J. Adam, *A Conquest of England* (1965), p. 127; Timothy Baker,
The Normans (1966), p. 112; Denis Butler, *1066. The Story of a Year*
(1966), p. 246; C. W. Barclay, *Battle, 1066* (1966), p. 81; D. J. A.
Matthew, *The Norman Conquest* (1966), p. 84

36 Bernard S. Bachrach, 'The feigned retreat at Hastings', *Medieval
Studies* 33 (1971), pp. 344–7; Brown, 'Battle of Hastings', loc. cit.;
Brown, *The Normans and the Norman Conquest*, pp. 171–2; Fuller,
Decisive Battles, p. 380; Morillo, *Battle of Hastings*, pp. 190–3, 212–13;
G. Slocombe, *William the Conqueror* (1959), pp. 153–4; Alan Lloyd,
The Making of a King (New York, 1966), p. 214

37 Jim Bradbury, *The Battle of Hastings*, op. cit., pp. 198–9; Bernard S.
Bachrach, 'The Alans in Gaul', *Traditio* 23 (1967), pp. 480–9;
Bachrach, 'The origins of Armorican chivalry', *Technology and
Culture* 10 (1969), pp. 166–71

38 BT, plates 66–7; *Carmen*, vv. 423–44, pp. 26–8; Wace, *Roman de
Rou*, vv. 8079–111, 8189–208, ii, pp. 186, 190; Poitiers, p. 194;
William of Malmesbury, *De gestis regum*, ii, p. 303; Brown, 'Battle of
Hastings', loc. cit., p. 20; Henry of Huntingdon, *Historia Anglorum*,
ed. Greenaway, pp. 394–5; P. Abraham, *Les Oeuvres poétiques de
Baudri de Bourgueil, 1046–1130. Carmen* (Paris, 1926), vv. 419–20

39 *Carmen*, vv. 527–30, p. 34; Freeman, *Norman Conquest*, iii, pp.
491–4; Morillo, *Battle of Hastings*, p. 161

40 Wace, *Roman de Rou*, vv. 8139–59, ii, p. 188; BT, Plates 70–1;
Poitiers, p. 196; Henry of Huntingdon, *Historia Anglorum*, ed.
Greenaway, pp. 394–5; J. Bradbury, *The Medieval Archer* (Woodbridge, 1985), pp. 22–32; Matthew Strickland, 'Military technology
and conquest: the anomaly of Anglo-Saxon England', *ANS* 19
(1996), pp. 353–82

41 Spatz, *Die Schlacht*, p. 62; Poitiers, pp. 198–200

42 *Carmen*, vv. 531–4, p. 34; BT, Plates 71–2; Wace, *Roman de Rou*, vv.
8859–60; Poitiers, p. 202; William of Malmesbury, *De gestis regum*, ii,
p. 304; Barlow, *Norman Conquest*, p. 211; Matthew Strickland, *War
and Chivalry*, op. cit., p. 5; J. Flori, *L'Essor de la chevalerie, XIe–XIIe
siècles* (Geneva, 1986), pp. 66–8

44 *Carmen*, vv. 551–8, p. 36; Poitiers, pp. 200–2; BT, Plates 72–3;
Freeman, *Norman Conquest*, iii, p. 501; R. H. Gordon, *The Battle of
Maldon: Anglo-Saxon Poetry* (1970), pp. 332–3; Morillo, *Battle of
Hastings*, p. 224

45 W. H. Stevenson, 'Senlac and the Malfosse', *EHR* 28 (1913), pp.

292–303; C. T. Chevallier, 'Where was the Malfosse? The end of the battle of Hastings', *Sussex Archaeological Collections* 101 (1963), pp. 1–13; Jim Bradbury, *The Battle of Hastings*, op. cit., pp. 208–11

46 Poitiers, pp. 202–4; *Carmen*, vv. 559–66, p. 36; van Houts, *Gesta Normannorum ducum*, pp. 168–70; E. Searle, ed., *Chronicle of Battle Abbey* (Oxford, 1980), p. 38; C. H. Lemmon, 'Campaign of 1066', loc. cit., pp. 97, 111–12

47 *Carmen*, vv. 573–6, p. 36; F. Michel, *Chroniques Anglo-Normandes*, op. cit., ii, p. 26; Freeman, *Norman Conquest*, ii, pp. 763–5

48 Douglas & Greenway, *English Historical Documents*, ii, p. 243; Poitiers, p. 204; Ordericus Vitalis, ii, p. 178; *Carmen*, vv. 577–96, pp. 36–8; also, ibid., pp. xliii–xlv; Cyril Hart, 'William Malet and his family', *ANS* 19 (1996), pp. 123–65

49 F. Lot, *L'Art militaire* (Paris, 1946), op. cit., i. pp. 284–5; F. Baring, 'The battlefield of Hastings', *EHR* 77 (1905), pp. 65–70; C. H. Lemmon, 'Campaign of 1066', loc. cit., pp. 100–1; Fuller, *Decisive Battles*, pp. 372–4; Korner, *Battle of Hastings*, p. 273; E. M. C. van Houts, 'The Norman Conquest through European eyes', *EHR* 110 (1995), pp. 832–53; van Houts, 'The trauma of 1066', *History Today* (1996), pp. 9–15; H. E. J. Cowdrey, 'Ermenford of Sion and the Penitential Ordinance following the Battle of Hastings', *Journal of Ecclesiastical History* 20 (1969), pp. 225–42

50 Lynn White, *Medieval Technology and Social Change* (Oxford, 1962), p. 37; David R. Cook, 'The Norman military revolution in England', *ANS* 1 (1978), pp. 94–102 (esp. p. 100); R. Bartlett, *The Making of Europe: Conquest, Colonisation and Cultural Change, 950–1350* (1993), pp. 60–84; F. C. Suppé, *Military Institutions on the Welsh Marches. Shropshire 1066–1300* (Woodbridge, 1994), pp. 1–33; C. W. Hollister, *Anglo-Saxon Institutions*, op. cit., *passim*

51 Florence, i, p. 228; William of Malmesbury, *De gestis regum*, ii, p. 306; Korner, *Battle of Hastings*, pp. 282–4; Morillo, *Battle of Hastings*, p. 225

52 *Vita Haroldi*, pp. 135–47, 168–73; Swanton, *Three Lives of the Last Englishmen*, op. cit., pp. 13, 38–40; M. Ashdown, 'An Icelandic account of the survival of Harold Godwineson', in P. Clemoes, ed., *The Anglo-Saxons* (1959), pp. 122–36; R. Wilson, *The Lost Literature of Medieval England* (1970), pp. 58–9; D. Rollason, *Saints and Relics in Anglo-Saxon England* (Oxford, 1989); C. Kightly, *Folk Heroes of Britain* (1984), p. 110

Epilogue

1 N. Hooper, 'Edgar the Atheling, Anglo-Saxon prince, rebel and crusader,' *Amglo-Saxon England* 14 (1985) pp. 197–214; Florence, i. p. 228; William of Malmesbury, *Gesta Regum*, ii. p. 307; Freeman, *Norman Conquest*, iii. pp. 766–67

2 Ordericus Vitalis, ii. pp. 180, 218; William of Poitiers p. 210; *Carmen*, vv. 620–30; R. Allen Brown, *The Origins of English Feudalism* pp. 30–31

3 ASC, 1066, 'D' version; Ordericus Vitalis, ii. pp. 180–82; William of Poitiers pp. 212–16; J. A. Giles, ed. *Lanfranc. Opera Omnia*, 2 vols (Oxford 1844), i. p. 57; Clarke, *English Nobility*, op. cit. pp. 114–15; C. H. Lemmon, *The Norman Conquest: its setting and impact* (1966) pp. 116–22; J. Beeler, *Warfare in England 1066–1189* (N. Y. 1966) pp. 25–33; E. H. Baring, 'The Conqueror's footprints in Domesday', *EHR* 13 (1898) pp. 17–25; G. H. Fowler, 'The devastation of Bedfordshire and the neighbouring counties in 1065 and 1066', *Archaeologia* 72 (1922) pp. 41–50

4 William of Poitiers p. 220; Ordericus Vitalis, ii. pp. 182–84; J. Nelson, 'The rites of the Conqueror', *ANS* 4 (1981) pp. 117–32

Index